Cihan Yüksel Muslu is Associate Professor at the University of Houston and holds a PhD in History and Middle Eastern Studies from Harvard University.

"*The Ottomans and the Mamluks* constitutes a significant contribution to Ottoman historical scholarship and presents a valuable and innovative example of historical and linguistic research. Through a close and extensive reading of narrative and documentary sources, Muslu traces the shifting terms of the Mamluk–Ottoman relationship, tracking the changing diplomatic protocols and language that signalled the growing strength of the Ottomans and the Mamluk responses to the diplomatic challenge ... Although the diplomatic encounters left few bleeding bodies in the field, Muslu nonetheless conveys the dramatic tension produced by significant diplomatic events at the Ottoman and Mamluk courts."

Amy Singer, Professor of Ottoman History and holder of the Chair in Ottoman–Turkish History at Tel Aviv University

"Dr Muslu uses rigorous and thorough analysis to support her groundbreaking assertion that the relationship between two Sunni Muslim powers, the Ottomans and the Mamluks, was just as complex and varied as between powers of different religions. Her unique periodisation, omitting the final five years of the Mamluk Sultanate (1512–17) and the build-up to the Ottoman takeover of Damascus and Cairo by Sultan Selim I, allows her to demonstrate that the Mamluks were actually dominant over the Ottomans for most of those years, contrary to common scholarly assumptions."

Anne Broadbridge, Associate Professor and Associate Department Chair at the University of Massachusetts, Amherst

THE OTTOMANS AND THE MAMLUKS

Imperial Diplomacy and Warfare in the Islamic World

Cihan Yüksel Muslu

I.B. TAURIS
LONDON · NEW YORK

New paperback edition published in 2017 by
I.B.Tauris & Co. Ltd
London • New York
www.ibtauris.com

First published in hardback in 2014 by I.B.Tauris & Co. Ltd

Copyright © 2014 Cihan Yüksel Muslu

The right of Cihan Yüksel Muslu to be identified as the author of this work has been asserted by the author in accordance with the Copyright, Designs and Patents Act 1988.

All rights reserved. Except for brief quotations in a review, this book, or any part thereof, may not be reproduced, stored in or introduced into a retrieval system, or transmitted, in any form or by any means, electronic, mechanical, photocopying, recording or otherwise, without the prior written permission of the publisher.

References to websites were correct at the time of writing.

ISBN: 978 1 78453 670 1
eISBN: 978 0 85773 580 5
ePDF: 978 0 85772 476 2

A full CIP record for this book is available from the British Library
A full CIP record is available from the Library of Congress

Library of Congress Catalog Card Number: available

Typeset in Garamond Three by OKS Prepress Services, Chennai, India
Printed and bound by CPI Group (UK) Ltd, Croydon, CR0 4YY

Benimle beraber ikinci doktoralarını bitiren sevgili Annem Semahat (Şenaltan) Yüksel'e ve Babam İbrahim Aydın Yüksel'e

CONTENTS

A Note on the Book and Transliteration viii
Acknowledgements x

Introduction 1
1. The Tools of Diplomacy 23
2. Perceptions in Transformation (*c*.1350–1402) 64
3. From Titulature to Geopolitical Affairs: An Age of Negotiations (1413–1451) 86
4. Imperial Ambition Resurrected (1453–1481) 109
5. From Captivity Narratives to a Peace Treaty: A New Era of Image-Building (1481–1491) 134
6. From Warfare to Alliance: The Intricacies of Imperial Diplomacy (1491–1512) 156
Conclusion 176
Appendix I: The Anatomy of a Typical Letter 188
Appendix II: Titulature 190
Appendix III: Missions and Envoys 192

Notes 276
Selected Bibliography 340
Index 365

A NOTE ON THE BOOK AND TRANSLITERATION

Those readers interested in further information about the embassies I discuss in the book should consult Appendix III for additional details about these and other cases I was not able to include in the main text.

For Ottoman–Turkish words, modern Turkish spelling and orthography are used.

For the words from the Mamluk context, all transliteration will be eliminated, except for the ayn and hamza.

For the sake of consistency, those words denoting terms, places, and people of the Islamic world (i.e. the Karamanids) that are going to form a part of Ottoman lands (except for Mamluk lands of course), the slightly Turkified version of the common forms in English will be used (i.e. the Karamanids instead of Qaramanids and Karamanoğulları). As for the names of their rulers (i.e. the Karamanids, etc.), the Turkish spelling and orthography is used, considering that eventually they were subdued by the Ottomans.

For the names of the Dulkadirid rulers, forms in English (Shahbudaq, Shahsuwar, 'Ala' al-Dawla) are used, with the exception of Nasir al-din Mehmed Bey. Instead of Muhammad, Mehmed is preferred.

For those words denoting terms, places, and people of the Islamic realm that never formed a part of either the Ottoman or Mamluk lands, all transliteration will be eliminated, except for the ayn and hamza (for instance, Shah İsma'il).

If there is an accepted English name for a city or region, this has been preferred (Damascus, Cairo, etc.). If there is no accepted English rendering for a city or region, then the familiar forms are used, such as Kayseri, Malatya (with one exception: I prefer Constantinople instead of Istanbul).

ACKNOWLEDGEMENTS

While it would be impossible to name every individual who has been involved in this project, I would like to thank many of those who have helped me during this long journey. First, I would like to acknowledge the friendly and accommodating staffs of Dar al-Kutub, the Süleymaniye Library, the Topkapı Palace Archive, the Topkapı Palace Library, and the Başbakanlık Archive.

By granting me a research fellowship, Koç University's Research Center for Anatolian Civilizations (RCAC) in Istanbul, Turkey allowed me to radically revise and expand my dissertation into this book. I thank them for this amazing opportunity to spend an entire academic year at their beautiful research center near such important archives and manuscript libraries. More than funding, this fellowship offered me an intellectual home during my stay in Istanbul and surrounded me with a vibrant and enthusiastic group of advanced scholars and graduate students. I am particularly thankful to the staff and to Scott Redford, RCAC's supportive director, who made this stay a very pleasant and memorable experience for my family and me. During the initial phase of this project, I also received financial and intellectual support from Harvard University, where I was granted a dissertation completion fellowship in 2005–6. I am also indebted to the generous fellowship of Türk Petrol Vakfı that funded my stay in Egypt. Its director Uğur Derman (now retired) has always been an adamant supporter of my work.

Acknowledgements

I am grateful to the administration at UT Dallas, particularly to Dean Dennis Kratz and Associate Dean Michael Wilson, who allowed me to take time off in my second year as a tenure-track assistant professor to take advantage of the RCAC fellowship. My special thanks go to the Interlibrary Loan staff of McDermott Library. The endless friendship, generous professional advice, and humor of my colleagues both encouraged and focused me.

My countless conversations with Cemal Kafadar on Ottoman history, research, and writing continued even after I completed my dissertation. From the inception of this project to its end, he has encouraged me to believe in my work, and his mentorship has been invaluable. Likewise, the guidance of Gülru Necipoğlu Kafadar at significant times during this project was enlightening. I particularly appreciate the guidance of Jane Hathaway who always found time for me in the midst of her demanding schedule.

While revising the manuscript, I particularly benefitted from the professional comments of Frédéric Bauden, Doris Behrens-Abouseif, Ann Broadbridge, Malika Dekkiche, Leslie Pierce, Amy Singer, and Derin Terzioğlu, who all read parts of this book at various stages. Their suggestions substantially improved my work. My local editor Sharon Duncan tirelessly polished my writing. Tomasz Hoskins, my editor at I.B.Tauris, always believed in this project. The patient and timely responses of Allison Walker, my production editor at I.B.Tauris, were encouraging for a first-time author. I am also grateful for the feedback I received from the anonymous reader who was a part of my review process at I.B.Tauris.

I am equally grateful to those who were closely involved in this project during its early phases when I was a graduate student at Harvard University. The support and intellectual guidance of Roy Mottahedeh, Michael Winter, and Hakan Karateke never faltered during those years. The guidance of Ekmeleddin İhsanoğlu, who was at that time the director of the Research Centre for Islamic History, Art and Culture, enabled me to build contacts with scholars such as Ayman Fuad Sayyid, who helped make my stay in Cairo both pleasurable and productive. The libraries of the French Institute and the American University of Cairo became my intellectual homes in Cairo. Finally, I cannot forget the timely help of Yusuf Küçükdağ in 2003.

My family and friends have shared with me both the pleasure and the agony of writing. Volkan Muslu has always believed that I could finish. My daughter, Dilara Muslu, has not only enriched my life but has also inspired me to dedicate myself to both my career and to her future. At the last stage of this project, I was blessed with the arrival of my son Emre Muslu. His presence convinced me that it is time to finish this project. My extended family—from my (now late) grandmother Hasibe Şenaltan to aunts, cousins, and my childhood friends—have always supported me with their prayers and love.

Finally, this book could not have been completed without the help of my parents, Semahat (Şenaltan) Yüksel and Aydın Yüksel, who introduced me to books and to the Ottoman language. My mother, who was my first language teacher, taught me the pleasures of learning and reading; my father was my first instructor in reading Ottoman script. They have given me endless emotional and intellectual support. The sacrifices they made so that I could first finish my dissertation and then complete this book have taught me what it means to be a parent. The only way I can pay my debt to them—if there is a way to do such a thing—is by doing the same for my children.

Despite the help I received from numerous people and institutions, this book will not be entirely free of mistakes, for all of which I am the only one accountable. As a final note, I emphasize that I am primarily trained in Ottoman studies. I hope that specialists of Mamluk history will regard with compassion the inevitable lapses in my knowledge of this area.

INTRODUCTION

In 1393 the Ottoman ruler Bayezid I (r.1389–1402) gave audience to the Mamluk emissary Amir Husam al-Din Hasan al-Kujkuni[1] in the Ottoman capital Bursa, an ancient city in northwestern Anatolia that flourished under Ottoman rule yet paled in comparison to the Mamluk imperial capital of Cairo.[2] According to a Mamluk source, while accepting the gifts sent by the Mamluk sultan Barquq (r.1382–9 and 1390–9), Bayezid commented that he was Barquq's slave, or *mamluk*.[3] With this exaggerated expression, Bayezid did not display false humility, but instead acknowledged his inferior political status. Despite his rapid expansion into the Balkans and through western and central Anatolia, the Ottoman sovereign was not yet the equivalent of his Mamluk counterpart, who ruled a prestigious regime that had dominated the central Islamic lands since the 1250s. Bayezid's predecessors had merely established themselves as vassals of first the Anatolian Seljuks and then of the Mongol Ilkhanids in northwest Anatolia, which existed as a frontier territory squeezed between the borders of the Byzantine Empire and multiple local Muslim magnates.

Four generations later, Bayezid II (r.1481–1512), Bayezid I's descendant and successor to the Ottoman throne, hosted another Mamluk ambassador in Çöke, a plain near the previous Ottoman capital of Edirne (Adrianople). Both the city and its green surroundings offered Bayezid safe haven from the political intrigues and frequent plague epidemics in Constantinople, the former Byzantine imperial center and the Ottoman capital since 1453. This ambassadorial audience, which took place in 1485, illustrates a radically different balance of power between the Ottoman and Mamluk rulers than the one in 1393.[4] The Mamluk ambassador Amir Janibak, who arrived during a pause in the Ottoman–Mamluk war that had begun in the spring of 1484, attempted to mend relations between the two courts.[5] He was hosted honorably and properly during his stay, but he quickly understood that there was little hope for him to successfully complete his mission.

An unidentified person in the Ottoman audience asked Janibak, "Who are you (the Mamluks) to rule over the Holy Cities, you sons of Infidels? This rule (or land) is more proper for our sultan [since] he is the son of the sultans and the sultans."[6] Even more telling was the fact that, during this entire exchange, Bayezid II did not utter a word to his visitor. Obviously, much had changed since the days of Bayezid I, who had declared his subservience to the Mamluk sultan. Soon after the Mamluk envoy's return to Cairo, military conflict between the two powers resumed.

These two vignettes, as later discussion will show, illustrate a drastic shift in the political status quo between the Ottoman and Mamluk courts. This shift, during which the Ottomans asserted their power first alongside and then gradually against the Mamluks, revealed itself primarily through diplomatic engagements. This book studies the diplomatic exchanges between the Sunni Muslim Ottomans and Sunni Muslim Mamluks from the 1360s to 1512. It illuminates an era when the first sustained encounters between these two powers gradually deepened into a regional rivalry and gave rise to the construction of a language and a set of behaviors for engagement. By studying the networks of diplomacy between the two leading Sunni Muslim empires of their time, this book attempts to better understand the place of this relationship within the image-making processes and historiography of each power.

An analysis of diplomatic exchanges indicates that the Mamluks factored significantly in the decision- and image-making processes of Ottoman sovereigns during their ascension to power. In an age when modern means of communication were not available, diplomatic embassies with thoughtfully planned ceremonies, attentively crafted official correspondence, carefully selected gifts, and cautiously prepared ambassadors played critical roles in the expression and dissemination of imperial ideologies between both political centers.[7] In Islamic courts the ceremonies and rituals that revolved around diplomatic encounters not only displayed remarkable regional variety,[8] but also—much like their Western or non-Muslim counterparts—went beyond mere repetitive and unchanging formalities: they served as primary battlefields where formulations of identity and sovereignty clashed, were negotiated, and were reformulated for both external and internal audiences.[9] Although it was different from modern diplomacy, a complex and developed diplomatic culture existed long before resident embassies were established in the eighteenth century.[10] A small misstep in diplomatic ceremonials most likely did not destroy the relationship between the capitals, yet the fact that both Ottoman and Mamluk chroniclers emphasized "the courtly insults" or the incidents during which diplomatic conventions and ceremonials were dismissed (or particularly upheld) reveals the value these societies attached to these ceremonies in their political cultures.[11]

The importance that both powers placed on these diplomatic communications also invites us to question the dominant perspective that Muslim rulers were historically obsessed with the idea of holy war, or *jihad*, which obligated them to exist in a permanent state of conflict with their non-Muslim peers.[12] This perception, which has been especially prevalent among non-specialists, has been particularly shaped by the frequent allusions to the tropes of *jihad* and *ghaza* (initially, an expedition for plunder[13]) in the diplomatic correspondence between Muslim rulers who recognized the powerful influence of these concepts on Muslim audiences and skillfully employed them in legitimizing their regimes and sovereignty.[14] The relationships of these Muslim powers with non-Muslims, however, went beyond warfare based on ideological and religious differences.[15] This oversimplified approach to interfaith contacts leads to the equally erroneous belief that the relationships between Muslim powers did not change, or that their diplomatic contacts were merely repetitive exchanges to keep up appearances or fulfill formalities while these powers focused on fighting "the infidels." Since both the Ottoman and Mamluk ruling classes adhered to Sunni Islam, their extended and multi-layered interactions confirm the complexity of inter-Muslim contacts. While the Sunni Ottomans crafted their image against the ideologically and geopolitically hostile Catholic Holy Roman Empire, they also crafted rhetorical language against the newly rising Shi'i Safavids under Shah Isma'il (r.1501–24) in Iran based on sectarian differences within Islam.[16] The diplomatic exchanges between the Sunni Ottomans and Sunni Mamluks, however, required a creative combination of diverse tropes and themes for both sides—one that not only sustained communication with but also conveyed superiority over the other. Until at least 1512, Ottoman–Mamluk interactions continued to display the same vitality and volatility they had since the fourteenth century. The relationship between these two Islamic powers should be imagined on a continuum that ranged from peaceful and fruitful contacts to exhausting wars and strategetic alliances, as is the case for most relationships between political powers. It was as complicated as the Ottoman–Habsburg or Mamluk–Crusader associations, and exuded an equally considerable sense of rivalry and competition. Political leaders in every phase of history shared this desire to protect their regimes and surpass their peers, regardless of their religious allegiances.

The Mamluks, the Ottomans, and the World

From the 1300s to 1512, the Ottomans transformed themselves from a minor Anatolian principality into a world power that challenged the venerable Mamluks. The earliest Ottoman–Mamluk diplomatic interactions, which began in the second half of the fourteenth century, should be understood within this context of unequal yet shifting power dynamics between the Ottomans, who attempted to carve a niche for themselves in the eyes of the prestigious Mamluk administration, and the Mamluks, who had built their domestic and international image on a complex yet effective mixture of ideological, political, and historical references.[17]

The earliest Mamluk sultans were slave-soldiers who took over the reign of their prestigious Ayyubid lords who ruled between 1171 and 1250.[18] The first Ayyubid ruler Salah al-din al-Ayyubi (d.1193) came from a Sunni Kurdish family in the service of the Zangids of Aleppo and Musul (the vassals of the Great Seljuks) and left an impressive legacy to his descendants and successors. In 1179 he ended the Shi'i Fatimid presence in Egypt, which had lasted since the tenth century, and recaptured Jerusalem from the Crusaders in 1187. His particularly celebrated image as a champion of faith was mostly based on his successes against the Crusader kingdoms that had been established after the First Crusade (1095–9) along the eastern Mediterranean coast and in northern Syria. After Salah al-din's death, his Ayyubid successors began to form an army comprised of slave-soldiers. During an extended period of political chaos that followed the death of the Ayyubid sultan al-Salih Ayyub (d.1240), Aybak al-Turkmani (r.1250–7), a commander of slave or *mamluk* origin, became the first Mamluk sultan when he married the Ayyubid child sultan's widowed mother. This marriage, which was an attempt to legitimize his sovereignty, helped the new sultan build relationships with his prestigious patrons.[19] Although Aybak's rule was often plagued by internal strife and chaos, his humble slave origins and subsequent rise to power served as a model for his Mamluk comrades.

After Aybak's reign and at least until the 1390s (or the end of so-called Bahri period of the Mamluk sultanate), attempts were made to institute dynastic succession. In fact, dynastic succession as a principle of political leadership was initially not questioned among the *mamluk* ranks.[20] The Mamluk regime gradually shied away from the dynastic impulse, but never altogether abandoned this principle. During the later Burji (Circassian) regime, the expression "kingship has no progeny" became a popular motto.[21] Thereafter, during times of accession, a Mamluk commander, who was either supported by a strong faction within the military or closely linked to the late sultan through ties of *khushdashiyya* (camaraderie) or patronage, was brought to power by a consensus or a quasi-election.[22] Occasionally, the new sultan replaced the young son of the previous sultan. In fact, he could be a grand amir who the late sultan had appointed as the *atabak* (also *atabeg*, the second-ranking military officer of the Mamluk state after the sultan)[23] of his young son before his death.

Although the Mamluk sultans who came to power through this system controlled the lands of Egypt and Syria until the Ottoman conquest in 1517, they were vulnerable to domestic and international criticism because of their non-Muslim slave origins.[24] Keenly aware of their humble beginnings, Mamluk sultans gradually honed a complex image that initially alluded to the glorious memory of their prestigious Ayyubid lords.[25] In a gesture of respect to their predecessor, early Mamluk sultans visited the tomb of their Ayyubid patron al-Salih Ayyub when they ascended to power.[26]

Following in the footsteps of their Ayyubid predecessors, the Mamluks established themselves as champions of their faith.[27] In fact, when faced with the approach of the Mongols in addition to the continuing Crusader presence in the coastal lands, they shouldered the task of fighting off these powers. The Mongols repeatedly attacked Mamluk and Anatolian Seljuk territories in the aftermath of Chingiz Khan's death (d.1224) and gradually encroached upon the politics of Anatolia and Syria. The Mamluks were the first to obstruct the advancement of the Mongols in the battle of 'Ayn Jalut in 1260.

The Mamluk success against the Mongols led various political groups in Anatolia to plead for Mamluk aid against successive Mongol attacks. Since the early thirteenth century, the Anatolian Seljuks who were a branch of the Great Seljuk dynasty in Iran controlled most of Anatolia from their capital, Konya in central Anatolia. The battle of Kösedağ in 1248, in which the Mongols heavily defeated the Anatolian Seljuks in central Anatolia, triggered a process of political disintegration in the region and paved the way to the rise of principalities (including the Ottomans) that had previously recognized Anatolian Seljuk suzerainty. From the 1260s onward, some of these Anatolian leaders—from the defeated Anatolian Seljuk ruler to the leaders of the principalities—sent letter after letter appealing to the Mamluk sultan Baybars (r.1260–77) to end Mongol control of the region.[28] In 1277, Baybars undertook his long-awaited campaign, defeated the Mongol army near Elbistan, and established Mamluk suzerainty in the region through symbolically loaded actions and ceremonies.[29]

Although Baybars retreated quickly from Anatolia and died soon after his return to Cairo, he still succeeded in establishing a Mamluk sphere of influence in the region.[30] The towns along his route through Anatolia remained under Mamluk control, and they outlined the frontier that would eventually separate the Mamluk sphere of influence from the Ottoman. This zone covered a vast region from the plain of Cilicia (near Çukurova in Turkey) to the west and the Taurus Mountains to the north and extended as far as Kayseri, where Baybars was crowned during his campaign in 1277. It included the urban centers south of Kayseri, such as Elbistan (which was close to the plain where Baybars defeated the Mongols), Malatya, Darende, Behisni, Kahta, Gerger, and Afşin. In this mountainous region, these settlements were connected mostly by passages and gates, such as Darb al-Hadas (a passage connecting Kayseri and Elbistan) and the Cilician Gates (known as Gülek Boğazı in Turkey), that were difficult to control and pass through. With its steep passages and mountains, the region served as a natural border between Anatolia and Greater Syria, and became part of the Mamluk northern frontier. The Mamluks ensured their control of this region by building vassal relationships with semi-nomadic Turkoman groups in the area and by appointing their leaders as Mamluk governors.

Despite its brevity, Baybars' campaign left such a permanent imprint on the region that two centuries later the Ottoman chronicler Neşri wrote a detailed account of the campaign and the subsequent solidification of vassalage ties between the Mamluks and the Karamanids.[31] Soon after Baybars' return to Cairo, the Karamanids not only became one of the most powerful principalities in Anatolia, but their formidable rivalry with the Ottomans also played a significant role in later Ottoman–Mamluk relations. Karamanid rulers later maintained their contacts with the Mamluks and even submitted requests to Cairo for appointments to govern various Anatolian towns.[32]

Some of these semi-nomadic principalities, such as the Dulkadirids and the Ramazanids, were geographically closer to the Mamluk northern frontier, and the roles they played in the Ottoman–Mamluk relationship cannot be overemphasized, as the following chapters will prove.[33] The Dulkadirids controlled the lands that extended from Elbistan to Antep, including Malatya and Kayseri, though the borders occasionally changed after the end of the thirteenth century. At times they even battled the Karamanids to defend the interests of their Mamluk patrons.[34] For the greater part of their relationship with the Mamluks and later the Ottomans, the Dulkadirids steadily sought for more autonomy. Although almost every Dulkadirid ruler visited Cairo and received the blessings of the Mamluk sultan at the beginning of his rule, these same leaders often refused to obey Mamluk authority as soon as they had an opportunity.[35] The Ramazanids established themselves on the plain of Cilicia with Adana at their center; the region lay slightly west of the Dulkadirid territory with occasionally overlapping borders and conflicting interests.[36]

Besides consolidating their presence in Anatolia, the Mamluks further promoted themselves with consecutive victories against the Crusader kingdoms and local Armenian powers.[37] These military achievements also enabled them to present their leader as a warrior-king (*Heerkönig*).[38] After the expulsion of the Crusaders from the region in 1291 and after the retreat of Chingiz Khan's successors to the affairs of Iran and central Asia, the Mamluks engaged in warfare against non-Muslim powers less frequently, aside from occasional skirmishes with the remnants of the Crusaders in Cyprus and Rhodes.[39] They also occasionally engaged in both diplomatic and military encounters with the successor states of Chingiz Khan and the Timurids, despite the fact that all of these entities had converted to Islam.[40]

While the Mamluk sultans often alluded to their roles as the defenders of Islam, these rulers also increasingly accentuated their positions as the custodians of Mecca and Medina (also called the Two Holy Cities or the Two Holy Sanctuaries of Islam) as central aspects of their images. They called themselves *Khadim al-Haramayn al-Sharifayn* (the Servitor of the Two Holy Sanctuaries) and claimed exclusive rights for the safety of the pilgrimage roads, the annual preparation and replacement of the *kiswa* (the black textile that covers Ka'ba), the annual *hajj* caravan, and the departure of the richly decorated yet empty palanquin called *mahmal* (or *mahmil*) that led the annual pilgrimage caravan from Cairo.[41] The Mamluk sovereigns fulfilled critical functions in the practice of *hajj*, which was a practice central to the spiritual world of the Muslims, and one of the Pillars of Islam. Among Muslim believers, these symbolic religious tasks honored the sovereigns responsible for them, and would at times foster competition between the Mamluk regime and other Muslim powers, including the Timurids and the Ottomans.[42]

After the Mongol sack of Baghdad in 1258, the transfer of the Abbasid caliphate to Cairo enhanced the prestige of the fledgling Mamluk regime.[43] Despite the gradual erosion of the caliphate's temporal authority since the ninth century and its lack of political power in Cairo, the caliphate occupied a place of some significance in the Mamluk worldview, and the caliphs were considered sources of symbolic authority when they sanctioned Mamluk sovereignty.[44] By re-using some of the architectural forms that had been used for the Abbasid caliphate in Baghdad, some Mamluk sultans further accentuated their associations with the Abbasid heritage.[45] Twice during the long Mamluk sultanate between 1250 and 1517, Mamluk commanders even considered the Abbasid caliph as a viable alternative for the sultanate.[46] On some diplomatic occasions, the Mamluk sultans also asserted that their proximity to the caliph was a sign of superiority and a token of God's blessing.[47]

The caliph's presence in Cairo attached a special status to the Mamluk rulers, even for some Muslim states as far away as western India.[48] For some leaders such as the sultans of Delhi (i.e. Tughlughs) and the Bahmanis, who founded their rule in the Deccan region of India in the mid-fourteenth century, their communication with the sultans of Egypt and the Abbasid caliphs were a matter of political recognition that helped to consolidate their regime.[49] The value that some Muslim sovereigns placed on the letters and titulature they received from the Abbasid Caliph indicates that the Sunni Muslim world still acknowledged its authority.[50] These titles revealed a ruler's status in the international arena while a *tashrif*, a robe of honor initially sent by the caliph to a ruler, further sealed his sovereignty.[51] Some Muslim rulers boldly challenged the Mamluk sultans for their roles as the protectors of the caliphate.[52]

The Mamluk sultans also embraced *mazalim* sessions as an integral part of their image.[53] Also known as *dar al-'adl*, these sessions were "the structure through which the temporal authorities took direct responsibility for dispensing justice."[54] During these sessions, the Mamluk sultans listened to the grievances of their subjects and addressed their issues, often with the help of legal scholars. Although it probably had precedents in the rest of the Islamic world, it has often associated with Nur al-din al-Zangi (d.1174), the Zangid ruler of Aleppo and Mousul, who was the patron of Salah al-din al-Ayyubi. Since then, it had been followed by the Ayyubids and subsequently by the Mamluks of Egypt and Syria.[55] Particularly for the Mamluk sultans, whose claims to sovereignty were vulnerable to criticism, this institution provided an opportunity for them to present themselves as proper and just Muslim rulers to a public that did not have any ethnic or linguistic ties with their leader. Although these sessions were not compulsory, the practice of *dar al-'adl* definitely belonged to the carefully groomed image of the Mamluk sultans.[56]

The Mamluk sultans also inherited Cairo from the Ayyubids, an imperial capital where the most prestigious Islamic institutions of higher learning (*madrasa*) were located; their architectural and financial patronage of these institutions elevated their status in the Islamic world.[57] While the charitable institutions reinforced an image of a pious and generous ruler, the colleges attracted numerous students and scholars to the Mamluk territories. The mere presence of these well-established thinkers aided the Mamluk sultans in crafting the religious ideology that further legitimized their regimes.[58] Most Mamluk sultans also fostered close relations with and offered patronage to sufis (Muslim mystics), some of whom were not natives of Mamluk society.[59] Additionally, Cairo served as a stage for symbolically loaded religious and secular processions, banquets, and festivals, during which the Mamluk rulers were occasionally present and appeared as generous benefectors of their people.[60]

During every diplomatic encounter between the two lands, the Ottomans contended with this strong and multi-faceted image of the Mamluk sultans and their well-established presence in Anatolia. In the late thirteenth century, the Ottomans first appeared in northwest Anatolia as one of the many frontier vassals of the Anatolian Seljuks. Most former Seljuk vassals were subject to the authority of the Ilkhanid Mongols, who established themselves in eastern Anatolia and in parts of Iran. As long as they paid their annual tributes to these new lords, however, those in western and northwestern Anatolia such as the Ottomans enjoyed more autonomy due to their geographical distance from Ilkhanid political control. In Anatolia, the semi-nomadic and Turkish-speaking Ottomans were surrounded by their superior Muslim peers such as the Germiyanids, who centered in and around the western Anatolian town of Kütahya, and the Karamanids, who recognized Mamluk suzerainty after Baybars' campaign in 1277.[61] Therefore, the Ottomans primarily turned their attention to the relatively defenseless Byzantine lands. In 1326 they adopted the old Byzantine town of Bursa as their capital, and then passed the Strait of Dardanelles to establish themselves in the Balkans. Their interest in the Balkans revealed itself when they carried their capital from the Anatolian town of Bursa to Edirne, a frontier city northwest of Constantinople that served as a gateway to the Balkans.[62]

The Balkan territories seized by the Ottomans had never before submitted to Islamic rule, and these conquests marked the Ottomans' increasing importance in the Islamic world. In 1453 the Ottomans further adorned this image by conquering Constantinople, the Byzantine imperial capital. This essential victory allowed the Ottomans to consolidate their expansion into the Balkans and Anatolia by securing the connection between these two regions in addition to monopolizing the straits that connected the larger Mediterranean basin with the Black Sea region. Beyond any geopolitical gain, the conquest also carried symbolic ideological meaning, since the city had been targeted by numerous Muslim rulers since the rule of the Umayyads in the seventh century. According to some traditions, the conquest of the centuries-old Byzantine capital at the hands of a Muslim ruler was foretold and celebrated by the Prophet

Muhammad.[63] With this process of military expansion, the Ottomans began to increasingly emphasize *ghaza* and *jihad*, concepts on which the Mamluk sultans had also partially based their prestige. Although both terms were used interchangeably in Ottoman–Mamluk diplomatic exchanges, recent studies suggest that the Ottomans gradually formulated a stronger claim on *ghaza* while the Mamluks always emphasized *jihad* as a part of their image.[64]

One significant difference between the Ottoman and Mamluk regimes was that the Ottomans strongly adhered to dynastic succession and did not divide their lands among the progeny of the previous leader. At times of accession, they almost always witnessed fierce struggles among male siblings that often ended with fratricide after one established his authority in the capital.[65] This practice meant that the Ottoman sultans also boasted of the nobility of their regime.

To a great extent, this historical and political background set the direction for the Ottoman–Mamluk relationship during this era. This relationship gradually shaped the politics at the heart of the Middle Eastern and Mediterranean regions, since geopolitical conditions became more volatile in response to the Ottoman expansion and the emergence of new formidable political rivals in the region, such as the Aqqoyunlus and the Safavids in the late fifteenth century.

The Ottoman intrusion into the Mamluk sphere of influence started in the fourteenth century and followed multiple phases of Ottoman advancement and retreat. Nonetheless, the gradual Ottoman regional infringement upon the Mamluks' borders not only brought their rulers into a more intense and increasingly competitive relationship, but also put the powers between these two imperial borders in an unstable position. These powers—the Karamanids, the Dulkadirids, the Ramazanids, and the others—had to closely follow the evolving relationship between the Mamluk and Ottoman capitals. While the Karamanids were subdued by the Ottomans by the late fifteenth century, both the Dulkadirids and Ramazanids remained under nominal Mamluk rule until they were annexed by the Ottoman ruler Selim I (r.1512–20). Until this event, even with their frequently shifting loyalties, these territories served as a buffer zone between the Ottomans and the Mamluks, particularly as the Ottomans expanded into this frontier region.

The rise of the Aqqoyunlus—first in Diyarbakır and then in Tabriz—brought drastic ramifications for both the Ottomans and the Mamluks in the fifteenth century.[66] The Aqqoyunlus arose from a confederation of tribes in the fourteenth century and lasted until 1502. Under the leadership of the young and ambitious Uzun Hasan (r.1457–78), the Aqqoyunlu polity gradually incorporated the lands of the formidable Qaraqoyunlu power in eastern Anatolia, Iraq, and Iran after 1467. Since the early fourteenth century, the Qaraqoyunlu confederation had been among formidable rivals of the Mamluks and then the Timurids.[67] After eliminating the Qaraqoyunlus, Uzun Hasan also defeated the Timurid ruler Abu Sa'id in 1469.[68] The emergence of this new power was initially welcomed by some European territories—first and foremost the Republic of Venice— that hoped it could offset the powerful Ottoman and Mamluk presence in the region.[69] The efforts of various European powers to build an alliance either against the Ottomans or the Mamluks (or both) were joined by Uzun Hasan, who vied for a chance to penetrate into both territories. This Muslim leader's attempts to collaborate with other Western powers prove the insignificance of religious affiliations or loyalties in the face of political and economic interests. Hasan's ambition troubled the Ottoman and Mamluk Sultans, who rightly considered the Aqqoyunlus a threat to their territories. In addition to endangering their geographical borders, the presence of the Aqqoyunlus complicated the relationship between the two sovereigns since Uzun Hasan (as well as his son and successor Sultan Yaqub, who ruled between 1478 and 1490) skillfully played them against each other.[70]

When the Shi'i Safavids under the leadership of the charismatic Shah Isma'il (r.1501–24) replaced the Aqqoyunlu polity in the early sixteenth century, they inherited the majority of the Aqqoyunlus' geopolitical position and political status while also agitating the relationship between Constantinople and Cairo. The Safavids' adherence to the Shi'i branch of Islam also altered the ideological dynamics between the Ottoman and Mamluk lands where the Sunni branch predominated. The Ottoman and Mamluk lands adjacent to the Safavid territory were particularly vulnerable to their ideological propaganda and territorial ambitions. For centuries after the retreat of the Fatimids to their original bases in North Africa after 1179, none of these regions had been controlled by a Shi'i ruling class or dynasty, and such a new and powerful Shi'i entity caused major repercussions for the larger Islamic world. The Safavid ruling class pursued a very strict and, at times, intolerant style towards people of other faiths, including the Sunnis. Following in Uzun Hasan's footsteps, Shah Isma'il conducted regular correspondence with multiple European courts, attempting to eliminate the Ottomans, the Mamluks, or both.[71] Ultimately, it was not the ambitious and rapid territorial expansion of Isma'il alone that worried his two Sunni Muslim neighbors, but rather his aggressive ideological stance.[72]

Additionally, the second half of the fifteenth century (when the Mamluk ambassador Janibak visited Bayezid II) witnessed the onset of great political and social upheavals, from the conclusion of the Reconquista in the Iberian Peninsula in 1492 to the circumnavigation of the Cape of Good Hope in 1498. Most of these world events either had major consequences for the Ottomans and Mamluks or were partly motivated by their presence in the eastern Mediterranean and Red Seas, facts which prove the connectedness of these two prominent Sunni Muslim powers with the rest of the world. On the western coast of the Mediterranean, policies set by the King of Aragon Ferdinand V (r.1479–1516) and the Queen of Castille Isabella I (r.1474–1504) before and after the Reconquista triggered a population movement that created enormous consequences for both the Ottoman and Mamluk societies. The Muslim presence in the Iberian Peninsula had been gradually established since the first waves of Muslim attacks in the early eighth century and had lasted under different Muslim powers until 1492. The Reconquista not only seized the kingdom of Granada—the final territory that remained in the hands of the Muslim Nasrid rulers—but also led to the expulsion of most of the Jewish and Muslim populations from the area.[73] These attacks did not entirely end the presence of either group in the peninsula, but they did begin a process of gradual assimilation and expulsion that lasted at least until the seventeenth century.[74] The expulsion of Jews and Muslims under the rule of Ferdinand and Isabella was not an isolated incident; the Portuguese king Dom Manuel I (r.1495–1521) issued a similar decree in 1496 under pressure from the Spanish Habsburg royal family.[75] Expelled Jewish and Muslim communities arrived in Ottoman and Mamluk territories in waves, while some also found safe haven in North Africa. This population movement not only changed the social makeup of the Ottoman and Mamluk societies, but also influenced the politics of both powers. Additionally, the Nasrids of Granada and the Hafsids of Tunis turned to both the Ottomans and Mamluks for assistance against the powers of the Reconquista.[76]

Fifteenth-century geographic explorations were also partially propelled by the Mamluk monopoly on the only known route to the Indian Ocean and the gradual Ottoman control of the Black Sea and western Anatolian coast.[77] Both Mamluk and Ottoman lands occupied prime geographical locations and lay at the crossroads of transit routes that led to the larger Mediterranean Sea, Black Sea, and Indian Ocean trade systems. Until 1498, ports in the eastern Mediterranean and the Red Sea under Mamluk authority offered the only known connections to the profitable Indian Ocean trade system. Although most powers of the Indian subcontinent also had commercial ties that lay further east, they highly valued their transactions with the West. Under Mamluk domination, Jidda (a port on the Red Sea coast and the closest port to the Muslim Holy City of Mecca) provided an outlet where ships from India and Southeast Asia could access the Arabian Peninsula, Egypt, and Syria.[78] Likewise, from its Mediterranean and Black Sea ports, Anatolia provided another land route to Syria and Egypt (and therefore to the Indian Ocean), and was connected to the Iranian trade zones and the rest of the Silk Road.

The commercial transactions between the Mamluk and Ottoman territories had a long history and involved both the direct exchange of local merchandise and the transit exchange of international products. Before the rise of the Ottomans, the Mamluk sultan Qalawun (r.1279–90) had signed treaties with the Byzantine emperor to ensure the flow of trade between their lands.[79] While imported spices from India and Arabia and high-quality fabrics generally came to Anatolia through Egypt, furs and slaves that the Mamluks depended on for the continuation of their military recruitment system reached the Mamluks through Ottoman lands that were linked to the Black Sea trade.[80] Mastic, the aromatic gum produced on the island of Chios, traveled to Egypt and Syria through Anatolia.[81] While Anatolia regularly bought local sugar, Egyptian cloth,[82] and dyes from Egypt and Syria, Egypt and Syria acquired Anatolia's timber,[83] mohair,[84] metals,[85] alum,[86] and possibly grain.[87] In the latter half of the fifteenth century, at least two cities under Ottoman rule, Bursa and Antalya, particularly flourished as both direct and transit trade centers between the Ottomans and the Mamluks, while the Mamluk city of Alexandria had a *fondaco* (hostel) for the Ottoman merchants.[88]

Although this pattern of commerce fluctuated over the centuries, particularly during times of war, it never disappeared entirely.[89] Despite the consistent economic activity between the Ottoman and Mamluk lands, references to merchants and commerce are usually vague in their diplomatic documents, as the following chapters will attest. While these references confirm the existence of these commercial networks, they do not allow us to estimate the volume of these transactions. Neither do they tell us how often mutual commercial interests and the well-being of traveling merchants were negotiated by ambassadors and the administrations they visited. Nonetheless, these omissions should not lead us to call into question the strong economic relationship between the two powers and the centrality of these transactions for the larger world economy.

The main agents of this intense traffic included local and foreign Muslim and non-Muslim merchants who, with their various religious and ethnic affiliations, exemplified the rich mosaic of Ottoman and Mamluk territories.[90] The presence of multiple European consuls and *fondacos* that served an internationally diverse community of tradesmen in prominent urban centers such as Alexandria and Cairo is a testament to the substantial investments of foreign merchants in Mamluk lands. The Catalan merchants under the protection of the

Crown of Aragon boasted a strong presence in the Mamluk lands until at least the 1430s or until the Crown's policies toward the Mamluk regime changed.[91] Although from the mid-fifteenth century onward the Republic of Venice claimed a substantial share of the eastern Mediterranean trade, an impressive cosmopolitanism prevailed in Mamluk cities: when the Venetian ambassador arrived in Cairo in 1489, he reported "the almost contemporary presence of ambassadors from Florence, Genoa, and Rome" in a bleak tone.[92] Likewise, foreign European merchants, especially Italians, established a strong presence in the Ottoman territories alongside Muslim and non-Muslim local merchants.[93] However, the dependence of foreign merchants on the generosity of the Ottoman and Mamluk rulers to conduct their business in the Black, Mediterranean, and Red Seas did not lead them to adopt a completely conciliatory policy towards their patrons. For instance, the Venetians, whose commercial interests were closely entangled with those of the Ottomans and Mamluks, engaged in expensive maritime wars with the Ottomans at least twice during the second half of the fifteenth century.[94]

This economic network was threatened by the circumvention of the Cape of Good Hope in 1498. After decades of expeditions funded by the Portuguese court, Vasco de Gama's new route became a pillar of the Portuguese king Dom Manuel's politics that targeted the destruction of the Venetian and Mamluk economies.[95] In India, Dom Manuel also hoped to discover a potential new Christian ally that could attack the Mamluks from the rear.[96] Overpowering the Mamluks would have allowed Dom Manuel both economic dominance and access to Jerusalem, but the support of an Indian ally never materialized, nor was the Portuguese navy able to seize complete control of the Red Sea trade. Although the Portuguese did attempt to gain control of this market with attacks on Jidda and on Aden in Yemen, they were thwarted by the Ottoman naval forces dispatched by Bayezid II at the request of the Mamluk sultan Qansuh al-Ghawri (r.1501–16).[97] As early as 1506 or 1507, Bayezid II began to send aid to the Mamluks in order to curtail these Portuguese incursions, but the Portuguese nonetheless extended their sphere of influence and secured the flow of trade by establishing a series of bases along the coast of the Indian Ocean.

Beyond their commercial ties with other world powers, the Ottoman and Mamluk territories carried spiritual significance for Christians and Jews. While the Ottoman Empire included many early Christian pilgrimage sites within its borders, the Mamluks ruled Jerusalem, the birthplace of both faiths. As a result, both lands received a steady flow of both Jewish and Christian pilgrims in addition to Muslims. The Ottoman and Mamluk lands attracted individuals such as Cyriac of Ancona (born c.1301 and died before 1457), the Christian Italian merchant and traveler who keenly studied the old Byzantine and Greek monuments.[98] While the number of these "antiquarian pilgrimages"[99] was relatively minor compared to the number of spiritual pilgrimages and business trips, their mere existence indicates the centrality of these territories to the self-perceptions of contemporary societies that claim a share of Hellenistic, Roman, or Byzantine heritage.

The affairs in and between the Ottoman and Mamluk lands carried the utmost importance for other regions that pursued international and regional trade and travel, since any political instability in either territory or between the two disrupted the land route connecting the Balkans with Anatolia, Iran, Greater Syria, and Egypt.[100] Such volatility also threatened the eastern Mediterranean ports under the control of either power or hindered the access to the Iranian trade routes that connected Anatolia to the rest of the Silk Road.[101] Any upheaval disturbed the traveling Christian, Jewish, or even Muslim pilgrims whose destinations were at the heart of their spiritual worlds, and any domestic unrest interrupted the transactions of European businessmen who fulfilled the steadily increasing demand for spices and other Eastern products. Any conflict with either the Ottomans or Mamluks increased customs charges for non-local merchants, temporarily suspended their transactions, or annulled the safe-conduct papers that were granted to non-Muslims.[102] Since the Mamluks and the Ottomans were central to the international politics of all powers that pursued higher ambitions in the Mediterranean Sea and Indian Ocean, any change in Ottoman–Mamluk contacts was closely followed by these other powers.

Overview

Within this complex historical, political, and economic context, the multilayered relationship between the Ottomans and Mamluks began to unfold. From their earliest exchanges in the mid-fourteenth century, the Ottoman and Mamluk sovereigns renegotiated and redefined their images through diplomatic encounters. The purpose of these missions extended beyond the overt messages that were either articulated in the correspondence or delivered orally by an ambassador. The composition of the letters, the titulature and tropes used in the correspondence, the selection of envoys, the behavior and treatment of ambassadors, and the choice of gifts were all as important as the actual messages. An overview of these tools that the Ottomans and Mamluks were familiar with and utilized in their encounters will clarify how this system of communication functioned and contributed to the image-making processes of these sovereigns. The overview in Chapter 1 suggests that the Ottomans initially imitated the Mamluks in their official ceremonies and diplomatic conventions, though they eventually outgrew and transcended the once superior or more prestigious Mamluk model.

As Chapter 2 illustrates, the relationship between the Ottomans and Mamluks displayed remarkable vitality and complexity from its earliest phase until 1402. The earliest Ottoman and Mamluk texts not only showed the Ottoman acknowledgement of Mamluk superiority, but also the Mamluks' growing awareness of the Ottomans and their military successes in the Balkans and Anatolia. The loyal and regular visits of Ottoman embassies to the Mamluk capital after almost every military success, the respectful tone of early Ottoman correspondence, and the impressive selection of gifts proffered to the Mamluk sovereigns all testify to the vital symbolic and regional importance of the Mamluk court to its younger counterpart. Despite their higher status, the Mamluks carefully followed the growing Ottoman presence along their own northern frontier in Anatolia while putting on a guise of indifference. After the Ottoman attacks to the northern Mamluk frontier in Syria in 1399, however, the Mamluk rulers became more overtly concerned about the potential threat of an intrusive Ottoman polity. This early phase of contacts became a critical period for the formation of the Ottoman image at the Mamluk court as well as for the evolution of Ottoman–Mamluk diplomatic discourse.

Chapter 3 demonstrates how the days following the major waves of Timurid attacks between 1384 and 1404 and the battle of Ankara (1402) brought new domestic and international challenges for both regimes. Pressured by these serious concerns, some of which challenged and even damaged their images in the international arena, both the Ottomans and the Mamluks maintained their diplomatic contacts with each other. While the Ottomans under the leadership of Mehmed I (r.1413–21) and Murad II (r.1421–44 and 1446–51) continued to pay their respects to their Mamluk counterparts with regular diplomatic embassies, they also sought further recognition from the Mamluk court. With one of the most elaborate Islamic chancery offices at their service, the Mamluk sultans Faraj (r.1399–1405 and 1405–12), al-Mu'ayyad Shaykh (r.1412–21), Barsbay (r.1422–38) and Jaqmaq (r.1438–53), whose reigns predominantly overlapped those of Mehmed I and Murad II, refined their perception of the Ottomans with every piece of news they received from Ottoman territories and responded by increasingly elevating their titulature.

Chapter 4 will explore how the Ottoman conquest of Constantinople in 1453 and the ambitious politics of the young Ottoman ruler Mehmed II (r.1444–6 and 1451–81) started a new chapter in the Ottoman–Mamluk relationship. Expressing himself primarily through diplomatic missions, Mehmed demanded a different type of recognition from the Mamluk court. His main counterparts, Sultans Inal (r.1453–61), Khushqadam (r.1461–7), and Qaytbay (r.1468–96), did not submit to Mehmed's appeals, although each negotiated with Mehmed in different ways. During this later phase, the two powers devised competitive rhetorical tropes that were communicated to each other's courts primarily through diplomatic correspondence, gifts, and ceremonies. At a time when the Ottomans asserted their superiority in almost every corner of the known world, these two powers challenged each other by questioning the other's right to sovereignty while claiming the exclusive right to lead the Islamic world. While their religious rhetoric had once served as a unifying factor, in the second half of the fifteenth century even their shared faith presented another opportunity to express rivalry or to bolster claims for superiority. The way by which the Ottomans and Mamluks recast this well-known trope in a new competitive manner proves their plasticity in this setting.

As Chapter 5 illustrates, in a physical manifestation of this charged diplomatic atmosphere, the two imperial armies exhausted each other in a long war between 1485 and 1491.[103] Despite the common perception that wars bring about a complete cessation of communications, this war between the Ottoman ruler Bayezid II and the Mamluk sultan Qaytbay presented new and creative opportunities to sustain the network between them and contributed to the complex process of the refinement of mutual perceptions.[104]

Chapter 6 studies the final 30 years of the Ottoman–Mamluk relationship until the death of Bayezid II in 1512. During this time of counterclaims and challenges, it was still Bayezid II to whom the Mamluk sultan Qansuh al-Ghawri first appealed for naval assistance in 1507 when the Portuguese navy approached the Arabian Peninsula and the Red Sea. Despite the increasing volatility of their diplomatic encounters and after an inconclusive and exhaustive war, the Ottoman and Mamluk rulers allied against a common enemy that threatened their shared political and economic interests. With his request, Qansuh al-Ghawri opened new horizons for Bayezid, who seized this opportunity to become involved in the politics of the profitable Indian trade system. In the coming decades after 1512, the Indian Ocean would witness a significant power struggle between the Ottomans and the Portuguese that grew out of this initial request for aid.[105]

The decision to study the multiple phases of this relationship from its inception until 1512 and to exclude the final five years preceding the fall of Mamluk regime to the Ottomans in 1517 is primarily a practical one, since a study that would include the final five years would undoubtedly produce a second volume. By omitting these years, the book also argues for an alternative to a common trend in Ottoman–Mamluk studies. Most scholarly studies to date have emphasized moments of conflict—particularly military campaigns—between the two empires before proceeding teleologically to the Ottoman conquest of Egypt.[106] This focus on the ultimate Ottoman victory neither acknowledges the ideological and political superiority of the Mamluks for the greater part of their long relationship with the Ottomans, nor accommodates the plasticity, flexibility, and adaptability of their mutual communications. One way to see the richness of their interactions is to turn our attention to the earlier diplomatic engagements that both the Ottomans and Mamluks tirelessly maintained under any conditions. Until the rise of the Shi'i Safavids, the Ottomans molded their image in the Islamic world in response to diverse factors and political actors such as the Timurids, but also in the light of the Mamluks' strong presence—a presence that quickly disappeared in the primary sources after 1517.

CHAPTER 1

THE TOOLS OF DIPLOMACY

The reach of Bayezid began to extend far into the lands of Rum. He became so well-known for his jihad against non-Muslims that he gained a great reputation. Al-Malik al-Zahir (Barquq) wrote him letters, sent him gifts, and sent him commander after commander (as ambassadors). He also sent Ibn al-Sughayr, the head of the doctors, to Bayezid. Since no rulers remained who had not sent letters and gifts to the Ottomans, al-Malik al-Zahir, the ruler of Egypt, feared for his ruin. He (Barquq) said that "I am not afraid of Timur because everyone will help me against him. Rather, I am afraid of Ibn 'Uthman (the Ottomans)," I (the author) heard Ibn Khaldun[1] saying. He (Barquq) repeatedly said, "for the ruler of Egypt there was no fear except from Ibn 'Uthman[.]"[2]

As the above passage implies, diplomatic exchanges were not merely routine missions, but rather served as seals of acknowledgement from the sender that recognized the recipient's sovereignty and political authority. By sending his emissaries to the Ottoman court, the Mamluk sultan Barquq recognized the Ottomans' status in the international arena—a status that would gradually increase from the fourteenth century until 1512.

This passage from Ibn Bahadur does not reveal, however, how different components of these missions contributed to this process of diplomatic acknowledgement. Although every mission had a specific and immediate task to discuss or negotiate, it often conveyed indirect yet equally important messages that were primarily disseminated through correspondence, gifts, envoys, and ceremonies such as ambassadorial audiences.[3] The fifteenth-century Mamluk historian Ibn Taghribirdi (d.1470) revealed the widespread recognition of these elements—at least in Mamluk society—when he repeated the old proverb, "The strength and greatness of a king is known from three things: his letter, his envoy, and his gift."[4] Contemporary Ottoman texts expressing parallel sensitivities have not yet emerged, but it is reasonable to assume that the Ottomans embraced similar principles.

When the Mamluks—the leading sovereigns of the Sunni Muslim world and the eastern Mediterranean—and the Ottomans—a minor but growing principality along the frontiers of the Byzantine Empire—initiated their earliest diplomatic contacts, they used envoys, gifts, letters, and ceremonies to disseminate and negotiate their imperial ideologies. Every individual or item that accompanied, welcomed, or hosted a diplomatic mission contributed to the non-verbal communication of diplomacy, and these elements often completed the actual message or enhanced its effect on its recipient.[5]

A closer look at the practices of the Ottoman and Mamluk courts, however, reveals the striking inequality between the established character of Mamluk court etiquette and the developing quality of the Ottomans during the period under investigation. The Mamluks relied on a stable body of regulations that was primarily inherited from their Ayyubid predecessors when they took over the Ayyubid imperial capital, Cairo.[6] The architecture of the ceremonial spaces in their citadel–palace—which had been constructed by the Ayyubids—was also deeply influenced by the traditions of the Great Seljuks.[7] Additionally, the possible Mongol influence on early Mamluk ceremonials should be taken into consideration, as well as other sources that made additional references to diverse Muslim and non-Muslim traditions.[8] The Mamluk sultans and their advisors merely modified this deeply-rooted framework to fit their changing political conditions and needs.[9]

During this period the Ottomans moved their capital three times—to Bursa, Edirne, and finally Constantinople—while the Mamluks remained in Cairo, a fact that also reflected the disparity between the settled Mamluk institutions and the emerging Ottoman ones. With each new capital and palace, the Ottomans further refined their court etiquette and ceremonies. They gradually built their own equivalents of the Mamluks' institutions and constructed parallel ceremonies, often by emulating other Islamic courts and by assimilating practices from the lands they conquered.[10] Although Ottoman rituals and institutions shared a number of characteristics with Mamluk practices, they were also strongly inspired by the Timurids.[11] During its second phase of construction after 1468, the Topkapı Palace in Constantinople served as a stage for the reformulation of Ottoman rituals and imperial ideology,[12] and this phase of reformulation had not yet ended in 1512. By this time, however, the Ottomans had clearly devised their own body of distinct regulations and conventions that carried traces of Islamic, Byzantine, and even Central Asian nomadic traditions.[13] To trace the gradual divergence of Ottoman and Mamluk ceremonials, as well as interpret the diplomatic interactions that will be discussed in the following chapters, an overview of their mutual diplomatic repertoire is necessary. This overview traces the typical sequence of a diplomatic mission, beginning with the selection of an ambassador and ending with his return home.

The First Step: Selecting an Ambassador

> For an embassy a man is required who has served kings, who is bold in speaking, who has traveled widely, who has a portion of every branch of learning, who is retentive of memory and farseeing, who is tall and handsome, and if he is old and wise that is better. If a boon-companion is sent as an envoy he will be more reliable; and if a man is sent who is brave and manly, skilled in arms and horsemanship, and renowned as duellist, it will be extremely good, for he will shew the world that our men

are like him; and if an ambassador be a man of noble family that
will be good too, for they will have respect for his ancestry and
not do him any mischief; and he should not be a wine-bibber,
a buffoon, a gambler, a babbler or a simpleton. Very often kings
have sent envoys bearing gifts of money and valuables and sued
for peace and shewn themselves weak and submissive; after
giving this illusion they have followed up by sending prepared
troops and picked men in the attack and defeating the enemy.
The conduct and good sense of an ambassador are a guide to the
conduct, wisdom, judgment, and greatness of his king.[14]

Although this passage from Nizam al-Mulk (d.1092), who established an almost legendary reputation as the experienced vizier of the young Seljuk Sultan Malikshah, was produced nearly three centuries before the first diplomatic exchange between the Ottomans and the Mamluks, it offered a timeless guide for a ruler choosing his diplomatic representatives. The fact that this guide appeared in a book that belonged to the same genre as *Mirror for Princes*—an advice book for rulers—revealed the intention of the wise vizier: to warn kings to select their envoys wisely. The brief section on the qualities of ambassadors in the encyclopedic chancery manual of the Mamluk scholar and secretary al-Qalqashandi (d.1418) also suggested that these principles resonated with fifteenth-century Mamluk perceptions.[15]

Rulers selected their envoys carefully.[16] In an age when modern means of communication were not available, the Ottoman and Mamluk sovereigns relied on their diplomatic representatives for a number of crucial tasks, from transmitting their images to negotiating treaties. The envoys sustained communications between the courts, carried oral messages (some of which were entrusted to them in confidence), and protected the honor of their sovereigns. While some served as mere messengers, a number gathered intelligence.[17]

Beyond their loyalty to their rulers, envoys ideally possessed linguistic competence and social skills. An envoy who knew the language of the court he visited was more likely to succeed there,[18] and the Ottomans frequently benefited from the services of subjects who could speak the correct languages in European courts.[19] Mamluk bureaucratic practices evinced a similar concern.[20] Envoys familiar with a local culture, who had already built connections with the members of a particular court, or who could appeal to the personal interests or hobbies of a recipient ruler, were also more likely to achieve their mission. During the period under investigation, a professional body of diplomats did not yet exist, but some individuals who shouldered this responsibility more than once rose to eminence as quasi-diplomats.[21]

Ottoman sources for this period only offer some tentative conclusions about how representatives were selected.[22] In choosing envoys, leaders generally examined a candidate's occupational background and social status, which would contribute to their imperial message and image.[23] The Ottomans tailored their embassies to the Mamluk court to make a particular impression at a particular moment; they chose prestigious military commanders to declare military victories and scholars of Islam to emphasize their dedication to their faith.[24] If a mission dealt with legal issues such as an inheritance or the negotiation of a treaty, they sent legal scholars.[25] By 1512, the Ottoman rulers—particularly Bayezid II— had started to rely increasingly on representatives from the *devşirme* (child levy) system for diplomatic missions to Cairo.[26]

The Ottomans' eventual preference for *devşirme* recruits mirrored the pattern of envoy selection at the Mamluk court. During the Bahri Mamluk reign (1250–1390), which preceded their diplomatic exchanges with the Ottomans, the Mamluks tended to send more than one ambassador, often one from the military class and one from the scholarly class.[27] Later, the Mamluk sultans frequently sent sufis and scholars to other Muslim courts, but generally dispatched *mamluks* to the Ottoman court.[28] This choice might have reflected practical concerns; both the Ottoman administration and the Mamluk amirs spoke Turkish—albeit different dialects—and therefore could communicate efficiently. The Mamluk sultans' growing reliance on *mamluks* for diplomatic missions also paralleled the increasing militarization in the Mamluk regime—an argument that must be tested by further study.[29] During the fifteenth century, this practice became so prevalent that these *mamluks* were occasionally appointed to positions (such as *ihtisab*) that were previously occupied by legal scholars.[30]

At first glance the role of ambassador was likely seen as an honor, since it demonstrated a ruler's confidence in an individual. In reality the position was demanding because it oscillated between two extremes. While envoys might receive the highest honors and prestige during and after their missions, they would often have to undertake great risk. The possibility always existed that the titulature accorded to a recipient in the correspondence, a specific message, a gift, or their own behavior might elicit the recipient's wrath.[31] Although the conventions of Islamic diplomatic practices demanded and described the good treatment of ambassadors, these conventions were occasionally violated.[32] Even if their lives were spared, envoys were sometimes subjected to abuse.[33] Occasionally, unforeseen conditions, such as the natural death of an envoy or even a ruler, plagued the success of a diplomatic mission.[34] As they struggled with an infinite number of possibilities, envoys would risk humiliation, their careers, their wealth, and sometimes even their lives when they undertook a diplomatic mission.

The Preparation of Letters: Content, Outlook, Interpretation, and Secretaries

While his ambassador prepared for departure, a ruler and his advisors crafted the correspondence and selected the gifts for the recipient ruler. Two separate letters were prepared on occasion, with the second piece (*qa'ima* or *tabat*) containing a reaffirmation of the initial message and/or a list of the accompanying gifts.[35] Since very limited information exists about the Ottoman practices that revolved around the preparation of diplomatic correspondence during this period, the rest of this section will focus on Mamluk practices.

Although they might sound mundane to modern ears, the external features of correspondence—such as the size of the paper or the formulas greeting the recipient—carried levels of meaning beyond their actual content. In Mamluk chancery practices, these features were hierarchically organized and selected according to the rank of the recipient and the intent of the sender. This order also revealed the ideologies and worldviews of rulers since, each ruler had a different title and therefore a different status in the medieval political world.[36] While caliphs always ranked first in this political system and were honored accordingly, during this period the Mamluk administrators categorized the other Muslim rulers with whom they regularly corresponded into three main groups.[37] The highest category included the rulers of Chingiz Khan's successors, such as the Ilkhanids, the Jalayirids, and the Timurids. The next category consisted of Anatolian dynasties, such as the Karamanids. Less significant Anatolian powers comprised the lowest ranking group.[38] Finally, non-Muslim powers were treated as a separate group and ranked among themselves.[39]

Rulers took these categories into account when choosing the external characteristics of a letter, such as paper size, the type of calligraphy used, and ink color.[40] The most valuable paper—and therefore the most prestigious—was full-sized Baghdadi paper, which was reserved for rulers from the highest category.[41] Additionally, a liberal usage of space on this same paper conveyed the wealth and superiority of its sender. By contrast, rulers of lesser rank would receive letters on half- or third-sized Baghdadi sheets;[42] the smallest size was used to correspond with rulers from Anatolian principalities or Ilkhanid governors and functionaries.[43] Only three references discussed the paper size used in Ottoman–Mamluk correspondence.[44] While one of the references is unclear, and the other two suggest that in the early fifteenth century Mamluk letters to the Ottomans were composed on third-sized Baghdadi paper.[45]

The internal characteristics of a letter were as important as its external appearance.[46] Each letter contained epistolary sections such as the introductory protocol (*fawatih*) and the ending protocol (*khawatim*), each of which was divided into further sub-sections.[47] A number of predefined transitional phrases and expressions ensured clear and smooth connections between the sections.[48] The introductory protocol of a letter held particular significance because it not only illuminated the nature of the power relationship between the recipient and the sender, but also clarified the theme or genre of the correspondence.[49] For instance, if a letter announced a military victory (*fathname*), both the language and the greetings in the introduction made this purpose clear.[50] This study will emphasize titulature or honorifics (*laqab*, pl. *alqab*) as the essential elements of the introductory protocol, although occasional references to other elements will also appear.

Titulature served as the primary indicator of how a sender and a recipient of a letter viewed each other.[51] Pages-long lists of honorifics in diplomatic manuals and collections of letters demonstrated that the use of appropriate titles was not merely an unchanging part of ceremonials but held great significance in Islamic diplomatic culture.[52] As political conditions shifted, titles were redesigned and adapted to the emerging power dynamics, and they reflected the status of the recipient in the eyes of the sender. For instance, the titles accorded to non-Muslim rulers referred generally to their Christian faith, while those that the Mamluks bestowed on the Ottomans acknowledged the recipients' warfare against the non-Muslims.[53] Conversely, the titulature that the Ottomans accorded to the Mamluk sultans evoked the leadership of the Mamluks in the Islamic world. Since a ruler's status was negotiated with the usage of titulature, a title that did not satisfy the expectations of its recipient could trigger a period of deterioration in a diplomatic relationship.[54]

As some political powers disappeared and new ones emerged, the hierarchical organization of their titles evolved.[55] Depending on the political climate, a ruler could be demoted to a lower level of appellation or promoted to a higher one by his peers. While independent from short-term political changes, most titles had a limited life span; some took on a higher or lower connotation while others fell into disuse.[56] The following chapters will show, however, a slow yet steady promotion in the titulature that the Mamluks used to address their rising Ottoman peers.[57]

Through various familiar tropes and themes, diplomatic correspondence mirrored the imperial ideologies of its senders and changed according to the political context and goal of a mission.[58]

Traditional references and citations were common, and some authorities on epistolary writing maintained that "each letter should contain at least one rhetorical concept from the Qur'an or Prophetic tradition."[59] Letter-writers often invoked the names of prominent figures in Arabic, Persian, and Islamic literature—first and foremost the Prophet—to make a desired point.[60] Among other tropes, seniority and age hierarchy were among the rhetorical tools used to maintain or improve diplomatic relationships.[61] Finally, whenever one Muslim sovereign needed to sustain positive contacts with another, he used the imagery of "two arms from a body" to remind the recipient of their shared religion.[62]

In Ottoman–Mamluk correspondence these tropes shifted over time, and familiar themes were gradually alluded to in drastically different ways. For example, the Ottomans tried to explain or even legitimize their succession policy (fratricide) in their early correspondence with the Mamluks.[63] As the Ottoman dynasty remained in power, however, they increasingly and proudly accentuated their succession practices in order to target what they believed was the weakest aspect of the Mamluk sultans' image: their background as recently converted slaves. In the past, other rulers such as Timur had denigrated the Mamluk regime with similar attacks.[64] The Turco-Mongol ruler, who rose to power in Central Asia in 1370s and died in 1405, claimed Chingizid heritage and founded the Timurid dynasty. These kinds of shifts prove the plasticity of these tropes and of the language of diplomacy, and rulers and their advisors skillfully employed them for maximum effect.

This rich amalgam of external and internal features—from paper size to titulature to tropes—produced eloquent yet complex texts that often elude literal translation. A greater understanding of these letters, therefore, depends upon a careful method of reading that pays attention to their historical contexts and the shifting meanings of expressions.[65]

Closely linked to this issue of textual interpretation are concerns about the preservation and the authenticity of letters. Far more Mamluk chancery manuals and compilations of letters exist than Ottoman, and these two types of texts served as the main depositories of official correspondence for the period under investigation. A compilation of letters mainly consisted of different samples of administrative and diplomatic correspondence occasionally accompanied by lists of titulature. A chancery manual may have included not only samples of letter writing, but also illuminated the diplomatic conventions of the time with descriptions of multiple administrative and bureaucratic practices, from court etiquette to the rankings of contemporary rulers. The earliest-known Mamluk versions of these documents date to the early fourteenth century.[66]

The completion of the seven-volume chancery manual *Subh al-A'sha fi Sina'at al-Insha'* by the Mamluk scholar and secretary Shihab al-din Abu al-'Abbas Ahmad b. 'Ali al-Qalqashandi (1355– 1418) in 1412 culminated this genre.[67] After a brief teaching career, al-Qalqashandi became a secretary in the Mamluk imperial chancery and produced works in different genres including law and the secretarial arts.[68] He became primarily known, however, for his encyclopedic *Subh al-A'sha*. Its rich content demonstrated the extent of the administrative structure and diplomatic etiquette that regulated the Mamluk court and provided information on the administration, rules, and ceremonials of earlier Islamic regimes such as the Fatimids. In addition to offering samples of correspondence, al-Qalqashandi covered numerous topics, such as the details that differentiated diverse types of internal and external correspondence, the titulature accorded to rulers depending on their rank in Mamluk perceptions, the types of papers and ink for diverse types of correspondence, and different types of ceremonials.

Ottoman works similar to al-Qalqashandi's did not exist before the sixteenth century. A few scattered compilations of letters (*münşeat*) emerged from the fifteenth century onward, but they were humble in both size and content, and were comprised mostly of internal correspondence.[69] The earliest available and most substantial *münşeat* was that of Feridun Bey, who died in 1555.[70] Even Feridun Bey's work, however, does not extend beyond a collection of letters and a list of honorifics. The earliest extant record that described the ceremonies and ambassadorial audiences at the Ottoman court dates to the mid-seventeenth century and was titled *Elçi Kanunnamesi*

(The Code of Ambassadors).[71] It was not until the early eighteenth century that the *teşrifat defterleri* (works that recorded codes of official court ceremonies, protocol, and etiquette) proliferated and were often used by officers of etiquette as reference books.[72]

In the absence of more comprehensive sources, therefore, we benefit from the scanty evidence available in Ottoman chronicles, traveler accounts,[73] anecdotes recounted by envoys,[74] and the accounts of various figures who entered the service of the Ottoman court.[75] Using the aforementioned seventeenth-century or later sources to reconstruct a fifteenth-century ambassadorial audience at the Ottoman court presents a methodological risk to researchers. Besides the inherent risks of recording an event long after it happened, the authors and copyists who reproduced the texts were also known to editorialize, often in an attempt to create a more glorious account.[76] Despite their shortcomings, these later sources are still occasionally cited due to the dearth of primary sources on early Ottoman ceremonials.[77] The paucity and vulnerability of primary sources, especially Ottoman ones, raise the thorny issue of credibility regarding Feridun Bey's *münşeat*, a main Ottoman depository for Ottoman–Mamluk correspondence and a primary source for this study. Although the authenticity of this source has been questioned in the past, for the period under investigation (after 1389), it proves to be relatively reliable.[78]

Since correspondence formed a crucial part of their public image, rulers prepared it carefully. Most letters from foreign rulers were performed orally at the time of their presentation to the Mamluk sultan, while others were performed publicly in congregational mosques.[79] Their preparation demanded not only multiple drafts, but also the cooperation of the ruler, his administrators or advisors, and members of the chancery (*diwan al-insha'*).[80] In the Mamluk administration, the *katib al-sirr* (the head of the Mamluk chancery or confidential secretary) served a critical role in the formulation of diplomatic correspondence. Depending on his personal skills and training, he often relied on the talents of the *katib al-insha'* (composition secretary), who was often more experienced in or more academically suited to the composition of formal letters.[81] The

Mamluk historian Ibn Taghribirdi's critical comments about a *katib al-sirr* of Barsbay's testify to the high standards some members of Mamluk learned class held for secretaries:

> The appointment of this ignoramus to a high position such as this [*katib al-sirr*] was counted one of the mistakes of al-Malik al-Ashraf [Barsbay], because his ignorance was a disgrace. For if al-Malik al-Ashraf were wise and intelligent, and he should receive from some distant ruler a letter containing elegant and eloquent prose and poetry, and he should wish his confidential secretary to reply with something surpassing it or at least equal to it (as al-Malik al-Nasir Muhammad ibn Qalawun and other great rulers used to do), he would know the shortcomings of the one whom he has appointed to this office.[82]

In addition to their eloquent writing, these secretaries often memorized the Qur'an because they were expected to incorporate its verses into their prose.[83] They also needed to be well-informed about the finer points of official correspondence and excel in employing them skillfully. In short, they were to be masters of literary composition (*insha'* in Arabic; *inşa'* in Turkish).

While the field of official correspondence was complex, a vague relationship connected the Mamluk and Ottoman practices of literary composition. Many scholars rightly argue that the Persian tradition influenced the Ottomans.[84] Although it is impossible to determine exactly where the influence of one specific tradition ended and another one began—particularly in a field such as Islamic diplomatic practices,[85] which drew heavily from both Persian and Arabic conventions—the possible influence of Mamluk *insha'* culture on the fledgling Ottoman culture should also be considered.[86] In their letters to the Mamluks, the Ottomans loyally followed the Mamluk rankings of Arabic titulature,[87] and, despite the fact that both the Ottoman and Mamluk ruling classes spoke Turkish, the official correspondence between the two lands was exclusively drawn in Arabic until the sixteenth century.[88]

The presence of Mamluk-trained scholars and administrators in early Ottoman institutions further supports the possibility that the Ottomans borrowed from Mamluk *insha'* practices. An early example of such a scholar was Shams al-din al-Jazari (1350–1429), a celebrated expert of Qur'anic reading (*qira'at*) and the art of composition.[89] After he fell out of favor with Mamluk administrators, the Ottoman ruler Bayezid welcomed him to Bursa with the utmost respect, and Shams al-din al-Jazari pursued his career there until Timur defeated Bayezid in 1402. The scholar's son, Muhammad ibn al-Jazari (also known as Muhammad al-Asghar), accompanied him to Bursa and later followed his father to the Timurid capital of Samarqand. In his later life, Muhammad eventually returned to the Ottoman lands and was given a post at the Ottoman court composing documents, possibly including official correspondence to other rulers.[90] Mehmed I also considered him for higher positions such as the vizierate, but hesitated because of Muhammad's publicly-known weakness for opium.[91] With his diverse background, Muhammad al-Asghar likely brought influences from both Mamluk and Timurid *insha'* practices to the Ottoman chancery. Ibn 'Arabshah (1392–1450), another Mamluk scholar who was competent in Persian, Turkish, and Arabic, served as the head of the chancery in the Ottoman ruler Mehmed I's court and probably occupied the official position of *nişancı*, which was the head of Ottoman chancery and the Ottoman equivalent of *katib al-sirr*. He originated from the Mamluk city of Damascus but left after it was conquered by Timur in 1400–1 and later trained in Samarqand. Besides translating some literary works for Mehmed I into Turkish, he composed Mehmed's letters to the Mamluk sultan al-Mu'ayyad Shaykh in Arabic.[92]

Among scholars who might have influenced Ottoman diplomatic correspondence, Molla Gürani (d.1488) was among the best known. He most likely came from a Persian-speaking background and spent many years learning and teaching in Mamluk territory.[93] Later in his career, he was introduced by some Ottoman scholars to the Ottoman ruler Murad II, who appointed him to tutor Mehmed II, the young prince and future sultan. Years later Mehmed II solicited the services of his old tutor to write his diplomatic correspondence—in particular the victory proclamation of Constantinople—to his Mamluk counterpart in Cairo.[94] Molla Gürani's prose, like that of other Mamluk-trained scholars, must have carried some elements of Mamluk style to the Ottoman institutions in which he served.

Mehmed II was not the only Ottoman sovereign who took great care in his exchanges with the Mamluks. A record from the late fifteenth century certifies that Mehmed II's son Bayezid generously rewarded a poet who composed a poem to accompany a letter to the Mamluk court.[95] Despite all their care, the Ottomans did not impress their Mamluk peers with the literary and rhetorical quality of their correspondence until the early sixteenth century. A letter Mehmed sent in 1456 following the Ottomans' military success in Serbia was criticized by the Mamluk chroniclers, who stated that the letter suffered from the ignorance or inexperience of scribes who did not know Arabic spelling and grammar.[96] In contrast, a later correspondence that was sent by Bayezid II to Qansuh al-Ghawri in 1511 was complimented by Ibn Iyas for its exceptional literary qualities.[97] The question remains open to investigation: did this compliment reveal a sincere assessment of the improving Ottoman chancery practices, or did it simply mirror the changing times and the increasing status of the Ottomans? It is perhaps not coincidental that during these later years, the Mamluks needed Ottoman help against the encroaching Portuguese threat.[98]

Preparing the Gifts

The recent interest of modern scholarship in gift practices affirms the universality of gift exchanges, and the Ottomans and Mamluks were no exception.[99] Gift selection was an important aspect of preparing for a diplomatic mission.[100] Islamic culture particularly valued this practice because it was mentioned in the Qur'an and came to be associated with the Prophet after the rise of Islam.[101] This cultural emphasis manifested itself in a new literary genre, *Kitab al-Hadaya* (Book of Gifts), which produced books dedicated to this entrenched practice. The earliest examples of *Kitab al-Hadaya* probably appeared sometime before the eleventh century.[102] While they are not among the most abundantly available records of Islamic culture—so far only seven manuscripts have been identified—their existence alone confirms the significance of this practice, especially since no similar genre has been discovered in any other Mediterranean society.[103]

The size and complexity of the vocabulary used to describe gift exchanges suggests that this practice was multi-faceted.[104] Notably, some words commonly used in Ottoman sources (such as *hediye* or *pişkeş*) have either Arabic or Persian roots and were used cross-culturally. While *hadaya, 'atiya, in'am, tuhfa* (meaning rarities), *hiba*,[105] *'aja'ib* (meaning marvels), and *muhadat*[106] appear most often in Arabic (mostly Mamluk) sources, *hediye*,[107] *don*,[108] *atiye, pişkeş* (or *peşkeş*),[109] *sacu*,[110] *armağan*,[111] *tuhfe*,[112] *yüz kızardan, yüz ağardan*,[113] and *belek*[114] occur most frequently in the Ottoman context. These words, though they could have been used interchangeably, did connote a hierarchical classification that illuminated the relationship between the recipient and the donor. The Arabic word *in'am*, for instance, connoted largesse or described donatives granted by a sovereign to his troops or soldiers, either to reward or ensure their loyalty during a long campaign.[115] The Persian word *peşkeş* suggested a tribute or even a bribe from the lower-ranking individual.[116] Likewise, the Turkish words *yüz kızardan* and *yüz ağardan* referred to an interaction between an inferior donor and a superior recipient, while the word *don* may have referred to attire presented as gifts.[117] These connotations also raised the question of whether an item was intended as a gift or as a bribe—an issue that has initiated long discussions among scholars of Islamic law but did not have a direct bearing on Ottoman–Mamluk diplomacy.[118] The gifts that were included in diplomatic missions were ideally protected by the same immunity offered to envoys. They were also closely connected with economics and trade in various ways—a connection which has been generally neglected by researchers because of the overwhelming ideological, cultural, and symbolic significance of gift exchanges.[119] Gifts were occasionally known to deliver secret messages at critical times.[120]

As both the extensive vocabulary for and the general emphasis on gift exchange in Islamic culture reveal, gifts played a more significant role in diplomacy than has been previously acknowledged.[121] Gifts—or the absence of them—and their value often complemented an envoy's mission with a hidden or implied message.[122] In one remarkable Mamluk–Ilkhanid exchange in 1301, both the Ilkhanid ruler Ghazan (r.1295–1304) and the young Mamluk sultan al-Nasir Muhammad (r.1293–4, 1299–1309, 1310–41) stated in their letters that they would judge the sincerity of the other's intentions for peace after seeing his gifts.[123]

As the case of Ghazan and al-Nasir Muhammad suggests, the rulers in this part of the world acknowledged the communicative power of gifts and were therefore particularly careful with their selection.[124] A passage in which the sixteenth century Ottoman chronicler Neşri depicted the Ottoman–Mamluk exchange after the successful Ottoman battle in Varna (1444) reflected this same realization:

> to the sultan of Egypt, [Murad II] sent Azeb Bey [as an ambassador], he sent a considerable number of infidel [prisoners of war] in their armors, they displayed armors [...] and when the sultan of Egypt saw these infidels in their armors [he said: "] Allah[!] May Ibn-i Osman (the Ottomans) be victorious [!",] that Friday he made the sermons in the mosques be read in the name of Murad Han and gave a substantial amount of goods to Azeb Bey[.][125]

Although no specific objects were exclusively given to either rulers or ambassadors (or to the administrators of a hosting court), gifts for rulers were always the most elaborate and expensive of the mission. Garments, furs, swords, weaponry, horses, saddles, helmets, tents, silver and gold artifacts, slaves, and porcelains were common offerings for rulers, and sometimes even cash or coins were sent. For some missions, fabrics or weaponry were the predominant offerings. In others, slaves—which were particularly valued as gifts—were exchanged between sovereigns, while robes of honor were bestowed primarily upon diplomatic representatives.[126] Hunting animals, such as birds, were also among favorite and valued gifts, as hunting was a privilege for sovereigns and other members of the court.[127]

Sovereigns also attempted to choose gifts that appealed to the personal interests of a recipient ruler in order to strengthen the ties between the two courts or to ensure the success of a mission.[128] For instance, the relationship between the Ottoman ruler Bayezid II and the Counts of Mantua in Italy (who were members of the Gonzaga family) originated with Count Francesco II's passion for horses.[129] The count, who wanted to enlarge his stables, began sending representatives to buy horses from Ottoman lands. Bayezid, who needed allies in European courts, wanted to keep the lines of communication open with the Gonzagas and began to send them horses and riding equipment. The presence of Bayezid's brother Cem in Europe gave the Ottoman ruler an additional incentive to play careful politics with European leaders, and he supplemented these gifts with relics of Christianity that carried great symbolic value for Christian rulers.[130]

Since their earliest diplomatic contacts, the Ottomans and Mamluks had taken part in this tradition of mutual gift exchange.[131] While the Mamluks sent Alexandrian or Aleppen textiles to the Ottomans, the Ottomans reciprocated with Bursan silk and Angoran wool. Alongside these more common items, both courts, with their strong interest in warfare and military skills, turned weaponry and horses into highly valued and frequent gifts.[132] Foreign weaponry acquired as spoils was primarily sent by the Ottomans to the Mamluks and served the additional purpose of showcasing their own military power.[133] Although in a number of other historical contexts sending artillery and weaponry indicated hostility, in the Ottoman–Mamluk context no evidence suggests that these objects caused or contributed to any conflict between the two lands.[134]

Rulers also took particular pride in giving items that the recipient would have found difficult to procure. Ottoman rulers often gave silver items to the Mamluk court, a gesture that was at least partially an allusion to their conquest of silver-rich Serbian and Bosnian lands.[135] Slaves or prisoners of war were common gifts from the Ottomans to the Mamluks, particularly when the purpose of the mission was to announce or to congratulate a military success, or to improve relations that had become strained.[136] The value of this particular gift did not solely stem from the economic cost of a slave, but also highlighted the drastic difference between the groups' access to slaves. While the Ottomans acquired slaves during their regular campaigns and frontier attacks in the Balkans, the Mamluks had to purchase the slaves upon which they built their military system.[137] Geography also played a part in this discrepancy, since the Ottomans were geographically closer to the routes of the slave trade than the Mamluks. Sending slaves or prisoners of war, therefore, became a particularly Ottoman way to announce success, wealth, and expanding political power, as well as accentuate the aspects of *ghaza* and *jihad* in their evolving image.[138] The Ottoman preference of offering fur to the Mamluk sultans likely also stemmed from geography and their relatively direct access to the northern Black Sea coasts and territories beyond.[139]

In return, the Mamluks sent the Ottomans spices and valuable Indian or Chinese textiles, which they easily obtained because of their control of the Red Sea and their proximity to the Indian Ocean trade system. Balsam, which European travelers referred to as a very valuable gift from the Mamluk sultan, was sent to the Ottoman court a few times, but only on very special occasions.[140] Although Chinese porcelains were among valuable gifts the Mamluk court sent to other rulers, it was never mentioned as a gift to the Ottomans.[141] On multiple occasions, however, the Mamluks conveyed exotic wild animals to the Ottoman court: elephants,[142] giraffes,[143] leopards or lions,[144] parrots,[145] and wild asses or mules.[146] These rare animals symbolized the wealth and power of the sender and could be seen as extraordinary signs of generosity to improve or maintain a relationship. Only a sovereign had the resources to maintain a menagerie.[147] Thus these exotic animal gifts performed a dual function: they not only underlined the Mamluk connection to distant lands, but also their escalating respect for the Ottomans. The fact that the Ottoman ruler Murad II requested an elephant from the Mamluk sultan Barsbay perhaps reveals this Ottoman ruler's recognition of his regime's need for a more elaborate courtly life-style.[148]

Along with the more traditional offerings, decapitated heads of prisoners of war, captured rulers, or enemy commanders were some of the gifts that delivered confusing, if not contradictory, messages. Depending on the relationship between the recipient and the sender, they might have symbolized either submission or a threat.[149] In 1507, Qansuh al-Ghawri was pleased when one of his commanders sent him the severed heads of Safavid soldiers as a symbolic gift that announced Mamluk military victory. His predecessor Qaytbay, however, did not hide his resentment when the Aqqoyunlu ruler Uzun Hasan sent him the head of the Timurid sultan Abu Sa'id in 1469. He gave the deceased ruler's head a proper Islamic burial with an accompanying formal procession.[150] Qansuh al-Ghawri behaved in a similar manner upon receiving the head of Uzbeg Khan, which arrived with a Safavid embassy from Shah Isma'il.[151] Likewise, when the Ottoman sultan Selim I sent the head of the Dulkadirid ruler to Cairo, Qansuh al-Ghawri interpreted his "gift" as a threat to the Mamluk regime, despite contrary statements from the accompanying Ottoman ambassadors.[152] As was the case with the titulature used in correspondence, this diversity of meanings lent a dynamic character to Ottoman–Mamluk interactions. In addition, because of the reciprocal nature of gift exchange, each occasion gave them a new opportunity to reevaluate each other and to adjust their mutual perceptions accordingly.[153]

While some gifts possessed a dynamic significance and value, others carried a designated status in the art of gift-giving. For instance, in socities that valued ceremonial clothing and appurtenances, robes of honor naturally held a special place in gift exchanges.[154] According to al-Qalqashandi, robes were ranked in a hierarchical order, and a particular robe that was granted by the caliph to a ruler was called a *tashrif*. Eventually, as caliphs lost their political standing, the word *tashrif* was applied to special robes that the sultan bestowed on his high-ranking administrators, governors, or vassals.[155]

In the language of gifts that both the Ottoman and Mamluk societies knew so well, robes could also connote a hierarchical relationship between a more prestigious giver and a lesser-ranking recipient.[156] The act of bestowing a robe upon an envoy was a generous and widespread gesture. While some scholars suggest that the ambassador who donned the robe of this host pledged his vassalage to him, this interpretation is hardly conclusive.[157] Particularly in Ottoman ceremonials, palace functionaries dressed an ambassador in a robe of honor before he entered the presence of the Ottoman sultan, and, in a number of cases, Mamluk ambassadors returned home wearing an Ottoman robe of honor.[158] It is unlikely to think that these Mamluk ambassadors would have returned to their own sultan's lands wearing this robe if the gesture had insinuated a shift in their loyalties. The gift was, at the very least, a reward for an ambassador. In fact, when a hosting sovereign was not content with the message or the deportment of an ambassador, he sometimes withheld the robe of honor as a clear sign of his displeasure.[159]

Although a robe was a fitting gift for a diplomatic representative, it was generally an inappropriate gift for a sovereign.[160] Rulers employed them, on occasion, to send a condescending or humiliating message to a recipient. Bayezid I took deep offense when Timur expressed his superiority over the younger Ottoman ruler by sending him a robe and, in his indignation, cited his noble origins and greater wealth than Timur.[161] Clearly, the relationship between Bayezid and Timur did not deteriorate merely because of a robe, but rather because of the cultural meaning that their diplomatic conventions invested in these textiles, along with these sovereigns' conflicting territorial ambitions. Remarkably, this same Ottoman sultan willingly accepted and put on a robe of honor he received from the Mamluk sultan Barquq, although this event is only recounted in Mamluk sources.[162] Likewise, the Mamluk sultan Barsbay worried deeply upon hearing a report that the Ottoman ruler Murad II had accepted and worn a robe from the Timurid sovereign Shahrukh (d.1447).[163] Barsbay had been hoping to join forces with Murad against the Timurids, and he feared that this gesture symbolized Murad's deference to Shahrukh. Later, when Barsbay heard that he was misinformed about the incident, the Mamluk sultan expressed great relief.[164]

Robes also manifested the significance of seniority and were frequently exchanged among the older and younger members of a family, as was the case with Bayezid II and his son Korkud.[165]

Likewise, Prince Korkud received a robe of honor from the considerably older Mamluk sultan Qansuh al-Ghawri during his stay in Mamluk lands. This event, which did not cause any friction between the two courts, indicated not only the precedence of age in these societies, but also suggested that, despite any expectations the prince may have had, he still ranked below the Mamluk sultan.

The meanings of robes and other attire were further complicated when the items were given from a ruler's personal wardrobe. Sovereigns occasionally gave their own clothes to individuals in their service, to envoys, or to other rulers.[166] For an ambassador, receiving a personal item from a sovereign was often considered an honor because these items were believed to carry the ruler's aura or charisma.[167] In a sense, the gifts seemed to complete a "spiritual transmission" that paralleled practices from both Islamic *sufi* traditions and Christian iconography.[168] In the Islamic tradition, a disciple of a *sufi* master was honored or promoted to a higher spiritual status when he received a robe that was presumed to have belonged to a previous spiritual leader.[169] Likewise, the followers of the Fatimid caliph (who was the Isma'ili imam) believed that their spiritual leader's cast-off robe would transport his "Baraka" or blessing to its new owner.[170] The fact that the Prophet's robe has long been regarded as a valuable Islamic relic also speaks volumes for the cultural value that Muslim societies placed on the outer garments of political or religious authorities.[171]

As with most diplomatic gift exchanges, the transference of a ruler's personal attire was open to a multitude of readings and prompted conflicting responses. When Murad II gave his robe to the Mamluk ambassador Taghribirdi (the only known occasion when an Ottoman ruler bestowed his own robe on a Mamluk ambassador), this gesture was read in both Ottoman and Mamluk contexts as a sign of Ottoman sultan's delight with a friendly message from his Mamluk counterpart.[172] However, the gesture could have served as a tool by which the sender expressed his superiority over the recipient. For example, in January 1479 the Ottomans and the Venetians signed a peace treaty that imposed harsh conditions on the Republic of Venice after 16 years of warfare. After signing the treaty, the ambassador of

Venice, Giovanni Dario, returned home accompanied by the Ottoman ambassador, Lütfi Bey. The Ottoman sultan Mehmed II sent valuable gifts to the Venetian doge with his ambassador, including a woven belt from his own wardrobe. When Lütfi Bey presented his sultan's gifts to the doge, he directed the doge to wear the belt "for love of his master."[173] This message of superiority became clearer as Lütfi Bey and his entourage behaved with the utmost arrogance during their stay in Venice.[174]

Occasionally, Ottoman and Mamluk rulers chose to redistribute the gifts they received to other political sovereigns or their own subjects.[175] This gesture allowed the recipient to transform his gift into his own "signs of grandeur."[176] By "regifting" what he accepted from another diplomatic mission, a recipient ruler demonstrated his generosity while also non-verbally articulating his own wealth and lack of need for the items.[177] The Mamluk Sultan al-Mu'ayyad Shaykh ordered that the gifts of an Ottoman mission be sold and that the revenue be used to construct his religious complex.[178] This generous offering, beyond serving the common good, also emphasized the ruler's piety—a prime asset for the image of any Muslim ruler. When gifts were granted to others or into the service of the community, they became public, however indirectly, and were not as easily forgotten as the other diplomatic gifts that remained behind palace walls. Even after the items were no longer physically present, the gesture of giving became part of a social memory and the ruler's enduring image.[179] This practice of regifting, therefore, gave rulers one more way to masterfully manage how they were perceived both domestically and internationally.

Finally, some gifts carried ideological significance. Since both the Ottoman and Mamluk rulers were Muslim, items that incorporated religious symbolism were particularly meaningful. Books, especially copies of the Qur'an, were often exchanged between the Muslim rulers.[180] Although they were rarely mentioned in descriptions of Ottoman–Mamluk gift exchanges, they often denoted a positive message or a hidden attempt to improve the relationship.[181] Even gifts that were seemingly intended for pious purposes, however, could decorate a stage on which rulers' political and ideological challenges clashed with each other. With their openness for multiple interpretations, gifts could render significant services in the exchange or evolution of imperial ideologies.

Arrival and Housing of the Ambassadors

Despite sparse information about early Ottoman ceremonial practices, evidence indicates that the Mamluks and Ottomans followed similar patterns when accepting foreign embassies.[182] Once the correspondence and gifts were entrusted to an ambassador, his entourage departed for the foreign court. When an embassy entered Ottoman or Mamluk territory, however, officials at the border (sometimes from the sending side, sometimes from the receiving side) sent an advance courier to inform the capital of the mision's arrival and request safe passage for the mission.[183] The receiving territory often provided an escort for the mission.[184] The Ottoman court sent a palace functionary called a *mihmandar* (meeter and greeter or guide; in the Mamluk context, the master of ceremonies) to the border to accompany diplomatic missions, although it is not known exactly when this practice began.[185]

Even at this early stage, a hosting ruler's greeting procedure might divulge his opinion of the incoming embassy and its sender.[186] In Mamluk practices, both the rank of the host's escort and the size of his entourage were determined by the host's perception of the sending ruler and their current relationship.[187] A high-ranking amir, a viceroy (*na'ib al-saltana*), or a chief chamberlain (*hajib al-hujjab*) met higher-ranking emissaries or royal guests while a *mihmandar* received the representatives of lower-ranking rulers.[188] On rare occasions, Mamluk sultans were even known to leave their palace in order to greet a political refugee or a visiting monarch in person.[189]

After entering the capital, the delegation was guided to its lodgings.[190] Missions to the Mamluk capital could be settled in the sultan's palace or in one of the minor palaces overlooking the polo-ground below the citadel; according to *Subh al-A'sha* this gesture indicated great respect for the sender.[191] Otherwise, the ambassador and his entourage were directed to a guest-house or "some place according to his rank" such as the royal mansion called the *dar al-sultaniyya*.[192] Alternately, some visitors were sometimes housed in the mansions of former administrators.[193]

Unlike the detailed descriptions in *Subh al-A'sha* and other Mamluk chronicles, sources contain little information about the lodgings of foreign representatives in Ottoman lands, particularly in the earlier capitals of Bursa and Edirne.[194] *Elçi Hanı*, Constantinople's hostel for foreign missions that was built in either 1509 or 1511, not only filled a practical need for housing, but also revealed the Ottoman Empire's gradual institutionalization of court etiquette and diplomatic conventions.[195] Although this edifice, which was probably built with funds from Hadım Ali Paşa, a grand vizier of Bayezid II, has not survived to the present day, it was most likely located on *Divan Yolu*, or the Council Road, the main processional route to the imperial palace and the center of government. Like their Mamluk counterparts, however, the Ottomans channeled different embassies to diverse locations; by the second part of the sixteenth century, merely three or four decades after the construction of *Elçi Hanı*, some embassies were directed instead to the imperial palaces of dynasty members or viziers.[196] It is not clear whether this choice was guided by a practical need for more space or by a desire to offer more comfortable accommodations to some particularly respected embassies.

If the Ottoman sovereign had left the capital, missions were sometimes guided to his encampment and occasionally were even ordered to accompany him during a military campaign. This arrangement occurred more frequently during the early years of Ottoman growth.[197] Other rulers, such as Bayezid II, spent considerable time in the old capital of Edirne and continued to accept missions either in the palace or in its vicinity.[198]

In both the Mamluk and Ottoman capitals, some missions were kept under house arrest or were accompanied by officers disguised as guides until the sovereign returned or they were granted an audience. These officers not only kept a close eye on the ambassador to ensure his security, but also to prevent him from sending intelligence back home.[199] This measure was not particularly effective, however, since we do know that ambassadors did correspond with their own sovereigns while abroad.[200] The surveillance, then, served perhaps as a psychological tactic to provoke a sense of anxiety and helplessness in the minds of ambassadors, an attempt that should be interpreted as a part of the image-building attempts of the hosting sovereign. Impressing ambassadors was a prime goal of the hosting sovereigns, and those accompanying the ruler during a campaign were exposed to a different type of power display.

In both Ottoman and Mamluk practices, allocations either in cash or in kind were also granted to diplomatic representatives.[201] These funds were independent from the conventional gifts bestowed upon an envoy and his entourage, yet they fulfilled a similar purpose: to display the donor's wealth, hospitality and generosity. This practice existed at the Mamluk court until the end of the Mamluk regime,[202] and, although some specialists of Ottoman history date the beginning of this practice to 1538, it is likely that it existed long before then and remained a regular practice until Selim III (r.1787–1807).[203]

An additional practice during the early stages of an embassy was the routine courtesy visits that an ambassador paid to prominent members of the hosting administration before being introduced to the ruler.[204] During these visits, the ambassador not only offered gifts to these individuals and cultivated acquaintances with important members of the hosting regime, but was also often apprised of the basic etiquette and ceremonial rules he would be expected to follow in his meeting with the sultan. This preparation and advice could help him avoid a major faux pas that could threaten his mission, if not his life. These networks also gave the ambassador easier access to the sovereign.[205] In Mamluk practices, the chief dragoman (interpreter or translator) emerged as a particularly influential figure who could help an ambassador build networks with high-ranking Mamluk officers and achieve success in his mission.[206]

The Crucial Day: Ambassadorial Audiences, Court Etiquette, and Ceremonial Spaces in Cairo

The most critical moment of any diplomatic encounter was the ambassador's audience with the hosting sovereign, and both the host and his guest prepared carefully. Ambassadors received detailed instructions from their own sovereigns, while the hosting sovereign and his advisors designed the ceremonies or processions for the ambassador.[207] Although the conventions of both courts overlapped substantially—particularly during the early stages of their relationship—the Ottomans increasingly developed their own ceremonial customs over time.

The ambassadors' processions from their lodgings to the audience hall enabled them to display their own sovereign's wealth and prestige to the hosting court as well as the common people.[208] In Mamluk ceremonials, the layout of the imperial capital allowed such public display and observation.[209] We know some missions captured the public's attention because narrative accounts recount their processions, especially if they included a noticeably large entourage or valuable gifts. On some occasions, ambassadors also recorded that they were picked up by Mamluk officers at or before daybreak and were accompanied by them during the parade to the citadel.[210] These processions, or at least parts of them, were likely also watched by the residents of the citadel and even by the sultan himself. Since at least the time of the Fatimids, diplomatic processions through Cairo had been occasionally observed by the ruler behind grilled windows (*shubbak*).[211] Later in the Mamluk citadel, similar windows were used to serve as a reminder of the ruler's presence or to incorporate it into the ceremonials.[212]

Although the Mamluk regime benefitted from the legacy of the preceding regimes in Cairo, these earlier practices did not remain untouched. Many of the Mamluk sultans changed the main ceremonial rules and regulations, some because of their personal tastes and some because they wanted to promulgate a slightly different imperial image and ideology.[213] Sultan Barquq particularly emerged as a figure of remarkable ceremonial innovation.[214] His sultanate has been identified as the moment of transfer from the Bahri to the Burji regime, and, although the preceding Bahri regime was not based upon dynastic succession, it was predominantly occupied by Sultan Qalawun and his descendants, who played significant roles in constructing the ceremonial spaces within the citadel. Barquq broke with many Qalawunid practices[215] and modified even basic traditions such as the days when the court (*diwan* in Arabic; *divan* in Turkish) convened or when *dar al-'adl* sessions were held—which were also the days when the sultan accepted foreign missions.[216] Barquq preferred morning or day sessions with ambassadors rather than al-Nasir Muhammad's custom of night sessions.[217]

During his reign, Barquq also changed the locations where diplomatic audiences were received. At the beginning of the fourteenth century—prior to the first diplomatic contact between the Ottomans and the Mamluks—the grand portico (*al-Iwan al-Kabir*) of the Mamluk citadel was established as a hall for administrative meetings, *dar al-'adl* sessions, and as a space to receive foreign envoys.[218] In Barquq's days this *Iwan* was used less frequently, and the *dar al-'adl* sessions moved to the Hippodrome,[219] where he also accepted foreign dignitaries.[220] Rumayla Square, under the citadel, was also increasingly used for processions, including ambassadorial audiences.[221]

Although some later Mamluk sultans preferred other venues, each of these audience halls consistently exhibited imperial power and prestige.[222] On the day of an audience, the sultan took his seat on an elevated throne or dais (*takht al-muluk*) at the far end of the hall, often with his legs crossed or folded "in the tailor's fashion."[223] His commanders and functionaries lined up to his right and left.[224] Once the embassy, which had been previously instructed about proper etiquette,[225] reached the outer gates of the palace, they dismounted from their horses and were stripped of their weapons by palace officers.[226] They passed multiple gates, finding a new hall and a new crowd of spectators behind each one.[227] Once the palace chamberlains (plu. *hujjab*) ushered the ambassador and his entourage into the main hall, the visitors kissed the ground,[228] and the *katib al-sirr* formally presented the ambassador to the sultan. Ambassadors, generally, were not permitted to sit during an audience. The *dawadar* (literally, the bearer and keeper of the royal inkwell)[229] took the letter from the ambassador.[230] He then gave it to the sultan, who opened it before giving it to the head of the chancery. Finally, the head of the chancery read the letter aloud.[231] The chief dragoman may have translated the message, which was then conveyed by the *nazir al-hass* and the *amir al-kabir* or the *dawadar* and the *katib al-sirr* to the sultan.[232] The ambassador's gifts were also presented to the sultan at this time, although little evidence survives about the particular rules concerning their presentation in the Mamluk court. Palace functionaries probably carried them into the audience hall on pillows.[233]

During the audience, the sultan appeared—or at least was expected to appear—to be a proud, silent, and inaccessible figure.[234] This imposing imperial image was also manifested in the sultan's gestures. To recognize an ambassador's presence, he might have merely nodded or stood.[235] If he wanted to honor his guest, he might have spoken to the ambassador,[236] since the ambassador was forbidden to speak directly to the sultan unless he was addressed first. Most of the time, the *dawadar* addressed the ambassador. Finally, the ambassador was seated at the banquet, often near the *hujjab* or dragoman.[237] While musicians sometimes played during the banquet,[238] on rare occasions the ambassadors enjoyed additional displays, such as the scene of bastinado that an ambassador from Naples witnessed during his audience in 1483.[239]

Ambassadorial Audiences from Bursa to Constantinople

In contrast to the enduring framework that governed ambassadorial audiences in the Mamluk capital, the multiple transfers of Ottoman capitals make it particularly difficult to reconstruct a general picture of their ceremonials in their earliest center, Bursa. Although it served as the Ottoman capital from 1326, the city was destroyed at least once by the combined Timurid and Karamanid forces in the aftermath of the Ankara battle (1402), which may have ruined existing ceremonial spaces or palaces. After the capital was transferred from Bursa to Edirne, most likely in the early fifteenth century, the processions that were performed in Bursa's architectural monuments and ceremonial spaces were soon forgotten.

The existence of some kind of pomp and ceremony, however, is confirmed by the accounts of the Mamluk ambassador Amir al-Kujkuni, who was sent to Bursa by Sultan Barquq in 1392.

In what survives from al-Kujkuni's accounts, no reference is made to his audience with Bayezid, nor does he describe the hall where he was given an audience. His statements as reported by the fifteenth-century Mamluk historian al-Maqrizi, however, suggest that Bayezid's official residence in Bursa was likely a conglomeration of numerous kiosks, pavilions, or houses constructed from wood.[240] To an observer from Mamluk lands—a place that had to import its wood and built its own citadel with stone—the use of this material was striking and was likely interpreted as a show of power and wealth.

The banquet that included the ruler, the high dignitaries, the present ambassadors, a group of soldiers, and possibly also the company of performing musicians was a tradition that began during Bayezid's reign.[241] The fact that the Mamluk ambassador al-Kujkuni mentioned the silver and gold cups and dishes from which Bayezid ate and drank suggests that he took part in such an event with the Ottoman ruler. Ibn al-Sughayr, the physician who accompanied al-Kujkuni upon Bayezid's request, corroborated his companion's statements and also added that Bayezid brought back numerous silver items when he returned from his *ghaza* against the Serbs (*Al-Aflak*).[242] According to Ibn al-Sughayr, even the thresholds of the Ottoman ruler's palace were covered with silver because the material was so plentiful in their lands.[243] This abundance of silver elicited a noticeable reaction from both al-Kujkuni and Ibn al-Sughayr, who came from the Mamluk lands where silver had become scare. This shortage eventually led to major adjustments in Mamluk monetary policy, which had been based on gold and silver for decades.[244]

Al-Kujkuni's account also stated that he accompanied Bayezid to the *hamam* (Turkish bath) in the Ottoman ruler's palace.[245] While this practice—which is not mentioned in any other source—could suggest the informality and simplicity that guided the etiquette of the yet-fledgling Ottoman polity, it might also indicate Bayezid's exceptional reverence for the Mamluk sovereign. The event gave the Mamluk ambassador another opportunity to observe Ottoman wealth: the items used in the Turkish bath, including the bathtub and the cup, were coated with silver.

After 1402 the Ottoman capital moved from Bursa to Edirne.[246] The capital changed for a third and final time to Constantinople in 1453, and after 1471 the new imperial Topkapı Palace, with its double-layered gates and gardens, became the main ceremonial space for state affairs and the receptions of foreign embassies. Until 1478, however, embassies were received at the new palace in Constantinople in much the same way as they had been at the Edirne palace.[247]

According to the account of the ambassador Bertrandon de la Broquière, who represented the count of Burgundy during a visit to the Ottoman ruler Murad II in Edirne, ambassadors were expected to first pay a visit to prominent members of the court such as the grand vizier and offer them gifts. This procedure was reminiscent of the courtesy visits foreign ambassadors made while visiting Mamluk lands.[248] When accompanied by satisfactory gifts, these visits could accelerate the process of scheduling an audience with the Ottoman ruler or help ensure the success of a mission.[249]

Much like the Mamluk tradition, missions were generally accepted in the Ottoman capital on the days when the sultan held court (*divan*).[250] The Ottomans also preferred to accept embassies on *ulufe günleri*, a day when the janissaries' salaries were distributed and the number of people present in the palace courtyard soared.[251] The crowd, filled with uniformed janissaries and other army members, must have made an impressive scene for foreign visitors.

As was also the case in the Mamluk tradition, the ambassador and his entourage marched to the Ottoman palace in a procession, often accompanied by minor officers of the palace. In Edirne they crossed a bridge over the Tunca River, while in Constantinople they marched via the Council Road, *Divan Yolu*. If the mission had been lodged in Pera, they were brought by boat to Sarayburnu and then proceeded from the coastal route to the outer gate of the palace. The mission's ambassador was likely the only figure allowed to ride on horseback during this phase of the procession,[252] but even he had to dismount when the group reached the palace's first gate, *Bab-ı Hümayun*. Upon entering the first court, they may have seen a yard filled with petitioners waiting to plead their cases before the sultan.[253] Then they might have been guided to the Middle Gate and the Council

Hall to meet with the grand vizier or other high dignitaries. On at least one occasion in Constantinople, however, the viziers emerged from the Council Hall to greet the ambassadors.[254]

Mehmed II generally embraced his father Murad II's ceremonial practices until at least 1478, first in Edirne and then in Constantinople. In both palaces, the locations where sultans accepted foreign missions connected the public sphere to the private chambers of the sultan. While the sultans used a colonnaded hall to accept missions in Edirne, Mehmed II used a splendid portico in Constantinople's Topkapı Palace.[255] This portico stood in front of the second gate (third gate after 1478), which led to the private courtyard of the ruler. Both halls were connected to the private chambers of the ruler by a paved path. On the day of the audience, the sultan left his private chamber in the company of a few servants, donned a robe at some point between his chamber and the audience hall, and entered the hall from a gate that connected the private courtyard with the middle courtyard.[256] He took his seat on an elevated dais and sat by crossing or folding his legs, although he reportedly sat on a carpet on some occasions.[257] Once he sat, the members of the court took their places around him.[258]

A vizier then escorted the ambassador into the ruler's presence, where the ambassador bowed once. After reaching the first step of the dais, he bowed deeply for a second time. Depending on his visitor's status, the sultan may have stood and approached him, or offered his hand to be kissed—a practice rarely mentioned in Mamluk sources.[259] When the ambassador stepped back, he kept his face turned toward the sultan until he took his seat. Again the sultan was seated first, then the ambassador, and finally the ambassador's entourage and the rest of the audience.[260]

Next, the hosting court staged a communal banquet. The sultan received his food on a golden tray while the rest of the participants were served, according to rank, with either silver or copper trays. Musicians may have performed during the banquet or even during the entire ceremony. While some sources state that by the reign of Murad II the sultan no longer ate in front of the audience and the food was quickly gathered,[261] others indicate the continuation of this practice in 1444 and even in 1455.[262] The departure of the sultan signaled the end of an audience. When the sultan rose to leave, everyone rose with him, and his courtiers loudly declared his greatness and glory. After sitting and rising for a second time to incite another wave of applause, the sultan returned to his quarters.[263]

In 1478 a second phase of construction began in the Topkapı Palace, and these architectural changes were accompanied by ceremonial modifications that further differentiated the Ottoman rituals from those of the Mamluks. A third set of outer walls and gates as well as subsequent garden and shore pavilions were added to the existing structure.[264] These changes ushered in a new imperial image that influenced almost every aspect of court administration and etiquette, including the diplomatic ceremonies where rulers presented their self-images to both internal and external audiences. As Mehmed II gradually disappeared from the public eye,[265] a more secluded image of the sultan emerged and distinguished the Ottomans from their Mamluk peers. Mehmed limited his public appearances to two religious holidays,[266] and when he did emerge from his palace, he was surrounded by a much larger retinue than before.[267]

These changes, which were masterminded by Mehmed II, were appreciated by other prominent figures. Prince Uğurlu Mehmed, the son of the Aqqoyunlu ruler Uzun Hasan, escaped from his father's court and came to Constantinople in 1474 after a brief stay at the Mamluk court. When questioned by the sultan, the prince, who had seen not only the processions in his father's palace but also Mamluk processions, reassured his host that the displays at the Ottoman court were unequalled.[268] While a guest and refugee enjoying the hospitality of the Ottoman ruler might have felt obliged to assess the Ottoman court in a positive light, the conversation still revealed the importance of palatial architecture and court etiquette to a ruler's appearance.

Although the architectural changes to the Topkapı Palace reflected the Ottoman sultan's gradual seclusion, they still connected the ruler to the outside world. In this regard, the new structure was similar to the Mamluk palace in Cairo. For instance, the third set of external walls that were added to the Topkapı Palace had three towers, one of which was called the Kiosk of Processions (*Alay Köşkü*).[269] Its grilled window overlooked the road where processions of ambassadors approached the palace's first gate. While we do not know if Mehmed ever used this particular kiosk for the purpose of observation, a miniature painting of the palace from 1596 depicts his great-grandson Murad III watching the procession of a Safavid mission from this location.[270] The other shore and garden pavilions, some of which were added during Mehmed II's time, were situated so that the sultan could enjoy panoramas of the city or sea.[271]

Mehmed II's increased seclusion also gave rise to a new style of ceremony that emphasized the role of the grand vizier as the highest-ranking administrator in the Ottoman Empire. Once an envoy and his entourage passed the Council Road and the Kiosk of Processions from which the sultan may have watched them, they reached the outer walls of the Topkapı Palace. After passing the first gate, the group was kept in the first courtyard until the grand vizier reached the Council Hall in the second courtyard. Then, on his way to the Council Hall, the ambassador might have observed a special ceremony called the Council of Victory (*galebe divanı*), or, depending on his rank, a display of valuable textiles. Sometimes wild animals were also exhibited on the left side of the court as a reminder of the sultan's wealth and his palace menagerie.[272] In some occasions, the ambassador arrived at the Council Hall and waited for the grand vizier's entrance.[273]

In this new style of ceremony, the Ottoman sultan did not attend this initial meeting in the Council Hall, but could observe it from a window that overlooked the venue.[274] The window, which was positioned so as not to reveal the sultan's presence, was reminiscent of the *shubbak* in the Mamluk citadel. The practice also resembled the use of similar windows by the Abbasids in Baghdad, since this window was obviously not for panoramic purposes but rather to groom the image of an "omniscient but invisible" sultan.[275]

Although no information has survived about how the ambassadors were seated in the Council Hall before the sixteenth century, a late seventeenth-century source stipulated that envoys from a Muslim ruler were to be seated on the same sofa with the *nişancı*.[276] Envoys from a non-Muslim sovereign, however, were to be seated on a single stool closer to the gate of the *divan* hall and across from the grand vizier.[277] This system, though it honored both Muslim and non-Muslim ambassadors, also differentiated between them.

Mehmed II further innovated the sultan's role and image when he stopped attending the communal banquet during diplomatic audiences.[278] This departure from tradition further separated Ottoman practices from those of their Mamluk counterparts and highlighted an increasingly secluded image of the Ottoman ruler. Instead, ambassadors were seated at the table of the grand vizier while his men were distributed to the tables of other high-ranking members of the *divan*.[279] After a brief rest following the banquet, the ambassador was then taken by the palace officers (*ağas*) to the gate of the treasury next to the Council Hall. There he donned a robe of honor and was taken to the Chamber of Petitions (*Arz Odası*) at the third gate where he would see the sultan.[280]

After 1478 the Ottomans built the new Chamber of Petitions (*Arz Odası*) adjacent to the Council Hall to receive foreign ambassadors. As a part of Mehmed II's restructuring measures, it lay at the entrance of the third courtyard and also linked the private and public spheres of the sultan. While the pavilion or tent-like structure served a function similar to the Mamluk *Iwan al-Kabir*, it differed architecturally from the elongated, colonnaded halls of the Mamluk citadel. During a diplomatic audience, the grand vizier and other dignitaries entered the Chamber of Petitions first, followed by the foreign ambassador. The ambassador was escorted by two men from the palace, possibly *ağas*, that held his arms.[281] After entering, the ambassador was expected to bow and to kiss either the sultan's hand or the ground.[282] At this point he may have been allowed to sit while the rest of the court remained standing.

According to a seventeenth-century handbook, the presentation of a foreign ruler's letter to the Ottoman sovereign differed slightly from Mamluk practices. The ambassador gave it to the *divan* member who stood physically closest to him (who was often the lowest-ranking vizier) who then handed it to the person next to him. In this manner—from the hands of the lowest-ranking person to those of the highest-ranking—the letter would reach the grand vizier. The grand vizier then placed the letter on a pillow that lay on the throne next to the sultan. No evidence exists that the letter was read aloud during the event.[283]

While Mamluk sources reveal few details regarding the presentation of gifts, Ottoman records trace a gradual refinement in this ceremony. Before the construction of the Chamber of Petitions, servants placed the gifts on pillows and carried them before the sultan.[284] Once the embassies moved to the Chamber of Petitions, however, gifts were passed in front of the Chamber window and were no longer brought inside.[285]

Either before or after the presentation of his gifts, an envoy might be invited to speak. Otherwise, according to Ottoman convention, he preserved his silence in the ruler's presence. Until Süleyman I's reign (r.1520–66) and depending on the situation, Ottoman rulers were known to address envoys directly,[286] though the grand vizier also performed this function. Depending on the need, a dragoman might aid their communication. Finally, the envoy was dismissed from the audience hall. According to seventeenth-century Ottoman handbooks, the ambassador was guided by palace officers to the outer yard of the palace where he often received additional gifts.[287]

Envoys were rarely invited to a second audience with the Ottoman sultan. If an ambassador did not receive a response and corresponding gifts for his sovereign during his audience, he waited in his residence for a response. Diplomatic negotiations often took place during a single session or in a series of meetings between administrators of the hosting court and the diplomatic representative. Often he was invited back to the palace or to the residence of a high-ranking officer to discuss his mission or to receive the sultan's response and gifts for his sovereign.[288] If he was invited to the palace to meet members of the imperial court, the envoy might have had a chance to watch the sultan from a distance while the ruler led his council or heard the complaints of his subjects.[289] Even these impromptu occasions, however, were carefully crafted by the hosting court to impress the ambassador.

After an Audience: Mamluk and Ottoman Processions

During the rest of their stay, foreign ambassadors were invited or were "accidentally" exposed to further processions such as weddings, circumcision festivals, military training, soldiers returning from successful campaigns, the arrival of other diplomatic missions, and religious celebrations. The boundaries between the performers and their audience were blurred during these occasions: the ambassadors who had been sent to perform and present their own sovereign's image were instead transformed into an audience for the hosting administration. As they offered a rare chance for the sovereign to display his might to his peer's representative, these occasions were carefully tailored in advance by the host and his advisors.

Due to the prestige of the Mamluk regime, Cairo offered an important stage for these kinds of diverse ceremonies and celebrations, some of which were further refined and added by the sultans to the diplomatic repertoire.[290] Unlike the ambassadorial audiences which generally only the members of the court and the diplomatic mission attended, the majority of these celebrations was open to the public and were often attended by the Mamluk sultan.[291] Many processions and urban celebrations in the city would have impressed a foreign dignitary, from the annual opening of the Nilometer to hunting parties led by the sultan.[292] Finally, the departure of the annual pilgrimage caravan and *mahmal* was among the highlights of Cairene urban life. As the empty litter and its entourage passed through the city, they reinforced the Mamluk sultan's leading symbolic role as the protector of Mecca and Medina.[293] Both Ottoman and Mamluk sources recorded that Ottoman embassies, in addition to other foreign Muslim dignitaries, observed this ceremony on multiple occasions.[294]

Additionally, many secular (often military) occasions were attended by foreign dignitaries. Ambassadors witnessed Mamluk troops engaging in training sessions and playing exhibition games similar to polo, events that were staged to highlight the soldiers' horsemanship and swordsmanship. These exhibitions of skills enhanced the Mamluks' image as a military regime. Since military parades and triumphal processions passed through the city, rulers and their advisors had the opportunity to impress both external and internal audiences at the same time.[295] A letter written by an Ottoman prisoner in 1485 corroborated the careful orchestration behind these kinds of occasions.[296] In this rare fifteenth-century captivity narrative, the author, who was forced to march in a triumphal procession following a Mamluk military victory, detailed how Mamluk commanders informed city authorities to prepare for the event. On the day of the procession, the businesses and shops of the city were closed. First, the severed heads of enemy soldiers were carried on lances to "salute" the crowds. Then the author of the letter and his fellow captives—likely in chains and scarcely clothed—were paraded through the city by Mamluk troops and cavalry men. Although the author did not remark on the presence of any foreign dignitaries observing his humiliation, numerous Mamluk chronicles indicated that ambassadors visiting Cairo were invited to watch similar events.[297] Among other triumphal processions, the parade of Mamluk troops as they escorted the captured king of Cyprus Janus in 1426 is a particularly well-known and frequently cited example. Sultan Barsbay, who was known for his renewal of old traditions such as sumptuous ceremonies and banquets, kept a large group of foreign dignitaries waiting until the procession with the King of Cyprus arrived at the citadel.[298] A later example that left a significant imprint on the social memory of the Mamluks was the parade that escorted the captured Dulkadirid ruler Shahsuwar through the streets of Cairo in chains.[299]

Over time, Mamluk chroniclers began to mention and even to lament the fact that Mamluk celebrations and official processions had decreased in frequency and become less impressive.[300] For instance, during the earlier years of the Bahri regime when they were more strongly influenced by the Mongols, the Mamluk sultans used tents for some audiences.[301] This practice gradually diminished as audiences moved to the citadel, a shift that reflected strong Ayyubid and some Abbasid influences. While a growing concern for the sultans' safety contributed to this shift, it also reflected their increasingly sedentary ruling style.[302] Unlike the increasingly invisible Ottoman rulers, however, the Mamluk sultans were expected to appear in public for certain events.[303] For example, the Mamluk emphasis on headgear and outfits—which particularly caught the eyes of Western visitors—might have grown out of the Mamluk sultans' need to leave an impression during their more frequent public appearances.[304] On various occasions Mamluk sultans accompanied foreign ambassadors to certain quarters of the city or to public ceremonies.[305] Even before Mehmed II's time, no ambassador visiting the Ottoman court was ever honored with a similar gesture by the Ottoman sultan.

Unlike the numerous occasions depicted in Mamluk sources, the Ottoman sources of this period mention neither triumphal processions and public ceremonies, nor their multiple days of spiritual commemoration.[306] Although the rise of a new ruler was marked by an accession ceremony, sources did not mention the presence of foreign dignitaries at these events. A few descriptions of imperial weddings and circumcisions mention the presence of diplomatic representatives.[307] Only from the mid-sixteenth century did sources include more frequent references to such festivities. This increased attention to the urban festivities brought about the rise of a new genre, *Surname* (Book of Festivities), which celebrated these occasions and the rulers who made them possible.[308]

It is almost unthinkable, however, that Ottoman political authorities did not benefit from such power displays and communal identity enforcers in an urban community where news from annual raids and imperial campaigns arrived frequently.[309] One brief reference in the chronicle of the Byzantine historian Doukas indicated otherwise. Doukas, while lamenting the fall of Constantinople to the Ottomans on May 29, 1453, stated that Mehmed II had left the city on June 18, 1453 and made a majestic triumphal entry into Adrianople just a few weeks later. The Ottoman ruler "had taken with him in wagons and horseback all the noble women and their daughters" to the previous Ottoman capital. Doukas' comments imply a well-orchestrated triumphal procession that he probably witnessed firsthand:

Mehmed's majestic triumphal entry into Adrianople was followed—and what a spectacle it was—by all the noblewomen and Christian governors and rulers streaming in and greeting him "Hail!" [...] Afraid that they might suffer the same fate as the City, they involuntarily made their submission with gifts. The tyrant was sitting on his throne, haughty and proud, boasting about the fall of the City. The Christian rulers stood there trembling and wondering what the future held in store for them.[310]

Doukas' generic reference to "Christian rulers" included vassals and ambassadors who had probably been waiting for Mehmed II's return to Adrianople since the fall of Constantinople, and Mehmed II conveyed his demands to this group. In addition to Doukas' account, the sixteenth-century Ottoman scholar and historian İbn Kemal described at least one triumphal procession in 1497 that was observed by the Mamluk ambassador Khayr Bey. His description, however, only detailed a performance that took place behind the gates of the Topkapı Palace and did not clarify whether this procession also passed through the imperial capital.[311] The scarcity of references to such occasions, particularly in pre-sixteenth century Ottoman sources, could also perhaps, ironically, indicate their frequency. It is possible that, because these celebrations and processions were so frequent, they became commonplace for domestic audiences and were thus omitted in local writings. They may have survived only in the writings of foreign observers.[312]

The Return of Ambassadors: Ambassadors as Conduits

After these mutual exchanges of performances and presentations were completed, ambassadors left with the permission of the hosting sovereign. An escort or guide from the hosting sultan often accompanied the missions, not only to keep an eye on them until they reached the border, but also to help them with their daily needs.[313] The success of the mission determined what the ambassador would carry back to his homeland. At the least, he left the country with an oral response and a promise that the sovereign would send his own representative with due correspondence. Many times, however, he returned home with both a letter and corresponding gifts, and perhaps even gifts for himself and his entourage. On some occasions, if the hosting sovereign was particularly pleased with the sender's message, he sent his own ambassador back with the group, along with an additional letter and gifts.

The return of ambassadors to their homes marked perhaps the second-most critical, though mostly ignored, part of a diplomatic exchange. After representing their own sovereign in another court, ambassadors were then expected to deliver the response of their host and describe the treatment they received. For this part of their mission, they served as storytellers whose recollections had the potential to change the relationship between the two courts. Depending on the circumstances, envoys may have slightly amended the language of their host's message, if not its content.[314] The reports of diplomatic representatives sometimes made the difference between war and peace, as we will see in the following chapters.

The impact of diplomatic missions on mutual interactions and cultural encounters should not be underestimated, although the evidence that proves this impact often falls through the cracks of history. Centuries would pass before the Ottoman genre of *Sefaretname* (the official travel report of an embassy) came to its fruition. Nonetheless, ambassadors clearly presented written or oral reports to their sovereigns, although they rarely survived the following centuries.[315] A small number of anecdotes recounted by the chroniclers suggested that envoys also served as channels of communication by transporting observations and items they gathered during their missions.[316] These anecdotes and objects not only gave a personal dimension to Ottoman and Mamluk diplomatic encounters, but also contributed to each society's social memory.[317]

An example from a parallel context gives a general impression of the vibrant social and cultural exchange that diplomatic representatives often facilitated. In 1449, Şükrullah, the poet and chronicler who was sent by the Ottoman ruler Murad II to the ruler of the Qaraqoyunlus, encountered a history of the Oghuz (Oğuz in

Turkish) during a meeting with Jihan Shah (r.1439–67). While this embassy was neither Şükrullah's first nor last,[318] it made the most enduring impact on Ottoman culture and society. The manuscript that Şükrullah saw included a genealogy that traced the ancestors of the Ottomans and the Qaraqoyunlus back to the same legendary character, Oghuz.[319] Through Şükrullah's chronicles, which were composed after his return to Ottoman lands, this genealogy became a part of official Ottoman historiography, which was undergoing a period of reconstruction under the supportive patronage of Murad II and his successors.[320]

On the surface, these delegations all looked similar: each had at least one ambassador, one letter, and appropriate gifts for the receiving ruler. The meanings of these components were shaped by both short-term considerations and long-term transformations. The rich potential and the multiple readings these configurations offer prove the resilience and plasticity of this powerful communication method among sovereigns or societies. They illustrate that sharing the same ideological world did not force the Ottomans and Mamluks to an exchange of empty messages and ceremonies. On the contrary; because these rulers shared the same ideological world, they had to be more creative and resourceful in order to convey their intentions effectively.

CHAPTER 2

PERCEPTIONS IN TRANSFORMATION (c.1350–1402)

Historians cannot explain the relationship between the Ottomans and the Mamluks in a linear fashion or with the facile view that it became increasingly hostile as the year 1512 approached. Even during the earliest phase of their relationship, the diplomatic exchanges between the two lands were of a complex and shifting nature and emphasized the dramatic contrast between the status of each power in the face of Ottoman growth and expansion.

These fluctuations arose partly from the changing internal dynamics of both powers. During this period the Mamluk regime experienced a major transformation in leadership: while the previous Bahri line of sultans had descended from the Qalawunids, the new Burji regime suggested the creation of a new political ideology. This change in the Mamluk capital coincided with the rising regional status of the Ottomans and the expansion of their geographical hegemony. The Ottomans began their contacts with the Mamluk sultans from the inferior position of a minor Anatolian principality among more impressive and respected regional peers such as the Germiyanids and the Karamanids. The Ottomans were on the rise, however, and by 1397 had emerged as a power capable of stopping the advance of a major Crusading army. In addition to their capital of

Bursa, they also renovated the city of Edirne, which would become a gateway to the Balkans and eventually the next Ottoman capital.[1]

As both polities changed, so did the mutual images they disseminated through diplomatic engagements. Among Ottoman rulers, Bayezid I left a permanent mark on the relationship between Cairo and Bursa. The timing of his missions to the Mamluk court demonstrated that the Ottomans closely followed Mamluk politics in Anatolia, emphasized their own successes in the Balkans, and carefully promulgated their own image as *ghazis* (the champions of *ghaza*). This particular image might have posed a discreet challenge to the Mamluks, who had partially based their political legitimacy on a similar claim that they were warriors of faith. Ottoman diplomacy also likely sought to compensate for their political and military maneuvers against other Anatolian Muslim powers and the controversies these actions had instigated.

The Mamluks were not passive and stagnant recipients of these Ottoman messages. From the perspective of the twenty-first century, the Mamluk sultans—settled far away in Cairo—may seem to have been distant from or irrelevant to late-medieval and early-modern Anatolian politics. Their diplomatic exchanges with the Ottomans suggested, however, that the Mamluks were, in fact, closely involved and even politically invested in the region.[2] As the Ottomans expanded their reach and advertised this expansion through diplomacy, the Mamluk sultans adapted to this new political reality by sending more frequent and more carefully planned missions. Perhaps most disturbing for the Mamluks, as the earlier passage from Ibn Bahadur's work suggests,[3] was observing the Ottomans receive international recognition from multiple foreign missions while they also became increasingly adept at sending missions to them.

The Earliest Ottoman References in Mamluk Sources

The writings of multiple Mamluk secretaries illustrate the slow shift in how the Ottomans were perceived by the Mamluk court during this earliest phase of their relationship. One of the earliest references to the Ottomans in Mamluk sources came from the writings of

Shihab al-din Ahmad Ibn Fadl Allah al-'Umari (1301–48), a prominent secretary who later rose to the position of *katib al-sirr* in the Mamluk chancery during the third reign of Muhammad b. Qalawun.[4] Two of al-'Umari's works, the impressive geographical treatise *Masalik al-Absar* and the chancery manual *Al-Ta'rif Bi al-Mustalah al-Sharif*, include the Ottomans in their depictions of political conditions in Anatolia (*Bilad al-Rum*). His works significantly influenced later Mamluk historians and scribes, therefore al-'Umari's opinions are particularly relevant in reconstructing the Mamluks' initial approach to the Ottomans.

In his description of a politically diverse and active Anatolia in *Masalik al-Absar*, al-'Umari paid relatively little attention to the Ottomans. Although each of his two sources—one a Genoese convert to Islam and the other a native of Anatolia—provided him with slightly different details about the region, they both listed the Ottomans among the minor powers.[5] Al-'Umari detailed the significant roles of the Germiyanids and the Karamanids in Anatolia, particularly when Ilkhanid authority waned after the 1270s.[6] The Germiyanids were portrayed as the most powerful, while the most detailed information belonged to the Karamanids. According to al-'Umari, the Karamanids wrote to the Mamluks requesting a document of investiture for their ruler to be officially titled as the *Sultan al-Rum* (the ruler of Anatolia).[7] The author's discussion of the Ottomans, in contrast, was tellingly placed immediately after a section about the petty rulers of Qawaya (identified as modern Geyve and called Kabia in Greek),[8] a political entity that would disappear around the late fifteenth century. He recounts the Ottomans' many defeats of the Christians,[9] particularly under the leadership of Orhan, Bayezid I's grandfather, who ruled between 1326 and 1362. Orhan's army of 25,000 men fought the Christians to become the masters of Bursa. Remarkably, al-'Umari also thought it worthwhile to mention that the Ottomans crossed to Gallipoli to battle the Byzantines for wealth and spoils, a story that evoked an early image of the Ottomans as *ghazis*. Al-'Umari conversely reported that Orhan signed treaties with and helped other groups in his vicinity when needed, an observation that reflected the syncretic nature of the frontier region where the Ottomans were establishing themselves.[10]

Despite some minor variations, al-'Umari's later chancery manual reinforced his earlier treatise when he summarized the status of the Ottomans in a single sentence.[11] He then cited the name of the Ottoman ruler (Orkhan ibn 'Uthman)[12] after he introduced the rulers of Qawaya and reiterated that Orhan's rank equaled theirs. As his manual was written as a reference book for scribes, al-'Umari listed the titulature that reflected each ruler's status at the Mamluk court. Although he did not give any specific instructions regarding titulature for the Ottomans, he referred to the rulers of Geyve as *al-Majlis al-Samiyy al-Amiri* (The Lofty and Commanding Seat or the Lofty Seat, the Commander)[13] with a stressed "y" at the end, and he likely used the same title for the Ottomans.[14] According to al-'Umari's later colleague al-Qalqashandi, among eight common *alqab* or titles, *al-Majlis* ranked fifth in importance.[15] In addition, the adjective *al-Amiri* referred to the position of *Amir*, which was a high-ranking army commander who could have been, but was not necessarily, an independent ruler.[16]

In his discussion of proper titulature for the many Anatolian Muslim rulers, al-'Umari first mentioned the Germiyanids in the section where he listed the names of the *Umara' al-Atrak* (Commanders of the Turks or Turcoman groups).[17] He stipulated that letters from the Mamluk sultan to the Germiyanid ruler should address him with the same title used for the Artuqid ruler of Mardin in southeastern Anatolia, which was *al-Maqarr al-Karim* (His Noble Residence),[18] but should use slightly less exalted language than the letters for the Artuqids.[19] He also specified that the Germiyanid titulature *al-Maqarr al-Karim al-'Ali al-Maliki* (His Noble, Sublime and Kingly Residence) should be accompanied by a brief *du'a'* or *salutatio* (salutation), which entailed pious invocations or greetings in addition to well-wishing formulas for the continuation of the addressee's rule.[20] This particular address ranked third among titulature and was therefore used for higher-ranking commanders.

The dissimilarity between the titles the Mamluks designated for the Germiyanids (*al-Maqarr al-Karim al-'Ali al-Maliki*) and the Ottomans (*al-Majlis al-Samiyy al-Amiri*) indicates the existence of an additional hierarchy between the Anatolian powers.[21] Despite the gradual erosion of its meaning over the centuries, the epithet of *Malik*, which was applied to the Germiyanids, was nonetheless a more prestigious one than the Ottoman title *Amir*.[22] Although the Karamanids received a comparatively simpler title than the Germiyanids, they were also ranked higher than the Ottomans.[23]

A second manual, one that appeared approximately three decades after al-'Umari's, demonstrated a slight shift in Mamluk attitudes toward the powers in Anatolia. Taqi al-din ibn Nazir al-Jaysh (d.1384), who served in the Mamluk chancery during the reign of Sultan Sha'ban (r.1363–76), completed his own manual in 1376.[24] While he relied heavily on al-'Umari's work, he incorporated minor changes in titulature that reflected the region's transforming political conditions. Although the Germiyanids were still called the most prestigious rulers in Anatolia and were addressed with the same title as before, Ibn Nazir al-Jaysh questioned their high status. He believed that the Germiyanids no longer outranked the Karamanids. He also recommended that *al-Majlis al-Samiyy* should remain in use for the Ottomans and that no change should be made in their relative status.[25]

Ibn Nazir al-Jaysh also noted that no records of Ottoman–Mamluk correspondence had survived except in al-'Umari's work.[26] It is likely, however, that by 1376 some contact had already been made between the two courts. The fact that both Mamluk administrators included the Ottomans in their manuals demonstrates that the Mamluks had become aware of this new power. Although they contain contradictory details regarding the chronology and purpose of the mission, later Ottoman and Mamluk chronicles include references to at least one embassy between the two powers before the 1380s. More evidence is needed in order to fully resolve the ambiguity that surrounds this case.[27]

Diplomatic Performance and Prince Bayezid's Wedding

Although the date of the earliest Ottoman–Mamluk diplomatic contact remains undetermined, we do know that a Mamluk mission attended the wedding celebration of Prince Bayezid in Bursa in 1381. The prince, who was the son of Murad I and would later become the sultan Bayezid I, married the daughter of the Germiyanid ruler Süleyman Şah (d.1387).[28] According to Aşıkpaşazade's account, the marriage was initiated by the bride's father, who likely realized that the Ottoman expansion in the region would eventually swallow his lands as well.[29] By marrying his daughter to Murad's son, the Germiyanid ruler hoped to spare his lands from destruction and ensure a continuing rule for his descendants, even if they became Ottoman vassals.

While Ottoman chroniclers referred briefly to other marriage alliances, they—particularly Aşıkpaşazade—emphasized the considerable number of foreign dignitaries present at Prince Bayezid's wedding.[30] After presenting their gifts, ambassadors were seated "according to their ranks,"[31] and the Mamluk ambassador was given "the first seat" in the assembly. After the other ambassadors took their places, Murad's governors and commanders were asked to present their gifts. According to Aşıkpaşazade, the ambassadors were surprised at the wealth of Murad's warlords and saw it as an indication of the ruler's own wealth. During the celebration, the Ottoman sultan spared no expense and treated his guests lavishly.

Since the Ottomans eventually overtook the entire Germiyanid territory, Aşıkpaşazade's narrative, which assumed the subservice of the Germiyanids, initially seems legitimate and even accurate to historians. At the same time, however, we cannot ignore the benefits this strategic relationship would provide the Ottomans, particularly in the 1380s. Although later historical developments would overshadow the once-obvious significance of the Germiyanids, the way al-'Umari and Ibn Nazir al-Jaysh depicted their power attested to their former prestige in Anatolia and at the Mamluk court. The number of diplomats at Prince Bayezid's wedding, particularly from the Mamluks, could also be seen as a show of respect to the

Germiyanid ruling family. Ottoman chroniclers paid special attention to this marriage alliance because it not only secured a part of the Germiyanid territories (as the bride's dowry) and linked the Ottomans with a prestigious ruling family of Anatolia, but also because this wedding marked perhaps the first Mamluk acknowledgement of Ottoman growth.[32] Conversely, the persistent silence of Mamluk chroniclers regarding the event testified to the continuing imbalance between the mutual perceptions of these two powers.

The colorful Ottoman accounts of the wedding also serve as a reminder of the overall importance of royal weddings and similar pageants in the image-building processes of sovereigns and the discourse of diplomacy.[33] These occasions often targeted both internal and external audiences, as they promulgated the aura of a wealthy, generous, and powerful ruler,[34] and Murad merely followed a successful tradition when he seized this opportunity to promote his image. Murad further asserted his status as a cultivated sovereign who was well-versed in court etiquette when he presented his gifts from the Mamluk sultan to Evranos Bey, a prominent frontier warlord under Ottoman rule, and sent Bey's gifts to the Mamluk sultan.[35] By redistributing his gifts rather than keeping them, Murad was not displaying a spontaneous or unusual act of generosity, but was following the lead of his Mamluk peers.[36]

Murad's preferential treatment of the Mamluk ambassador offers insight into the diplomatic etiquette of the time and reveals how a sovereign would treat the representative of his superior. By presenting the first seat and valuable gifts to the Mamluk envoy, the Ottomans made his ambassadorial precedence clear. Beyond the fulfillment of diplomatic etiquette, the respectful treatment of this ambassador could have helped dispel Mamluk anxiety about rising Ottoman power. Prince Bayezid's wedding inaugurated a series of diplomatic and military engagements that gave the Ottomans greater control in Anatolia. During the celebrations, Murad purchased the rulership of some Hamidoğulları territories in south Anatolia from their ruler, Hüseyin Bey (d.1391). In what was perhaps an attempt to alleviate a rising Karamanid concern about the Ottoman acquisition of these territories, Murad also engaged one of his daughters, Nefise

Sultan, to the prince of the Karamanids.[37] According to some researchers, this Ottoman acquisition caused the earliest signs of conflict between the Ottomans and the Karamanids.[38] By hosting the Mamluk ambassador exceptionally well amidst these strategic operations and calculations, Murad perhaps attempted to reassure him—and hence his sovereign—that Ottoman territorial ambition would not pose a threat to Mamluk interests in the region. Although Mamluk sources did not reveal any concern at the Mamluk court regarding this fledgling regional power, the Mamluk sultan Barquq was aware of the recent Ottoman growth in both the Balkans and Anatolia. In a sense, the wedding of Murad's son provided the Ottoman ruler with an opportunity to refresh networks with his peers while also reconnecting with his own vassals and governors.[39]

In the years that followed Prince Bayezid's wedding, Ottoman chronicles continued to report the arrival of Mamluk missions, while Mamluk sources barely mentioned the Ottoman ones—an indication that the balance of power between the two groups had not yet changed in the eyes of Mamluk chroniclers. After returning from a difficult but successful campaign against the Serbians in 1386, Murad intended to march on the Karamanids, who had attacked Ottoman lands under the leadership of Alaaddin Ali Bey (d.1397–8), the husband of Murad's aforementioned daughter Nefise. While Murad prepared for this campaign, an envoy of the Mamluk sultan Barquq arrived with a message. The message's content and form of address were so unusual that the Ottoman chronicler Neşri, who rarely depicted scenes of diplomatic exchanges from these decades of Ottoman history, devoted considerable space in his account to it:

> After Murad Han Gazi came to Bursa, an important envoy came from the sultan of Egypt with lavish gifts [.] Gazi Murad Han showed him the utmost respect, and hosted him with great banquets [.] The message that the envoy brought was the following: 'I [the Mamluk sultan Barquq] am the one who prays to God for the *Sultan al-Ghuzat wa al-Mujahidin*. May he accept me as a son and not differentiate between me and his son Bayezid [.] I might seem far from them [Murad and his son] but I feel a

spiritual closeness to them [.] For them I have such longing and sympathy that I would join his holy wars, if I could. And he displayed humility and longing [.] Gazi Murad Han, too, displayed great courtesy and humility, and sent a letter expressing his longing [.] To [Barquq's] envoy he gave many gifts, and to every gift that the sultan of Egypt sent, he responded with one hundred gifts and sent those gifts with the envoy [.][40]

Due to the submissive tone of Barquq's message, the passage at first seems to suggest the chronicler's biased, if not entirely inaccurate, picture of Ottoman–Mamluk relations. Even if Neşri did embellish the wording of the message, Barquq's humble appeal could also be explained by the age difference between himself and Murad. At the time of this event, Barquq was younger than Murad and had only occupied the Mamluk throne for four years. Particularly for rhetorical purposes, the trope of ranking seniority by age and experience came frequently to the fore in Islamic diplomatic practices and, at times, could subvert the true political status and power of the parties involved.

Barquq's address to Murad might have also indirectly conveyed a salute to Murad's longevity as a ruler and his success in domestic affairs. The young Mamluk sultan had recently risen to power following the decades-long rule of sultans from the Qalawunid lineage. Although in the future he would receive a special place in Mamluk history as the first sultan of the Burji regime, Barquq's power was unsettled and destabilized at the time of his message. Murad, in contrast, had endured his share of dynastic competition and domestic unrest, yet had managed to remain in power since 1362.

The titulature that Barquq used to address Murad also attracted the attention of later Ottoman chroniclers to the extent that Müneccimbaşı, a seventeenth-century successor of Neşri, reduced his account of the event to a discussion of the titulature alone. According to Müneccimbaşı's report, a Mamluk envoy brought lavish gifts and a letter that addressed Murad as *Sultan al-Ghuzat wa al-Mujahidin* (The Sultan of Champions and of Warriors of the Faith), a title that honored the Ottoman ruler's success against the non-Muslim powers of the Balkans.[41] Beyond illustrating the place of titulature in contemporary diplomatic conventions, Müneccimbaşı's exclusive focus suggests that the letter carried an implicit approval of Murad's actions from the Mamluk sultan. Since a Muslim ruler who fought against another Muslim ruler would not have been called "a warrior of the faith," Murad may have asked for his more prestigious, albeit younger, counterpart Barquq's blessings before marching upon the Karamanids. This exchange also may have grown out of Murad's desire to calm the Mamluk capital while legitimizing his own aggression; Barquq's response could also have signaled a shift in Mamluk policy toward the Karamanids.[42]

The First Known Ottoman Ambassador: Yazıcı Salih

For the next few years, while both capitals were likely preoccupied with the Karamanids and other Anatolian political affairs, the Ottomans and the Mamluks continued their tentative diplomatic relationship. Both Mamluk and Ottoman sources recorded at least one Ottoman embassy to Mamluk territory headed by Yazıcı Salih, a member of the Ottoman chancery, in 1388.[43] Although the goal of this mission remains indefinite, its timing indicates some possibilities. One theory suggests that the embassy was sent to announce Murad's 1387 victory against the Karamanids in the battle of Konya.[44] If this was the case, then this embassy was the first that the Ottomans sent to the Mamluks in order to announce their successes in Anatolia against other Muslim rulers. The envoy may have also extended an invitation to the upcoming circumcision festival of several Ottoman princes and perhaps even approached the topic of Timur's aggression in the region.[45]

Yazıcı Salih, who was called "Yazıcı" ("Secretary" or "Scribe," a nickname for his post), deserves special attention as the first recorded Ottoman ambassador. Considering the modest size of fourteenth-century Ottoman bureaucratic institutions, Salih likely served as a secretary of the Ottoman chancery. No information is available about his educational background, but his skills in Arabic and Persian indicate that he had training in both languages.[46] He may have visited Egypt for his education, as his two famous sons Yazıcıoğlu Mehmed and Ahmed Bican would later do. The *madrasas* in Mamluk lands were among the most prestigious educational institutions in the fourteenth-century Muslim world.

Yazıcı Salih's literary activities in Turkish, along with his skills in Arabic, may have prompted Murad to appoint Salih as an envoy to Barquq's court. Sultan Barquq preferred Turkish to Arabic,[47] and he was particularly fond of being read to in Turkish during his leisure time. Barquq's inclination for the Turkish language also manifested itself in his patronage; he chose a Turkish-speaking scholar from Ottoman lands, Şeyh Bedreddin (1358–1416), to tutor his son Faraj.[48]

Yazıcı Salih's mission to Barquq's court must be reexamined in light of the Mamluk sultan's particular interests. The envoy authored a book of astrology in Turkish titled *Şemsiyye*, which became one of the most popular books of fourteenth-century Anatolian literary culture.[49] Although *Şemsiyye* was completed in 1408, long after its author returned from his mission, Salih may have previously revealed his passion for literature or composed other works in Turkish.[50] As astrology was a favorite pastime at the Mamluk court, this parallel between the interests of the Mamluk sultan and the literary activities of Yazıcı Salih may not have been a coincidence. While emphasizing the significant yet largely neglected role the Turkish language played in Ottoman–Mamluk cross-cultural interactions, these interchanges also raise the question of whether ambassadors themselves could be interpreted as gifts. By choosing an envoy who shared and honored the interests of the recipient, a sending ruler often helped to secure the success of a mission.

Barquq and Murad always greeted each other with kind and generous gestures, and their relatively friendly relationship manifested itself for a final time in 1389, after Murad was killed by non-Muslim Balkan forces on the Kosova battleground. Barquq endowed a golden-inlaid candlestick, a silver-inlaid vessel, and the Qur'an in multiple volumes to Murad's mausoleum, probably when extending his condolences to the new Ottoman sultan Bayezid for the loss of his father.[51] The gesture was Barquq's last salute to Murad I.

A New Ruler, a New Image in Bursa

In 1402, after Bayezid fell captive to Timur in the Battle of Ankara, a heated conversation reportedly took place between the two rulers, which was recorded in a Greek chronicle:

> [Timur said to Bayezid:] "yet you dared to march against me with falconers, *zağarcı*, and hounds, as if you are dealing with a child." It is reported that Bayezid had 7000 falconers and zağarcı hunters, in addition to 6000 hounds. When Bayezid heard Timur's mocking words, he answered as follows: "King, you are a Tatar, i.e. Scythian. You are greedy; you seize, you live as befits a thief, and you are not aware of the value of falcons and hounds. But I, Murad's son and Orhan's descendant, the scion of kings, must maintain hunters, falcons, and hounds." This response enraged Timur; he ordered his prisoner bound.[52]

Bayezid's alleged response to Timur acknowledged the multiple changes that the ambitious Ottoman ruler initiated at his own court and within its ceremonial practices. Multiple authors, some in a critical manner, attested to the fact that Bayezid increased the size of his court,[53] enjoyed frequent hunting parties,[54] and often ordered musicians to play for his personal enjoyment as well as for state occasions such as ambassadorial audiences.[55] These kinds of changes were often attempts by a ruler to reformulate his claims to sovereignty and his imperial ideology. Clearly, Bayezid pursued different ambitions than those of his father.

Naturally, the Mamluk sultan Barquq felt the impact of this new reformulation of the Ottoman court.[56] Al-Qalqashandi, who was an eyewitness to these events, recorded that Bayezid and Barquq corresponded regularly. Although the author completed his aforementioned manual in 1412 (ten years after Bayezid's death), al-Qalqashandi's treatment of the Ottomans primarily focused on

Bayezid's reign. While describing the political situation in Anatolia, al-Qalqashandi first summarized al-'Umari's description in the *Al-Ta'rif*[57] but also explained that the political context had changed since the time of his former colleague: the Germiyanids had long disappeared from the political scene, and the Ottomans were the new masters of Anatolia. In one section that described attire in the Anatolian region, he examined the apparel of Ottoman envoys who visited Cairo during the days of Barquq. In his earlier treatise, al-'Umari had focused on the outfits of the Germiyanids.[58]

Despite his shift in perspective, al-Qalqashandi agreed with his former colleague that the Ottomans remained among the petty powers of the larger Islamic world. While he acknowledged the rise of the Ottomans in Anatolia, he questioned yet did not amend al-'Umari's titulature for them.[59] In al-Qalqashandi's hierarchy, the Ottomans were still well below the rulers of *Hind* (India),[60] who the Mamluks addressed as *al-Maqam al-Ashraf* (His Most Noble Station), the highest form of address after *al-Janib al-Karim*, which was accorded only to the caliphs.[61] Neither did al-Qalqashandi consider the Ottomans equal to the Timurid rulers, who ranked just below the rulers of *Hind* and held the title of *al-Maqam al-'Ali* (His Sublime Station).[62] In the same way as his predecessors, however, al-Qalqashandi acknowledged the role of the Ottomans in *jihad*, the warfare against the non-Muslims along the frontiers of Islam. For both al-'Umari and al-Qalqashandi, the *jihad* of the Ottomans was the defining characteristic of this fledgling power's identity in the diplomatic arena.

Early Diplomatic Correspondence

While narrative sources highlighted Anatolian politics as the primary focus of Ottoman–Mamluk interactions, their earliest-available diplomatic correspondence,[63] which survived in Feridun Bey's sixteenth-century compilation, also addressed the issues of piracy and trade. In a letter dated September 1391, the Mamluk sultan Barquq, after acknowledging the arrival of an Ottoman ambassador, reported that he sent a letter to the Genoese demanding (using the verb *amara*: "to order") the release of Muslim captives and their goods. Although historians have yet to identify a particular incident, the Mamluks may have intervened—as they occasionally did—on the behalf of the Muslim captives. A Genoese embassy had returned Muslim prisoners—including prominent Mamluk merchants—to Barquq only a few years before.[64] Bayezid expressed his gratitude for the Mamluk sultan's initiative and further requested that Barquq pardon two Ottoman merchants who were imprisoned in Mamluk territory for violating Mamluk law while conducting business.[65] The patrons of these merchants were prominent members of the Ottoman army and administration.

Beyond emphasizing the importance of trade networks between Ottoman and Mamluk territories, the letters referred to an old and well-known trope in Islamic diplomatic and chancellery practices: unity in religion. Since the letters concerned the release of Muslim merchants from the hands of non-Muslims, allusions to the rulers' shared faith were fitting: both powers freely reminded each other that their lands were like two arms from the same body. Similar references surfaced in other Ottoman–Mamluk correspondence whenever the political context demanded or facilitated this particular kind of rhetoric.

The titulature used in the letters concurred very closely—if not exactly—with the guidelines of al-'Umari and Ibn Nazir al-Jaysh.[66] While Barquq referred to Bayezid with the expression *al-Janab al-Munif* (His Exalted Honor), the Ottoman sultan responded with the title *al-Abwab al-Sharifa* (the Noble Portals), an expression that was also used in Mamluk sources.[67] *Al-Janab al-Munif* is not the exact titulature al-'Umari and Ibn Nazir al-Jaysh assigned to the Ottomans (it was *al-Majlis al-Samiyy*), but it ranked only one level higher. This slight elevation either signaled a change in the Ottomans' status since the time of Ibn Nazir al-Jaysh or presents a possible inconsistency between the descriptive handbooks and the actual usage of titles. Otherwise, the similarities between the Mamluk manuals and the Ottoman collection of letters are promising and lend credence to each of the texts.

The Earliest Ambassadorial Report
about the Ottoman Court

The next instance of Ottoman–Mamluk diplomatic contact was significant in the history of both powers. In 1392 a Mamluk embassy headed by the Mamluk governor of Karak, Amir al-Kujkuni, arrived in Bursa to discuss Anatolian affairs. The ambassador's goal was to dissuade Bayezid from marching against the Karamanids and Qadi Burhan al-din, the ruler of Sivas, whose Anatolian territory fell within the Mamluk sphere of influence.[68] This mission again demonstrated the close involvement of the Mamluk sultanate in Anatolian affairs, despite the fact that no Mamluk ruler since Baybars had either dispatched or personally led any military expedition to the region.

While Amir al-Kujkuni's visit may have seemed like a typical diplomatic mission, Barquq's choice of envoy was one of the earliest signs that the Ottoman ruler Bayezid had succeeded in altering how the Ottomans were perceived by the Mamluks. The ambassador had become one of Sultan Barquq's most trusted companions in recent years. After rising to power in 1382, Barquq was deposed in 1389 by an internal faction. He was entrusted to the governor of Karak, Amir al-Kujkuni, who not only allowed his prisoner to accept visitors and food, but also visited him personally. A year later, al-Kujkuni helped Barquq escape to recapture the Mamluk throne. The Mamluk sultan did not forget his old friend; he granted al-Kujkuni additional fiefs and promoted him to a higher amirate while still allowing him to keep his governorship in Karak. The two remained close until al-Kujkuni's death in 1398.[69] It is telling that Barquq entrusted this Ottoman mission to his confidant, who was additionally well-known for his conversational skills.

The Mamluk records of this mission show that the entire negotiation was both clarified and buttressed through symbolically loaded diplomatic gestures and gift exchanges. Barquq sent impressive gifts (including a robe) with al-Kujkuni, and in return Bayezid treated the Mamluk envoy with the utmost respect. Bayezid gladly accepted the gifts and wore the robe of honor, a gesture that was at least an indication of his respect for Barquq but may have signaled his acceptance of Mamluk suzerainty.[70] Finally, according to another Mamluk source, Bayezid told al-Kujkuni that he was Barquq's slave, as discussed in the Introduction.[71] Bayezid's subservient attitude suggests that he did not contest Barquq's intervention on behalf of the Karamanids and Qadi Burhan al-din and that the Ottoman ruler still accepted his inferior position.[72]

This negotiation with the Mamluks was nonetheless profitable for the Ottomans. Bayezid asked the caliph—and therefore the Mamluk sultan—for a diploma of investiture that officially granted him the title of *Sultan al-Rum*. Bayezid likely gave his word that he would not march upon the Karamanids and Qadi Burhan al-din in exchange for this diploma; Mamluk chroniclers later reported that peace was negotiated between Bayezid and these two powers.[73] Bayezid believed that being called *Sultan al-Rum* by the Mamluks was a privilege, and this new title may have given the Ottomans a sense of superiority over their Anatolian rivals.[74] Soon, al-Kujkuni returned to Mamluk territory accompanied by an Ottoman ambassador and gifts, which indicated the success of his mission.

For the first time in Ottoman–Mamluk relations, the brief remarks of Mamluk chroniclers were substantiated by colorful accounts from al-Kujkuni and Ibn al-Sughayr.[75] These accounts not only provide us with the earliest ambassadorial reports of the manners, rituals, and diplomatic ceremonies at the Ottoman court, but also include further information on the history of its ruling family, society, and economy.[76] According to al-Kujkuni (and Ibn al-Sughayr), Bayezid sat every day on an elevated dais—from which he could see his standing subjects—and received those who had complaints and grievances. This dispensation of justice by the ruler probably caught al-Kujkuni's attention, who could not help but notice its parallels to *mazalim* sessions in Cairo.[77]

New Issues, New Performances: Timur, Refugees, and the Battle of Nicopolis

After 1394 and until Timur defeated Bayezid in the Ankara battle, Timur's encroachment in the region prompted a series of diplomatic exchanges between Cairo and Bursa. Mamluk chronicles also recorded the hasty arrivals and departures of other Anatolian dignitaries to and from Cairo during the same time period. The almost concomitant or consecutive timing of these missions suggests that the Mamluk capital was busily involved in negotiations for a regional alliance against Timur. Bayezid sent at least three missions to Cairo to address the topic, although little information has survived regarding these missions.[78] In response, the Mamluk sultan sent Amir Tulu back to the Ottomans.[79]

While Amir Tulu's primary purpose was to discuss a potential alliance, he also brought back news about Shams al-din al-Jazari, a famous Mamluk scholar. Shams al-din al-Jazari had gone to Bursa after his estrangement from the Mamluk regime and was treated generously by the Ottomans.[80] Amir Tulu's detailed descriptions of the scholar's lavish lodgings and large salary suggest that the Mamluk sultan may have been disturbed by the fact that this famous scholar had found a new patron. Since the Mamluk sultans' legitimization of their sovereignty partially relied on the presence of such scholars in their territory, Ottoman rulers conflicted with another pillar of the Mamluk sovereigns' images when they offered new careers to Mamluk scholars and bureaucrats.[81]

In subsequent years the Ottoman court also rose to prominence as a safe haven for political refugees. After escaping from Timurid attacks, two rulers in the region, Qara Yusuf of the Qaraqoyunlus (d.1420) and Ahmad the Jalayirid of Baghdad (d.1410), originally appealed to the Mamluk court for protection. In fact, the Jalayirid ruler had previously taken refuge in Mamluk lands in 1394 and was welcomed warmly by Barquq.[82] When Ahmad appealed for a second time, however, he brought Qara Yusuf, and they came to Mamluk lands at a time when they were plagued by the civil strife that broke out during the early days of Sultan Faraj (who came to power after his father Barquq's death). As the young and inexperienced Mamluk sultan was already facing internal strife as well as the Timurid menace, Qara Yusuf and Ahmad were denied protection.[83] This incident presents an aberration in the long history of Mamluk sultans who patronized and aided other local rulers such as the Dulkadirids and Karamanids.[84] Qara Yusuf and

Ahmad then petitioned the Ottoman ruler and spent approximately eight months in the Ottoman court between 1399 and 1400. By providing a safe haven for refugees and emigrants, the Ottomans found another way to step into the political arena and to cause the Mamluks concern.

After his trip to Ottoman lands, Amir Tulu also brought back news of the Ottoman victory in the battle of Nicopolis.[85] This military encounter, which took place in September of 1396, marked the first time that the Ottomans faced a Crusading force that combined both Western European and Balkan powers.[86] After Amir Tulu returned home, an Ottoman embassy from Bayezid arrived to officially deliver the news of his victory to Barquq. The embassy, which was accompanied by an unusually large entourage and numerous slaves that were sent as gifts, was given an audience in Cairo on June 8, 1397, eight months after the battle. Mamluk chronicles dwelled at great length on this particular diplomatic encounter, in part because Bayezid and his advisors used this victory as an opportunity for self-promotion at the Mamluk court. The impressive embassy ostensibly communicated Bayezid's respect for Barquq, but it also asserted the Ottoman image as warriors of faith, a theme that had already surfaced in earlier Mamluk sources.[87]

Bayezid's diplomatic efforts yielded significant returns. Barquq generously honored the Ottoman diplomatic representatives from the moment they arrived until the day they left. He ordered that banquets and festivities be held to celebrate the happy news of the Ottoman victory. Although the embassy brought a large and impressive array of war spoils, hunting birds, and fabrics,[88] sources particularly emphasized the presence of slaves.[89] Not only was the sheer number of slaves significant, but their high status and the manner in which they were presented to Barquq also stirred great excitement among the audience.[90] For example, several high-ranking war prisoners wearing full armor were presented to the Mamluk sultan.

Since slaves did not accompany every mission the Ottomans and the Mamluks exchanged gifts (particularly so many in a single mission), Bayezid's choice of gift conveyed multiple messages in this political context. His overt message showed respect and told the

Mamluks that the Ottomans cherished and valued their friendship. The gift may also have demonstrated, however, a cleverly implicit message, since the prisoners displayed a richness of resources for which the Mamluks paid dearly.[91]

Although the Mamluk sultan Barquq ordered banquets and festivities to celebrate the "happy" news of the Ottomans' victory, he was perhaps also troubled by it. The defense of Islam and war against the non-Muslims stood among the pillars of the Mamluk sultans' image, since, as the heirs of the Ayyubids, they shored up their claims for power by defeating the Crusaders, the Armenian princes, and the Chingizid armies.[92] Bayezid's military success in the Balkans seemed to almost infringe on the Mamluk sultan's spiritual domain. Barquq's reported comments to his confidant Amir al-Kujkuni on Bayezid—which appear at the beginning of Chapter 1—manifest his awareness of and his concern about this new threat.[93]

An Ottoman Display of Power: Penetrating the Mamluk Frontier in Northern Syria

Bayezid's embassy following the battle of Nicopolis was not the last occasion that prompted the Mamluks to reassess the Ottomans. In 1399–1400 Bayezid attacked Malatya and its nearby towns, which had been under intermittent Mamluk suzerainty since at least 1277. Bayezid, after the Mamluk sultan Barquq's death, first sent an ambassador to Cairo demanding Malatya and its surrounding strongholds. After the expected negative answer arrived, Bayezid captured Elbistan, Malatya, and Darende by force.[94] As a ruler who ambitiously extended the territories under his hegemony both to the east and to the west, Bayezid profited from the chaos that shook the entire Mamluk domain after the death of their capable sultan. His decision demonstrated that the Ottomans' regard for Mamluk supremacy had changed, and this act of territorial ambition began to sow the seeds of alienation between the two lands.

Bayezid's maneuver also marked the first time that the Ottomans came into direct contact with the Dulkadirids.[95] Malatya had been under the authority of a Dulkadirid governor appointed by the

Mamluk sultan, and the fact that the Sultan Faraj was unable to defend his vassals at this critical time must have been an embarrassment for his regime. The capture of Malatya was likely one of the first times that a Mamluk sultan failed to protect one of his dependents.[96] Bayezid's attack led to the rise of a new Dulkadirid leader, Nasir al-din Mehmed Bey, who had been previously dismissed by Cairo. Amidst changing regional dynamics, Nasir al-din Mehmed Bey (r.1399–1442) stayed in power for almost half a century. Although he continued to acknowledge Mamluk superiority and protection over the Dulkadirid entity as usual, he also maintained regular contacts with Bayezid's successors. From all the possible candidates in the region, he married one of his daughters to the Mamluk sultan Jaqmaq and another to the Ottoman ruler Mehmed I.[97]

The disruption caused by the Ottoman attack on the Dulkadirids was soon overshadowed by Timur's ambitions. His further penetration into the Anatolian and Syrian regions and his hostile correspondence with Bayezid forced the Ottoman sultan to mend his relationship with the Mamluks. At least two Ottoman missions arrived in Cairo with the goals of restoring relations and requesting help against Timur. Emir Ahmed, who may have been a previous ruler of Amasya, headed one of these missions.[98] He brought a valuable convoy of gifts that included ten slaves, ten horses, silver artifacts, and additional gifts for the Mamluk commanders;[99] their high value suggests the gifts were a peace offering.

The fact that an alliance was even considered by the Mamluk *diwan* so soon after Bayezid's attack on Mamluk lands raises the question of whether Şeyh Bedreddin, Faraj's tutor, had begun to influence the young sultan's attitude toward the Ottomans. Bedreddin, who had been born in the then-Ottoman frontier town of Adrianople and was selected by Barquq to tutor his son sometime after 1383, only exerted enough influence, however, to create a moment of discussion in the Mamluk council. The members of the Mamluk *diwan* reminded Faraj that Bayezid had attacked Mamluk lands during the chaotic days following his father's death, and questioned how the young sultan could trust Bayezid.[100] Faraj ultimately followed his council's advice, and the

Ottoman ruler was left alone in his conflict with Timur. Mamluk attitudes toward the Ottomans had changed completely since the days of al-'Umari's works.

Bayezid's aggressive policies toward the Mamluks were also viewed unfavorably by those with strong networks in both Mamluk and Ottoman lands. The author Ahmedi (d.1413), for example, criticized Bayezid in his verse chronicle entitled *İskendername*—a book that belonged to the genre of advice literature (*nasihat-name*) that exerted great influence on later Ottoman chronicles. He wrote his work at a time when Bayezid had already been defeated by Timur and the survival of the Ottoman polity appeared doubtful. Ahmedi had initially planned to present his work to the Germiyanid ruler, but after 1402 he instead offered it to Bayezid's eldest son Süleyman,[101] a gesture that made the critical tone of the text even more meaningful. Perhaps the author intended to warn the next potential ruler of the Ottomans against the mistakes his father had committed.[102]

While Bayezid had instituted many controversial policies that were derided by other authors,[103] Ahmedi disapproved those that endangered the Mamluk lands where he had spent time as a student during Barquq's reign.[104] Even though he hoped to find a new patron in the court of his son Süleyman, Ahmedi still referred to Bayezid as *Bey* and to Barquq as *Sultan*; his conscious choice of titles revealed that the author did not dispute Barquq's higher status. In *İskendername*, Ahmedi clearly expressed his disapproval of Bayezid's attack on Malatya:

> By command of the Creator—May He be Honored and Glorified—the appointed hour of death arrived for the Sultan of Egypt.
>
> Hearing this, he [Bayezid] set his sights on Syria. He proclaimed, "Egypt is mine!"
>
> He did not say, "He [the ruler of Egypt] died. I, too, will die. Just as he died, I, too, will die."
>
> . . . . . .
>
> Thinking it was his opportunity, he [Bayezid] took the road. With the army, he arrived in Mildeni.

After besieging it for some time, he conquered it. He turned his reins back to his capital.

He arrived and made provisions to stay for the Winter, (and then) to return for the conquest of Syria in the Summer.

All this that he did was his precaution. He could not know that it was preordination.[105]

With these words Ahmedi insinuated that the Ottoman–Timurid conflict interrupted the Ottoman relationship with the Mamluks at a critical moment. Would Bayezid have further encroached on Mamluk lands if he had ruled longer, as Ahmedi implies in his verse? Like other counterfactual questions in history, this one is doomed to remain unanswered. Apparently, the "preordination" Ahmedi alluded to amounted to a disastrous defeat for the Ottomans. Bayezid, who was utterly defeated and captured by Timur in the battle of Ankara in 1402, died in captivity. Henceforth, the Ottoman territories descended into chaos and witnessed an intense power struggle between Bayezid's surviving sons for approximately the next 11 years. In the meantime, the provincial Mamluk capital of Damascus was soon devastated by Timurid troops, and the young Mamluk sultan Faraj barely escaped Bayezid's fate before he submitted to Timur's authority. Timur's successful attacks shattered the Mamluk sultan's image and his political legitimacy as the Sultan of Muslims and Islam, the Protector of the Holy Cities, and the Invincible Defender of Muslim Lands.[106] In the post-Timurid days, both the Ottomans and the Mamluks—in their own fashions—would need to devise new ways to salvage their humiliated names and to recreate and promulgate new images of political legitimacy.

CHAPTER 3

FROM TITULATURE TO GEOPOLITICAL AFFAIRS: AN AGE OF NEGOTIATIONS (1413–1451)

In the aftermath of the Timurid invasions, both the Ottomans and the Mamluks began recovering their previous territories and prestige. While the Ottoman rulers Mehmed I and Murad II returned their attentions to the Balkans, their Mamluk counterparts al-Mu'ayyad Shaykh, Barsbay and Jaqmaq advanced against the remaining Crusader forces in Cyprus and Rhodes.[1] Both sides' increasing emphasis on *jihad* and *ghaza* served as the central pillar of this new phase of image reconstruction,[2] but this emphasis should not be taken at face value. Both powers, while speaking of "the infidels" in their diplomatic correspondence, simultaneously yearned to reestablish their superiority over their surrounding Muslim powers.

Even during this phase of reconstruction and reconsolidation, the frequent appearances of Ottoman and Mamluk ambassadors in each other's capitals, bearing carefully prepared letters and impressive gifts, illustrates the centrality of this particular network for both sides. Although it is often dismissed as a quiet era for Ottoman–Mamluk contacts, this period was one of significant changes: the greatest promotion of Ottoman titulature in the

Mamluk correspondence took place during these four decades; the expansion of the Ottoman sphere of influence both in the Balkans and Anatolia was simultaneously pronounced and acknowledged in a clearer fashion; and the charity of Ottoman rulers as a component of their images came to the fore. Amidst their ambivalent domestic and international situations, the diplomatic language of both parties shifted slowly and surely.

Ottoman Interregnum

The use of titulature in Mamluk sources revealed the extent of the chaos caused by the Timurid attacks on Ottoman lands. Al-Qalqashandi, who completed *Subh al-A'sha* in 1412 (a time when the civil strife in the Ottoman polity had not come to an end), primarily focused on the reign of Bayezid in his discussion of the Ottomans. In contrast, he discussed the post-Bayezid period in two brief sentences, despite the fact that he outlived the Ottoman ruler by more than a decade. Even though he emphasized the rise of the Ottomans in his work, the section that listed the titulature accorded to various rulers gave the appellations previously accorded to the Ottomans by al-'Umari without any amendment (*al-Majlis al-Samiyy*). He also omitted any examples of titulature exchanged between any Ottoman—or even any Anatolian—and a Mamluk sovereign. In a later section, he included a copy of the titles by which the Mamluk governor of Damascus addressed the late Ottoman ruler Bayezid I.[3] This letter opened with a *salutatio*, followed by the prestigious title of *al-Maqarr al-Karim*. It is likely that al-Qalqashandi was unsure how to describe the relationship between the Ottoman and Mamluk rulers during this unsettled time. Therefore, for safety's sake, he included the titles by which a Mamluk governor should address an Ottoman ruler. The brevity of al-Qalqashandi's comments on the post-Bayezid period reflects the ambiguity the Mamluk scholars felt towards the Ottomans during this tumultuous time of Ottoman rule.

An Overview of Changing Titulature between 1402 and 1451

Despite the relative silence of Mamluk sources on the topic, Ottoman rulers did make contact with Cairo during this era. In fact, an undated piece of Mamluk correspondence—which was probably written between 1405 and 1408—responded to a letter from Bayezid's eldest son Süleyman. After he declared his sultanate in Edirne, Süleyman (r.1402–11) was probably the first of Bayezid's princes to reach out for the recognition of the Mamluk sultan. The Mamluk response to the young ruler proves that al-Qalqashandi was correct to question the old Ottoman titles from al-'Umari and Ibn Nazir al-Jaysh.[4] The Mamluk sultan Faraj saluted Süleyman with the following composition: *Za'uf Allah Ta'ala Ni'ma al-Janab al-'Ali al-Amiri...* (May God Almighty multiply the prosperity of His Grand Honor, the Commander...) This particular title not only ranked higher than the former convention of *al-Majlis al-Samiyy al-Amiri*, but also closely coincided with an address from earlier correspondence between Bayezid and Barquq (*al-Janab al-Karim*).[5] In his letter Faraj expressed his gratitude to Süleyman for restarting the communication that was so active in their fathers' days. Besides a few vague references to Süleyman's continuing clashes with his brothers, the letter does not contribute significantly to our knowledge of Ottoman political events. In closing, Faraj listed and offered thanks for Süleyman's generous gifts: Greek (rum) slaves "whose beauties were beyond description"; furs of sable, squirrel, and fox; carpets; silver utensils and vessels. With such an impressive collection, Süleyman was clearly attempting to convince the Mamluk sultan that he, rather than one of his brothers, had seized control of his father's domain.[6] The letter and the gifts may also explain why Mamluk authors called Süleyman the successor of Bayezid I.[7]

According to Mamluk sources, Mamluk officials henceforth addressed Süleyman's successors Mehmed I and Murad II with the honorifics of *al-Janab al-'Ali al-Amiri*—a title that exactly matched Süleyman's in terms of status and ranked higher than the earlier title of *al-Majlis al-Samiyy*. Not surprisingly, the Mamluk scribes also proudly recorded the imperial titulature with which the inferior Ottoman rulers respectfully addressed the Mamluk sultan: *al-Maqam al-Munif* (His Exalted Station).[8]

The correspondence that was collected by the Ottoman official Feridun Bey, however, depicted a slight contradiction with Mamluk sources. According to Feridun, the Ottoman rulers began to address the Mamluk sovereigns with the title *al-Janab al-'Ali* while the Mamluk sultans bestowed the title of *al-Maqarr* on the Ottoman sovereigns rather than the lower-ranking *al-Janab*. Otherwise, the rest of the Ottoman titulature in this collection showed a striking resemblance to the Mamluk versions.

Remarkably, this discrepancy between the Mamluk and Ottoman sources disappeared at an unknown point during Murad II's reign. According to an anonymous Mamluk collection of letters, the Mamluk sultan Barsbay addressed Murad with *al-Maqarr al-Karim* for the first time in 1433.[9] Along the same lines, al-Sahmawi (d.1464), who became the head of the Mamluk chancery during Barsbay's reign, listed the following titles for Ottoman rulers (as well as for the Qaraqoyunlu ruler Iskandar bin Qara Yusuf, who died in 1438) in his 1436 manual: *Al-Maqarr al-Karim al-'Ali, al-Kabiri, al-'Alami, al-'Adili, al-Mujahidi, al-Mu'ayyadi, al-Ghawthi, al-Ghiyathi, al-Za'imi* [...] *'Izz al-Islam wa al-Muslimin, Sayyid al-'Umara fi al-'Alamin, Muqaddam al-'Asakir, Mamhad al-Duwal, Mashid al-Mamalik, al-Za'im al-Juyush al-Muwahhidin, 'Awn al-'Umma, Ghiyath al-Milla, Zahir al-Muluk wa al-Salatin, 'Adad 'Amir al-Mu'minin*.[10] Al-Sahmawi also noted that most of the Anatolian powers that were mentioned in al-'Umari's and Ibn Nazir al-Jaysh's works had, by that time, acceded either to Ottoman suzerainty or superiority.[11] Despite the ambiguity that remained after the Timurid invasion, the fact that Mamluk sources acknowledged the gradual rise of the Ottomans' diplomatic status through shifting titulature shows the ongoing dynamism of their diplomatic encounters. The Ottomans still had not, however, reached the level of the Timurids, who were assigned the title of *al-Maqam* according to al-Sahmawi's chancery manual.[12]

The earlier disparity between the Mamluk texts and Feridun Bey's collection possibly reflected an exercise in editorial discretion by

Ottoman officials. The loyalty of these Ottoman bureaucrats to their patrons, however, had its limits: while they might have changed the honorific of their own sovereigns from *al-Janab* to *al-Maqarr*, they never completely reversed the power dynamics between the Ottoman and Mamluk sovereigns. According to both the Mamluk scribe Ibn Hijja and his Ottoman colleague Feridun Bey, the Ottoman rulers Mehmed and Murad respectfully referred to their Mamluk peers as *Sultan al-Islam wa al-Muslimin* (The Sultan of Islam and Muslims), *Malik al-Muluk fi al-'Alam* (The King of Kings in the World), *Hami Sukkan al-Haramayn al-Sharifayn* (The Protector of the Residents in Two Holy Cities), *Sultan al-Haramayn* (The Sultan of Two Holy Cities), and *Hafiz Bilad Allah* (The Protector of God's Domain).[13] While these honorifics acknowledged the central position of the Mamluks in the Muslim world, both Ottoman and Mamluk sources reveal that the Mamluk Sultans Faraj, al-Mu'ayyad Shaykh, Barsbay, and Jaqmaq never addressed their Ottoman counterparts as sultan. Mehmed and Murad were recurrently called *Amir*.[14] Some honorifics incorporated the title of sultan, such as *Zahir al-Muluk wa al-Salatin* (The Support of the Rulers and the Sultans),[15] but still did not designate the Ottoman rulers as sultans.[16] Despite this omission, the Ottoman image as *ghazis* was mutually reemphasized via epithets such as *Nusrat* (or, more often, *Nasir*) *al-Ghuzat wa al-Mujahidin* (Victorious One of *Ghazis* and *Mujahids*).[17] The consistent use of *Amir* for the Ottoman rulers, as opposed to the Mamluk sovereigns' uncontested monopoly of the title of sultan (and its derivatives such as *sultani* or *mawlawi*), shows that even the Ottoman secretaries— who in retrospect adjusted their own patrons' statuses—knew the boundaries of editorial discretion.

From Fratricide to Granada

An exchange in 1415 marked the beginning of an intense series of letters between the Ottoman ruler Mehmed I and the Mamluk sultan al-Mu'ayyad Shaykh. The two rulers, whose reigns overlapped almost completely (Mehmed I died six months after al-Mu'ayyad Shaykh), had much in common. In the aftermath of the Timurid invasions, both leaders tried to suppress internal conflicts, consolidate their authority at the political center, and, in particular, reestablish their sovereignty in their old domains. Their correspondence, therefore, focused on Anatolian affairs,[18] though it also referred to Ottoman expeditions in the Balkans.[19] While Mehmed fought in both the Balkans and in Anatolia, al-Mu'ayyad Shaykh organized three campaigns to northern Syria and southern Anatolia.[20] Six of the seven surviving letters between these two sovereigns either referred to Anatolia or were sent before or after a campaign that one of them undertook in the region.[21] In these letters both rulers particularly emphasized the significance of ending any "rebellion" or "disobedience" against their authority; especially for the Mamluks, the surrounding Anatolian territories had always belonged to them, and they were merely reclaiming what was theirs.[22]

Alongside these issues of regional geopolitics, the correspondence between Mehmed and al-Mu'ayyad Shaykh broached the delicate subject of Ottoman dynastic practices. In his first letter in 1415, Mehmed recounted not only his recent military conflict with the Byzantines, but also his own struggle against his brothers to secure the Ottoman throne.[23] Mehmed may have been trying to legitimize his adherence to the Ottoman practice of fratricide by portraying it as a way for him to return his attention to the more important issues of *jihad* and *ghaza*. Surprisingly, Mehmed's comments about his succession struggle did not elicit any comment from al-Mu'ayyad Shaykh.[24] In his response the Mamluk sultan merely expressed his happiness about Mehmed's success against the Byzantines.

The Ottomans understood the unusual character of their succession practices, and the timing of a later piece of Ottoman correspondence implied a close connection between their dynastic struggles and their claims to sovereignty in the international arena. Almost two years had passed since the Ottoman ruler Mehmed's successor Murad II had come to power in June 1421, and one year had passed since the Mamluk ruler Barsbay had taken the throne in April 1422. While both capitals went through their own power struggles at the highest levels of their administrations, both sovereigns delayed the usual diplomatic gesture of sending a goodwill mission to the other until the dust settled in the streets. Like his father Mehmed before him, Murad sent his first representative to the Mamluk court after eliminating his two primary rivals from his own family and before departing on a major campaign in Anatolia.[25] While the execution of these rivals did not necessarily end the challenges that tested the Ottoman ruler's authority, it was only after their deaths that Murad felt confident enough to announce his sovereignty to the Mamluk sultan.

Although the Mamluk sultans were familiar with bloody succession struggles, they were not as used to them in a dynastic context.[26] In his biography of Bayezid I, al-Maqrizi recounted in a surprised and disapproving tone how the Ottoman ruler rose to power after killing his brother.[27] The same chronicler also gave a surprisingly detailed account of Murad's rise in 1423 and his subsequent mission to Cairo.[28] In a possible attempt to divert attention from Ottoman dynastic politics, the delegation brought impressive gifts from the new ruler and enjoyed an equally generous reception by Barsbay.[29] Al-Maqrizi's writings, beyond demonstrating that the author was surprisingly well-informed about Ottoman affairs, also show us that the Ottoman practice of fratricide still drew considerable attention in Mamluk society.

In addition to their respective succession struggles, the aggressive policies of the Karamanid principality were a common topic between Mehmed and al-Mu'ayyad Shaykh, especially until 1421. Mehmed's letter regarding his successes against the Byzantines and his succession to the throne decisively acknowledged the conventional role of the Mamluk sultan in Anatolian affairs.[30] Although his letter did not explicitly refer to the Karamanids, it was composed while Mehmed was in İnegöl—where he camped before moving into Karamanid territory—and was entrusted to the judge of İnegöl.[31] The embassy, whether it was sent to convince the Mamluk sultan of the legitimacy of Ottoman dynastic practices or assuage any fears that might arise from Ottoman penetration into the Karamanid territories, presumably completed its mission with success: the Ottoman ambassador returned with another Mamluk ambassador and corresponding gifts—a sign that his reception had been positive.[32]

A closer look at the items that were exchanged during this mission reveals a clear difference between the economic values of the Ottoman and Mamluk gifts. While the Ottoman gifts were comprised primarily of various types of fabrics from Anatolia and Europe, the Mamluk gifts displayed a richer variety and included two horses, two saddles made of gold and silver, and goods from India and Alexandria. The diverse geographical origins of the Mamluk gifts emphasized the differences between the resources available to each sovereign.

Despite the imbalance between their statuses, al-Mu'ayyad Shaykh's last letter to Mehmed confirmed his acceptance of the Ottomans' involvement in Anatolian affairs—a recognition that had been given to Bayezid but had been lost in the aftermath of the Ankara battle. In al-Mu'ayyad Shaykh's last campaign against the Karamanids in 1419, the Mamluk armies, under the command of the Mamluk sultan's eldest son Ibrahim and aided by the Karamanid ruler's brother Ali Bey and the Dulkadirid ruler Nasir al-din Mehmed's troops, routed the Karamanid armies and brought back the severed head of the Karamanid prince Mustafa.[33] The father of the beheaded prince, the Karamanid ruler Mehmed Bey, was also captured and was brought to Cairo in chains on January 6, 1420.[34] This entire episode was proudly described in a Mamluk letter (or *fathname*) to the Ottoman court.[35] Al-Mu'ayyad Shaykh spent the rest of the year in poor health and died on January 3, 1421; Mehmed died six months later.

A letter to Mehmed from al-Mu'ayyad Shaykh's son and successor Ahmad—who was a minor at time he took the throne—reached the Ottoman capital after Mehmed's death.[36] The letter celebrated the Ottoman successes in the Balkans but also expressed Ahmad's wishful thinking: if he could, he would march to Granada to save the Muslims from the oppression of the Spanish kings. Since he was unable to do this alone, the Mamluk sultan suggested that something could be achieved by enlisting the help of a King Janosh, a loyal "friend" of the Mamluk court. This Janosh was possibly the king of Castille, John II, who pursued a policy of treaties and tribute with the Muslim rulers in the Iberian Peninsula. If this text was accurate, it showed the wide range of issues that the Ottoman and Mamluk courts addressed during this time of transition. Perhaps the new sultan was trying to counterbalance the growing Ottoman control in the Balkans by emphasizing his own network of ties along another frontier of Islam.

An Age of Victory Proclamations and Negotiations

Of the approximately 18 surviving Ottoman and Mamluk letters that were written between 1421 and 1451 (after the deaths of al-Mu'ayyad Shaykh and Mehmed), 11 are either victory proclamations or congratulatory responses to such proclamations.[37] In these texts, as expected, references to the tropes of *jihad* and *ghaza* or to the suppression of a disobedient inferior dominated the language of diplomacy between Cairo and Edirne.

The Ottomans took the lead in the game of image-building with consecutive campaigns in the Balkans. Among the victory proclamations that have been discovered so far are those that announced the capture of the strategic stronghold Güvercinlik (Golubevich along the Danube, which had been controlled by the Serbian despot) and a simultaneous victory against the Albanians in 1427; the recapture of the same stronghold from the Hungarian King Sigismund (d.1437) the next year; the celebrated and significant conquest of Thessalonica (Selanik) after years of siege in 1430; the fall of Smederova (Semendire) in 1438; and the battle of Varna in 1444, which took place amidst a political crisis in Edirne. Both Ottoman and Mamluk chronicles referred to additional diplomatic exchanges for which the actual correspondence has not been found. Chroniclers from both sides tirelessly depicted the arrival and departure of these Ottoman missions as well as the slaves and artifacts they proudly displayed in their processions. Disseminating the news of these victories was so important to the Ottoman rulers that some of their letters pleaded for announcements in the sacred cities of Mecca and Medina.[38] It is not surprising that the Mamluk administration, after facing this bombardment of victory announcements, promoted the Ottoman sultan's appellation from *al-Janab al-'Ali* to *al-Maqarr al-Karim*.[39]

The Mamluk responses to these victory announcements included countless celebration banquets, the return of Ottoman missions with equally valuable corresponding gifts, and verbal affirmations of the Mamluk sultans' reported joy. While most of the Mamluk sultans carefully followed the established etiquette while conveying their good wishes for their peer's success along the frontiers of Islam, however, Barsbay and Jaqmaq refused to passively or humbly celebrate Murad II's continued assertion of his position.

Barsbay kept pace with the Ottomans by turning his attention to Cyprus, whose rulers positioned themselves as the descendants of the Crusaders in the eastern Mediterranean.[40] Each of Barsbay's three consecutive attacks was successful, but it was not until the last one in July 1426 that Cyprus' King Janus (r.1398–1432) was captured and brought to Cairo along with other valuable slaves and spoils. This campaign held a special place in Mamluk military history not only because it involved maneuvers on both land and sea and proved their unusual military prowess in both spheres, but also because the captured sovereign was one of the scions of the kings of Jerusalem and the Crusader states. As a result of this expedition, Cyprus became a tributary vassal of the Mamluks.

As the Mamluk army triumphantly paraded its prisoners—including King Janus—through Cairo, Barsbay publicly proclaimed his military success and also refreshed his image as a *ghazi* ruler. The Mamluk sultan who was committed to rebuilding and reviving the old ceremonials and pomp of the Mamluk regime invited all the foreign envoys who were in Cairo to the procession.[41] The entire group of spectators was forced to wait until the parade arrived[42] and then watched while the army brought Janus in chains and forced him to kiss the ground in front of the Sultan. As a sign of the Mamluk Sultan's generosity and wealth, the other spoils of war were either distributed among the Mamluk commanders or sold in the markets. The delegations that witnessed this procession included the envoys of the Hafsid sultan, the Timurid ruler Shahrukh, the leader of the Bedouin tribes, the Dulkadirid ruler, and the Ottoman ruler Murad II.

At the same time, Barsbay's victory announcement demonstrated the fluidity of roles between the sender and the recipient in diplomatic relations. While the foreign representatives in Cairo were originally sent to spread the names of their own sovereigns, they also bore witness to the Mamluk victory. In addition to this public occasion, Barsbay probably sent the prominent ambassador Taghribirdi al-Hijazi al-Khassaki al-Ashrafi to the Ottoman capital to announce his success for a second time.[43]

Although their military campaigns to the Balkans and to Cyprus provided both the Ottomans and the Mamluks with opportunities to reconsolidate their images, they were not entirely motivated by religious ideology. While past campaigns against the Mongols and the Crusaders had provided the Mamluk sultans with opportunities to craft their images as warriors of faith,[44] the Mamluk attacks on Cyprus also reflected their geopolitical concerns. The eastern Mediterranean coast under Mamluk control had been intermittently attacked by various groups, including the pirates who often used Cyprus as a base. These aggressors attacked the ships that traveled between Anatolian and Mamluk ports, captured the goods of Muslim merchants, enslaved the Muslims, and slowed trade between Mamluk lands and Anatolia. Depending on the political conditions of the time, the Mamluk sultans followed different policies in dealing with these threats. While the Mamluk sultan Faraj achieved minor success with two small flotillas, his successor al-Mu'ayyad Shaykh (who first considered attacking the island) signed a treaty with the King of Cyprus, who promised to close the island to pirates.[45] The fact that al-Mu'ayyad Shaykh opted for a treaty instead of attacking Cyprus demonstrates that his decision-making process was not entirely influenced by ideological concerns. Finally, Barsbay and his successor Jaqmaq led recurrent attacks on Cyprus and Rhodes (respectively), partly because they wanted to protect their coasts and partly to prevent an alliance between the rulers of Cyprus and the Timurids. Such an alliance would have left the Mamluk rulers surrounded by opponents to the east and to the west.

The fact that Barsbay sent an embassy to Murad II in 1433–4 to announce his "victory" against the Muslim Aqqoyunlus further reinforces the idea that rulers used each military occasion to polish their images as successful military commanders, even when the victory was not an ideological one.[46] The Mamluk sultan presented this campaign not as an act of *jihad* but rather as an undertaking that brought the unruly Aqqoyunlu ruler to obedience. In fifteenth-century international politics, as in modern times, self-presentation and perception mattered more than the reality, and, after congratulating Murad for another success against the Hungarians, Barsbay framed his campaign as a clear-cut victory. In reality, Barsbay's campaign was not completely successful. After a long and exhausting siege with no concrete territorial gains, he retreated with a substantially reduced and resentful army and only the nominal subservience of the Aqqoyunlu ruler 'Uthman.[47] Nonetheless, the Mamluk sultan, who had been hosting victory missions, countered these celebrations with one of his own. At the end of his letter, Barsbay also reminded Murad II of his "holy conquest" (*al-fath al-qudsi*) of Cyprus seven years before.[48] Barsbay's letter also confirmed that the Ottoman sphere of influence had geographically expanded in the previous decades and also included the Aqqoyunlus now.[49]

Fraternity and Solidarity

While communications between the Ottomans and the Mamluks had always been couched in language that alluded to tropes of fraternity and solidarity, it was not until 1427 that missions were exchanged to discuss the possibility of an alliance between the two lands. In the past Bayezid had investigated the possibility of an alliance against Timur, but his investigations were not well-received because there had been recent Ottoman attacks on Mamluk territory.[50] In 1427, in the aftermath of the Cyprus campaign, Barsbay was still engaged in skirmishes with pirates along his coasts when he received an intelligence report about a Western army approaching Ottoman lands. Seeing an opportunity for alliances on both land and sea, he sent an envoy to Murad II with the suggestion that the two rulers reinforce their ties of friendship and brotherhood against this approaching threat.[51]

By the time Barsbay's envoy (Taghribirdi al-Ashrafi, who may have also carried the victory proclamation after the Cyprus campaign), reached Murad with the Mamluk ruler's proposition, the Ottomans had already encountered an allied army of Hungarians and Serbians and had conquered the frontier castle of Güvercinlik between the summer of 1427 and the winter of 1428. Even after this victory, Murad II was so pleased to hear Barsbay's offer that he gave the envoy an ornate golden robe and a hat from his own wardrobe in addition to other valuable gifts for Barsbay.[52] Even though Barsbay's offer of friendship was not followed by any real logistical support, it nevertheless contributed to the development of a mutually positive attitude on both sides.

In 1429, soon after Taghribirdi's return, an Ottoman envoy, Hoca Cemaleddin, brought the official news of the conquest of Güvercinlik to Cairo.[53] Barsbay, who may have wanted to properly respond to the honor that Murad had bestowed upon Taghribirdi, ordered an imperial procession and a great celebration in honor of the Ottoman envoy. According to Mamluk sources, the envoy was given a spectacular audience at the foot of the citadel in the presence of Mamluk administrators, scholars of law, and the general public.[54] He presented a letter that described the Ottomans' successful campaign as well as valuable gifts from Murad II that expressed his appreciation for Barsbay's offer.[55]

One theory suggests that the valuable gifts Murad II sent to Barsbay were a response to the impressive ceremony that the Ottoman envoys had witnessed in the Mamluk court after the Cyprus campaign.[56] The Ottoman gifts included 50 slaves of European origin (*rum*), 15 doves and various hunting birds, a great amount of sable, squirrel, lynx, and fox fur, and also 20 pieces (*qita'*) of European silk cloth for *mahmal*. The Ottoman ruler may have chosen to send a large and valuable group of European slaves in order to counter the excessive number the Mamluks had acquired during their campaign to Cyprus. Apparently, the silk cloth for *mahmal* did not stir up any negative feelings in Cairo—further evidence that gifts were interpreted differently depending on the message that accompanied them.[57] This particular gift from Murad should also be evaluated within the context of the simultaneously evolving tension (1424–35) between Barsbay and Shahrukh over *kiswa*.[58] By sending textiles for *mahmal* rather than *kiswa*, Murad may have been implying his respect for Barsbay's prerogative and expressing his solidarity with the Mamluk sultan against Shahrukh's insolence.

A letter that Murad sent to Barsbay between 1429 and 1430 can be also evaluated in light of this atmosphere of alleged fraternity and solidarity. In 1428 Murad signed a truce with the Balkan powers after a period of intense warfare, then sent a letter to Barsbay informing him of the truce.[59] Murad II explained that he was not initially interested in the King of Hungary's pleas for peace, as he believed that waging war against the non-Muslims was the way of the *Muhajirin*, those first Muslims who went to Medina upon the orders of the Prophet Muhammad and later created the seed of the first Muslim army to fight against the people of Mecca. After too much warfare had exhausted the people of both lands and blocked the roads of commerce, however, Murad II had signed a three-year truce. The tone of Murad II's letter to his Mamluk counterpart sounds humble, even apologetic, as if the Ottoman ruler felt the need to legitimize the truce in the eyes of the Sultan of Islam, as Murad II called Barsbay in the letter. Barsbay responded to this letter with a tone of approval. He reminded Murad II that the Prophet had also signed a truce with the people of Mecca and that it was understandable for him to sign a truce with the non-Muslims. Barsbay added that the conditions of this truce had great benefits for the Muslims. At the end of the letter, the sultan expressed his pleasure that Murad II had confided in him.

Although these texts frequently referred to their Islamic historical heritage, Prophetic traditions, and even Qur'anic verses in order to embellish a point, discussing the religious basis for a political decision was not common in Ottoman–Mamluk diplomatic relations. The fact that Murad II made a case for his treaty through the revered and shared memory of early Muslim history indicated his deep dissatisfaction with the recent events in the Balkans. Murad II's letter not only showed his effort to explain and legitimize his actions in the eyes of another Muslim ruler who occupied the same ideological circle, but may have also been an attempt to salvage his name in a land where he was called *Sahib al-Ujat* (Master of Frontiers) or *Nusrat al-Ghuzat wa al-Mujahidin* (Victorious One of *Ghazis* and *Mujahids*).[60] In response, Barsbay consoled his fellow sovereign in a dialectic manner with an example from their mutual heritage.

Ignored Refugees

For an impressively long period between 1402 and 1451, sources did not record any diplomatic conflict or military engagement between the two powers, although two separate circumstances could have easily instigated tension. The first case, which was only recorded in Mamluk sources, concerned two members of the Ottoman dynasty, the siblings Süleyman and Sara (Hundi?).[61] Their father Orhan, who was the son of Süleyman, was blinded and imprisoned by his uncle Mehmed I before they were born, and both children were born into a state of partial captivity. When Orhan passed away in 1429 or 1432, his servant (possibly called Doğan) escaped with the brother and sister to Mamluk territory. They were welcomed by the Mamluk ruler Barsbay, who had just returned from his "victorious" campaign to the Aqqoyunlus in 1433.[62] Although they received hospitable treatment at the Mamluk court, the Mamluk authorities reprimanded them when they tried to return home in 1437.

It is not clear why the siblings or Doğan wanted to return to Ottoman lands, and, at this point, the accounts in different Mamluk sources diverge from one another. One version suggests that the Ottoman ruler Murad II requested that Barsbay return his relatives. When Barsbay refused—in part because he was concerned for their lives—Murad II then convinced Doğan to bring the two back to Ottoman lands. After the entire group was caught on a ship in Alexandria and brought back to Cairo, Doğan was executed. Other members of the group were also severely punished while the young prince endured a minor punishment and was soon returned to the Mamluk barracks. The Ottoman princess eventually married Barsbay and, after his death, Jaqmaq. Her children did not survive to puberty, and Jaqmaq later divorced her.[63]

At the same time that the Mamluk sultan hosted these two Ottoman family members, the Ottoman ruler Murad II also provided a safe haven for Janibak al-Sufi, Barsbay's main political rival. Barsbay had imprisoned Janibak at his accession, but he later escaped and found his way to Ottoman lands.[64] The chronological overlap of these two cases suggests that negotiations may have taken place concerning the fates of these individuals.

Surprisingly, neither of these potentially incendiary incidents damaged the relationship between Murad II and Barsbay. Both rulers were invested in other political fronts, and they shared a mutual distrust of Shahrukh, the ambitious Timurid ruler. In 1424, a major crisis erupted between the Mamluks and the Timurids when Shahrukh—who was known for his piety and his political ambitions—sent the *kiswa* to Barsbay with his ambassadors.[65] Although it was disguised as a diplomatic gesture, this action was, in fact, a direct challenge, since the annual replacement of this textile was a jealously guarded prerogative of the Mamluk sultans. With this "gift," Shahrukh infringed on the Mamluk sultans' rights and asserted a claim for leadership of the Islamic world. After this diplomatic transgression, his relationship with Barsbay would remain tense.

Shahrukh's ambitions also manifested themselves in further diplomatic exchanges with Anatolian powers when he attempted to reclaim control of territories that had once recognized his father Timur's authority. When he heard the news of Shahrukh's efforts, Barsbay was disturbed:

Ṣafar, 839. The Sultan received the news that Shâh Rukh ibn Tîmûrlank had sent robes to Sultan Murâd Bak bin 'Uthmân, ruler of Asia Minor, to Emir Ṣârim ad-Dîn Ibrâhîm ibn Qaramân, mentioned above, and to Qarâ Yuluk and his sons and Nâṣir ad-Dîn Bak ibn Dulghâdir, with the understanding that they were his viceroys in their territories. All of them put on his robes, and this distressed the Sultan, namely, that ibn 'Uthmân [Murad II] had put on his robe, until it was said to him that he had done so in a social gathering, in derision of it.[66]

This passage illustrated not only the extent of Shahrukh's ambitions, but also the significance of robes in fifteenth-century Islamic diplomacy, particularly when both the recipient and the sender were heads of state. Since robes asserted or reaffirmed a sender's superiority over a recipient, Barsbay was understandably concerned upon hearing that Murad II had worn Shahrukh's gift.[67] Both of these gift-giving episodes involving Shahrukh remind us that this diplomatic practice was not taken as a mere ceremonial obligation but could serve as a way to claim or acknowledge power.

Barsbay, who interpreted Shahrukh's diplomatic maneuvers as signs of potential military aggression, approached Murad II, along with other sovereigns in the region, for an alliance that same year.[68] Sources, however, did not say anything further about Barsbay's appeal for help, perhaps because the internal dynamics in Shahrukh's territories prevented the Timurids from pressing the Mamluks further and made such an alliance unnecessary.[69] The death of Barsbay in 1438 certainly ended this quest, and his successor Jaqmaq, once he was able to secure his reign, treated Shahrukh more carefully.[70]

Changing Roles

The death of Barsbay sparked a succession struggle that lasted until Jaqmaq was able to consolidate his authority in Cairo. Although he adopted a cautious policy toward the Timurids, Jaqmaq also recognized the increasing prestige of the Ottomans in subtle ways. He sent a messenger to Murad barely two months after taking the throne (September 10, 1438) and first reported Barsbay's death in a letter dated October 28, 1438.[71] The new Mamluk sultan recounted the events that surrounded his accession with unusual detail and particularly emphasized the roles of the caliph, prominent scholars, and religious leaders who unanimously supported him. Jaqmaq explained how, after a quasi-vote that included high commanders of the army and administration, he replaced Barsbay's young and inexperienced son after initially serving as his regent. While minimizing his role in this alleged *fait accompli* and vote, Jaqmaq also asserted his legitimacy as a ruler by referring to the Prophet's well-known saying: "My community does not agree on a mistake."[72] In an unusual passage, the new sultan also told Murad II that he had sent the elephant the Ottoman ruler had requested from Barsbay, since the late sultan had not been able to oblige before his death.[73] The letter addressed Murad II with the title *al-Maqarr al-Karim*, which had been the conventional address for the Ottoman rulers since at least 1433.

The detailed explanations in Jaqmaq's letter to Murad II, which have an almost defensive tone, catch one's attention. After all, it was the Ottoman rulers—first Süleyman and then Mehmed—who had once sought recognition from the Mamluk rulers and tried to explain their controversial succession practices. This shift in the way the Ottoman rulers were viewed by the Mamluk sovereigns suggests that even during these relatively calm years between 1402 and 1451, the Ottomans and Mamluks continued to negotiate for more refined statuses. Murad II returned a delayed response to Jaqmaq with a quasi-congratulatory letter and simultaneously announced his new conquest of Smederova. Murad II's letter also referred, although briefly and generically, to the valuable gifts Jaqmaq had sent with his ambassador.

Jaqmaq responded to Murad II's announcement with a celebratory letter that has been preserved in both Ottoman and Mamluk sources. Although there is no way to confirm the accuracy of the extant gift list that survives only in the Ottoman version of the text, it deserves attention due to the value of the listed items. While many valuable yet usual items—from swords to rare fabrics—were listed,[74] the most remarkable gift was placed at the top of the list, in a spot parallel to its symbolic significance in the ideological and spiritual worlds of both powers. It was "a Holy Book in the hand of Caliph 'Uthman." The Qur'an was among the gifts that were customarily exchanged between Muslim courts, yet this copy was special because Caliph 'Uthman had played a crucial role in establishing the definitive version of the Holy Book. In Abbasid ceremonials, the Qur'an of 'Uthman fulfilled a symbolic task: if the caliph chose to receive someone, this copy would be placed in front of him, next to other ceremonial appurtenances that had come down from the

Prophetic age.[75] Undoubtedly, the Mamluks did not send 'Uthman's own Qur'an that had been used in Abbasid ceremonials, but a copy that had been written by the caliph himself. The symbolic significance of the gift indicated the Mamluks' high esteem for the Ottoman court, and the survival of this particular gift list showed that the Ottomans shared their reverence for the text.[76]

While this exchange of letters between Edirne and Cairo unfolded over the course of two years, another phase in Mamluk–Timurid relations also began. Jaqmaq sent Shahrukh a letter dated February–March 1439 that announced his accession to power, but its content contrasted deeply with his letter to Murad II.[77] As usual, Jaqmaq appropriately addressed Shahrukh with the very high-ranking title of *al-Maqam al-Sharif*, which was equivalent to the Mamluk sultans' titulature. Yet, at least in the surviving copy, he only announced Barsbay's death and did not give any further details. Murad II, in contrast, had been bestowed with the lower-ranking title of *al-Maqarr al-Karim al-Amiri* yet had been honored by Jaqmaq with additional explanations that Shahrukh did not receive.

Seven months later, in November 1439, Jaqmaq accepted a Timurid mission that brought an unexpected message from Shahrukh. According his ambassador, Shahrukh had heard of Jaqmaq's accession, yet "he wished to be confirmed in the knowledge of the event."[78] Sources are not clear whether Shahrukh had received Jaqmaq's letter and not been satisfied by its content or if he had not received it at all. In either case, in order to avoid unnecessary tension, Jaqmaq honored the ambassador with a robe and additional gifts and ordered the preparation of another letter to Shahrukh.

When the next Timurid embassy reached Cairo in September 1440, Jaqmaq was ready to smooth over any misunderstanding with the Timurids: this time Cairo was well-prepared to host his guests, and Jaqmaq's own son was sent to welcome the group. The residents of the city enjoyed the lavish decorations in honor of the mission and observed the procession in amazement. Shahrukh's representatives brought gems, camels, silks and other textiles, fur, and musk, and they were also granted a generous daily allocation for their expenses during their stay. Before his departure the Timurid ambassador was granted a robe of honor which, according to Ibn Taghribirdi's description, exceeded any other robe given to any previous ambassador in quality and richness. The gifts that he carried back to Harat were equally impressive.[79] The Mamluk court's generous and extremely proper gestures showed that the Mamluk sultan and his advisors did not want to affront Shahrukh.

The Indirect Discourses of Diplomacy: Commerce, Pilgrimage Caravans, and Fatwas

While a discussion of diplomatic exchanges is helpful in tracing the evolution of mutual images and perceptions, such a discussion falls short in reflecting the complexity of the Ottoman–Mamluk relationship. The extensive commercial networks that existed between the two territories are among the most important yet neglected aspects of this relationship. Both Ottoman and Mamluk sovereigns frequently wished in their correspondence for these networks to improve,[80] and, on rare occasions, they asked for specific favors to that end.[81] For example, in a letter dated August 1436, Murad II requested the Mamluk sultan's help in retrieving an inheritance for the daughter of an Ottoman merchant who died in Mamluk Tripoli. The fact that this daughter was married to an Ottoman *qadi* named Husameddin, who acted as both Murad II's representative and the deceased merchant's agent, gives only a glimpse into the complex networks between these societies.

Beyond the usual exchange of diplomatic missions, the sovereigns also engaged in indirect communication. The annual pilgrimage caravan's departure from Cairo held great significance for all Muslim rulers, and many loyally sent their annual alms and gifts for the journey to Mecca and Medina. Although the Ottoman rulers had sent alms in the past, sources for the first time mentioned that Mehmed I and Murad II had established pious foundations (*Evkaf al-Harameyn* in Turkish) to support the Two Holy Sanctuaries, their residents, and the members of Prophet's family.[82] While these gifts did not function in the same way as those carried by ambassadors, they conveyed various messages to the Mamluk sultans, to the public, and to the larger world of Islam.[83] These gifts and donations helped rulers craft their images both at home and in Mamluk lands as auspicious, generous, and pious. The honorific that Murad II received in Mamluk correspondence during these decades, which was "Shelter of the Poor and Needy," was probably adopted after such a display of generosity.[84]

Depending on their context and their manner of delivery, however, these gifts could also become tools by which other Muslim rulers countered an essential facet of the Mamluk's imperial image and ideology. The Timurid ruler Shahrukh, for example, felt the wrath of the Mamluk sultan when he attempted to send *kiswa* for the caravan.[85] Similar propositions to send the silk cover of the ceremonial palanquin *mahmal* were also occasionally but not always seen as challenges to Mamluk authority.[86] There are no records that indicate the Ottomans affronted the Mamluks in this manner.

In 1444 another indirect yet influential engagement between the Ottomans and the Mamluks took place. While Murad II was engaged in a difficult campaign in the Balkans, the Karamanid ruler İbrahim Bey (d.1464) formed an alliance against him[87] and attacked Ottoman lands in the east. In a letter sent to Cairo, Murad asked if it was legally permissible for him to wage war against İbrahim Bey who, although a Muslim himself, was disturbing the Muslims living in Ottoman lands and distracting the Ottoman ruler from *jihad*.[88] The scholars who formulated responses to this question included respected Mamluk intellectuals. Five surviving fatwas from various scholars, such as the celebrated Ibn Hajar (d.1449), agreed that it was permissible to fight against the Karamanids. Some took the argument even further and claimed that shedding the Karamanid ruler's blood was permissible according to Islamic law.[89]

By posing his question, Murad II cleverly gained Jaqmaq's consent to attack the Karaminids without offending the Mamluk sultan. Normally such an attack would have caused resentment at the Mamluk court, since the Karamanids had been Mamluk vassals for decades. Once the scholars had announced their legal opinions, however, it became more difficult for Jaqmaq to overstep their wishes. Soon after receiving the legal opinions he expected, Murad II marched on the Karamanids in July 1444.[90] İbrahim Bey ultimately signed a treaty with the Ottomans and accepted Ottoman suzerainty. Murad II, through a seemingly deferential ploy, deftly maneuvered his intrusion into the Mamluk sphere of influence.

Soon after his campaign into the Karamanid territory, Murad II relinquished his power to his 12-year-old son Mehmed II for almost two years. Barely four months after he stepped down, a Crusading alliance seized the opportunity to attack the Ottomans while they were under the sovereignty of a child ruler. The Ottoman armies under Murad's command engaged the Crusading army in Varna on November 10, 1444. The young Mehmed II sent at least two diplomatic missions to Cairo during his brief tenure, and the first one announced his father's military success. Mehmed II dispatched Azeb Bey, who had been a commander in the battle,[91] and his convoy entered Cairo on January 31, 1445 accompanied by prisoners of war.[92] Mamluk chroniclers' depictions of the embassy, however, clarify that the Mamluk public audience—if not the administration—was unaware that there had been a regime change in Edirne. A later Ottoman mission finally brought the news that Murad II had relinquished power to his son Mehmed II. The letter conveyed a particularly respectful, perhaps even submissive, tone from the young Ottoman ruler.[93]

Mamluk sources did not record that Murad II reclaimed the reins of the Ottoman government from his son in 1447. Neither did any mention the crucial battle of Kosova, which took place between the Ottoman and the Crusading armies in October 1448. The sources only recounted that the Mamluk ambassador Amir Qanim al-Tajir departed to Edirne on July 25, 1449. He accompanied the Ottoman ambassadors that had likely come to announce the Ottoman army's victory in Kosova.[94]

Two years after Qanim's departure, Cairo received the news of Murad II's death in March 1451.[95] In his history of dealing with the prestigious Mamluk regime, Murad II clearly followed a different path than that of his great-grandfather Bayezid. His tactics were persistently based on diplomatic communication and negotiation rather than physical aggression. As the shifting titulature and diversification of issues in the letters revealed, it was perhaps because of the peaceful nature of his diplomacy that he was successful in establishing an equal—if not more prestigious and reputable—perception of the Ottomans, both in Mamluk Cairo and in the broader international arena. The laudatory obituary that Ibn Taghribirdi wrote for him attests to this fact:

> Sultan Murad Bak died when he was in the full years of his maturity. Because of his possession together of intelligence, prudence, determination, generosity, bravery, and leadership, he was the best ruler of his time in the East and the West. He spent his whole life in endeavor on the path of God the Exalted, made a number of invasions, gained a number of victories, conquered lofty forts, citadels, and cities from the enemy and those deserted [by God]; but he was devoted to the pleasures which men's appetites love; perhaps his state was like that mentioned by one of the pious who had been asked about his religion and said, "I tear it with sins and mend it with prayers for forgiveness"; and he is the more deserving of God's pardon and generosity because he had to his credit famous monuments and was the cause of great benefits to Islam and of defeats to its enemy, so that it was said of him that he was a wall for Islam and Mohammedans—God pardon him and give him Paradise in return for his youth; for through his excellence he was the highest glory to the human race—God the exalted be merciful to him.[96]

This short yet powerful passage summarizes Murad II's direct and indirect diplomatic achievements: his military success in the Balkans, his broadening political authority and influence, and his charity and pious patronage. Even after his death, this last quality was reinforced by Murad II's will, which stipulated donations and endowments for residents of the Two Holy Sanctuaries and the members of the Prophet's family.[97]

CHAPTER 4

IMPERIAL AMBITION RESURRECTED (1453–1481)

Upon hearing of Murad's death, the Mamluk sultan Jaqmaq quickly prepared a mission headed by Amir Asanbay to express his condolences to Mehmed II, Murad's son and successor.[1] When Asanbay returned in December of 1451, he was accompanied by an Ottoman diplomat who officially announced Mehmed's second enthronement. The Ottoman mission confirmed Mehmed's satisfaction with Jaqmaq's swift diplomatic gesture, and the ambassador proffered slaves and furs to the Mamluk sultan on December 23, 1451. For the rest of their stay, the embassy enjoyed the utmost generosity from the Mamluks including a daily stipend of 100 *dinars* (gold coins); they also received an additional 3,000 *dinars* for their return trip.[2] At the time, no one guessed that the young Mehmed, who had previously deferred to the Mamluk sultan's position, would later attempt to radically alter the power dynamics between the two lands.

No one expected the young Ottoman ruler to conquer Constantinople, yet the city fell to Mehmed II's armies after a two-month-long siege on May 29, 1453. In addition to transforming the geopolitics of the eastern Mediterranean and the Middle East, this conquest reshaped the status and the image of the Ottoman sovereign. For three more decades, Mehmed not only pursued an expansionist policy in almost every direction, but also consistently professed the Ottoman Empire's new role in the region with institutional and ceremonial changes.[3] Mehmed was not content to cast himself—as his father Murad had done—as a ruler who dominated the Balkans and southeastern Europe. He also wanted to be known as the Caesar or Kaiser (Kayzer in Turkish) of Rum and as the foremost leader of the Islamic world.

Mehmed II's territorial and ideological ambition was just one of the many threats to the conventional Mamluk sphere of influence in Anatolia. While the death of the Timurid ruler Shahrukh in 1447 mitigated the possibility of a Timurid attack, the simultaneous rise of the Aqqoyunlu leader Uzun Hasan posed a new danger. As Mehmed reformulated his territorial and political claims and disseminated his new image, however, his main Mamluk contemporaries (Inal, Khushqadam, and Qaytbay) did not bow to the Ottoman sultan's desires. Their responses to his overtures, though they shifted slightly from one ruler to another, generally preserved the status quo that relied on the Ottoman admission of Mamluk superiority and the Mamluk acknowledgement of Ottoman geographic expansion.

The disparity between the Mamluks' goals and the Ottomans' ambitions brought the two powers into intermittent conflict that was primarily enacted through diplomatic discourse rather than armed struggle. Although sources diverged from one another about the details of particular incidents, both Ottoman and Mamluk chroniclers related that the misuse of honorific titles and the negligence of diplomatic etiquette either mirrored or caused troubles between the two courts, while new tropes were formulated and old ones were recast in a more daring manner than before. Diplomacy became the battleground for both Ottoman and Mamluk ambitions.

The Ottoman Conquest of Constantinople

An Ottoman embassy headed by Celaleddin al-Kabuni arrived in Cairo on October 27, 1453, barely five months after the conquest of Constantinople, the Byzantine imperial capital.[4] The mission's purpose was to announce Mehmed II's conquest and to extend the Ottoman ruler's congratulations to Inal, the new Mamluk sultan who had come to power in March 1453.[5] The Mamluk society's excitement about the arrival of the Ottoman mission conveyed the significance of this particular conquest for the larger Islamic world. Sultan Inal had ordered the decoration of the cities along the mission's route, and, as the group entered Cairo, the Mamluk capital launched into a celebration that lasted for days.[6] Artisans and shop owners decorated their stores, and the imperial drums were beaten from dawn until dusk. Neither of these practices was usual for greeting foreign missions.[7]

The mission was given an audience only two days after its arrival, another gesture that indicated the Mamluk administration's special regard for its guests. On October 29, 1453, Inal received Celaleddin al-Kabuni in a special ceremony held in the *hawsh* (a courtyard where ceremonies took place in the citadel).[8] In addition to the approximately 30 slaves from Constantinople's noble class and two captured clergymen, the ambassador also brought nine cages (or baskets or trunks) of sable fur, nine of bobcat fur, nine of ermine fur, and nine of squirrel fur along with nine ornate textiles, nine colored textiles, and nine oblong pieces of atlas cloth.[9] Afterwards, in an unusual gesture, Inal descended from the citadel with the ambassador to observe the city and its special decorations for the occasion.[10]

Mehmed II also took great care with the mission's victory proclamation. He asked his former tutor, Molla Gürani, to craft the victory announcement using the most elegant and impressive language possible. Along with the letter's explicit message of victory, Mehmed also sent the implicit message that this scholar who had once been in the service of the Mamluk sultan was now his own servant. After all, patronizing scholars, intellectuals, and artists was one of the responsibilities of a powerful sovereign. Mehmed's efforts with this letter proved how highly he valued the Mamluk court and how strongly he believed in the importance of diplomatic correspondence in spreading a sovereign's image to the international arena.

Two separate variants of the Ottoman victory proclamation for the Mamluk court have been preserved: one in Feridun's collection, and the other in both al-Biqaʿi's chronicle and in an anonymous letter collection.[11] Although these two texts are similar in their general structure and content, their expressions, tropes and tone differ from each other.[12] Except for Feridun's usual devaluation of the Mamluk sultan's title from *al-Maqam* to *al-Maqarr*, both versions use respectful and appropriate honorifics. In Feridun's version, however, the rest of the Mamluk sultan's epithets include two additional adjectives that could be rendered as "Elevated Paternal."[13] This combination respectfully alluded to the Mamluk sultan's seniority in terms of age and experience. Considering the reverence that Islamic societies have displayed for seniority, this gesture was fully compatible with Islamic diplomatic practices and shows the 21-year-old Mehmed's respect for the 72-year-old Inal.

In contrast to Mehmed's initial reverence for the Mamluk sultan's seniority, Feridun's version of the Ottoman ruler's letter also revealed his discreet but escalating ambitions for a more prestigious image. In one passage, Mehmed declared that it was time to reestablish communication between the two rulers while clearly distinguishing his own role and position from the Mamluk sultan's: "Now this is the time to reconnect between the person who shouldered the responsibility of enabling the pilgrimage for the pilgrims and pious people and the person who shouldered the responsibility of preparing and equipping the people of *ghaza* and *jihad*, as he inherited this task from his fathers and ancestors [.]"[14] Mehmed's artificial division of labor almost completely dismissed the Mamluk sultan's claims and earlier accomplishments against the Crusaders and others that had been at the core of their image and sovereignty claims since the beginning of their regime.[15] Furthermore, Mehmed's reminder that he inherited his pursuit of *jihad* from his ancestors underscored the dynastic origin of the Ottoman rulers while alluding indirectly to the Mamluk sultan's slave origins. This implicit statement was probably the beginning of a new trope in Ottoman–Mamluk diplomatic exchanges—one that would be visited more frequently in later episodes of this relationship. Both this statement and the allusions to Inal's seniority, however, did not appear in al-Biqa'i's version of Mehmed's letter.

There are two possible yet conflicting ways to interpret these two different texts. It was not unusual to send two separate letters with a single mission, and Feridun's version referred to the existence of a second letter. Both of these letters may have been sent together to Inal.[16] The fact that the adjectives implying Mehmed's reverence for Inal's seniority did not appear in al-Biqa'i's version might have indicated that Mehmed and his advisors did not want to sound repetitively submissive in both texts. At the same time, the absence of the first letter's bold statements alluding to the Ottoman ruler's dynastic heritage and leading role in defending the Islamic world could have revealed the Ottoman regime's search for a more balanced tone.

The fact that al-Biqa'i's version of the text employed a more respectful and less dramatic tone raises the other possibility that a group of advisors, along with Mehmed, reviewed the draft and crafted a more appropriate version for the Mamluk audience. The existence of two separate variants suggests that multiple drafts were created before a final and conclusive text was reached—a process that again proves the care and attention that the Ottoman ruler gave to his appearance at the Mamluk court. It is likely that Feridun's bolder version more accurately reflected Ottoman self-perception, and for this reason it was collected and preserved for a domestic audience.

During the Ottoman ambassador's stay in Cairo, Inal entertained his guest by inviting him to ceremonies that were regularly held in the *hawsh*. On one occasion in November 1453, he dressed Celaleddin in a valuable robe trimmed with sable.[17] When the Ottoman embassy prepared to return home, he selected Yarshbay al-Inali al-Ashrafi to accompany them and to carry his own letter to Mehmed. Yarshbay departed on December 22, 1453, barely two months after the Ottoman ambassador's audience.[18] The correspondence he carried conveyed a celebratory tone and contained an itemized gift list with 16 entries including gold weaponry, a rich variety of textiles and clothes, and animals such as an elephant.[19] After Amir Yarshbay's departure, the Ottoman ambassador remained in Cairo for two more days to certify that the Ottoman ruler's gifts for the Sharifs of Mecca were dispatched safely.[20]

Despite their complimentary tones, both of Inal's letters maintained a reserved attitude towards the Ottoman ruler. In one, Inal expressed his own gratitude for Mehmed II's goodwill message after his own succession to the Mamluk throne and acknowledged his reverence for Mehmed's noble family.[21] Nonetheless, he addressed Mehmed with the usual title of *al-Maqarr al-Karim* (although Feridun's version recorded the higher title of *al-Maqarr al-Sharif*).[22] The title of *sultan* was not used, but the rest of the title affirmed Mehmed's responsibility for and role in *jihad* and *ghaza*, as usual. In a slightly novel gesture, the titular title *al-Nasiri* (Victorious) was added to Mehmed's appellations.[23]

The treatment that the Mamluk ambassador Yarshbay received in Constantinople was equally important for the future of Ottoman–Mamluk relations and Mehmed II's image in Cairo. Although Yarshbay spent the entire winter in the Ottoman capital and finally returned to Cairo on August 1, 1454 with Mehmed's letter of thanks, the only known record of his experience at the Ottoman court appeared as a few statements in Ibn Taghribirdi's account.[24] Ibn Taghribirdi confirmed that Yarshbay returned to his sovereign Inal wearing a robe of honor—one that was probably in the Ottoman fashion—from the Ottoman ruler. Yarshbay informed Inal that Mehmed Bey (certainly not "Sultan Mehmed") had hosted and honored him in the most generous manner possible.

While no exchanges between the Ottoman and Mamluk capitals were recorded for the next few years, one diplomatic incident between 1454 and 1455 indirectly revealed Inal's positive yet reserved attitude toward the Ottomans. An embassy from the Karamanid leader İbrahim Bey arrived in Cairo between December 1454 and January 1455; its mission was to present the sovereign's complaints about Mehmed. At the time of Mehmed's accession in 1451, İbrahim Bey had attacked Ottoman territory, and by 1454–5, Mehmed had initiated two separate campaigns against the Karamanids. When the Karamanid ambassador presented his grievances at the Mamluk court, however, Inal was not inclined to listen.[25]

When the next Ottoman mission appeared in Cairo on April 24, 1456, one year after Mehmed's successful campaign to Serbian lands,[26] the members of the Mamluk administration respectfully celebrated the ambassador's arrival.[27] The mission was again led by Celaleddin al-Kabuni and was granted an audience only three days after its arrival. The gifts included a selection of war spoils: approximately 30 slaves, different kinds of furs, and different styles of silk and woolen textiles. Intriguingly, Ibn Taghribirdi particularly praised the fact that the gifts were presented to the sultan on porters' heads, which was apparently a tradition among the rulers of Mashrik (by which he likely meant the Timurid and Chingizid traditions).[28] The Mamluk chronicler may have wanted to highlight the fact that the Ottoman ruler was well-trained in diplomatic etiquette and treated the Mamluk sultan in a befitting manner.

As it brought the news of a major military success in the Balkans, it was not surprising that Mehmed's letter strongly emphasized the ideals of *ghaza* and *jihad*. It started with the conventional appellation of *Sultan al-Haramayn* and other expressions of respect for the Mamluk sultan,[29] then announced the fall of the Serbian despotate to Ottoman subjugation. During this critical campaign, the Ottomans had seized significant castles (including Novo Brodo, which fell to the Ottomans on June 1, 1455) and regained the control that they had lost in 1444. Mehmed also informed the Mamluk sultan about the upcoming circumcision festivals of his two sons, Bayezid (the future Bayezid II) and Mustafa, which would take place in 1455–6 in Edirne.

Inal ordered the preparation of a Mamluk embassy to accompany Celaleddin al-Kabuni's return. Meanwhile, the Ottoman ambassador spent time in Cairo, rested, and observed public occasions such as the departure of the annual pilgrimage caravan. The Mamluk sultan appointed Amir Qanibay (d.1458), who was the *mihmandar* and *muhtasib* (market inspector) of Cairo, to be his ambassador.[30] The mission's departure was delayed by a rumor that reached Cairo on June 25, 1456 that Mehmed II had unexpectedly succumbed to the Black Death. After they received the reassuring news of Mehmed's health,[31] celebratory drums were beaten in Cairo for three days, and both embassies departed on July 9, 1456. The Mamluk sultan's letter to Mehmed, while celebratory and cheerful in tone, still addresses the Ottoman ruler with the usual *al-Maqarr al-Karim* combined with titles that emphasized his role in *jihad*.[32] Inal's generous gifts for the Ottoman ruler and the young princes included swords, saddles, textiles, and an elephant.[33] Qanibay returned to Cairo almost a year later after his departure—after being treated with the utmost hospitality.[34]

At around the same time that these missions left Cairo, Inal received the news that the Karamanid leader İbrahim Bey had seized the Cilician strongholds of Tarsus, Adana, and Gülek from their Mamluk governors.[35] Henceforth, reasserting Mamluk authority in Karamanid territory became a pillar of Inal's politics, though he also took care not to disturb Ottoman interests in this pursuit.[36] After a delay caused by the approaching winter, Inal sent troops under the command of the future sultan Khushqadam to his northern border with the Karamanids. At least one Ottoman chronicler stated that Inal received the Ottoman ruler's blessing for this maneuver as well as Ottoman logistical support for his troops.[37] Since this incident broke out around the time of Qanibay's mission to the Ottoman court, it is possible that the ambassador had also been ordered to broach this topic with Mehmed II. In the end, the Mamluk troops successfully repelled the Karamanids and inflicted serious damage to the heart of their territories.[38]

At the time of Inal's death in 1461, the Ottomans and the Mamluks enjoyed a fairly stable and balanced relationship, in part because Mehmed II had seemingly upheld the conventions of diplomatic etiquette. Likewise, Inal had continued his contacts with the Ottoman court, showed respect to Ottoman ambassadors, and displayed enthusiasm—at least superficially—for the Ottomans' military successes. In Mamluk correspondence, the Ottoman involvement in *ghaza* was acknowledged and even praised. Inal, however, still preserved the balance of power between the two lands by addressing the Ottoman ruler with the same titulature his predecessors had used.

In evaluating Inal's approach to foreign policy, it is important to remember that the Mamluk sultan did not pursue aggressive policies on every front.[39] Although he clashed with both the Karamanid leader İbrahim Bey and the Qaraqoyunlu ruler Jihan Shah, he maintained good relations with the Aqqoyunlus.[40] Perhaps due to his advanced age, Inal was a cautious ruler, seasoned in battles and political conflicts, and particularly careful when making decisions that could strain his diplomatic relationships with surrounding powers.

Diplomatic Etiquette and Political Rivalry

When he was asked why the relationship between the Ottomans and the Mamluks deteriorated, the fifteenth-century Ottoman chronicler Aşıkpaşazade enumerated a list of reasons.[41] Though his chronology contained some inaccuracies, Aşıkpaşazade particularly blamed the Mamluk sultan Khushqadam, who consolidated his rule in Cairo four months after Inal's death, for the escalating tension between the two Islamic powers. According to Aşıkpaşazade, "The conventional rule of etiquette was mutually dismissed, and both parties started to dislike each other."[42] The Ottoman chronicler, who claimed that Khushqadam created enemies in every direction, was not entirely misleading; in fact, the relationship between the Aqqoyunlus and the Mamluks also deteriorated considerably during these years.[43] Khushqadam had commanded the Mamluk troops that had terrorized the Karamanid territory during Inal's reign, a tactic that gave some indication about his future style of rule.[44]

While Khushqadam's rise to power in Cairo certainly played a critical role in the increasing volatility of Ottoman–Mamluk relations, Mehmed's territorial and ideological ambitions also manifested themselves in a more aggressive manner during this time. In the following decade, Mehmed turned his attention to Anatolia and penetrated further into the Mamluk sphere of influence, a move that strained the relationship between the two capitals and also transformed the language of diplomacy between them.

Not surprisingly, in Aşıkpaşazade's eyes, it was not Mehmed II's ambitions but rather Khushqadam's neglect of diplomatic etiquette that triggered the volatility between the two rulers. In the summer of 1461, Mehmed personally led a campaign to the Anatolian coast of the Black Sea where he subdued the Isfendiyarids and ended the Trebizond Empire on August 15, 1461. The Isfendiyarids (also called the Candarids) had been among the Anatolian powers that had autonomously emerged in the post-Seljuk period, been subdued by Bayezid I, and finally regained their autonomy in the aftermath of the battle of Ankara. With the conquest of the Trebizond Empire, Mehmed also eradicated the last vestiges of the Byzantine Empire in the region. Mehmed's annexation of these lands was an important step in his unification of Anatolian lands under Ottoman authority. After returning to his capital, Mehmed accepted the many foreign missions that arrived to congratulate his success, but noticed the absence of a Mamluk ambassador among the foreign dignitaries. Apparently, Mehmed felt offended that Khushqadam had not sent him a goodwill mission. In return, Mehmed did not send a mission to congratulate the novice ruler for his accession to power.[45] Aşıkpaşazade's analysis of this event focused on Khushqadam's failure, and the Ottoman chronicler either conveniently ignored or was unaware that the early months of Khushqadam's reign were particularly chaotic as the new sultan consolidated his authority. This negligence that reportedly troubled Mehmed (and Aşıkpaşazade) so deeply, however, went unmentioned in Mamluk sources.

Mehmed II's strong reaction to Khushqadam's neglect grew out of a new Ottoman self-perception that was rooted in the conquest of Constantinople. Despite the aggravating economic pressure that his continuous conquests would put on the empire's budget, Mehmed minted the first official gold coin of the Ottoman Empire.[46] The royal protocols that Mehmed put on his coins reflected this new attitude: As the new sovereign of the former Byzantine imperial capital, Mehmed presented himself to the world as "The Sultan of two lands and the Khan of two seas, the Sultan, Son of a Sultan, Mehmed, son of Murad Khan, May God perpetuate his sultanate!"[47] and "The one who mints gold [coins], the master of glory and victory on land and sea, Sultan Mehmed, son of Murad Khan, May his victory be exalted!"[48] It was not a new practice for Ottoman rulers to stress their dynastic heritage; both Mehmed I and Murad II—Mehmed II's predecessors—also emphasized that they were the sons of rulers on their coins. The language on Mehmed II's coins went beyond stressing the "noble" lineage of the Ottomans; it also alluded to the empire's geographical borders and to its wealth. Moreover, he transformed the royal insignia (*tuğra*) by adding "Forever!" to the earlier expression of "Victorious!" that was probably first used by his father Murad.[49] The manner in which Mehmed II presented himself to the world differed from that of his ancestors, and he expected his fellow sovereigns to respond accordingly.

Another diplomatic incident offered a glimpse into the discrepancy between Ottoman expectations and Mamluk perceptions as well as the role of etiquette in their relationship. Remarkably, it appeared in both Ottoman and Mamluk sources and therefore provides an excellent opportunity to compare their mutual perceptions. In 1464,[50] three years after Mehmed II took offence at the absence of a Mamluk embassy, the Mamluk sultan sent an envoy with lavish gifts, supposedly to apologize to the Ottoman ruler.[51] Mehmed accepted the apology and responded to this act of goodwill with an Ottoman envoy. Since Mehmed envisioned himself in a higher position than his father had occupied, however, the letter that Mehmed sent to the Mamluk sultan opened with the address "Our *Brother*, the *Servant* of the Holy Sanctuaries" rather than with the conventional address of "Our *Father*, the *Sultan* of the Holy Sanctuaries."[52] By addressing the 62-year-old Khushqadam in this manner, the 32-year-old Mehmed perhaps inadvertently disregarded the diplomatic convention of reverence for seniority in order to clearly convey his bold message. In the past he had respectfully upheld this rule of etiquette when communicating with the Mamluk Sultan Inal, who was also his senior.

In his description of Mehmed II's insolence, Aşıkpaşazade nonetheless blamed the Mamluks for the Ottoman envoy's troubles during his visit to Cairo. The night before his audience with the Mamluk sultan, the Ottoman envoy was mistreated by the Mamluk commanders. When he was invited into the presence of the Mamluk sultan the next morning, the envoy, still offended by his poor welcome the night before, refrained from kissing the ground and stated that he had not come to kiss the ground but to bring greetings from his sultan. After neglecting an essential ritual of the Mamluk court and boldly explaining his actions, the ambassador was treated badly during the audience. In Aşıkpaşazade's account the envoy was cast as an unfairly humiliated representative who had only demanded the recognition befitting his ruler. When the envoy returned to Constantinople, he reported his negative experiences at the Mamluk court, much to Mehmed's displeasure.

The Mamluk chronicler Ibn Taghribirdi narrated the same events in a drastically different manner, thus implying that the story was adapted to the needs and agendas of the narrator and his audience.[53] Ibn Taghribirdi did not refer to any attempts by Khushqadam to ameliorate his relationship with the Ottomans, but instead began his story with the arrival of the Ottoman mission on June 4, 1464. This version stated that the mission was warmly welcomed to Cairo by a group of Mamluk commanders and then escorted to their lodgings.[54] In the Mamluk account, the problems began the next day, during the audience. When the envoy approached the circle where Sultan Khushqadam waited for him, the Mamluk commanders, such as the *mihmandar* and the *dawadar*, ordered the envoy to kiss the ground, an act required of every foreign envoy at the Mamluk court. When the Ottoman envoy disregarded the instructions, the Mamluk sultan was deeply offended.

An affront that was apparently worse than the envoy's refusal to kiss the ground was the unusual opening of the Ottoman letter. During the audience, Mehmed II's correspondence was read aloud by the *katib al-sirr*. It addressed the Mamluk sultan as *al-Maqarr al-Karim* (His Noble Residence), which was, according to Ibn Taghribirdi, an unusual epithet. Although Ibn Taghribirdi's descriptions of the titulature did not match Aşıkpaşazade's, both authors conveyed that the titulature defied convention. The envoy then presented Mehmed's gifts: 30 slaves, furs from various animals and colorful fabrics, and the Mamluk sultan distributed them among his commanders.

The Ottoman ambassador must have noticed Khushqadam's dissatisfaction because he quickly explained that he was neither familiar with nor had he been instructed about Mamluk court etiquette prior to the audience. He further added that even God accepted late prayers and that he would kiss the ground in front of the sultan more than once. When the Mamluk sultan demanded an explanation for the inappropriate titles in Mehmed's letter, the Ottoman envoy claimed that the secretaries who composed the text did not know the correct titles for a Mamluk sultan. Despite the ambassador's apology, he left the citadel without receiving a robe of honor, and the absence of this gesture clearly signaled the Mamluk sultan's displeasure.[55]

A few days after the audience, when the Mamluk sultan's anger had subsided, the Ottoman ambassador seized a chance to mend relations. He attended the prayer on the first day of the Ramadan feast, which was an official public event attended by the sultan and his administration.[56] After he participated in the communal prayer, the ambassador was granted a robe and was seated underneath the Mamluk commanders. As he watched the rest of the ceremony from his seat, the ambassador was deeply impressed by the way that the commanders, bureaucrats, and judges of all ranks kissed the ground when they approached the sultan. Unlike Aşıkpaşazade, who did not report an apology, Ibn Taghribirdi insinuated that the incident did not turn into a major disaster only because the ignorant ambassador apologized again in a subservient manner. He further argued that the first affront due to the ambassador's ignorance was forgivable, but the second affront of the misused titulature was not, a distinction that indicates how seriously the Mamluk society took these ceremonies and rules.[57]

The treatment that the Ottoman ambassador received during the rest of his stay suggested, however, that Khushqadam had not completely forgiven the ambassador's misdeeds or the misuse of titulature in the letter. On June 15, the Mamluk sultan gave the ambassador a silk travel robe (*khil'a al-safar*), granted *salariyya*[58] to his entourage, and permitted them to leave the Mamluk lands. Although he had already chosen Sudun al-Kisrawi for the task, he decided not to send his own ambassador back with the Ottoman mission. Instead, Khushqadam "ordered" ("*amara*") the ambassador to convey the Mamluk sultan's gifts to Constantinople himself. This time, the ambassador hesitated to follow this order and proposed that they could be conventionally carried by a Mamluk ambassador at a later time.[59]

These two different accounts of the same diplomatic exchange nevertheless highlighted the agency of envoys in interstate relations. There is no obvious explanation for the letter's inappropriate epithet, though it does not seem realistic to think that the Ottoman chancery did not know the proper titulature for a Mamluk sultan. Since Mehmed questioned and even rejected the idea of Ottoman inferiority, one also wonders if the Ottoman envoy was instructed not to kiss the ground during his audience. Ibn Taghribirdi's account gave many details about the ambassador's apologies, so it is equally likely that the envoy was merely ignorant, or that the Ottoman ruler did not intend to cause a diplomatic incident, at least not one so serious. Perhaps the unlucky envoy slightly revised the details of his visit to save himself from Mehmed's wrath. Since he blamed the Mamluk administrators for the incident, it is also worth considering their role in this diplomatic crisis.

Aşıkpaşazade's account of the incident also stated that the Ottoman envoy's experience directly impacted the treatment of the next Mamluk ambassador to arrive in Constantinople. This ambassador may have been al-Sayyid al-Sharif Nur al-din 'Ali al-Qurdi, who was sent by Khushqadam in December of 1464 to request an alliance against the Aqqoyunlu leader Uzun Hasan.[60] The death of the Karamanid leader İbrahim Bey in July 1464, followed by a succession struggle between his six surviving sons, had suddenly disrupted the political equilibrium in the region. It was almost expected that the Ottomans and the Mamluks would become involved in this struggle, but Uzun Hasan also entered the conflict when some of the Karamanid princes fled to his territory.[61] This development disturbed Khushqadam, who also learned that Uzun Hasan had seized control of Gerger, a frontier town under Mamluk control.[62] Despite the ill feelings that had been brewing in both capitals, Khushqadam decided to approach the Ottoman ruler for assistance.[63]

Unfortunately, Khushqadam's offer was not accepted by the Ottoman sultan. Nur al-din 'Ali al-Kurdi was reminded of the way that Khushqadam had treated the Ottoman envoy during his previous visit.[64] According to Aşıkpaşazade, Mehmed expressed his disappointment to the Mamluk envoy with the following words:

> [Mehmed II said:] "Isn't it regrettable that someone who is ignorant of law (*kanun*) and etiquette (*kaide*) rules on a throne

and in a land such as Egypt's [? Mehmed] honored the envoy [,] hosted him well [,] offered him lavish goods [,] and endowed upon him gifts that were matching with his might [.]"[65]

Aşıkpaşazade, who was the only chronicler to record this conversation, made Mehmed II's displeasure clear. Presumably, Mehmed claimed that even though the Mamluk sultan ruled in the old lands of Islam, he did not know how to treat an envoy. By contrast, Mehmed saw himself as an ideal ruler who generously and hosted the Mamluk envoy in the customary manner, despite the humiliation his representative had endured in Cairo.

Mehmed II's reported comments also compared the differences between Ottoman and Mamluk rulers in the sphere of legislation. He alluded to his own codification efforts as the first Ottoman ruler who formally arranged legal and courtly etiquette, or *kanun* and *kaide*.[66] Even though the Mamluk sultans possessed judicial functions during *mazalim* sessions, they never possessed any legislative authority.[67] This role sharply contrasted with the active role that the Ottoman sultans, beginning at least with Mehmed II, shouldered in establishing their codes of law *kanunname*. This short passage showed Mehmed's own power in legislation while pointing out the limits of Khushqadam's power and sovereignty claims.

While he waited for his ambassador's return from Constantinople, further developments in the region increased Khushqadam's concern. Uzun Hasan returned the keys of Gerger to the Mamluk sultan but demanded a generous fee for his "loyalty" in return. In the meantime, the news about Mehmed II's involvement in Karamanid affairs reached Cairo. Not surprisingly, Mehmed had championed the succession of his relative Ahmed Bey, whose mother had descended from the Ottoman dynasty. Khushqadam was displeased to hear that Mehmed had sent his own troops to support Ahmed.[68]

Tensions rose even further when the Mamluk ambassador Nur al-din 'Ali al-Kurdi returned to Cairo and complained about the unfair treatment he had received in Constantinople.[69] Considering Mehmed II's later dealings with the Aqqoyunlus, it would have made sense for the Ottoman ruler to consider the Mamluk sultan's offer for an alliance. Mehmed's refusal to do so indicated his sensitivity about his image and reputation in the international arena. The titulature in the letter Mehmed sent back with Nur al-din 'Ali al-Kurdi confirmed this tension: for the first time in a letter found in a Mamluk source, the Ottoman ruler addressed the Mamluk sultan with the title *al-Maqarr al-Karim* instead of *al-Maqam al-Sharif*.[70]

The Dulkadirid Rivalry

In the Ottomans, the Dulkadirids found an ally that they could pit against the Mamluks, particularly during their succession crises. The sensitive balance between the three lands was shaken when Khushqadam decided to overthrow the Dulkadirid ruler Malik Arslan, the son and successor of Suleyman Bey (r.1442–54). An assassin appointed by Khushqadam killed Malik Arslan during a Friday prayer in October 1465,[71] and two of his brothers emerged as likely candidates for succession: Shahbudaq, who was supported by Khushqadam, and Shahsuwar, who was supported by Mehmed II. Merely one month after the assassination, Khushqadam appointed Shahbudaq to his deceased brother's position while Mehmed simultaneously appointed Shahsuwar as governor of Bozok and Artukova as well as other regions. Mehmed sent messengers to solicit Khushqadam's support for his own candidate in January–February 1466.[72]

Other letters testified to the extent of the Ottomans' political investment in their ally. While the civil war between the Dulkadirid brothers lasted for two years, the diplomatic representatives of Mehmed II and Khushqadam traveled between Cairo and Constantinople; at least three letters that were composed in Constantinople in November 1466 have survived to the present day.[73] One of the letters proves that, at least in the eyes of the Ottoman administration, the affairs of the Dulkadirids and the Karamanids were connected. It described the allegedly chaotic conditions in Karamanid territory after the loss of their leader İbrahim Bey and claimed that they needed an outside power—the Ottomans, of course—to intervene. Mehmed had supported his relative Ahmed since at least 1463, and, although Ahmed's rise to power in 1465 temporarily defused the tension in the region, he soon started to defy his Ottoman protector and cousin. The Ottoman letter also implied that Shahsuwar, who was already under the protection of Mehmed, also desired the support of the Mamluk sultan. After reassuring Khushqadam that the purpose of his letter was only to strengthen the ties between the two capitals, Mehmed asked the Mamluk sultan to support Shahsuwar. In his other letter, Mehmed respectfully reiterated his hope that Khushqadam would welcome Shahsuwar's rise to power. The close chronology between Mehmed's two letters indicated the intensity and frequency of the diplomatic negotiation between the two capitals. Contrary to Mehmed's request, however, Khushqadam did not change his position or withdraw his aid from Shahbudaq.

Two Ottoman chroniclers claimed that in 1466 or 1467—the same year that diplomatic traffic between the two capitals was at its height—Mehmed II decided to march on the Mamluk territory.[74] The reason for this abrupt decision was not clearly defined, but one chronicler surmised that Mehmed had decided to reconquer the strongholds of his great grandfather Bayezid I that had been lost after the battle of Ankara. According to both sources, however, Mehmed changed his mind at the last minute and instead directed his army to the Karamanid territory, whose ruler Ahmed had angered his Ottoman protector when he refused to join the campaign against the Mamluks. This Ottoman campaign was the first of several that resulted in the complete subjugation of the Karamanids.

The Mamluk chronicles from the same time acknowledged that the Dulkadirid affair strained the relationship between Khushqadam and Mehmed.[75] After two years of civil war, Shahsuwar finally ousted his brother in October of 1467 with the support of Ottoman regiments. After Shahsuwar consolidated his authority in Dulkadirid territory, Mehmed emerged as a victorious benefactor while Khushqadam, who had backed the losing candidate, seemed defeated. This loss must have been a major blow to the Mamluks' authority in the region.

Shahbudaq and the Mamluk sultan did not accept their defeat readily. In September of 1467, Khushqadam prepared another major military force to assist Shahbudaq. His sudden death in October of

1467, however, diverted the Mamluks' attention from the Dulkadirid territory to the well-known succession struggles in Cairo. At the time, no one could have guessed that the rivalry between Shahsuwar and Shahbudaq only marked the first round of a long, strenuous struggle between the Dulkadirids, the Mamluks, and the Ottomans.

A New Ambition for Mehmed II

The Ottoman chronicler Aşıkpaşazade recounted an additional incident that clarified the widening scope of Mehmed II's ambitions and further escalated the tension between the Ottomans and the Mamluks. Apparently, a pilgrim that had traveled to Mecca complained to the Ottoman ruler that the water wells along the pilgrimage routes were in need of repair.[76] In response, Mehmed dispatched his envoys to the Mamluk governors with money to repair the wells but no diplomatic gifts. A Mamluk chronicler also recounted that in 1461 Mehmed sent a messenger to the Mamluk governor of Aleppo to warn him about the lack of security on the roads to Jerusalem. In a threatening tone, Mehmed stated that he could invade Mamluk territories if the conditions of the pilgrimage roads did not improve.[77] While the details of these narratives differ, they are similar enough to show that Mehmed aspired to a leading status in the Muslim world—one that exceeded his inherited role along the frontiers of Islam. Beyond interfering in the political affairs of the region, he had begun to infringe on the Mamluk sultan's ideological sphere of influence.[78]

According to Aşıkpaşazade, the interference of the Karamanids escalated the conflict between Mehmed and Khushqadam regarding the pilgrimage roads.[79] After hearing of Mehmed's threats, the Karamanid ruler İbrahim Bey sent an envoy to the Mamluk court. The envoy, who hoped to strain the relationship between Cairo and Constantinople, presented his sovereign's interpretation of Mehmed's actions to the Mamluk sultan. He claimed that Mehmed was using the conditions of the water wells as an excuse to dishonor the Mamluk sultan by sending money. According to Aşıkpaşazade, "The Mamluks believed in [Karamanids'] lies."

Even though Aşıkpaşazade blamed the Karamanids for this incident, he also mentioned two controversial choices by Mehmed. He first conceded that Mehmed had already violated the conventions of diplomatic etiquette by sending envoys directly to Mamluk governors rather than to the Mamluk sultan. Second, since the maintenance of the pilgrimage roads was traditionally the responsibility of the Mamluk sultan, Mehmed had undermined Khushqadam's authority by indirectly questioning his ability to fulfill this responsibility. These kinds of challenges had created problems between the Mamluk sultans and other Muslim sovereigns before.[80] Finally, Mehmed had further compounded the affront by not sending any gifts to the governors. Even without Karamanid interference, the Mamluks clearly saw the Ottoman sultan's actions as a threat.

This new development in Ottoman–Mamluk relations was quickly reflected by Mehmed's diplomatic language. After the conquest of Constantinople and the geographic expansion that followed, the Ottoman ruler became more assertive: in his surviving correspondence, Mehmed increasingly emphasized his noble origins as well as his almost exclusive claim for *jihad*. He was the first Ottoman sovereign who attempted to change the diplomatic status of the Mamluk sultans by demoting their honorific from *al-Maqam* to *al-Maqarr*. Finally, he insinuated that the Mamluk sultan—or at least Khushqadam—did not deserve to rule in Egypt and Syria because he was not well-versed in "law and etiquette (*kanun ve kaide*)." While Mehmed was redesigning and reformulating his claims through these tropes, Khushqadam passed away and eventually was succeeded by Qaytbay. Upon his succession, Qaytbay was forced to face Mehmed's challenges to the traditional position of the Mamluk sultanate.

Qaytbay and Mehmed II

No correspondence between Mehmed II and Qaytbay has been discovered, so it was the conflicting accounts of other Ottoman and Mamluk sources that revealed the complexity of their relationship. In a gesture that implied his intention to follow diplomatic etiquette and improve relations, Mehmed sent what he claimed was a goodwill mission to congratulate Qaytbay. Ironically, Mamluk annals did not record the arrival of this mission but did describe the arrival of a group from the Aqqoyunlu leader Uzun Hasan among the events of 1468–9.[81] From 1467 to 1473, both Constantinople and Cairo witnessed the frequent arrivals and departures of Ottoman and Mamluk embassies.[82]

After his accession, Qaytbay seized an opportunity to address the lingering Dulkadirid issue and to seal his legitimacy and sovereignty with a military success against Shahsuwar. During almost every campaign season for the next five years (1466–71), Mamluk troops departed from Cairo. None of their expeditions was resoundingly victorious. Finally, the Mamluk commander Yashbak min Mahdi began to turn the tide of the conflict in 1470–1.[83] Shahsuwar eventually fled to the castle of Zamantı. After a long Mamluk siege and extensive negotiations with Mamluk ambassadors, Shahsuwar finally surrendered on the condition that the Mamluk sultan spare his life. Qaytbay took no chances, however, and Shahsuwar was hanged in Cairo barely one month after his surrender in August 1472. While Mamluk sources reported the satisfaction his subjects took in this success, they also acknowledged the sense of disapproval that prevailed in some circles concerning Shahsuwar's execution. Amir Tamraz al-Shamsi, the primary agent to negotiate Shahsuwar's terms of surrender, did not hide his anger upon hearing that its terms were not upheld.[84]

Although the Mamluk chroniclers noted the frequent missions between Cairo and Constantinople during these intense days, none divulged the tasks of these missions.[85] In contrast to the vague references in Mamluk chronicles, Aşıkpaşazade offered a clearer explanation for this series of communications. Aşıkpaşazade argued that Mehmed and Qaytbay came to an agreement: Qaytbay would leave the Dulkadirid territory to Mehmed if Mehmed would cease to support Shahsuwar. Qaytbay broke his promise and further escalated the tension, however, when he executed Shahsuwar and installed Shahbudaq in his place.[86] Although Mamluk sources did not document the event, Ibn Aja recorded the arrival of a representative from Mehmed to Yashbak's camp soon after 'Ala' al-din al-Husni departed for Constantinople. The Ottoman ambassador told Yashbak that Mehmed approved of the Mamluk expedition and offered him logistical support.[87] This message, although lacking any details to this effect, suggests the existence of an agreement between Mehmed and Qaytbay. Intriguingly, Ibn Iyas noted that in July of 1472, 'Ala' al-din al-Husni returned to Cairo from his mission to the Ottoman capital and was angry at Amir Yashbak for an unidentified reason.[88] Perhaps he too was upset about the fact that Amir Yashbak and Qaytbay had violated their agreement with Shahsuwar and damaged the Mamluk administration's credibility with Mehmed.

While it is unclear whether Mehmed was involuntarily ousted from the Dulkadirids' succession struggle or chose to step back to remind Shahsuwar of his dependent position,[89] the chronological overlap between the reassertion of Mamluk suzerainty in Dulkadirid territory and the consolidation of Ottoman authority in Karamanid territory merits attention. In leaving the Karamanids to the Ottomans, the Mamluks chose to keep control over the Dulkadirids. The overlap between these two events, which would bear important repercussions for the future of the region, could not have been a mere coincidence.[90]

The Mamluks' elimination of Shahsuwar and their establishment of Shahbudaq's leadership did not end the Ottoman–Mamluk rivalry. Soon, Shahsuwar's nephew 'Ala' al-Dawla replaced his uncle as the Ottoman-backed candidate while Shahbudaq still enjoyed Mamluk support and preserved the upper hand. After Mehmed declared his support for 'Ala' al-Dawla by giving him a robe in his capital in 1478–9, this new phase of negotiations was interrupted by Mehmed's death in 1481.[91]

Diplomatic Etiquette II

Amidst these struggles for superiority and power, diplomatic discourse played an important role in expressing the dissatisfaction of each sovereign. According to Aşıkpaşazade, Mehmed II sent an ambassador to Cairo with valuable gifts to ameliorate his relations with Qaytbay after the execution of Shahsuwar. This ambassador, however, was not treated well, and when Qaytbay sent a return mission to Constantinople, he appointed his *muhtasib* as its leader.[92] Mehmed was displeased by the social status of the Mamluk envoy, who was merely the inspector of the Cairene market, and the valuable gifts the Mamluk ambassador presented did not change his initial impression.[93]

The social status of this Mamluk envoy highlighted the discrepancy between the way the Ottomans were perceived in Cairo and the way the Ottomans viewed themselves. While Mehmed envisioned himself as a "grand ruler (*ulu padişah*)," the Mamluk sultan did not send an envoy that corresponded to this high status. While Qaytbay may have been bothered by Mehmed's involvement in foreign affairs and had chosen this envoy to subtly express his discontent, the Mamluk sultan may have simply not realized that the Ottoman ruler expected a different level of recognition.

The Ottomans and the Mamluks temporarily neglected the Dulkadirid and Karamanid conflicts when the more pressing matter of the growing Aqqoyunlu influence reemerged on the region's political spectrum.[94] Despite Aşıkpaşazade's allegation that their relationship deteriorated, the diplomatic traffic between Qaytbay and Mehmed did not wane between 1472 and 1474. On the contrary, these events suggest that the two rulers probably set their disagreements aside and joined together to stop Uzun Hasan's expansion.[95] In 1472, when the Mamluk commander Yashbak marched against Uzun Hasan, he sent the veteran diplomat Ibn Aja to inform the Ottoman ruler about his actions.[96] Simultaneously, the Ottoman troops led by Mehmed himself also marched towards the Eastern frontier. In April 1473, Amir Yashbak defeated Uzun Hasan near Bire in southeastern Anatolia,[97] marking the end of the long-standing tensions between the Mamluk sultans and the Aqqoyunlu leader. Since at least 1464, Uzun Hasan had challenged the Mamluks in every possible manner, both ideologically and politically. He had interfered with Karamanid affairs, he had indirectly challenged the Mamluk sultan by sending him the defeated Timurid ruler Abu Sa'id's head, and he had formulated both messianic and ideological assertions through his correspondence.[98] The fact that most of these tactics involved diplomatic communication again proves the significance of diplomacy in the formulation and expression of imperial ideologies.

Four months after he was defeated by the Mamluks, Uzun Hasan battled the other prominent ruler in the region. In August of 1473, the Ottoman ruler Mehmed gained the upper hand in the battle of Otlukbeli, forced Uzun Hasan to flee, and captured important members of the Aqqoyunlu dynasty and administration. In a display of military prowess disguised as a diplomatic gesture, Mehmed sent a victory mission to Cairo carrying the head of Zaynal Mirza, the oldest son of Uzun Hasan.[99]

As soon as he heard the news of the Ottoman victory, Qaytbay diligently followed the rules of diplomacy and prepared a mission to congratulate Mehmed. He chose a trusted and experienced representative, Barsbay al-Ashrafi, for the mission. When Barsbay succumbed to an untimely death near Aleppo, Qaytbay first chose Amir Almas to replace him before changing his mind. In the end, it was Yashbak al-Jamali, who ranked higher than Amir Almas, who led the Mamluk delegation to Constantinople. The delayed mission moved quickly with its heavy gifts, including a camel caravan that carried wheat and oats. When they reached the frontier city of Kayseri after 70 days, they were enthusiastically welcomed by the Ottoman Grand Vizier Mahmud Paşa. The mission then continued to Constantinople where it was accepted by Mehmed. Besides treating them well, Mehmed offered them a generous stipend, probably 300 *dinars* per day.[100]

While Yashbak was probably still enjoying its hospitality, the Ottoman palace was shocked by the death of Mehmed's son Prince Mustafa in June of 1474. Qaytbay, wanting to preserve his newly mended relationship with Mehmed, quickly sent another mission to express his condolences. The embassy departed Cairo on June 3, 1474. The treatment that this mission received provides an almost flawless case study of diplomatic ceremonies as described in later Ottoman protocol books. After taking the land route, the mission was welcomed by representatives of Prince Bayezid, Mehmed's other son who was the governor of Amasya. After receiving Mehmed's consent to accompany the mission, the prince escorted the entire company to Üsküdar in 18 days. The city had been prepared to welcome the mission and staged three days of ceremonies in honor of the Mamluk ambassador.[101] The ambassador's audience with the mourning sultan went well, and the mission departed one month later.[102] Soon after in August of 1474, an Ottoman mission appeared in Cairo. Although Ibn Iyas claimed that this mission was sent to intervene on behalf of the previous Syrian governor Inal al-Hakim, it also probably conveyed Mehmed's appreciation for the condolence mission.[103]

The last recorded communication between Mehmed and Qaytbay concerned Kasım Bey, who had inherited the leadership of the Karamanids from his elder brother Ahmed in 1473-4. Much like the case between the Dulkadirids and the Mamluks, after the Ottomans took control of the Karamanid territory in 1476, the surviving members of the Karamanid dynasty had an unstable relationship with the Ottomans. After surrendering the majority of his lands to the Ottomans, Kasım Bey, in the company of his family and closest followers, escaped to the Taurus Mountains close to the Mamluk frontier. The group occasionally skirmished with Ottoman troops, and in 1476-7, as the circle around him narrowed, Kasım Bey sought refuge at the Mamluk court. A letter dated March-April 1477 described the escape of the Karamanid ruler and requested that the Mamluks send him to the Ottoman court in chains.[104] Two months later, an Ottoman ambassador arrived in Cairo. After accepting him in a generous manner, Qaytbay gave his answer to the envoy, who soon departed.[105] Nothing else about this visit was divulged in any Mamluk chronicles, yet we know from later incidents that Kasım Bey was never sent to the Ottoman ruler but instead was transferred to Aqqoyunlu lands. Sources did not record any other exchanges between Mehmed and Qaytbay before Mehmed's death at his encampment in Gebze in 1481. Before his death, Mehmed had mobilized both his army and his fleet without revealing the target of his expedition.

Mehmed II's Last Destination[106]

Only two Ottoman chroniclers, Tursun Bey and İbn Kemal (who was, in fact, adopting Tursun Bey's account), recorded that Mehmed II's last campaign targeted Mamluk lands. No other Ottoman or even Mamluk chroniclers made this claim.[107] In evaluating Tursun Bey's argument, it is important to remember that it was written under the patronage of Mehmed's son and successor Bayezid II and during the days of the Ottoman–Mamluk war from 1485 to 1491. The chronicler may have cited that Mehmed had been marching to Mamluk territory in an attempt to legitimize Bayezid's later decision to go to war with Qaytbay. Although Mehmed's ultimate plans concerning the Mamluk regime merits further discussion, the evidence does not conclusively prove that Mehmed was marching to Syria in April of 1481.

Nonetheless, Mehmed increased the volatility of the relationship between the two courts. As he transformed the image of the Ottoman sovereign, he expected others—including the Mamluk regime—to adjust their view of the Ottoman administration as well. Although the Mamluk sultans did not completely give in to this expectation, Mehmed still left his imprint on Ottoman–Mamluk encounters.

CHAPTER 5

FROM CAPTIVITY NARRATIVES TO A PEACE TREATY: A NEW ERA OF IMAGE-BUILDING (1481–1491)

In 1485 the new Ottoman ruler Bayezid II (r.1481–1512) hosted the Mamluk envoy Janibak, who, as discussed in the Introduction, had been sent by the Mamluk sultan Qaytbay to improve the relationship between the two capitals.[1] Cilicia had witnessed clashes between Ottoman and Mamluk troops with no definitive result since 1484. While armed conflict between two lands generally signals the end of their diplomatic engagements, this particular war presented new opportunities for communication and exchange between the two lands.

According to Janibak's oral report, which was recounted in a Mamluk source, an unidentified Ottoman spoke during the ambassadorial audience, questioning Qaytbay's right to rule and asserting that Bayezid, with his dynastic lineage, was a more legitimate leader.[2] The remark was out of line even for wartime. Molla Gürani, Mehmed's aged and revered tutor who had spent long years in Mamluk lands, rushed to Janibak's aid and reprimanded the individual: "Don't speak about the rulers of Egypt, you dishonor yourself." Janibak, who may have been encouraged by Molla Gürani's remarks, also replied with a provocative rhetorical question defending the Mamluks' right to rule: "Who was the father of our Prophet Ibrahim and Prophet

Muhammad?" Despite this tense verbal exchange, the Ottoman ruler still showered the Mamluk ambassador with gifts at the audience. Soon after Janibak's return to Cairo, however, the Ottomans and Mamluks returned to their military conflict.[3]

This episode displayed the maturation of the new Ottoman tropes that would dominate their future diplomatic encounters with the Mamluks. The anonymous Ottoman at Janibak's audience directly attacked the legitimacy of the Mamluk sultans by alluding to Qaytbay's slave origins and his relatively recent conversion to Islam as opposed to Bayezid's dynastic lineage and established religious heritage. The Ottomans believed that they deserved to rule over the Holy Cities since they were descended from generations of Muslim rulers and not from non-Muslim slaves.

The Mamluk sultan's sovereignty revolved around his protectorate of Mecca and Medina (as well as Jerusalem), and the Mamluk regime had jealously guarded this role against other Muslim sovereigns. References to Islam had functioned as a part of Ottoman–Mamluk diplomatic language, yet in the past (at least until Mehmed II's attempts to intervene in the protection and maintenance of the pilgrimage roads in 1461) they had merely served as unifying factors between the two Muslim lands.[4] In this phase of formulating new sovereignty claims, however, even their shared faith and its symbolism presented an opportunity to bolster claims for superiority. In fact, the protectorate of the Holy Cities became the major source of contention between Bayezid and the Mamluk sultan Qaytbay and his successor Qansuh al-Ghawri. Rather than merely respecting this position, Bayezid yearned to possess it.

The Mamluk ambassador's response to this well-formulated challenge showed that his regime was inventing new ways to counter Ottoman claims for superiority. Janibak, by alluding to the humble origins of Islam's two most iconic figures (the Prophets Muhammad and Abraham) as well as their great achievements, underscored the insignificance of pedigree in spiritual or ideological leadership. This line of argument skillfully emphasized the weaknesses of dynastic regimes and argued for the meritocracy on which the Mamluk ruling system was supposedly based.

While the story of Janibak's mission illustrated only one episode during this era of warfare, it was a representative one. As the following pages will emphasize, every mission, captivity story, and agent in the peace process served to reinforce the tropes that had been expressed in previous diplomatic encounters and also to formulate new ones. Under these conditions, this particular war should be viewed as an integral part of the image-building process for both sides.[5]

From 1481 to 1485

Bayezid's brother Prince Cem took refuge in Mamluk lands in July 1481, an event that certainly changed the relationship between the new Ottoman ruler and Qaytbay and culminated in the Ottomans' controversial treatment of Janibak in 1485. After the death of the Ottoman ruler Mehmed II, his two sons Bayezid and Cem engaged in a literal race of dynastic succession from their provincial capitals, Amasya and Konya. After Bayezid reached the imperial capital first, the two brothers engaged in a relentless succession struggle. Cem's troops were defeated in the vicinity of İnegöl, and, in the ensuing chaos, Cem suddenly appeared in Aleppo to request asylum from the Mamluk sultan Qaytbay.

A ruler—particularly the Mamluk sultan of Egypt and Syria, the protector of the Sacred Shrines, and the Sultan of Islam and the Muslims—could not close his doors to a political refugee. Refusing Cem's request would have disgraced Qaytbay, yet Cem's case undoubtedly presented a dilemma: if Cem succeeded in seizing power from his brother, Qaytbay would not want to miss an opportunity to aid the future Ottoman ruler. If Bayezid remained in power, however, protecting his rival would incur the Ottoman sovereign's wrath.[6]

Even Ottoman chronicles diverged from one another regarding the complex case of Cem's reception in Mamluk lands. While they unanimously depicted Bayezid's growing resentment toward the Mamluk administration, they offered two conflicting reasons for it. One group stated that the Ottoman ruler was angry at the Mamluk sultan for siding with Cem, while the other claimed that Bayezid's wrath stemmed from the fact that his brother was not hosted in the manner accorded to an Ottoman crown prince.[7] In either case, Cem's presence at the Mamluk court escalated the tension between the two imperial capitals. For the next seven to eight months (probably between July 1481 and April 1482), Cem was hosted by the Mamluk sultan and honored with multiple banquets, processions, and public occasions. He also became the Ottoman dynasty's first male member to make his pilgrimage. Cem finally left the Mamluk territories to face his brother Bayezid again and was defeated for a second time in the spring of 1482.[8] Soon after this defeat, Cem departed to Rhodes, planning to pursue his legitimate claim to the Ottoman throne in the Balkan territories.

Due to the intervention of European powers that included the Master of Rhodes, the Pope, and the King of France—all of whom benefitted from Bayezid's generosity—Cem's plan never came to fruition. Cem's imprisonment in European courts not only caused personal aggravation to the unlucky prince and to his immediate family (which he had entrusted to the Mamluk authorities), but also troubled Bayezid, whose political and military actions in Europe were severely limited due to Cem's presence. Bayezid was probably torn between two desires: his urge to protect the honor of the Ottoman dynasty, which had been damaged by Cem's imprisonment, and his need to preserve his own rule by ensuring that Cem would not be released. After four years of diplomatic traffic and gifts (most of them relics), the unlucky prince died unexpectedly.[9] Some in the Mamluk administration had never approved of Cem's departure from the Mamluk lands, and Qaytbay closely followed the Ottoman prince's adventures in Rhodes and Europe and unsuccessfully negotiated for his safe return.[10] Although Cem never returned, his stay in Mamluk territories left a permanent mark on the Ottoman–Mamluk relationship.

A second issue that evolved almost simultaneously with the Cem affair involved another grave breach of diplomatic etiquette. During his last years, Mehmed hosted an embassy from the Bahmani ruler Shams al-din Muhammad Shah (r.1463–82) and reciprocated with his own ambassador, Muhyiddin Çelebi.[11] The Ottoman envoy completed his mission and began the journey home with another

Bahmani representative. When the two envoys arrived in Jidda (the Red Sea port under Mamluk authority) in 1481, the news of Mehmed II's death had begun to spread. According to Ibn Iyas, the governor of Jidda refused to grant passage to the envoys and seized their gifts and goods, including a dagger adorned with valuable gems.[12] Ibn Iyas also insinuated that Qaytbay participated in the plot and had desired the dagger for himself, and his suspicions were echoed by his Ottoman peers. Soon afterward, however, Qaytbay ordered that the envoys be released and their gifts be returned by a Mamluk delegation headed by Janibak. Despite Qaytbay's change of heart, his initial appropriation of diplomatic gifts that were intended for another ruler seriously violated the diplomatic practices of the time.

After the Cem affair, a third issue emerged as the Dulkadirids once again became a source of conflict.[13] After Bayezid defeated Cem for a second time in the spring of 1482, the Ottoman ruler spent the rest of the summer near the province of Karaman in Anatolia, where Cem had once served as governor. Whether by force or by appeasement, Bayezid reinforced his authority in a province that was particularly close to the Mamluk sphere of influence and where he was less popular than his brother.

In another attempt to consolidate his authority in Anatolia, Bayezid "invited" the Dulkadirid ruler 'Ala' al-Dawla, who was his own father-in-law, to his encampment.[14] With this invitation in the spring of 1482, Bayezid's Anatolian rally (or punitive campaign) culminated when 'Ala' al-Dawla severed his connections with his Mamluk protectors and paid homage to the Ottoman sultan. After all, Bayezid had just defeated his own Mamluk-supported brother and was threatening the Dulkadirid region with his army.

Scholars overwhelmingly attribute the start of the Ottoman–Mamluk war in 1485 to 'Ala' al-Dawla's shift in loyalty.[15] This approach, however, underestimates Bayezid's abilities as a leader and places him in a passive position. During his father's reign, Bayezid had served as the governor of Amasya close to the northern Mamluk frontier.[16] While there, Bayezid became familiar with the dynamics of local politics—particularly with Mamluk–Dulkadirid relations—

and this acquaintance deepened when he married 'Ala' al-Dawla's daughter, Ayşe Hatun.[17] At least once before, in 1472, he had offered safe haven to his father-in-law when the Mamluks intervened in the Dulkadirid succession struggle and sided against him.[18] Bayezid certainly knew that a rapprochement with his father-in-law might pave the way for a conflict with the Mamluks.

Dulkadirid and Ottoman troops arrived in Malatya in the spring of 1484, approximately one year after Bayezid and 'Ala' al-Dawla formed their alliance. After a successful siege, the combined forces launched into Mamluk territory, triggering a long and exhausting war. Armed conflict was suspended after Mamluk troops ambushed and routed the allied forces near Malatya on September 23, 1484. By sending Janibak's delegation to Bayezid in 1485, the Mamluk sultan attempted to repair the damage caused by both this conflict and the diplomatic crisis that grew out of the Bahmani mission. Janibak, who had experience in diplomatic missions and had earned the Mamluk sultan's trust, shouldered the delicate task and dutifully accompanied the Bahmani mission to the Ottoman court.

A Critical Mission in Çöke

Janibak's aforementioned audience and tense verbal exchange took place in this delicate diplomatic climate: the Ottoman–Mamluk relationship had been troubled since Cem's asylum in Mamluk territory and the appropriation of the Bahmani gifts in Mamluk lands. Bayezid probably interpreted these acts to mean that the Mamluk administration did not recognize his right to the Ottoman throne. Moreover, a couple of months before Janibak's arrival, Bayezid had already accepted foreign dignitaries from the Hafsid Sultan 'Uthman (r.1435–88) of Tunis, the Aqqoyunlu ruler Sultan Yaqub (Uzun Hasan's son who ruled between 1478 and 1490), the Shirwanid ruler Farrukh Yassar (r.1462–1501) of Azerbaijan,[19] and the King of Hungary Matthias Corvinus (1458–90).[20] These delegations congratulated Bayezid on his accession and for his first military achievements: the conquests of Kilia and Akkerman on the northern Black Sea coast in the summer of 1484. Amidst these diplomatic missions, Bayezid likely noticed the absence of a Mamluk delegation, as did the famous scholar and chronicler İbn Kemal.[21]

The unusually detailed accounts of Janibak's audience in both Ottoman and Mamluk sources prove this particular encounter's significance for both powers, but particularly for the Ottomans. As was the case when Bayezid I married the Germiyanid princess, Janibak's audience overlapped with the arrivals of multiple foreign dignitaries. Later accounts emphasized this particular convergence of diplomatic missions as a turning point in the consolidation of Bayezid's international recognition.[22] The missions included representatives of the Mamluk, Bahmani, and Golden Horde rulers (who were among the descendants of Chingiz Khan) in addition to Hungarian, Polish, and Neapolitan ambassadors. The Neapolitans, who were sent by King Ferdinand I (r.1458–94), had recently reclaimed Otranto from the Ottomans.[23] These audiences were scheduled for March 16, 1485 and lasted at least two days.[24]

On the first day, Bayezid accepted the Mamluk ambassador Janibak first, then the Bahmani ambassador that had accompanied the Mamluk delegation, and finally the embassy from the Golden Horde ruler Murtaza Han (r.1481–1502). When the Mamluk ambassador entered into the sultan's presence, Molla Gürani, who was sympathetic to the Mamluks, had already taken his seat at the sultan's right side. The ambassadors kissed the sultan's hand and Janibak was seated on the left side of the sultan with the Bahmani ambassador next to him.[25] When they presented their sovereigns' letters, each bowed before the sultan. Both delegations had brought impressive gifts: while those from the Bahmani ruler included valuable textiles that were carried on pack animals along with the controversial dagger, the gifts from the Mamluk court included a leopard[26] as well as gold coins and two letters from the caliph. The Golden Horde ambassador presented equally remarkable gifts that included some unique items such as expensive furs and whales' teeth.[27]

Janibak's encounter with the Ottoman ruler was naturally surrounded by layers of diplomatic ceremony and symbolism. Even though the two lands were at war, the Ottomans still gave ambassadorial precedence to the Mamluk representative, and the

Mamluk's gift of a leopard could have been an attempt to mend relations. The most remarkable items in the ceremony, however, were likely the letters of Caliph al-Mutawakkil II. According to Ibn Iyas, one of the letters was a *taqlid* that recognized the Ottoman ruler as the sovereign of *Bilad al-Rum* and predicted that God would soon grant non-Muslim lands to Bayezid. In the second letter, the caliph advised him to end his conflict with the Mamluks.[28] Unfortunately, these two letters have not been mentioned in any other Ottoman source, nor have they been found in any archives.

Almost eight months after his audience with the Ottoman ruler, Janibak returned to the Mamluk imperial capital wearing a precious robe of honor from Bayezid.[29] Although the Ottoman court had honored diplomatic etiquette by hosting the ambassador well, the mission did not achieve its ultimate goal of establishing peace between the two lands. Soon after Janibak's return, armed conflict between Ottoman and Mamluk troops resumed in Cilicia.[30]

War: An End of Contacts and Communication?

During the next six years, both sides occasionally gained the upper hand but failed to decisively defeat the other. For instance, an Ottoman campaign that started off with the successful invasion of Cilicia in the summer of 1485 was followed by continual Mamluk attacks that ultimately reversed the Ottoman advance in the region.

Naturally, the progress of this war between the two prominent powers of the Sunni Muslim world and the eastern Mediterranean coast was followed closely by the European powers. After the Ottomans suffered a major defeat outside Adana in February 1486, Bayezid sent a larger force under the command of his son-in-law Hersekzade Ahmed Paşa, who was then captured by the Mamluk commander Amir Azbak's troops on March 15, 1486.[31] Andrea Gritti, who was sent by the consul of Venice as an ambassador to Bayezid, called the debacle "the greatest defeat ever inflicted upon the Ottoman House."[32] The capture of the Ottoman commander, who was also the governor general of Anatolia, was a particular disgrace for the Ottomans.[33] Along with other prisoners of war, Hersekzade

Ahmed Paşa was carried off to Cairo in a "humiliating"[34] manner for a victory procession. He was, however, soon released from captivity on the condition that he negotiate for peace with Bayezid on Qaytbay's behalf.

While both Ottoman and Mamluk sources recorded Hersekzade's captivity and his diplomatic mission for the Mamluk sultan, they recounted this episode in drastically different ways. The Mamluk chroniclers only mentioned the release of Hersekzade in passing; some seemed to disapprove of the fact that the Mamluk sultan initiated his mission while others dismissively suggested that the gesture would not bear fruit. They stated dryly that Hersekzade returned home with gifts and that he planned to discuss the issue of peace.[35]

As opposed to the brief accounts in Mamluk sources, at least one Ottoman chronicler, Aşıkpaşazade, provided a colorful account of Hersekzade's captivity and his alleged arrangement with the Mamluk sultan.[36] Aşıkpaşazade's version also recounted the moment when the Mamluks made Hersekzade kiss the ground in front of the Mamluk sultan. This exercise, which adhered to the usual etiquette of the Mamluk court, must have felt particularly humiliating and awkward for the Ottoman governor general.

As a Mamluk sovereign who began his military career as a slave, Qaytbay was understandably intrigued by the Ottoman method of recruitment, which was based on the child levy (*devşirme*), as well as by Hersekzade Ahmed Paşa's own career path. Hersekzade, as a prince of the ruling house of Herzegovina, had been raised and educated in the Ottoman palace school.[37] He had climbed the ladders of promotion and married one of Bayezid's daughters. Qaytbay's inquiries gave way to the Mamluk sultan's observation about the similarity between his background and Hersekzade's: "Paşa, you are a slave, and I am a slave, why did you come to my lands?" After this attempt to forge a bond with his captive, Qaytbay broached the topic of his struggle with Bayezid. According to Aşıkpaşazade, the Mamluk sultan only alluded to the topic of peace and reconciliation until Hersekzade volunteered to serve as his agent of peace.

Aşıkpaşazade's presentation of Hersekzade—as a captive who boldly took the reins of conversation into his own hands—drastically challenged the common perception about the conditions of his captivity. It transformed Hersekzade from a helpless captive into a powerful negotiator who prodded his captor to action. This intriguing yet unrealistic anecdote revealed how the Ottomans wanted to depict themselves: despite his captive status, the Ottoman commander was still in charge of his own fate. Clearly, Ottoman self-perceptions had significantly evolved: only a century before, Ottoman chroniclers had proudly recorded the mere presence of a Mamluk ambassador at Prince Bayezid's wedding. The story of the later encounter between the passive Mamluk sultan and his bold Ottoman captive starkly contrasted with these earlier records.

Qaytbay's willingness to release Hersekzade with gifts for Bayezid suggested that the Mamluk sultan was, in fact, genuinely interested in suing for peace. He may have not wanted to send his own ambassador to the Ottoman capital because Amir Janibak, who had left only a year ago, had already returned home with empty hands. Qaytbay's use of an Ottoman representative demonstrated not only the flexibility of this diplomatic culture, but also the realistic and even pragmatic approach of these sovereigns to international relations. It is doubtful, however, that Hersekzade ever became a strong advocate for Ottoman–Mamluk peace; his initiatives at Qaytbay's request did not bring any concrete results.

Recurrent defeats made the Ottomans keenly aware of their geopolitical weaknesses, and in the spring of 1487, the Ottoman army—this time led by Davud Paşa—launched a campaign against a group of semi-nomadic tribal leaders. The Ottomans intended to assert themselves in the region and contest the well-established Mamluk authority among these tribes. In a sense, the Ottoman campaign was a tactical one: this operation was probably not successful because later events indicated that the Dulkadirid ruler 'Ala' al-Dawla, unbeknownst to the Ottomans, had switched his loyalties to the Mamluks in the spring of 1488.[38]

Despite its careful plans, the Ottoman military experienced a humiliating defeat in the battle of Ağaçayırı on August 16, 1488. After an intense two-day encounter, some Ottoman soldiers began to flee while others, including many experienced Ottoman commanders, died on the battlefield. Toward the end of the second day, when the commander general Hadım Ali Paşa realized that the majority of his commanders were dead or had fled from the battlefield, he too had to retreat. The most humiliating consequence of the battle was probably the pillage of Ottoman encampments by men of the Turkoman principalities, including 'Ala' al-Dawla's men. Bayezid, upon hearing the news of the defeat and the deserting commanders, ordered some of them executed while dismissing others from their positions. Even Hadım Ali Paşa, his favorite commander, was demoted.[39]

At this point in the conflict, another method of wartime communication came through individuals who, by all appearances, championed the peace process independently. The first such attempt came from the highest ranks of the Ottoman administration. According to Ibn Iyas, who was the only chronicler to record this event, Davud Paşa sent a messenger to Cairo in May 1489, ten months after the battle of Ağaçayırı.[40] The envoy apparently suggested that "if the Mamluk sultan sends an ambassador now, perhaps peace is conceivable."[41] Since the Mamluk armies had resoundingly defeated the Ottomans only ten months earlier, the condescending and arrogant tone of the message was not well received. The offence was further compounded by the fact that the envoy was sent by a high commander rather than the Ottoman ruler himself. Qaytbay, whose attempts to establish peace had already been rejected twice by Bayezid, responded negatively to this overture. Aware and proud of his army's success in Ağaçayırı, he vowed that he would not send an ambassador to Constantinople until certain conditions were met: the release of some Mamluk merchants that were under Ottoman arrest, as well as the relinquishment of some castles that Ottoman troops had reinvaded the past summer. Qaytbay's response was a public display of bravado that targeted the Ottoman embassy, the broader international arena, and his own domestic audience. Whether they were uninformed about Davud Paşa's attempt or chose not to mention it because of its failure, Ottoman sources did not document this exchange.[42]

Both the defeat in Ağaçayırı and 'Ala' al-Dawla's "treason" showed the impact of local Turkoman tribes on the Ottoman–Mamluk rivalry. In response to 'Ala' al-Dawla's change of heart and realignment with the Mamluks, the Ottomans decided to support Shahbudaq, an alternative candidate within the Dulkadirid family.[43] 'Ala' al-Dawla's cousin and rival, who was previously supported by the Mamluk regime, marched against the allied forces of 'Ala' al-Dawla and the Mamluks with the help of Mihaloğlu İskender Bey, the famous frontier commander who hailed from a prominent frontier warlord family that facilitated the Ottoman expansion into the Balkans. They were ultimately defeated, however, and Mihaloğlu İskender Bey, along with his son and other prisoners, was captured and conveyed by 'Ala' al-Dawla to Cairo and presented to Qaytbay during an impressive victory procession in June–July 1489.[44] Five months after the Ottoman commander's arrival in Cairo, Shahbudaq appeared in the Mamluk imperial capital to express his regrets and pledge his allegiance to the Mamluk ruler, as his cousin 'Ala' al-Dawla had done a year before.[45] Shahbudaq's reversal once again revealed the fragility of Ottoman suzerainty in these territories.

In what may have been an attempt to preserve his dignity, Bayezid responded to this disheartening news by organizing a festival in honor of his two grandsons' circumcisions and his three daughters' weddings in November–December 1489.[46] Such public celebrations gave the Ottoman sultan an opportunity to appear confident and indifferent to his recent reversals, which were presented to the public as inconsequential events.[47] Six months later, Qaytbay, who had previously reduced the number of expensive public ceremonies during his reign,[48] ordered a circumcision festival.[49] Although it primarily honored his own son, the son of Bayezid's brother (and rival) Cem also took part in the ceremony. These concurrent events raise the question of whether this celebration was intended as a display of Mamluk generosity or as a more aggressive declaration of superiority. The question must remain unanswered, but it suggests that these imperial encounters must have been more complex than they first appeared.

Despite the display of both confidence and wealth in these Ottoman and Mamluk celebrations, the prolonged military conflict between the two lands had evolved into a war of attrition that strained both powers' resources in different ways.[50] Bayezid, who was not necessarily worried about financing a single war, was, in fact, embroiled in multiple military endeavors. Although his raids in the Balkans and southeast Europe were mostly successful, bad news from the Mamluk front regularly arrived in the capital. The situation culminated when, in the spring of 1490, Mamluk contingents under the command of Amir Azbak penetrated into the heart of the Karaman territory. From January to October 1490, Mamluk troops pillaged the Ottoman provinces in the area and recaptured some strongholds such as Kevere.[51] Although the Mamluk armies inflicted heavy casualties on the Ottoman forces, Qaytbay still struggled to finance his war effort.[52]

During the Mamluk campaign that ravaged the Ottoman province of Karaman, Qaytbay sent one of his commanders, Mamay al-Khassaki, to Constantinople to negotiate for peace. Mamay, who was accompanied by 'Ala' al-Dawla's ambassador, arrived in the Ottoman capital on July 4, 1490. The two ambassadors found an angry Bayezid preparing for battle, and Mamay's claim that the commander Azbak had acted without Qaytbay's consent did not slow the Ottoman ruler's efforts. The Dulkadirid ambassador was treated badly in Constantinople, and the Mamluk ambassador was not released until December 1490–January 1491[53] amid concern that Mamluk troops in Karaman might retaliate if his treatment worsened. Mamay was probably put under house arrest while he and his retinue, including their horses, were provided with service and food.[54]

Although they included other detailed descriptions of these days, most Ottoman chronicles did not record Mamay's unusual treatment in Constantinople. The chroniclers' selective approach implied that not even the Mamluk attack on the Karaman province legitimized the house arrest of a Mamluk ambassador. In the past, Bayezid's father Mehmed, even during times of strained relations, had preferred to prove his just and legitimate sovereignty by granting the appropriate treatment to Mamluk ambassadors.[55] Bayezid's behavior, in contrast, undermined the image of a just Ottoman sovereign and was conveniently overlooked.

After Bayezid decided to personally lead his military campaign against the Mamluks, an opposing faction among his advisors became more vocal. According to Ottoman chroniclers, Molla Arab (d.1496, Alaaddin Ali al-Arabi or Zeyneddin Ali al-Arabi in some sources), who was the *Şeyhülislam* of Constantinople (*the chief mufti or jurisconsult of the capital*) at the time, emerged as the most prominent member of this opposition and as a self-appointed agent of peace.[56] He had originally come to Bursa to study under Molla Gürani, the scholar who reportedly spoke in favor of the Mamluk sultan during Janibak's contentious audience. After completing his studies, Molla Arab began to climb the ranks of the Ottoman legal system and ultimately succeeded his mentor to become the *Şeyhülislam* during Bayezid's reign.[57] By the time he achieved this rank, the Ottomans and the Mamluks had been at war for three years. As a native of Aleppo, Molla Arab was particularly eager for peace and enlisted the help of his personal networks in Mamluk lands for his cause.[58]

In July 1490, under tense conditions, a council convened in Beşiktaş on the coast of the Bosphorus, a place that served as a meeting point for the Ottoman army before it crossed to Anatolia. Almost all Ottoman chroniclers agreed that Bayezid planned to travel to Üsküdar the following day before continuing his march to Cilicia. It was at this council that some individuals—including Molla Arab— actively lobbied for peace between the Ottomans and Mamluks. As a scholar of law and religion, Molla Arab based his argument for peace on the ideology of *ghaza* while others (no specific names are mentioned) argued exactly the opposite. In Molla Arab's view, two prominent Muslim sovereigns should not waste their resources on infighting but rather focus their energies against the enemies of Islam. The Ottoman chronicler Bihişti, who completed his work in 1511, recorded this perspective: "It has been a long time since your ancestors and you have been occupied with punishing and fighting against the non-Muslims for the sake of faith [.] It is not a good sign that now Your Highness has been fighting against the Muslim brethren [.]"[59] The frontier war lords of the Balkans (called *"Rumeli Beyleri"*) also expressed their opposition to the war and considered the time inconvenient for a campaign against the Mamluks.[60] Bayezid, who had recently been troubled by a series of devastating fires, epidemics, and natural calamities on the Ottoman home front, may have witnessed a weakening of public morale and felt his own confidence waning.[61] In fact, a later Ottoman chronicler explicitly stated that Molla Arab interpreted these natural events as bad omens while trying to convince Bayezid to make peace.[62]

The timely arrival of the Hafsid ruler 'Uthman's delegation from Tunis to the Ottoman capital added an international dimension to the Ottoman–Mamluk conflict and bolstered the argument of the peace lobbyists. Concerned with the advance of the Spanish Reconquista in Muslim Spain, 'Uthman's message requested that Bayezid and Qaytbay end their conflict. In addition to valuable fabrics and artifacts, the Hafsid ambassador also presented a rare copy of the Qur'an and a compilation of *hadith* (Prophet's expressions) as gifts from his ruler.[63] This appeal for peace was not the first that Bayezid had received from the Maghreb and Spain; as early as 1486, Bayezid had accepted a delegation from the Nasrid rulers of Granada that expressed concern about the threat of the Reconquista.[64] The Hafsids, however, had a stronger claim to the Sunni leadership of North Africa than the Nasrids.[65] The delegation arrived at a critical time when some members of the Ottoman administration were looking for ways to sway the angry sultan. Their pleas and symbolically meaningful gifts intensified the controversy about the Ottoman–Mamluk war both domestically and internationally.[66]

Bayezid's own position on the Mamluk war was perhaps the most intriguing and complex, and Ottoman chroniclers unanimously recorded that the Ottoman ruler needed to be persuaded to sign for peace.[67] Mustafa Âli even noted that, at first, "scholars, army commanders, advisors, and viziers" were afraid to endorse a peace plan because they did not want to incur Bayezid's wrath.[68] After costly, ineffective campaigns and facing pressure at home and in the international arena, Bayezid acknowledged—albeit reluctantly—the need for such a plan. Bayezid decided not to march to Cilicia after the Beşiktaş council. Instead, he accepted a Mamluk diplomatic mission, possibly the one headed by Mamay (who, according to Mamluk chronicles, had not been released since his arrival in 1490).

A couple of days later, Bayezid returned to Edirne, leaving his men—including Molla Arab—to start the peace process.

Negotiations for Peace

Bayezid chose Ali Çelebi, who had been his prayer leader (*imam*) during his days in Amasya, to lead his diplomatic mission to Cairo. Like Qaytbay, who chose his ambassadors mostly from his own *mamluks* (*Khassakiyya* or Sultan's own recruits), Bayezid probably wanted a trusted ally to speak for him. Bayezid had previously appointed Ali Çelebi to the judgeship of Bursa, a high post in the Ottoman legal system,[69] and his familiarity with Islamic law was useful for such a mission. The scholar's presence would also enhance the Ottoman ruler's image as a Muslim sovereign, and Bayezid's choice did indeed catch the attention of Mamluk chroniclers.[70] After likely being endowed with plenipotentiary powers, Ali Çelebi left the Ottoman capital with the Mamluk ambassador Mamay in December 1490.

Like Bayezid's, Qaytbay's approach to the peace process was depicted differently by Ottoman and Mamluk authors. According to Ottoman sources, Qaytbay desperately sought peace while Bayezid, out of piety and concern for Muslim pilgrims and the residents of both lands, graciously consented to the Mamluk sultan's offer.[71] While the Ottomans presented Qaytbay as regretful and submissive, Mamluk chronicles instead depicted Qaytbay as a ruler who, despite being troubled by its cost, was committed to the war effort.[72] They also described the arrival of the Ottoman peace mission in April–May 1491 with a similar view of the Mamluk sultan: Qaytbay, rather than Bayezid, had the upper hand and benevolently chose to accept both Bayezid's mission and his offer. Some Mamluk sources even entitled this section of their narratives "the peace offer of the Ottoman ruler."[73] Moreover, they also gave the impression that Qaytbay was unexpectedly yet pleasantly surprised when Ali Çelebi accompanied Mamay on his return to Cairo. At the moment of their arrival, Qaytbay, who had intended to lead his own army into battle, had been busily preoccupied with campaign preparations.

The discrepancies between the Ottoman and Mamluk stories not only revealed how much appearances mattered for these regimes, but also concealed the truth about who started the peace process. Once the process had begun, however, both sides seized the opportunity for resolution. As the Ottoman ambassador neared Damascus in April 1491, the entire city prepared to welcome the mission, including its governor Qansuh al-Ghawri al-Yahyawi, its four leading judges, and other prominent residents. The entire delegation, which consisted of an impressive retinue of Ottoman commanders and servants, paraded through the city to its lodgings. The accounts affirmed that both the Ottoman mission and the residents of Damascus were well-prepared for this initial encounter, and Damascene author Ibn al-Himsi, in a tone of excitement and relief, recounted that Ali Çelebi brought the keys to the castles that the Ottomans had captured during the war.

The next phase of this critical diplomatic stage was equally impressive. Qaytbay generously hosted the delegates who reached Cairo in April–May 1491 and accepted the keys to the castles from Ali Çelebi during a public ceremony in the citadel. In what may have been a condition of the peace treaty, Qaytbay also released his Ottoman prisoners of war including Mihaloğlu İskender Bey,[74] and even honored some prisoners (including İskender Bey) with robes. Qaytbay also designated one of his prominent commanders, Janbulat (who came from Qaytbay's own *khassakis*), as his peace envoy to the Ottoman court and entrusted him with valuable gifts for Bayezid.

During the Ottoman mission's three-month stay in Cairo, the process of the Mamluks' image rehabilitation steadily intertwined with the ongoing peace negotiations. Qaytbay oversaw ceremonies that highlighted both the religious leadership and the military prowess of the Mamluk regime, two roles that had been contested by the Ottomans during the recent war. In the month of Rajab, when the judges in the imperial capital traditionally ascended to the citadel to celebrate the beginning of the three holy months, Qaytbay accepted them in the presence of the Ottoman ambassador. After the sultan was presented with the *kiswa* and the textile for the post of Abraham (*Maqam Ibrahim*), both items were paraded through the city with the *mahmal* leading the pilgrimage caravan.[75] This ceremony must have been planned to remind Ali Çelebi of Qaytbay's leading position in the Muslim world as the custodian of the Holy Cities and Shrines of Islam.[76] As a part of the same procession, the Mamluk regime also included a display of Mamluk lancers that engaged in a mock battle at the foot of the citadel. Ibn al-Himsi proudly recounted that the Ottoman ambassador, after witnessing military exercises that he could not have seen anywhere else, received numerous gifts from Qaytbay for his return home.[77] Thereafter, Ali Çelebi undertook his pilgrimage while Qaytbay's letter, gifts, and a corresponding Mamluk mission were prepared. In August 1491, Ali Çelebi and the Mamluk ambassador Janbulat passed through Damascus on their way back to Ottoman lands.[78]

After he accompanied Ali Çelebi to Constantinople, Janbulat's reception at the Ottoman court starkly contrasted with Mamay's earlier experience and signaled the Ottomans' acceptance of the peace treaty. According to Ottoman chroniclers, "a heavy delegation from Egypt" arrived on October 11, 1491. The adjective "heavy," which had never been used to describe a Mamluk mission, referred to Janbulat's valuable gifts and impressive retinue. After Janbulat participated in the *'id* prayer (the prayer on the first day of two religious celebrations) with the Ottoman administration and the sultan, the peace was concluded when the Mamluk ambassador returned to Cairo with equally impressive gifts for himself and for Qaytbay.

Although the actual text of the treaty has not been recovered, Ali Çelebi and Janbulat probably took a preliminary draft of the document to Constantinople. Remarkably, only Italian sources referred to any stipulations that impacted the commercial contacts between the two territories: they reported that the Mamluk merchants were once again granted the right to resume the slave trade with the Black Sea territories and vice versa.[79] Ottoman and Mamluk sources, in contrast, only conveyed a clear sense of relief and simply related that the roads between the two lands were reopened for trade and pilgrimage.[80]

Just as every aspect of the war had been closely intertwined with the image-building efforts of both sovereigns, so were their stipulations for peace. The negotiations concerning the frontiers loomed large in the writings of Ottoman and Mamluk chroniclers, who recorded that the three castles (Adana, Tarsus, and Gülek) that had been taken by the Ottomans during the war were returned to the Mamluks, while both sides agreed that the Gülek pass north of Adana would serve as the frontier between the two lands.[81] According to some Ottoman chroniclers, Bayezid insisted that the revenues of these strongholds be dedicated to the Holy Sanctuaries as they had been in the past.[82] This alleged stipulation underscored Bayezid's religiosity and piety—characteristics at the core of his image—and insinuated that it was the Ottoman ruler who most valued the Holy Sanctuaries. Although this part of the negotiation was never mentioned in Mamluk sources, Qaytbay supposedly acquiesced to this condition. This discrepancy between the accounts of the Ottoman and Mamluk chroniclers calls into question whether the Ottoman chroniclers added this stipulation in an attempt to salvage the honor of their sovereign, who clearly did not have the upper hand in the peace negotiations. It is also possible that the Mamluk chroniclers tried to protect their sovereign's name by not recording the restrictive condition, since it indirectly interfered with the Mamluk sultan's authority over his own lands. While we cannot answer this question until the actual document is found, these conflicting reports shed light on how closely this occasion was interconnected with the sovereigns' representations both at home and abroad.

As already depicted by Hersekzade's experience, captivity narratives contributed to this process of restoring the perceptions of both sovereigns, and the story of the Ottoman commander Mihaloğlu İskender Bey's captivity in Mamluk lands deserves particular attention. This captivity story, which Ottoman and Mamluk sources again recounted differently, particularly reinforced the existing tropes of Ottoman and Mamluk diplomatic discourse. The commander was released during the peace negotiations after spending almost two years in captivity.[83] Ottoman sources emphasized a conversation that allegedly took place between Qaytbay and Mihaloğlu İskender Bey on the day he was released. The Mamluk sultan, while honoring the warlord, apparently alluded to the familiar trope of *ghaza* when he stated, "I heard you are a *ghazi*, go and continue with such wars."[84] Ottoman correspondence and gifts for the Mamluk court had always underscored this aspect of Ottoman identity, especially after the Ottomans had noticed that this trope was particularly welcomed and celebrated by the Mamluks.

Mamluk witnesses to the encounter between Qaytbay and İskender Bey recorded their own versions of the event. According to a Mamluk source, Qaytbay asked the warlord a few questions about Islamic law, and the audience was shocked when İskender Bey could not answer them.[85] This anecdote manifested the common Mamluk perception of the Ottomans as ignorant in matters of religion.[86] Equally fascinating is the placement of this anecdote in Mamluk sources. The story appeared in a text that recounted the conversations in the Mamluk sultan Qansuh al-Ghawri's salons during the holy month of Ramadan. In this collection, Mihaloğlu İskender Bey's story appeared immediately after the section that narrated the Mamluk ambassador Janibak's daring verbal exchange in Bayezid's presence. The arrangement of these two particular anecdotes revealed an obvious rhetorical maneuver: the author of this text intended to counterbalance the impact of Janibak's humiliating experience with a scene that reflected İskender's alleged ignorance and Ottoman ignorance in general.[87] This tactic was used to create the impression that, although the Ottomans claimed the leadership of the Islamic world and the protectorate of the Sacred Shrines, they did not deserve such positions.

Most Ottoman chroniclers found ways to reassure their readers that the Ottomans and the Ottoman sultan were nonetheless superior to the Mamluks and the Mamluk sultan. One way in which the Ottoman chroniclers reasserted Ottoman superiority was by comparing the Ottoman dynastic lineage with the slave background of the Mamluk ruling class—a trope that had appeared in Janibak's account and the captivity story of Hersekzade Ahmed Paşa. The title that the Ottoman chronicler İbn Kemal gave to the section in which he enumerated the reasons for Ottoman–Mamluk animosity was a manifestation of this tactic: "[This section] narrates the reasons of the terror that happened between the Sovereign of the Time and the

Sultan of Egypt, the causes of animosity between this noble dynasty and the one coming from a bad origin [...]"[88]

İbn Kemal's predecessor Tursun Bey more directly reminded his readers of the Ottomans' "noble dynasty." He portrayed Bayezid as the son of a sultan who was too lofty to rule Egypt himself. For the chronicler, Bayezid's superior status to Qaytbay's was so obvious that only his "*kul*" (someone under his service) was an appropriate ruler for Egypt.[89] When narrating the departure of Hadım Ali Paşa and Hersekzade Ahmed Paşa in 1488 before the humiliating defeat of Ağaçayırı, he claimed that the Arab lands would have been conquered by a single march of the Ottoman ruler, but that leading the Ottoman army against the army of a slave-origin sultan was beneath Bayezid's rank.[90] This narrative subjectively ignored, however, the fact that Qaytbay did not lead his own army either. While or after the two armies battled, Ottoman chroniclers used the theme of dynastic lineage in their texts as a device to balance the Ottoman losses to the Mamluks. The legacy of this war was not limited to human casualties and expenses; the revision and reformulation of their mutual perceptions formed another facet of this vibrant and creative phase of interaction.

Beyond the officially appointed Ottoman and Mamluk ambassadors, the appearance of diverse intermediaries such as Hersekzade Ahmed Paşa, Davud Paşa, Molla Arab, and the Hafsid sultan during this peace process invite us to revisit our understanding about the nature and the limits of these sovereigns' authorities. In particular, the involvement of Molla Arab as a self-appointed agent of peace revealed the existence of a vocal and independent public opinion in at least parts of Ottoman society, a concept that runs against the preconceived notion of Oriental societies that supposedly submitted to the despotic fists of autocrats.[91] Bayezid was constrained by strong opposition within his own administration. In much the same way, Qaytbay struggled with multiple internal dynamics and factions in order to sustain the costly war and maintain the loyalty of his commanders and soldiers.[92] Through their carefully tailored diplomatic missions, these sovereigns disseminated the image of an absolute ruler and attempted to act accordingly, yet these images did not necessarily match the realities they faced at home. As illustrated so far, an entire war historiography was crafted by Ottoman chroniclers on one side and Mamluk chroniclers on the other. Each side diverged from the other, yet they shared a common goal: the vindication of their ruler's decisions and the maintenance of their awe-inspiring, carefully constructed images.

CHAPTER 6

FROM WARFARE TO ALLIANCE: THE INTRICACIES OF IMPERIAL DIPLOMACY (1491–1512)

A heightened sense of rivalry lingered between Cairo and Constantinople after the Ottoman–Mamluk war of 1485–91. In the wake of Safavid expansionism and the Portuguese encroachment of the Red Sea, the flexibility that had pervaded the Ottoman–Mamluk relationship since its beginning reemerged, and both powers swiftly transformed their predominantly contentious and occasionally hostile relationship into one of balanced and almost constructive competition. This swift shift not only reveals the complexity and plasticity of intra-Muslim engagements, but also contests the common notion of the Islamic world as a static and monolithic entity.

The conciliatory stance that the two lands adopted toward each other after the peace treaty did not abate their rivalry. As they channeled their military resources to address other conflicts, they also formulated new tropes that continued to foster a sense of competition between them. Bayezid had already begun to emphasize his dynasty-based sovereignty claims and Muslim heritage and to contrast his background with the slave-based and non-Muslim origins of his Mamluk counterparts. He began to contend for the leadership of the Islamic world when, in the past, the Ottomans had respected the authority of the Mamluk sultans in this regard. Finally, Bayezid's success in developing a formidable navy added an additional layer to the Ottoman image of *ghazi* and further altered his relationship with the Mamluks. Henceforth, the Ottoman ruler was not merely known as *Sultan al-Mujahidin* (the Sultan of Warriors of Faith) or *Sultan al-Ujat* (the Sultan of Islamic Frontiers), but also as *Qahraman al-Ma' wa al-Tin* (the Hero of Land and Sea).

A Shift in Ambassador Selection

Fewer missions were exchanged between Cairo and Constantinople in the years after the war. Despite this slower pace, each mission was carefully prepared by its sender and conscientiously hosted by its recipient. These considerable diplomatic efforts have been overshadowed, however, by the drastic events that came after this period.

During this new era of careful diplomacy, a shift was mutually discernible in ambassador selection. The Mamluk sultans began to rely increasingly on their own *mamluks* or *khassaki* whereas the Ottoman rulers, particularly Bayezid II, preferred representatives from either the *devşirme* ranks or from their imperial households. Davud Paşa (d.1501), a late fifteenth-century Ottoman bureaucrat from the *devşirme* class, was the first Ottoman ambassador to visit Cairo after the peace treaty. Almost three months before his journey to Mamluk lands, the Ottoman army defeated the Croatian army in the Battle of Krbava on September 9, 1493.[1] A seasoned diplomat, Davud Paşa may have announced this substantial victory in Cairo.[2] He likely traveled to the Mamluk court in 1494 while he was still serving as an *imrahor* within the Ottoman sultan's household.[3] İbn Kemal's exceptionally complimentary eulogy for Davud Paşa depicted a person who deserved to represent the Ottoman ruler at the Mamluk court; he was talented in the art of composition (*inşa'*), known for his good manners, often praised as a conversationalist, and was "everyone's favorite due to his good nature."[4] After Davud Paşa's assignment, Bayezid was so satisfied with his services that he appointed him to the prestigious position of *nişancı* (also called *tuğrakeş*), then to the governorship, and finally to the vizierate.

As Ibn Iyas's account revealed, Qaytbay and the rest of the Mamluk administration felt the need to counter Davud Paşa's mission with an assertive performance. Accompanied by an impressive entourage of prominent Mamluk commanders, Qaytbay descended from the citadel and proceeded to his new palace, which—despite a strained economy—had been built during the Ottoman–Mamluk War.[5] Qaytbay then distributed 50 gold coins to each of his Mamluks before returning to the citadel. In a surprised tone, Ibn Iyas recorded that Qaytbay's public appearance was his first in a long time and also explained that the Ottoman ambassador was present for this occasion and would be able to report the news of this impressive ceremony.[6] It is particularly telling that Qaytbay chose to distribute money to his Mamluks in the presence of the Ottoman ambassador. After all, they had performed exceptionally well against the Ottoman army—an army that had utterly defeated the Croatians but had never been able to destroy the Mamluks.

The task of responding to this Ottoman mission fell to Dawadar al-Thani Mamay, who had endured an unpleasant stay during his previous diplomatic mission to Constantinople.[7] He was no less prestigious a representative than Davud Paşa and came from the sultan's *khassakis* (or own recruits). As one of Qaytbay's leading commanders and as the second *dawadar*, he occupied a high-ranking position within the Mamluk administration.[8] Ibn Iyas particularly praised this commander for his sense of reason and insight.[9] Unlike his previous visit, Mamay received an appropriate welcome at the Ottoman capital.[10] By treating Mamay generously, Bayezid not only preserved his own name and honor, but also seized an opportunity to display the great wealth he had amassed in his recent victory against the Croatians. While the practice of giving slaves to ambassadors was unusual, in November 1494 Mamay reentered Damascus loaded with gifts from Bayezid that included (perhaps female) slaves and an ornate robe that was allegedly worth 3,000 *dinars*.

A year after Mamay's return, Mamluk chronicles recounted the return of another ambassador from an Ottoman mission. Qaytbay's appointment of Shaykh 'Abd al-Mu'min al-'Ajami as his ambassador to Bayezid's court departed from his previous preference for Mamluk commanders. Shaykh ʿAbd al-Muʾmin was appointed as the shaykh of a *zawiya* founded by Qaytbay.[11] This particular post, along with his name (al-ʿAjami), suggests that he was a Muslim mystic who probably arrived in Mamluk territory from Persian-speaking lands; he likely spoke Turkish as well. While many Mamluk sultans, including Qaytbay, had hired and protected individuals with similar backgrounds, Bayezid was also well-known for his strong interest in Islamic mysticism.[12] The overlap between Bayezid's predilection and Shaykh ʿAbd al-Muʾmin's position explains Qaytbay's seemingly unconventional choice, one that again affirms the fact that these embassies—even during this misleadingly quiet period—were carefully orchestrated by their senders.

After its ambassador was carefully selected, Shaykh ʿAbd al-Muʾmin's mission also took a rare and expensive array of gifts to Constantinople: textiles, predatory animals (probably a lion), a giraffe, a red parrot, and numerous other valuables.[13] As Bayezid's interest in hunting was well known and the Topkapı Palace housed a menagerie during his time, these gifts were obviously tailored to the sultan's tastes.[14] In return, Shaykh ʿAbd al-Muʾmin reported that although Bayezid was preoccupied with preparing his men for battle, the Ottoman ruler did not intend to march against the Mamluk army. Qaytbay's relief at hearing this news revealed the Mamluk ruler's continuing concern about a potential renewal of warfare.[15]

This pattern of regular yet cautious exchange was interrupted by Qaytbay's death on August 7–8, 1496. Although his son al-Nasir Muhammad (r.1496–8) took the throne immediately, a civil war consumed the Mamluk territories for four years.[16] Many of Qaytbay's commanders fell victim to the factional rivalry, and Mamay—who had recently returned from a second diplomatic mission to Ottoman lands—was killed in a skirmish. On March 8, 1497, his head was carried on a lance to Cairo.[17] Mamay's death at the hands of his fellow warriors was a tragic end for someone who had survived the significant risks of diplomatic missions.

During the years of uncertainty that followed Qaytbay's death, Bayezid began to emphasize a new side of his image with a fresh group of Ottoman ambassadors. After a long succession of envoys that had come from either the scholarly class (such as Ali Çelebi) or from *devşirme* recruits (such as Davud Paşa), Bayezid made an unorthodox choice for this prestigious position. He dispatched Kemal Reis, the famous Ottoman admiral and former pirate who had brought his significant talent to Bayezid's navy, in 1498–9.[18]

Kemal Reis' appointment mirrored a new development in the Ottomans' international policy and imperial ambitions.[19] Outwardly his mission was to deliver the Ottoman revenues from the pious endowments of the Holy Sanctuaries as well as the annual gifts and alms for the pilgrimage caravan. İbn Kemal also explained another practical consideration behind the admiral's selection: the land routes to Cairo were unsafe, and the sea had become the preferred method of transfer. Bayezid's efforts to construct an imperial navy that boldly challenged the domination of veteran forces such as Venice were well known, and he had always aspired to control the maritime routes of the Black and Mediterranean Seas.[20] Intelligence reports that the Ottoman ruler received from abroad communicated the weakness of the Mamluk navy, and one report even suggested that the Mamluks could be defeated if approached by sea.[21] In this context, Kemal Reis' appointment was probably Bayezid's way of flaunting a degree of maritime power that the Mamluk sultans had always yearned for yet had failed to achieve.

Ironically, it was Kemal Reis' return to Constantinople rather than his arrival in Cairo that caught the attention of Mamluk audiences. On his way, Kemal Reis engaged in a difficult sea battle before defeating a flotilla of the Hospitallers of Rhodes on November 18, 1498 and seizing at least five ships and substantial spoils. The famous sea captain returned home in triumph, and on the day he offered his spoils and captives[22] to Bayezid, the Mamluk envoy Khayr Bey (the governor of Aleppo who had been appointed by the young Mamluk sultan al-Nasir Muhammad in September 1497) was also present at the Ottoman court.[23] Bayezid also accepted the gifts of Malkoçoğlu Bali Bey, a famous frontier warlord who had returned from a campaign in the Balkans, on this same day.[24] The Ottoman ruler concluded his lavish display of power by giving some of his captured slaves to the Mamluk envoy. For Bayezid, this victory procession presented a unique opportunity to not only impress the Mamluk ambassador, but also to advertise his image as a *ghazi*-sultan who had an impressive navy at his service and financial resources at his disposal. He might not have been able to defeat the Mamluk armies on land, but he intended to shake the Mamluk sultan's secure position in the Islamic world with his fleet.

Since a new sultan was sitting in the Mamluk throne when Khayr Bey returned to Cairo in March 1499, Bayezid's message of Ottoman maritime success did not reach its intended audience. Khayr Bey, who apparently made some important contacts with the members of the Ottoman court during his mission, kept his appointment in Aleppo, which was geographically close to the Ottoman sphere of influence. He exchanged correspondence, some of it secretly, first with Bayezid and then with the sultan's son and successor Selim I.[25] Later, during the battle of Marj Dabik in 1516, Khayr Bey shifted his loyalties and fought for the Ottomans against the Mamluk army. This change of heart (or, in the eyes of the Mamluk regime, this act of treason) opened up a new career for Khayr Bey. In light of these subsequent developments, Bayezid's unusual generosity to the ambassador during his visit to Constantinople may have communicated the Ottoman ruler's expectation for his future services.

After his return to Cairo, Khayr Bey presented his ambassadorial report to the new Mamluk sultan, Qansuh al-Zahir, who was the maternal uncle of Qaytbay's son al-Nasir Muhammad. The new sultan had taken his nephew's place after he was killed in a bloody coup d'état, and Mamluk sources recorded Bayezid's disappointment when he heard that Qaytbay's son had been deposed and murdered.[26] As a ruler who had risen to power through dynastic succession, he was likely enraged that a son of a sultan had been killed by his own men. Even though the superiority of dynastic succession was among the tropes Bayezid and his image-makers had preached while crafting Bayezid's public image, al-Nasir Muhammad's fate may have also reminded the Ottoman ruler of the fragility of his own regime despite his outwardly well-established dynasty. One Ottoman chronicler also suggested that a marriage had been planned between Qaytbay's son and one of Bayezid's daughters, and Bayezid may have also been disappointed to miss a chance to be related to a Mamluk sultan who came from a dynastic lineage.[27]

Although he was not necessarily involved in the coup d'état that killed his nephew, the new Mamluk ruler felt the need to both exonerate and announce his new regime. To this end, Qansuh al-Zahir sent Amir Qansuh al-Khazinadari as his representative who stayed in Edirne between November 11 and December 2, 1500.[28] According to an expenditure record, the Ottomans spent 25,000 Ottoman coins hosting the Mamluk mission—a substantial sum that did not include the cost of the gifts for the delegation or for the Mamluk sultan.[29] When he passed through Damascus in May 1501, Amir Qansuh al-Khazinadari discovered that the Mamluk sultanate had changed hands three times during his 15-month diplomatic mission. Sultan Qansuh al-Zahir, who had sent this ambassador to Bayezid, had been replaced by Sultan Janbulat in July 1500. Janbulat was then replaced by Tumanbay in January 1501, and Tumanbay had been replaced by Qansuh al-Ghawri in March–April 1501.[30] Upon his return to Cairo, the ambassador presented his report to the new sultan.

A Note on Titulature

There is a gap in Ottoman–Mamluk correspondence between 1466 and 1502. While narrative sources and other archival documents attested to frequent diplomatic exchanges even during the war, no letters from these decades have come to light.

The post-1502 letters depict a confusing picture. On the one hand, some evidence displays a shift, one that seems almost too drastic to be plausible. In a letter dated to 1502 and preserved in Feridun Bey's collection, Bayezid addressed Qansuh al-Ghawri with the appellations *al-Hadra al-'Aliyya* (His Sublime Excellency). According to the classifications of both al-Qalqashandi and al-Sahmawi (whose work was chronologically the closest to Bayezid's and Qansuh al-Ghawri's era), this title had once been very prestigious. Over time, however, it had gradually lost its importance.[31] In his response to Bayezid's letter, Qansuh al-Ghawri addressed the Ottoman ruler as *al-Majlis al-'Ali* (The Sublime Seat) or *al-Majlis al-Sami* (The Elevated Seat), forms of titulature that ranked substantially lower than *al-Hadra* or *al-Maqarr*. Despite the shifting balance of power between them, it is unlikely that these rulers would have addressed each other by these lesser titles. It would be difficult to explain this drastic shift as a result of editorializing by an Ottoman compiler or copyist, as this change put the Ottoman sultan in an inferior position. On the other hand, a partially recovered and undated document suggests a continuation of the previous conventions, and it reveals that Qansuh al-Ghawri might have addressed the Ottoman sultan with *al-Maqam al-'Ali*, a title that ranked higher than *al-Maqarr*, and referred to himself as *Akhuhu Qansuh* (His Brother Qansuh).[32] As previously illustrated, Bayezid's father Mehmed II had sought these formulations in the past, yet his attempts had not yielded any concrete results.[33]

This discrepancy between the partial archival evidence and Feridun Bey's collection should not entirely de-legitimize the correspondence in Feridun Bey's work. It is possible, however, that the works of al-'Umari (d.1348), Ibn Nazir al-Jaysh (d.1384), al-Qalqashandi (d.1418), and al-Sahmawi (d.1464) might not be sufficient to interpret the titulature from the early sixteenth century. Although their works are critical in evaluating the titulature that was exchanged during an earlier phase of Ottoman–Mamluk relations, they were produced at least four decades before Bayezid reportedly addressed the Mamluk sultan by *al-Hadra al-'Aliyya*. No administrative handbook that could guide an analysis of early sixteenth-century titulature is available, and scholars who study titulature in the Islamic world suggest that the meanings and the ranks of these formulations occasionally changed over time.[34] In examining the correspondence between Bayezid II and Qansuh al-Ghawri, the honorific titles by which these two sovereigns addressed each other simply elude analysis.

From Regional to International Politics

During the last 12 years of Bayezid's reign, Qansuh al-Ghawri, despite his kingdom's internal turmoil, retained the Mamluk throne and witnessed major shifts in Ottoman–Mamluk diplomacy. The rise of the ambitious Safavid leader Shah Isma'il, in addition to the gradual encroachment of Portuguese maritime power in the Indian Ocean and the Red Sea, relegated both sultans' usual preoccupations—such as the Dulkadirids—to the backs of their minds. Even during this era of instability, however, neither Qansuh al-Ghawri nor Bayezid stopped refining and perpetuating their mutual perceptions and images.

In matters of diplomacy, Qansuh al-Ghawri and Bayezid addressed each other respectfully and cautiously without forgetting their mutual rivalry. The first set of surviving letters between the two rulers mirrored this careful yet contesting spirit. It was likely no coincidence that, when the Ottoman ambassador Silahdarbaşı Haydar Ağa (who had possibly joined the Ottoman service as a young *devşirme*) arrived in Cairo in November–December 1502 with a letter dated August 1502, his mission arrived only four months after Shah Isma'il's first penetration into Mamluk territory in August 1502.[35]

The Ottoman letter had been appropriately crafted for the occasion. The formulaic prayer that would normally have served as an *invocatio* invoked a God who chose sovereigns from the masses. The prayer also paid the usual respects to the Prophet Muhammad but emphasized a particular aspect of the Prophet's life: "Peace be upon the Prophet who became the messenger of God after an extended period of chaos," a statement that alluded to the disarray that surrounded the Mamluk sultan's rise to power. The rest of the letter similarly stressed the sovereignty, leadership, and qualities of a good ruler in an almost overbearing tone. This long, strongly didactic introduction was then followed by statements that flattered the new sultan and congratulated him for restoring peace in the Mamluk lands.[36]

Qansuh al-Ghawri's response to Bayezid, although it was formulated respectfully and appropriately, still asserted the Mamluk sultan's prestigious position. In a delayed response to Kemal Reis' display of Ottoman maritime power in 1498–9, it addressed the Ottoman ruler as "the Hero of the Land and Sea" and the "Shadow of God."[37] At the same time, however, the Mamluk sultan reminded

Bayezid of his vast territories and the impressive array of people who were under his control and patronage. Qansuh al-Ghawri then saluted the regime that he had inherited with extended descriptions of Mamluk lands and sovereignty. Although he may have been an inexperienced ruler (as Bayezid's letter had insinuated), he was certainly aware of the prestige and grace that defined the Mamluk regime. As a new ruler with still-contested authority, Qansuh al-Ghawri could not afford to alienate Bayezid, but neither did he bow to him.

Beyond their insinuations and verbal dueling, these letters also addressed practical political issues. Both Bayezid's and Qansuh al-Ghawri's letters referred to oral messages that had been entrusted to the Ottoman ambassador Haydar Ağa as well as the Mamluk ambassador Hindubay al-Khassaki, who accompanied him back to Ottoman lands. Although these issues were not mentioned in the letters, Haydar Ağa was most likely sent to discuss the new threat of Shah Isma'il as well as request the return of Prince Cem's daughter, who had stayed in Cairo after her father's departure in 1482.[38]

Due to the new Safavid threat along both sovereigns' frontiers and the fledgling nature of the new Mamluk sultan's authority, the Ottoman envoy Haydar Ağa was received favorably by Qansuh al-Ghawri. During his 70-day stay in Cairo, the Ottoman ambassador was hosted by the sultan at least three times, and each time he was invited to watch the *furusiyya* exercises (martial and recreational activities) of the Mamluk elite.[39] On each occasion, the Mamluk sultan bestowed robes of honor upon him and held a celebratory banquet. Before he departed, Haydar Ağa was given female slaves,[40] an unusual gesture that was probably a response to the slaves the Mamluk ambassador Khayr Bey had received from the Ottoman ruler in 1497. The ambassador returned to Constantinople with both Prince Cem's daughter and an array of impressive gifts.[41] At a time when the Safavids posed a real threat to both Ottoman and Mamluk powers, Qansuh al-Ghawri must have wanted to acknowledge the value of his powerful ally in the region.

For the next couple of years, every diplomatic mission between Constantinople (or Edirne) and Cairo always addressed the unexpected rise of the young Safavid leader Shah Isma'il, even in the face of more pressing concerns. One such concern was the Ottomans' harboring of Dawlatbay, the Mamluk governor of Tripoli (in Lebanon), in 1504–5.[42] After an initial attempt by the Dulkadir leader 'Ala' al-Dawla, the Ottoman ruler Bayezid stepped in to negotiate with the Mamluks on Dawlatbay's behalf. This intervention—which went unnoticed in Mamluk sources—was documented by two letters in Feridun Bey's compilation. The surviving part of Bayezid's letter dated August–September 1504 started with a verse on God's forgiveness, then requested pardon on behalf of the rebellious governor.[43] The Mamluk sultan's response kindly asked Bayezid to advise Dawlatbay to return home and to obey his sovereign.[44]

While these exchanges primarily discussed Dawlatbay's fate, both texts also revealed that their senders were preoccupied with Shah Isma'il and the atrocities that were being committed by Safavid troops. In Qansuh al-Ghawri's letter, the Mamluk sultan quickly shifted the discussion from Dawlatbay to an analogy between the Safavids and the Chingizid, whose atrocities epitomized violence for the Mamluks. Qansuh al-Ghawri claimed that the Safavids did not have any mercy for women, children, or scholars of religion, and he argued that their aggression had to be stopped.

The rise of the Safavids was closely monitored by the major political actors in the region because they controlled the Iranian Silk Road and were closely connected to many European courts. Although he often apologized for his indiscretions after the fact, Shah Isma'il's occasional penetrations into Mamluk and Ottoman territories caused grave concerns in Cairo and Constantinople. While some hoped that the Safavid leader would stop the expansion of the Ottomans, others wished that he would end the Mamluk regime's costly and arbitrary control of many Mediterranean ports. With his strong ideological rhetoric and devotion to the Shi'i branch of Islam, Shah Isma'il also posed an ideological threat to the Sunni Ottoman and Mamluk regimes.[45]

While the Safavids were on the rise, the world also witnessed the dawn of the Portuguese maritime empire and its circumnavigation of the Cape of Good Hope. This new development placed the Mamluks and the Ottomans at the center of world politics.[46] According to Mamluk sources, the penetration of Portuguese ships into the Red Sea and their threats to the Holy Sanctuaries in Mecca and Medina began to give the Mamluk sultan sleepless nights. Qansuh al-Ghawri invested considerable funds to prepare ships and renovate his strongholds along the shores of the Red Sea and the Indian Ocean.[47]

As early as during Qaytbay's reign, the Mamluks had received requests from other Muslim rulers for maritime help in Iberia, India, and along the North African coast.[48] Their repeated appeals showed that, for many Muslim rulers along the outskirts of the Islamic world, the title of the Sultan of Islam and the Muslims was not empty but conveyed power, and they expected Qansuh al-Ghawri to act on his title. Although later sources and studies often depicted this period as a time of Mamluk decline, these contemporaries believed in the Mamluk sultan's superior position and assumed he had extensive financial resources at his disposal.

While Bayezid and Qansuh al-Ghawri attended to international affairs and regional issues of mutual interest, neither sovereign abandoned the refinement of his image through diplomatic embassies. In July 1507, an Ottoman ambassador was visiting Cairo when the Mamluk sultan received the distressing news that Safavid troops were violating the Mamluk frontier.[49] Qansuh al-Ghawri immediately called his entire administration to an emergency meeting, and within a month Mamluk troops departed for Malatya to stop the Safavid invasion. While Qansuh al-Ghawri may have felt humiliated to receive this news while hosting an Ottoman ambassador, his swift actions displayed the efficiency and preparedness of the Mamluk regime when it faced a crisis and most likely helped to rehabilitate his image with his Ottoman guest.

Three months later, the Mamluk sultan's military success enabled him to salvage his name from its earlier humiliation. Two Ottoman delegations—including that of Kemal Reis—were present in Cairo[50] when the Dulkadirid ruler 'Ala' al-Dawla's messenger arrived with the news of the Safavids' defeat. This victory was confirmed by a display of the severed heads of Safavid soldiers. Qansuh al-Ghawri ordered that the heads be hung in Bab al-Zuwayla, and this victorious public display undoubtedly targeted his foreign guests as well as his domestic audience. A couple of days later, the Mamluk sultan bestowed a robe of honor on the Ottoman envoy and other gifts on his entourage before they left Mamluk lands.[51]

The timing of this procession was advantageous for the Mamluk sultan. On September 26, 1507, only 15 days before the announcement of the Safavid victory, Kemal Reis had been granted an audience with Qansuh al-Ghawri and had greatly enhanced the Ottoman image at the Mamluk court.[52] Ibn Iyas expressed his admiration for the seaman's life story, which was filled with warfare against the non-Muslims, and explained that the *"khawass"* (servant) of Ibn Osman (the Ottoman ruler) had engaged in "jihad against the Franks day and night." This brief yet meaningful passage indicated that Kemal Reis' appearance at the Mamluk court had not only portrayed the Ottomans as the leading *ghazis*, but had also signaled the rise of Ottoman sea power. This display made the case that Bayezid deserved the title by which Qansuh al-Ghawri had addressed him since at least 1502: the Hero of the Sea and Land.[53] Thanks to the news from 'Ala' al-Dawla's messenger, the Mamluk sultan was still able to salvage his honor and prove to the Ottoman envoy that he was capable of defeating their common enemy.

A Royal "Guest" in Cairo: Prince Korkud

Although the episode must have reminded Bayezid of the unpleasant Cem affair, his communications with the Mamluk sultan were not disrupted when his son Prince Korkud took refuge in Mamluk lands.[54] The two leaders, in light of international developments, had resolved to work more collaboratively, and in April–May 1509, Qansuh al-Ghawri appointed Amir 'Allan, his *dawadar*, as an ambassador to Bayezid. Amir 'Allan was sent to convey his wishes for the Ottoman sultan's recovery from illness,[55] and his status as a *dawadar* revealed the prestige of the Ottoman court in the eyes of the Mamluk sultan.[56] As 'Allan prepared for his long trip, Prince Korkud suddenly appeared at the Mamluk port of Damietta in May 1509.[57] Qansuh al-Ghawri dispatched a large convoy of high-ranking administrators to welcome the Ottoman prince, and this gesture set the tone for the rest of Korkud's stay in Mamluk lands. For the next 14 months, Korkud was not only honored by the sultan with banquets, but was also hosted on numerous special occasions that included the Prophet's birthday (*mawlid*) and other religious celebrations. On June 29, 1509, during the annual *mawlid* celebration, the Mamluk sultan seated Korkud to his right, above the Shafi'i judge. Moreover, in honor of his royal guest, the sultan dressed "in gala," which he had never done at any previous *mawlid*.[58]

Korkud, whose relationship with his sultan-father was strained and who was a junior figure to the aged Mamluk sultan, was aware of his lower status and respectfully kissed the Mamluk sultan's hand at their first meeting.[59] Qansuh al-Ghawri also acknowledged the difference in their ranks when, on several occasions, he bestowed robes of honor on the prince. Despite the exceptional value of these robes, the gesture again symbolized the hierarchical relationship between the superior donor and the inferior recipient.[60]

The Mamluk chronicler Ibn Iyas compared the Mamluks' special treatment of Korkud to their previous treatment of Korkud's uncle Prince Cem. The difference must have been at least partially due to the increasing prestige of the Ottomans in the international arena. Since the Prince Cem incident, the two powers had fought each other in an exhausting war—an event that showed the Ottomans were willing to engage the Mamluks militarily. At the same time, Prince Korkud's reception also showed Sultan Qansuh al-Ghawri's awareness of both world politics and his own surrounding international climate. While harboring an Ottoman prince could have brought both parties to the brink of war and did trigger multiple exchanges between the two capitals, the event was soon overshadowed by the escalating aggression of Shah Isma'il and the Portuguese penetration into the Red Sea. Given these circumstances, the Mamluk sultan knew that he would need Bayezid's help against both enemies and offered to mediate the Korkud affair rather than encourage the prince's potential insurgency against his father. In fact, since the negotiations for Korkud's safe return to Ottoman lands and for Ottoman help against the Portuguese attacks developed hand-in-hand, the presence of the Ottoman prince in Cairo may actually have assisted Qansuh al-Ghawri's diplomatic efforts.[61]

Under these special conditions, Qansuh al-Ghawri probably revised Amir 'Allan's mission to the Ottoman court. 'Allan, who had been preparing to depart just as the Ottoman prince arrived, took an impressive collection of gifts to Constantinople and hoped to convince Bayezid that the Mamluk sultan was ready to collaborate with him in the Korkud affair. Evidence from both Ottoman and Mamluk sources indicated that 'Allan was welcomed, honored with impressive gifts, and was given an audience on January 26, 1510.[62] After a ten-month mission, 'Allan returned to Cairo wearing a robe that had been granted to him by the Ottoman ruler and carrying allocations for Korkud from Bayezid.[63] While sources did not divulge anything about 'Allan's negotiations in Constantinople, Qansuh al-Ghawri acknowledged his *dawadar*'s success with a promotion.[64] Shortly thereafter, Korkud requested the Mamluk sultan's permission to return home in July 1510.[65] As was the case in many matters of diplomacy, 'Allan's mission should only be considered a successful first step in a long negotiation process.[66] In late June of 1510 and again in August of 1510, the Ottoman court hosted two more Mamluk missions that addressed the same issues as 'Allan's: one headed by Amir Yunus al-'Adili and the other by Amir Kasabay.[67]

Prince Korkud, who occupied a tenuous position as a royal guest, refugee, and diplomatic pawn, nonetheless witnessed special displays of power by the Mamluk sultan. On November 28, 1509, Muhammad Bey, the commander of the Mamluk fleet, escorted war prisoners from a skirmish in the Mediterranean Sea to Cairo.[68] While Muhammad Bey's primary task had been to find timber for ship construction, he had become engaged in an unexpected confrontation with the "Franks" and had defeated them in October–November 1509.[69] His victory procession in the Mamluk capital, which was witnessed by both the public and Korkud,[70] celebrated a rare maritime success for the Mamluks in the presence of the Ottoman prince whose father presided over the powerful Ottoman navy. The impression was short-lived, however: the same Mamluk fleet was destroyed in an unexpected encounter with the Rhodesian fleet in

August–September 1510.[71] The annihilation of the Mamluk fleet ended Qansuh al-Ghawri's hopes for countering the recently formulated Ottoman claims to maritime domination.

Three pieces of correspondence between Bayezid and Qansuh al-Ghawri survived this era of intense diplomatic traffic, and each reflected a special rhetorical strategy that was tailored to Korkud's case. Qansuh al-Ghawri alluded to the Qur'anic anecdotes about the relationship between Joseph and his son Jacob and invited Bayezid to treat his own son with mercy. He also offered detailed stipulations concerning Korkud's allowance and his appointment to a new province in the Ottoman Empire. Bayezid's responses to these letters both referred to the same tropes of Joseph and Jacob while discussing the conditions of Korkud's return.[72]

None of these letters, however, referred to the Ottoman maritime support the Mamluks had requested. In one of his letters, Qansuh al-Ghawri expressed an expectation for his ambassador to return with gifts that had been listed in an additional Mamluk letter.[73] The Mamluk sultan was in immediate need of Ottoman help because of the aforementioned destruction of the Mamluk fleet in August–September 1510,[74] and this other letter may have contained Qansuh al-Ghawri's request for maritime help.

The Ottomans' naval aid arrived in January 1511 under the command of Selman Reis and accompanied by an Ottoman ambassador; it was comprised of approximately 300 ships, timber, gunpowder, and iron.[75] During the Ottoman ambassador's audience, Qansuh al-Ghawri displayed unusual respect and humility when he kissed Bayezid's letter and placed it over his eyes.[76] Apparently, the Mamluk sultan was deeply touched by the contents of the letter, which, according to convention, were recited publicly. The letter also contained the unfortunate news that Kemal Reis, who had visited Cairo twice and had been hosted with particular honors, had disappeared in a storm on his way to Alexandria.[77] When Ibn Iyas complimented the language and the composition of the letter,[78] it was the first time in the history of Ottoman–Mamluk exchanges that an Ottoman letter had evoked positive comments from the Mamluks about the quality of its prose.[79]

The Last Performances of the Mamluk Court for Bayezid

Five days after his audience with the Ottoman ambassador, Qansuh al-Ghawri called the European consuls in Mamluk lands to a public meeting where he confronted them about their waning loyalty. In the presence of these consuls and his own administrators, he announced that the Mamluk governor of al-Bira had captured some of Shah Isma'il's messengers,[80] and that the letters they were carrying at the time invited the sovereigns of these European consuls to an alliance against the Ottomans and Mamluks. The fact that the Mamluk sultan publicly reprimanded this group only five days after the Ottoman ambassador's audience with the Mamluk sultan could not have been a coincidence; Qansuh al-Ghawri probably designed this public occasion to impress the Ottoman ambassador and may have even consulted him about the situation.[81] These European consuls, which Ibn Iyas generically called the "Franks," included a representative from Venice, where Bayezid had conducted a long and successful war nine years earlier.[82] At this critical moment in 1511, the entire political world seemed to revolve around the Ottomans and the Mamluks.

While this particular collaboration raises the question of whether Bayezid aided the Mamluks merely out of his concern for his son, the first Ottoman maritime aid had already reached Mamluk lands before the eruption of Prince Korkud's case. In September 1507 (two years before Korkud's appearance in Damietta), Kemal Reis had brought a small Ottoman fleet to Alexandria.[83] Moreover, Ibn Iyas also mentioned that Yunus al-'Adili—Qansuh al-Ghawri's ambassador to Bayezid in 1510–11—had also offered to pay for Ottoman aid. Bayezid, however, refused any payment and provided the needed materials free of charge.[84] By generously contributing to the defense of the Holy Cities, Bayezid may have also been seizing an opportunity to break the Mamluk monopoly in the leadership of the Sunni Muslim world. In short, while Bayezid would have sent help in any case, his aid might normally have cost the Mamluk sultan either an economic or a political concession. The presence of Korkud in Mamluk lands and Qansuh al-Ghawri's intense efforts on his behalf possibly diminished this cost.

The last known letters between the Ottomans and the Mamluks during Bayezid's reign were exchanged between Khayr Bey, the Mamluk governor of Aleppo, and the Grand Vizier Hadım Ali Paşa or his successor Hersekzade Ahmed Paşa. In a letter dated June 4, 1511 that specifically addressed the Ottoman grand vizier, Khayr Bey raised the possibility of an alliance between Bayezid and Qansuh al-Ghawri against the Safavids.[85]

In June–July 1512, one year after Khayr Bey's letter, the Mamluk sultan Qansuh al-Ghawri hosted 14 ambassadors in Cairo.[86] Their missions reflected a wide geographical range from the Venetians to the Hafsids to the Ottomans, and this impressive congregation asserted the lasting centrality of the Mamluk imperial capital in world events.[87] The primary purpose of the Ottoman mission, however, was to inform the Mamluk sultan about the accession of Bayezid's son Selim, which had taken place in April 1512. A few days after receiving this news, Qansuh al-Ghawri learned that his friend and foe Bayezid had passed away.[88]

The death of Bayezid marked the end of a complex but flexible diplomatic phase between the Ottomans and the Mamluks, and no one could predict how their relationship would change in the future. The two powers had faced each other in a long and seemingly fruitless war over the previous three decades, yet they set aside their lingering problems when faced with threats from the Safavids and the Portuguese. Likewise, although their enduring rivalry over the allegiance of the Dulkadirids, Ramazanids, and Turgudoğulları (another semi-nomadic tribal confederation in mid- and south Anatolia) did not disappear entirely, it diminished in the wake of these other dangers.[89]

Even though Bayezid and Qansuh al-Ghawri did not threaten each other during this phase, they continued to refine their mutual images through ceremonies and processions. Perhaps in their own political culture, the practices of image-building and the crafting of mutual perceptions were too important to neglect under any conditions. The Ottomans particularly valued opportunities to impress the Mamluks, and records from the Ottoman treasury certified that, among all the diplomatic missions the Ottoman court hosted between 1500 and

1511, the Mamluk embassies always received the most valuable gifts and allocations.[90] It was only toward the end of his reign that Bayezid began to host Safavid missions with the same generosity.[91]

The Ottoman public must have also valued this relationship with the Mamluks because Ottoman chroniclers—who wrote under the patronage of Bayezid primarily for domestic audiences—started to devote sections of their narratives to the deterioration of the Ottoman–Mamluk relationship well before the Ottoman conquest of Egypt. Bayezid's attempts to construct a historiography for the Ottoman dynasty turned him into a patron of chroniclers,[92] and his increasing desire to craft an imperial story gave the Mamluks—his primary rivals in battle and in diplomacy—a new place in Ottoman imperial rhetoric.[93]

The Mamluks both acknowledged and countered these Ottoman claims for supremacy. Even though these occasions conflicted with Qaytbay's general reforms and cost-cutting measures, every interaction with an Ottoman ambassador was filled with ostentatious ceremony and impressive displays of generosity. Obviously, Qaytbay recognized that these diplomatic performances and his own imperial image were intertwined. The special treatment of Ottoman missions continued during Qansuh al-Ghawri's reign, but neither Qaytbay nor Qansuh al-Ghawri gave in to Ottoman rhetorical pressures.[94] In the eyes of the Mamluk sultans, the Ottomans were still ignorant of religious rules and new to the world of Islamic culture and tradition. The Mamluks still saw themselves as the true patrons of the ageless learning institutions as well as the protectors of Mecca, Medina, and Jerusalem.

Beyond their consistently honorable treatment of Ottoman embassies, a shift in the attitude of the Mamluk sultans from Qaytbay to Qansuh al-Ghawri is nonetheless visible. From the moment he signed the Ottoman–Mamluk peace treaty in 1491 until the day he died, Qaytbay worried about an Ottoman attack.[95] For his successor Qansuh al-Ghawri, who was mostly preoccupied with the Portuguese, the Safavids, and the protection of pilgrimage routes, Bayezid appeared less threatening, or at least a less imminent threat.

This same sense of reprieve also pervaded the biography that Ibn Iyas wrote for Bayezid in his chronicle. In this biography the Mamluk chronicler did not mention the war, an event that occupied substantial space in the earlier sections of his chronicle. Since Bayezid's death took place in 1512—two decades after the peace treaty—and after the Ottoman's offer of maritime aid, Ibn Iyas may not have expected any escalating Ottoman aggression towards the Mamluk regime. His silence in Bayezid's biography about this Ottoman ruler's earlier aggression perhaps proved the flexibility of the Mamluk social memory and the adaptability of the Ottoman–Mamluk relationship that accommodated both wars and alliances within a span of three decades. Most importantly, it was probably the richness of both powers' diplomatic resources—from titulature to gifts—that enabled them to march swiftly, though not completely, from war to alliance and from one end of the diplomatic spectrum to the other.

CONCLUSION

1512 and its Aftermath

In 1512 Bayezid II's son Selim and his supporters forced him to abdicate the Ottoman throne. Two months after he was deposed, Bayezid died while traveling to Dimetoka, an old Byzantine town in modern-day Bulgaria. Despite the long war that had plagued his earlier relationship with the previous Mamluk sultan Qaytbay, the relationship between the Ottomans and Mamluks had steadily improved after Qansuh al-Ghawri's accession in 1501. Nonetheless, Qansuh al-Ghawri, who had offered a safe haven to the sons of Selim's brother and prime competitor Prince Ahmed, watched the transfer of power at the center of the Ottoman Empire closely.[1] It was only after Selim had eliminated his brothers and secured his position that the Mamluk sultan sent the ambassador Amir Aqbay al-Tawil to congratulate the new ruler.[2] Besides the contest for the Ottoman throne, the Mamluk Sultan was also concerned about the rising power of Shah Isma'il and the menace of the Portuguese navy. In fact, he had conferred extensively with Bayezid about these two issues before the end of his reign.

These same two issues were also the first to be addressed in the correspondence between Qansuh al-Ghawri and Selim I, the new Ottoman sultan.[3] Selim, who had once been the governor of Trabzon near the eastern border of the Ottoman Empire, was no stranger to the Safavid threat. During his term as governor, Selim expressed deep concern about their expansion and once even raided the Safavid territory in retaliation for Shah Isma'il's penetration into Ottoman lands. Not surprisingly, as soon as Selim secured the Ottoman throne, he returned his attention to this old adversary.

Selim's policies toward the Safavids also affected his relationship with the Mamluks. When the Ottoman army advanced on the Safavids during the summer of 1514, Qansuh al-Ghawri, as a cautionary measure, led his army to the border between the Ottoman and Mamluk territories. The Mamluk sultan's concerns about an Ottoman attack were unfounded, however, and Selim and Shah Isma'il faced each other on the plain of Chaldiran on August 23, 1514. After the triumph of the Ottoman army, Selim sent messengers to Qansuh al-Ghawri to complain about a different issue: the Dulkadirid ruler, 'Ala' al-Dawla, had refused to support the Ottomans against the Safavids.[4] When Qansuh al-Ghawri recused himself from the affair[5] and did not protect 'Ala' al-Dawla, Selim sent his men to seize the Dulkadirid territory.[6] The Ottoman commanders of this campaign were Vizier Sinan Paşa and Ali, who was 'Ala' al-Dawla's nephew. Ali had joined the Ottomans after his father Shahsuwar was executed in Cairo in 1472. By sending him to battle his own uncle, the Ottoman ruler imposed his own candidate on the Dulkadirid polity as his predecessors had done before him. Ali defeated 'Ala' al-Dawla, and the Dulkadirids' ruler's severed head, along with the heads of his son, his vizier, and other prominent members of his administration, were taken to Qansuh al-Ghawri in July 1515 by an Ottoman mission.[7]

While the Ottoman mission's letter, which announced their victory over the Dulkadirids, did not necessarily use a threatening tone, the severed head of the Mamluk sultan's old vassal conveyed a mixed message, as such "gifts" often did in a diplomatic context. Qansuh al-Ghawri, who was distressed by the offering, demanded an explanation. When they were asked about their sultan's intentions, the Ottoman ambassadors Karaca Ahmed Paşa and Zeyrekzade Rükneddin Molla asked for the Mamluk sultan's pardon, offered him additional valuable gifts, and explained that Selim's only ambition was to eliminate Shah Isma'il. Although, according to Ibn Iyas,

Qansuh al-Ghawri was not completely convinced, he responded properly to this mission by sending back valuable gifts and some special items that Selim had requested. For Ibn Iyas, however, the apologies of the Ottoman ambassadors were a ruse.

A complete treatment of the subsequent correspondence between Qansuh al-Ghawri and Selim and the further development of their conflict is beyond the scope of this study.[8] Soon after the Ottoman mission returned, however, the Ottoman and the Mamluk forces faced each other in Marj Dabik on August 24, 1516. The Ottomans defeated the Mamluk army and killed the Mamluk sultan in battle. Prince Kasım, who was a son of the deceased Ottoman prince Ahmed and a nephew of the current Ottoman sultan, fought with the Mamluk army, was captured by Ottoman troops, and was executed upon Selim's order. The adventurous prince was the last of a long and influential succession of refugees that circulated between the Ottoman and Mamluk courts.

The next battle between the Ottoman and the Mamluk armies took place outside of Cairo and ended with another Ottoman victory on January 23, 1517. In February 1517, Selim triumphantly entered Cairo. Even though the incorporation of the old Mamluk lands into the Ottoman Empire would take time, the Ottomans were the new rulers of Egypt and Syria. In addition to doubling the size of his Empire, Selim became the first Ottoman sultan who was called the servitor of the Holy Cities or *Khadim al-Haramayn al-Sharifayn*, a title that had been jealously guarded by the Mamluk sultans since they first acquired it in the thirteenth century. From this point on, the Ottomans carried out the responsibilities that the Mamluks had once owned and treasured. As a representative of the Ottoman sultan, the Ottoman governor of Egypt was responsible for protecting Muslim pilgrims and for the security of the Holy Cities. The Ottomans were finally the most immediate rivals of the Portuguese in the Red Sea, and they controlled the trade routes of the eastern Mediterranean. The Ottoman conquest of Egypt also engendered dramatic consequences for Cairo. Following the Ottoman conquest, the city, after serving as an imperial capital for centuries, became a provincial capital once again.

The drastic impact of the Ottoman conquest prompted contemporary chroniclers and their succeeding colleagues to describe and recount the historical process that intensified the hostility between the two Islamic powers.[9] Ottoman chroniclers emphasized political events, particularly those that triggered tension and enmity between the two parties. This trend explains why Ottoman sources in general did not say much about the contacts between the Ottoman ruler Mehmed I and al-Mu'ayyad Shaykh, the energetic and active Mamluk sultan who sent his son to Anatolia for punitive campaigns against the Karamanids and Dulkadirids, or those between Murad II and his Mamluk counterparts (primarily Barsbay). As shown in Chapter 3, the intense and frequent diplomatic exchanges during these decades particularly transformed the way in which the Ottomans were perceived by Mamluk society. Mamluk chroniclers treated the topic of Ottoman–Mamluk relations in a similar manner. Although they mentioned most of the Ottoman missions that came to Cairo during Murad II's reign and described the arrival of the Ottoman naval aid that Qansuh al-Ghawri had requested from Bayezid II, they also focused primarily on political events that aggravated the relationship.

These patterns in the narratives of Ottoman and Mamluk chroniclers undoubtedly contributed to the contents of modern studies, which primarily investigate the evolution and the consequences of the hostility between the Ottomans and the Mamluks. Some new studies, however, dispute the deeply-held convictions about the ultimate Ottoman plans against the Mamluks, while others even question the evolution of Selim's plan for the Mamluk regime.[10]

Before the accession of Selim—whose intentions concerning the Mamluk territories are beyond the scope of this study—three Ottoman rulers had shown aggression towards the Mamluks: Bayezid I, Mehmed II, and Bayezid II. Although Bayezid I penetrated into the Mamluk sphere of influence, the evidence suggests that he was primarily interested in conquering Constantinople and had no plans for a larger attack on Mamluk lands. While his great-grandson Mehmed II did alter the tone of the communication between the Ottomans and the Mamluks, he never engaged in open warfare with them and his intentions for the

Mamluk territory (or the target of his last campaign) remain unclear.[11] Of these three rulers, only Bayezid II engaged in an actual war with the Mamluks, but after facing strong Mamluk resistance, even he had to adapt his plans and adopt a more conciliatory tone with the Mamluk sultan. It is important to remember that during this long and complex relationship that almost lasted for two centuries (1360s–1517), only eight years were marked by active military conflict between the two powers.

While it is not responsible scholarship—at least in the absence of conclusive evidence—to embrace the idea that the Ottomans were "destined" to end the Mamluk regime, neither can we dismiss entirely the possibility that Mehmed II's last campaign was to the Mamluk lands or that Selim I had long planned to defeat the Mamluks. As already suggested in Chapter 5, some members of the Ottoman administration during Bayezid II's time opposed the idea of an attack on Mamluk lands, while other documentary evidence suggests that some individuals in the Ottoman ruler's inner circle may have favored an attack.[12] It is possible that—as was the case with the Ottoman attack on Constantinople prior to 1453—an Ottoman attack against the prestigious Mamluk regime was a lingering discussion rather than a unanimous agreement among the members of the Ottoman ruling class. Since the people of the time were divided or conflicted about this project, modern researchers also have a responsibility to examine all possibilities about how the Ottomans' designs against the Mamluks were formed.

The Language of Diplomacy: Titulature, Tropes, Envoys, and Gifts

Despite the tension and mutual animosity that imbued these writings, both Ottoman and Mamluk primary sources revealed another phenomenon of their diplomatic relationship: both sides stressed the formative influences of diplomatic communication. They attributed deterioration in the relationship to the neglect of diplomatic etiquette and attributed improvement to the enforcement of these traditions. Although both Ottoman and Mamluk authors consistently condemned the breach of these rules in their own cultures, each also blamed the other for such offenses.[13] In part, the unflagging interest of Ottoman and Mamluk chroniclers in diplomatic etiquette has determined the content of this study. During an age when transportation and communications were limited, every component of foreign missions became a way to formulate messages and exchange mutual perceptions. The significance that the men of this time attached to these practices in their political culture suggests that important nuances of Ottoman–Mamluk relations were buried in the accounts of these exchanges.

These accounts reveal two major types of transformations in Ottoman–Mamluk diplomatic practices: correspondence and ambassador selection underwent multiple phases that probably emerged independently from other short-term political concerns. Within correspondence practices, the classification of titulature as described in Mamluk chancery manuals reflected gradual changes in hierarchy. During the time of the fourteenth-century Mamluk official al-Qalqashandi, the Abbasid caliphs were addressed with the title *al-Janib* while the late-fifteenth-century official al-Sahmawi did not even include this particular title in his classification.[14] The disappearance of *al-Janib* from regular usage was not unlike the parasol (*chatr* or *mizalla*), an item that had once been an essential part of Mamluk ceremonies as a sign of royalty and sovereignty but was never mentioned in the context of Ottoman–Mamluk diplomatic encounters.[15] These institutional modifications suggest that even the bureaucracies of the region made allowances for the natural progression of change.[16]

As well as these long-term transformations, additional shifts in diplomatic conventions and culture were brought about by short-term political changes. These changes suggest that even by the late fourteenth century the communication between the Ottomans and the Mamluks went further than the cordial exchange of goodwill missions. The Mamluks had interacted with other Anatolian political powers before the Ottomans settled in the region, and (as discussed in the Introduction) the same themes that dominated these earlier interactions became cornerstones of Ottoman–Mamluk relations.

For instance, the idea that the Mamluk sultans were superior to the Anatolian rulers was initially upheld by the Ottomans. Within that limited and inferior position, however, the Ottomans began to use their diplomatic encounters with the Mamluk regime to impart significant messages that refined or reinforced their image.

The Mamluks' gradual promotion of the Ottoman ruler's titulature (from *al-Majlis al-Samiyy* to *al-Maqarr al-Karim* or *al-Maqam*), which happened during a misleadingly quiet era, demonstrates how the gradual geographic expansion and political rise of the Ottomans was reflected in diplomatic culture.[17] By the end of this era, the Ottomans had surpassed the Karamanids who, in the second half of the fifteenth century, still received the title of *al-Janab* as they had in the fourteenth century.[18] Despite his newly-elevated status, the Ottoman ruler Mehmed II was not content with the title *al-Maqarr* and responded by demoting the conventional Mamluk honorific from *al-Maqam* to *al-Maqarr*.[19]

Another indicator that mirrored the changing Ottoman expectations for their diplomatic interactions with the Mamluks was the appearance of certain resilient tropes of Islamic diplomatic culture. The trope of seniority occasionally appeared in the conversations between the Ottoman and Mamluk capitals, at least until the reign of Qaytbay.[20] On at least two occasions, this well-known theme of age hierarchy was used to show the junior sender's respect for the senior recipient. However, in a third case between the senior Mamluk sultan Khushqadam and the young Ottoman ruler Mehmed II, Mehmed expressed his ambition by dismissing the age hierarchy between them and addressing the Mamluk sultan as his peer.[21] Unfortunately, although such a correspondence would provide an excellent case study, we do not have an example of a letter where a young Mamluk sultan who was the son of another sultan (as opposed to a sultan from slave origins) addressed an experienced Ottoman sultan.

Symbolic references to their shared Islamic religion were particularly conspicuous in Ottoman–Mamluk correspondence. On occasions when either ruler wanted to maintain a positive relationship or improve an ailing one, he often alluded to the idea of Muslim brotherhood and fraternity through the familiar symbolism of "two arms from a single body."[22] Frequent references to *jihad*, *ghaza*, and the protection of the Holy Cities also prove the prevalent and influential role of Islam in this diplomatic relationship.

Over time the Ottomans found their own niche in the diplomatic manifestations of ideological and religious discourse. Although they were not located in the heartlands of Islam and had inherited no Islamic institutions (such as a *madrasa*), because of their location they were often involved in warfare against the Byzantines and other non-Muslim Balkan powers. The Ottomans knew how to benefit from their military successes along the frontiers of the Islamic world, and Mamluk chronicles frequently reported the arrival of an Ottoman mission to announce yet another victory against the non-Muslims. In the eyes of the Mamluks, these acts of war legitimized the Ottomans as defenders of Islam or as the *Sultan al-Mujahidin* or *Sahib al-Ujat*. Although there are no signs indicating that the Mamluk sultans, who seemed to welcome these announcements, were disturbed by them, it is valid to ask whether they considered these victories to be infringements on their role as the defenders of Islam.

In this light, the common perception that a united Islamic front, or *Dar al-Islam*, existed and fought against the lands under non-Muslim authority (*Dar al-Harb*) in the Mediterranean basin must be revisited. The shifting role of this theme and the alleged dichotomy between *Dar al-Islam* and *Dar al-Harb* also remind us that religious affiliations were uttered and reinforced by politicians only when they were also politically expedient. Even though Islamic discourse was closely integrated into the Ottoman–Mamluk relationship, these communications did not change the fact that any relationship between two powers is shaped by the rules of Realpolitik. While both sides invoked the trope of Muslim brotherhood, neither hesitated to use military force against their "brothers" when necessary.

As the Ottomans expanded the borders of Islam and formulated new claims in the international arena, they searched for more solid ground from which to counter the Mamluks and their deeply rooted legitimacy in the Islamic world. As discussed in Chapter 1, both the Ottoman and Mamluk ceremonies shared some characteristics and influences, and were primarily crafted under the influence of earlier and contemporary Muslim and non-Muslim courts.[23] The Ottoman and Mamluk palaces, the main areas where these ceremonials were staged, however, gradually changed to reflect different understandings of imperial images and sovereignty.[24] For instance, the Ottomans embraced the idea of a more secluded sultan, although the degree of this seclusion fluctuated to accommodate contemporary conditions.[25] Earlier Ottoman rulers such as Bayezid I had embraced the practice of *dar al-'adl* where *mazalim* jurisdictions were practiced, but his successors ceased to lead such councils.[26] The gradual abandonment of this old Ayyubid practice was one more way in which the Ottoman regime found its own voice while formulating its sovereignty claims. Additionally, as suggested in Chapter 4, beginning with the reign of Mehmed II, the Ottomans began to incorporate the strength of their own dynastic system into their discourse.[27] The methods of Ottoman dynastic succession, particularly fratricide, had intrigued the Mamluks as early as Bayezid I's reign.[28] They also tried to legitimize their attacks on Anatolian Muslim powers by arguing that these principalities (such as the Karamanids) were preventing them from carrying out their warfare against the non-Muslims.[29]

Later in their diplomatic relationship, the Ottomans started to challenge the Mamluks' prestige by using the same tropes in new ways. Rather than explaining or justifying their practice of fratricide, they began to assert the superiority of their dynastic practices.[30] Although dynastic succession had always been an important factor in Islamic sovereignty claims, it became even more important as this world expanded geographically. Many emerging local rulers did not have any affiliation with the caliphate or the Prophet's descendants, and the maintenance of political authority in a single family's hand for successive generations emerged as an important achievement. Within this new context, the Ottoman dynasty seemed successful, and even as it went through multiple succession crises among its family members, the authority of this particular family was never contested. As the descendants of successive Muslim rulers, Ottoman sultans were also able to claim priority in conversion, a powerful trope that had been previously used by Timur against the Mamluk sultans, most of whom were not born Muslims.[31] In response to these claims to authority, the Mamluks occasionally asserted the meritocratic nature of their succession system and derided the ignorance of the Ottomans in matters of religion.

As the Ottomans began to recast their succession practices in a positive light, it is equally telling that, towards the end of this period, it was the Mamluk sultans who felt the need to explain their methods of succession. In the cases of Jaqmaq and Qansuh al-Zahir, these new rulers, after eliminating the sons of their predecessors, found themselves writing letters to legitimize their actions. For example, in a letter from Jaqmaq to Murad II, the new Mamluk sultan underscored the fact that he had taken power after a quasi-election by the caliph and the leading Mamluk commanders.[32] This so-called system of election was one of the recurrent motifs that the Mamluks employed to strengthen their claims to sovereignty.[33] While no sources mentioned any negative reaction from Murad II, later narrative accounts gave a different picture when Qansuh al-Zahir took the Mamluk throne. While the actual correspondence between the Ottoman sultan Bayezid and the Mamluk sultan Qansuh al-Zahir has not been found, other sources implied that Bayezid did not welcome the enthronement of Qansuh al-Zahir, who came to power by eliminating al-Nasir Muhammad, the son of Sultan Qaytbay.[34]

As indispensable agents of diplomatic communication, envoys shouldered many responsibilities: they delivered messages and gifts, they represented their rulers, and they were often entrusted with confidential matters. Envoys bore witness to processions and celebrations that reflected the image the hosting ruler wanted to present, and at times even triggered hostility between sovereigns when they reported the nature of their treatment abroad. Like most political leaders, both the Ottoman and Mamluk rulers were aware of the rich potential that ambassadors offered and selected them carefully. The social and occupational standings of envoys were often intertwined with the messages they carried, and both regimes increasingly began to select representatives from the *mamluk* or *devşirme* class as opposed to the members of the learned class. Although internal politics might have influenced this shift, both regimes also used ambassadorial selection to tout their diverse yet equally efficient recruitment systems.

Gifts were not exchanged merely to fulfill the rule of reciprocity, but also to communicate messages. Their selections reinforced important tropes, served as a means of indirect communication, and occasionally rendered additional or mixed messages. The mostly Ottoman gesture of sending slaves or prisoners of war as gifts not only bolstered the trope of Ottoman involvement in *ghaza* and *jihad* along the frontiers of Islam, but also showcased the rich economic resources of the Ottoman regime. Likewise, sending alms or pious endowments to the Sacred Shrines implied the Ottoman desire to participate in the highly valued religious discourse among Muslim sovereigns. In short, diplomatic gifts, with their almost endless capacity to convey a breadth of messages, enriched the communication between rulers.

The evidence in this book exemplifies how much we can learn about the richness of the Ottoman–Mamluk relationship by looking at these diplomatic encounters. While the Ottoman conquest of Egypt does occupy a legitimate place in Ottoman–Mamluk studies, we should revise our approach to the earlier phases of this diplomatic relationship, which were equally active and complex.[35] In every period, image-building was important and intense, and the writers of this time, without the benefit of foresight, did not consider these years calm or uneventful. Due to Murad II's efforts to amplify the Ottoman image at the Mamluk court during a "peaceful" period, a substantial promotion in Ottoman titulature occurred. Ironically, the significant role that the Mamluk administration played in Ottoman political culture and its ideological world was almost completely forgotten after the Ottomans ended the Mamluk regime.

Indirect Diplomacy and Communication

This study does not fully explore the rich texture that lay behind the façade of official contacts. While it attempts to incorporate the accounts of ambassadors and captivity narratives as components of these Ottoman–Mamluk exchanges, it cannot address informal ties through commercial networks, among pilgrims and mystics that roamed in search of a spiritual master, or among travelling students and scholars that sought intellectual connections. Neither does it adequately analyze the influence of scholars that were trained in Mamluk lands yet built their careers in Ottoman institutions (or vice versa). A significant portion of Ottoman–Mamluk relations were probably hidden in the stories of individuals, from envoys to merchants, who circulated between these two lands and whose experiences might have indirectly contributed to the history of this relationship.

Neither does this work adequately treat the significance of patronage—another pillar of the image-building process—in the rivalry between the Ottoman and Mamluk sovereigns. The literary patronage of both Ottoman and Mamluk rulers particularly deserves further attention. Beyond its major political upheavals and geographical explorations, the fifteenth century also witnessed the simultaneous rise of Turkish-speaking military and ruling elites to the leadership of at least five major powers in the Islamic world: the Ottomans, Mamluks, Safavids, Mughals, and Uzbeks. While this observation does not ignore the existence of the primarily Arabic-speaking courts and dynasties in the rest of the Islamic world, it is remarkable that this vast region was ruled by Turkish-speaking courts.[36] Scholars, artists, and poets who wanted to benefit from the generosity of these potential new patrons started to produce works in their language, and the translation of classical literary works of Arabic and Persian literature and culture into different dialects of Turkish in Ottoman and Mamluk lands was a manifestation of this phenomenon.[37] By no means did this relatively new movement reduce the production of works in Arabic or Persian in any of these courts, but they did increase the variety of literary, scholarly, and artistic patronage.[38] The question of what these Turkish productions meant or signified for these rulers' imperial ideologies or their representations both to the domestic and foreign audiences deserves separate study. In addition to contributing to the study of the phenomenon called "the rise of empires," the story of the Ottoman–Mamluk rivalry should also find its place within the history of literary patronage. For historians, it is encouraging to note that the expansive horizons of Ottoman–Mamluk studies have not yet been exhausted.

APPENDICES

APPENDIX I: THE ANATOMY OF A TYPICAL LETTER (DIACRITICALS ARE USED)[1]

1. Introductory protocol (*iftitāh* or *fawātih*): The order of the following sub-sections can vary.
   a. *l'invocatio:* Formulas referring to and praying to God. This section also has sub-sections that are not included here.
   b. *l'intitulatio:* This section and the next reveal the identity of both the sender and the recipient. The identities and the mutual hierarchies of the sender and the recipient are expressed through titulature, which consists of *laqab* and *na't*. For the main and secondary *laqab* (which are generally rendered as titles in this study), see Appendix II. *Laqab*s are generally followed by adjectives that refer to the person's position or function (*mawlawī, amirī*, etc.). They are followed by composed appellations such as *Rukn al-Islām wa al-Muslimīn*.
   c. *l'inscriptio:* See above.
   d. *la salutation:* A formula greeting the recipient.
2. Text (*matn*).
   a. *l'expositio* (or *l'narratio*): This sub-section announces the reason for the diplomatic visit.

b. *Le disposition:* This sub-section concludes this section and often suggests solutions or desired results for the visit.
3. Final protocol (*iḫtitām* or *ḫawātim*): Has multiple sub-sections such as final prayers and the date.

APPENDIX II: TITULATURE (DIACRITICALS ARE USED)

Main and Secondary Titles (Alqāb Makāniyya and Alqāb Mufarraʻa) (listed in al-Qalqashandi's order)	al-ʻUmari (d.1348)	Ibn Nazir al-Jaysh (completed his manual in 1376)	Al-Qalqashandi (completed his manual in 1411–12)	Al-Sahmawi (probably completed his work during Barsbay or Jaqmaq's time) (d.1464)
Al-Jānib (?)			The Abbasid caliph in Cairo	This title does not exist
Al-Maqām (His Station)			The Mamluk rulers (varies) (also for the Ilkhanid rulers)	The Mamluk rulers
With a secondary title: Al-Maqām al-Ashraf				The Bahmanid rulers of India
				The Timurid rulers (an example from Faraj to Timur)
Al-Maqarr (His Residence)	The Germiyanids	The Germiyanids (but questions)	The Ottomans but from a Mamluk governor to the Ottoman ruler	The Ottomans (with al-Karīm)
With a secondary title: Al-Maqarr al-Karīm				
Al-Maqarr al-ʻĀli				

Appendix II

Al-Janāb (His Honor)	The Ottomans		
Al-Majlis al-Sāmiyy (His Lofty Seat)	The Ottomans	The Ottomans but he questions it	
Majlis			
Al-Ḥaḍra		A very prestigious title in earlier centuries. Used to address the caliphs or the Mongol Khans.[1] Gradually lost its prestige	The rulers of Bornu
		With no "al," for low-ranking officials, scribes, and scholars	

APPENDIX III: MISSIONS AND ENVOYS[1]

Note

In entries with multiple ambassadors, the ambassadors' names are numbered chronologically.

Dates	Ottoman	Mamluk	Purpose/details	Source
Shawwal 767/June 1366[2]	>		To pledge assistance to the Mamluks in their campaign against Cyprus.	Al-'Ayni, *'Iqd al-Jumān*, Süleymaniye Carullah 1591, 548a. Al-Maqrizi, *Kitab al-Suluk*, 3:121. Ibn Iyas, 2:33, 38.
773/1371	>	∨	To attend the circumcision festival for Prince Bayezid and Prince Yakub, the two sons of Murad I. (According to Hadidi, this festival took place right after the battle of Sırpsındığı.)	For the claim that a Mamluk ambassador brought valuable gifts for this celebration, see Hadidi, *Tevârîh-i Âl-i Osman*, ed. Öztürk, pp. 90–2. For the date of the circumcision, see Hadidi, pp. 90–2; Müneccimbaşı, *Jami' al-Duwal*, Süleymaniye Esad Efendi 2103, 688a. For an alternative dating (767), see Uruç, ed. Öztürk, 26; Mustafa Âli, *Künhü'l-Ahbâr*, TTK, 2009, 25b.

Dates	Ottoman	Mamluk	Purpose/details	Source
783/1381–2		✓	To attend the wedding of Prince Bayezid (the future Bayezid I) with the Germiyanid Princess.	Aşıkpaşazade, ed. Giese, pp. 52–5. Müneccimbaşı, *Jami'*, 688b. Neşri, ed. Unat and Köymen, 1:205–9. Neşri, ed. Öztürk, pp. 94–6.
787/1385–6		✓	To congratulate Murad I for his military success in Macedonia and Albania. This mission preceded his campaign against the Karamanids in the spring of 788/1386. A unique copy of Neşri's chronicle records that the Mamluk sultan Barquq, after hearing of Murad's plans to campaign against the Karamanids, requested the legal opinions of four Mamluk judges. (According to Müneccimbaşı, it was Murad who solicited the legal opinion.)	Neşri, ed. Unat and Köymen, 1:217–19. Neşri, ed. Öztürk, pp. 100–1. For the claim that Barquq solicited legal opinions about the Karamanids, Neşri, ed. Öztürk, p. 101n1258. For the claim that Murad solicited legal opinions against the Karamanids, Müneccimbaşı, *Jami'*, 687a–b. For the historical context, see Uzunçarşılı, "Murad I"; İnalcık, "Murad I."

		The four judges decided that it was legitimate to fight against the Karamanids. This report needs further investigation; the chronicler (or a copyist) may have confused a similar incident that took place during Murad II's reign. See below for this event in Murad II's reign.	Neşri, ed. Unat and Köymen, 1:239.
788/1386 or 790/1388	Yazıcı Salih	Probably to respond to the previous Mamluk envoy or to announce Murad's 1387 victory against the Karamanids in the battle of Konya. It may have invited the Mamluk sultan to the circumcision festival of Bayezid's three sons. During these years, the Ottoman and Mamluk rulers may have been discussing a possible alliance against the Karamanids.	Neşri, ed. Öztürk, p. 109. Bursalı Mehmed Tahir, *Osmanlı Müellifleri*, 1:195, 3:307–9.

Dates	Ottoman	Mamluk	Purpose/details	Source
Was given an audience on 10 Safar 790/February 19, 1388.	>		Ottoman ambassadors presented gifts to the Mamluk sultan. Their gifts were accepted and reciprocated.	Ibn al-Furat, *Tarikh*, 9:24. Ibn Hajar, *Inba'*, ed. Habashi, 1:349. Ibn Iyas, 2:390.
JA (Jumada al-akhira) 791/June 1389			Sources do not explain their reason for coming. Bayezid I came to power.	
After Murad's death in JA 791/June 1389		∨	The Mamluk sultan Barquq endowed a copy of the Qur'an among other things to the mausoleum of Murad I when the Ottoman ruler died.[3]	Uzunçarşılı, "Murad I," p. 595. See Karatay, *Topkapı Sarayı Müzesi Kütüphanesi Arapça Yazmalar Kataloğu* (Istanbul: Topkapı Sarayı Müzesi, 1962), vol.1, # 168.
6 Shawwal 793/ September 6, 1391 (the date on the letter)		Sa'd al-din Sa'd Allah al-Baridi	Barquq sent this letter to discuss the release of some Muslim merchants who were captured by Genoese ships.	Feridun, 1274, 1:116–17. In this and in the following letter, the titulature is mixed.

⟩		To thank Barquq for his previous intervention and additionally to ask for the release of two Ottoman merchants who were being kept in Mamluk prisons.	Feridun, 1274, 1:117–18.
Appointed as an ambassador in Muharram-Safar 794/December 1392. Departed in ZH (Dhu al-Hijja) 794/ October 1392.	1 ⟩ Amir Husam al-din Hasan al-Kujkuni	To secure peace between the Karamanids, the Ottomans, and Qadi Burhan al-din, the ruler of Sivas.[4] In the previous year, Bayezid had captured the frontier town of Kayseri, which was under Karamanid authority yet close to the Mamluk-Syrian frontier. According to Mamluk sources, al-Kujkuni successfully completed his mission.	For Bayezid's attacks on Qadi Burhan al-din's and Karamanid lands, see Neşri, ed. Öztürk, 145. Ibn al-Furat, *Tarikh*, 9:313, 339, 347. Ibn Hajar, *Inba'*, ed. Habashi, 1:434, 439, 453. Ibn Qadi Shuhbah, *Tarikh Ibn Qadi Shuhbah*, 1:424, 471, 476, 4:43.

Dates	Ottoman	Mamluk	Purpose/details	Source
The news of al-Kujkuni's return arrived in Cairo in Ramadan 795/July 1393.			When al-Kujkuni returned to Cairo, he was accompanied by an Ottoman ambassador. The Ottoman envoy may have also brought a request for investiture.	Al-Maqrizi, *Durar*, ed. Jalili, 1:451–2. Al-Maqrizi, *Kitab al-Suluk*, 3/2:790. Ibn Bahadur, 23b-24a.
Returned to Cairo in ZQ (Dhu al-Qada) 795/September 1393.			For Ibn al-Sughayr who accompanied Amir al-Kujkuni, see p. 51, 79.[5]	For a different chronology, see Ibn Iyas, 1:462.[6]
JU (Jumada al-awwal)-Rajab 796/March–May 1394	1 >	v	To bring an offer of alliance from Bayezid against Timur. Barquq responded to this offer positively.	Ibn al-Furat, *Tarikh*, 9:382. Ibn Hajar, *Inba'*, ed. Habashi, 1:471. Al-Maqrizi, *Kitab al-Suluk*, 3/2:813.
Shawwal 796/July 1394	>		To bring Bayezid's message that he was ready to send aid to the Mamluk sultan. Interestingly, the next entry in Ibn al-Furat's account reports the arrival of Qadi Burhan al-Din's envoy, who brought a similar invitation for alliance.	Ibn al-Furat, *Tarikh*, 9:386. Ibn Taghribirdi, *Nujum*, trans. Popper, 13:148.

ZH 898/September 1396			The battle of Nicopolis.	For the first arrival of the news to Mamluk lands, see Ibn al-Furat, *Tarikh*, 9:456, 465–66. Ibn Qadi Shuhbah, *Tarikh*, 1:583.
798/1395–6	2 >	Kadı Zeyneddin Sefer Şah b. Abdullah al-Rumi (who died on his way to Cairo)[7]	To build an alliance against Timur.	Al-'Ayni, *'Iqd al-Juman*, 614a–b. Al-Maqrizi, *Kitab al-Suluk*, 3/2:873.
Tulu returned to Cairo in Safar or 19 Ra I (Rabi al-awwal) 799/ November or December 21, 1396.	<1	Amir Tulu min 'Ali Shah	In addition to his diplomatic mission, Amir Tulu was also possibly instructed to see Ibn al-Jazari, who had fled to Ottoman lands the year before. On his return to Cairo, Amir Tulu also brought the news of the Nicopolis battle and generous gifts from Bayezid.	Ibn Hajar, *Inba'*, ed. Habashi, 1:525. For Ibn al-Jazari's escape to Ottoman lands, see Ibn Hajar, *Inba'*, ed. Habashi, p. 510.
Arrived to Bulaq on 23 Sha'ban 799/ May 22, 1397 and then to Cairo on 11 Ramadan 799/ June 8, 1397.	>		To announce the battle of Nicopolis. The mission first reached to the coast of Bulaq and was welcomed by officers from Cairo. It brought at least 60 prisoners of war.	Al-'Ayni, *'Iqd al-Juman*, 615b. Al-Maqrizi, *Kitab al-Suluk*, 3/2:879. Ibn Hajar, *Inba'*, ed. Habashi, 1:525.

Dates	Ottoman	Mamluk	Purpose/details	Source
(The news of this victory had reached Cairo in Safar-Ra I 799/November–December 1396)			(Piloti suggests 200), including a prominent Hungarian knight called Hoder (or Koder), as gifts.	Ibn Iyas, 2:490. Piloti, *Traité*, p. 229.
			Ibn Iyas mentions the arrival of an Ottoman envoy at that time, but claims that the envoy came to announce Timur's arrival in Erzincan.	Johannes Schiltberger, *Als Sklave im Osmanischen Reich*, pp. 50–1.
15 Shawwal 801/ June 20, 1399			Sultan Barquq died and was succeeded by his son Faraj.	
Shawwal-ZH 801/ July–August 1399	1 >	<2	To request Malatya. The new Mamluk sultan Faraj rejected this request.	Johannes Schiltberger, *Als Sklave im Osmanischen Reich*, pp. 74–5. Ibn Hajar, *Inba'*, ed. Habashi, 2:55. Ibn Taghribirdi, *Nujum*, trans. Popper, 14:5, 8. Al-'Ayni, *'Iqd al-Juman*, 645b.

ZH 801/August 1399		In August 1399, news about the fall of Malatya to the Ottomans reached Cairo. Bayezid took Malatya and Elbistan and besieged Darende.	See the sources in previous entry.
Was given an audience on 20 ZH 803 (15–16 ZH 803)/ August 1, 1401	Emir Ahmed (?)	To repair diplomatic relations in the aftermath of the Ottoman attack on Malatya and to build an alliance against Timur.	Al-Maqrizi, *Kitab al-Suluk*, 3/3:1069. Ibn Taghribirdi, *Nujum*, trans. Popper, 14:33–4. Ibn Iyas, 2:633.
		According to al-Maqrizi (and Ibn Iyas), the Ottoman ambassador brought various gifts—including slaves, textiles, horses and silver objects—for the sultan and his commanders.	For the name of the ambassador, see Yınanç, "Bayezid I," p. 382; Ibn al-Sayrafi, *Nuzhat al-Nufus wa-al-abdan fi Tawarikh al-Zaman*, ed. Hasan Habashi (Cairo, 1970–94), 2:118.
		He does not mention the purpose of the gifts while Ibn Taghribirdi states that the ambassador offered reconciliation and alliance against Timur—an offer that the Mamluk administration did not accept.	
27 ZH 804/July 28, 1402		The Battle of Ankara.	

Dates	Ottoman	Mamluk	Purpose/details	Source
25 Ra I 808–5 JA 808/September 20, 1405–November 28, 1405			Faraj was replaced by his brother al-Malik al-Mansur. 'Abd al-'Aziz for 70 days.	
The correspondence was probably composed between 808/1405–6 and 813/1410–11[8]	1 >	<2	This partially surviving Mamluk correspondence is a response to an earlier letter from Bayezid's son Süleyman. In the letter, the Mamluk sultan both lists and offers thanks for Süleyman's gifts.	BNF MS 4440, 50b-51a.
25 Muharram 815/ May 7, 1412			Faraj was deposed for a second time and later executed on 16 Safar 815/May 28, 1412.	J. Wansbrough, "Faradj," *EI*[2], 2:781.
Sha'ban 815/ November 1412			Sultan al-Mu'ayyad Shaykh came to power.	P.M. Holt, "Al-Mu'ayyad Shaykh," p. 721.
5 Ra II (Rabi al-akhar) 816/July 5, 1413			Mehmed I came to power, possibly in Edirne.	İnalcık, "Mehmed I," pp. 391–2.

ZH 817/February 1415	Kıvam al-melik ve al-din, the judge of İnegöl		To acknowledge al-Mu'ayyad Shaykh's accession to power. The Ottoman letter, which was composed in İnegöl, includes a list of Ottoman gifts (various types of textiles).	Feridun, 1274, 1:145. Ibn Taghribirdi, *Nujum*, trans. Popper, 17:29. Ibn Hajar, *Inba'*, ed. Habashi, 3:55.
			İnalcık claims that Mehmed I sent this mission just before his Karamanid campaign. However, in ZH 817-Muharram 818/ February–April 1415, the news of Mehmed's victory over the Karamanids had already reached Cairo. This mission may have brought the news of victory.	For the Mamluk awareness of the Ottoman success against the Karamanids, see al-Maqrizi, *Kitab al-Suluk*, 4/1:299. İnalcık, "Mehmed I," pp. 391–2.
Sha'ban 818/ October 1415		Qurtbay al-Khas-saki	To respond to the previous Ottoman ambassador. This exchange should be evaluated within the context of both rulers' military maneuvers in Anatolia, but particularly al-Mu'ayyad Shaykh's campaigns in Syria and southern Anatolia.	Feridun, 1274, 1:145–6.

Dates	Ottoman	Mamluk	Purpose/details	Source
The Ottoman mission arrived in Cairo on 5 Sha'ban 819/September 28, 1416, with a letter composed on 16 Safar 819/April 15, 1416	2> Tursan Bey (or Turasan or Turahan)	<1 Rustam al-Mu'ayyadi al-Khassaki (the name is from the Ottoman letter)	To respond to a preceding Mamluk embassy headed by Amir Rustam.	For the date when the Ottoman letter was composed and when it arrived in Cairo, see Ibn al-Hijja, *Qahwat*, ed. Veselý, pp. 178–83.
		<3 An undated Mamluk response	According to Ibn Hajar, the Ottoman ambassador was given a generous reception in Cairo and hosted in *Dar al-Ziyafa*. The valuable gifts the ambassador brought were sold and the revenue was spent on the construction of Sultan al-Mu'ayyad Shaykh's complex. Later, the Ottoman ambassador was hosted in a special banquet where ambassadors of other rulers were present.	Ibn Hajar, *Inba'*, ed. Habashi, 3:98. Al-Maqrizi, *Kitab al-Suluk*, 4/1:366, 385 (mistakenly identified as the ambassador of Süleyman ibn Osman, instead of Mehmed)
Probably hosted in a special banquet on 4 Safar 820/March 23, 1417				For the undated response of al-Mu'ayyad Shaykh, see Ibn al-Hijja, *Qahwat*, ed. Veselý, pp. 183–7. It must have been composed after September–October 1416.
			Al-Mu'ayyad Shaykh responded to this mission with a letter.	Ibn Bahadur, 37b.
Departed between Safar-Ra I 820/March–May 1417			According to Ibn Taghribirdi, when al-Mu'ayyad Shaykh left	For the details concerning the departure of Turasan Bey, see Ibn Hajar, *Inba'*, ed. Habashi, 3:127; Ibn Taghribirdi, *Nujum*, trans. Popper, 17:42–3.

Cairo for a campaign to the north in Safar 820/March 1417, he took Qaraqoyunlu, Aqqoyunlu, Ramazanid, and Ottoman dignitaries with him. The Ottoman dignitary may have been Turasan Bey. It is likely that the ambassadors were allowed to return on their own at some point, probably before 2 Ra II 820/May 18, 1417. (For another Ottoman mission that arrived on this date, see below).

The Mamluk sultan also sent an ambassador from Damascus to the Karamanids on 8 Ra I 820/April 25, 1417.

Dates	Ottoman	Mamluk	Purpose/details	Source
Arrived on 2 Ra II 820/May 19, 1417	>		When al-Mu'ayyad Shaykh was still on his campaign in Amik (or according to al-Maqrizi, in Kayseri), an Ottoman ambassador visited his encampment.	Al-Maqrizi, *Kitab al-Suluk*, 4/1:403 (again mistakenly identified as the ambassador of Süleyman, instead of Mehmed).
			No details of the meeting are known. Four months later, however, al-Mu'ayyad Shaykh received the news that Mehmed I had captured the Karamanid capital along with the Karamanid ruler Mehmed Bey and his son Mustafa (see the next entry). Mehmed may have informed al-Mu'ayyad Shaykh about his plans to attack the Karamanid territory with this embassy.	Ibn Hajar, *Inba'*, ed. Habashi, 3:128, 133. Ibn Bahadur, 38b.
Arrived in Aleppo on 8 Sha'ban 820/ September 20, 1417	>		To inform that Mehmed successfully captured the Karamanid ruler and his son and established his authority in Karaman lands.	Al-Maqrizi, *Kitab al-Suluk*, 4/1:416 (again mistakenly identified as the ambassador of Süleyman, instead of Mehmed).

APPENDIX III

Arrived in Cairo on 7 Safar 823/ February 22, 1420 with a letter dated 4 Shawwal 822/ October 24, 1419	Hacı (al-Hajj) Hayreddin Halil Bey	To announce Mehmed I's campaign against the prince of Wallachia (Mircea) and conquering the castle of Giurgiu (822/1419–20). According to al-'Ayni, the Ottoman ambassador offered the Mamluk sultan 30 slaves, many hunting birds, and silk textiles, among other gifts. The Mamluk officers gave the embassy particular care and attention during a special ceremony.	Feridun, 1274, 1:164–5. Al-'Ayni, *'Iqd al-Juman*, 759b. Al-Maqrizi, *Kitab al-Suluk*, 4/1:522. Ibn Hajar, *Inba'*, ed. Habashi, 3:212. Ibn al-Sayrafi, *Nuzhat al-Nufus*, 2:466.
Was given an audience on 25 Safar 823/March 11, 1420 (Ibn Hajar dates the event to Muharram 823/January–February 1420)			
Assigned as the ambassador in Muharram 823/ January–February 1420, left on 23 (?)	Qachqar al-Chaghatay	To announce the Mamluk sultan's eldest son's successful campaign against the Karamanid ruler Mehmed Bey. The Mamluk sultan ordered the composition of a letter to the	Ibn al-Hijja, *Qahwat*, ed. Veselý, pp. 287–90. Al-Maqrizi, *Kitab al-Suluk*, 4/1:519; and for the stay and departure of Molla Fenari, see ibid., p. 525.

Dates	Ottoman	Mamluk	Purpose/details	Source
Ra I 823/April 7, 1420 with the previous Ottoman convoy (see above) and Molla Fenari, who was returning to Bursa from his pilgrimage			Ottoman sultan announcing victory and describing how he received the Karamanid sovereign as his captive from his Mamluk vassal, the Dulkadirid ruler. This letter is the last one that was composed for the Ottomans during al-Mu'ayyad Shaykh's reign.	Ibn Hajar, *Inbaʾ*, ed. Habashi, 3:197, 212, 216–17.
8 Muharram 824/ January 13, 1421		∨	The Mamluk sultan al-Muʾayyad Shaykh died.	
The letter was composed on 27 Safar 824/March 3, 1421			To congratulate Mehmed for his recent success in the Balkans. This letter was sent by al-Muʾayyad Shaykh's son Ahmad. It arrived after the death of Mehmed I. Although it mentions Hayreddin Halil Bey's mission, the mission of this particular Ottoman ambassador had been responded to before with Qachqar al-Chaghatay's mission.	Feridun, 1274, 1:165–6.

23 JA 824/June 25, 1421	Mehmed I who was often addressed in Mamluk sources as *Ghiyath al-din Abu al-Fath* died and Murad II came to power in Bursa. The news of Mehmed's death reached Cairo in Rajab 824/July 1421.	İnalcık, "Murad II," *DİA*, 31:164. Al-Maqrizi, *Kitab al-Suluk*, 4/2:599.
8 Ra II 825/ April 1, 1422	Sultan Barsbay came to power. His accession was recorded by the Ottoman chronicler Neşri.	Neşri, ed. Öztürk, p. 257.
Among the events of 825/1421–2	Although al-Maqrizi does not mention any diplomatic missions in these years, he, in a surprisingly detailed and accurate manner, recounts the struggle of Murad II with his uncle Mustafa (executed in the winter of 1422) and Murad's siege of Constantinople.	Al-Maqrizi, *Kitab al-Suluk*, 4/2:624–5. İnalcık, "Murad II," *İA*, 8:599–601.

Dates	Ottoman	Mamluk	Purpose/details	Source
Ra II 826/March–April 1423			Al-Maqrizi recounts the battle of Nicea between Murad and his younger brother Mustafa, the capture and execution of Mustafa. See the Ottoman mission that arrived on 26 Muharram 827/December 30, 1423.	Al-Maqrizi, *Kitab al-Suluk*, 4/2:634. İnalcık, "Murad II," *İA*, 8:601.
7 Sha'ban 826/July 16, 1423–25 Ra II 841/October 26, 1437	?	?	The news that Amir Janibak, Barsbay's prime competitor, escaped from prison in Alexandria reached Cairo on this date. Until his beheading on 25 Ra II 841/October 26, 1437 in Diyarbakır, Janibak remained a constant threat against Barsbay's authority. Janibak sought refuge in the court of the Ottoman sultan Murad II, among others, during his long opposition. Although no correspondence between Barsbay and Murad about Janibak has survived, it is likely that such an exchange took place.	For a primary source account treating Janibak's incident, see Ibn Taghribirdi, *Nujum*, trans. Popper, p. 18. Al-Maqrizi, *Kitab al-Suluk*, 4/2:639.

27 Sha'ban 826/ July 25, 1424	>	It is not clear if this group was a diplomatic mission or a group intended to complete their pilgrimage and bring gifts from Murad II.	Ibn al-Sayrafi, *Nuzhat al-Nufus*, 3:28.
		Barsbay also responded them with gifts for Murad.	Muhanna, "New Clothes," p. 191.
Arrived on 26 Muharram 827/ December 30, 1423	>	To deliver rich and extensive gifts to the Mamluk sultan from Murad II.	Ibn Bahadur, 46b.
			Al-Maqrizi, *Kitab al-Suluk*, 4/2:656.
		Sources do not reveal the purpose of the mission. Immediately after this entry in his account, Ibn Bahadur reports that Murad killed his brother Mustafa. Perhaps Murad felt the need to explain his dynastic politics.	For this particular instance of fratricide, see İnalcık, "Murad II," *DİA*, 31:165–6.
Given an audience on 17 Ramadan 829/July 23, 1426	>	To deliver lavish presents from Murad II. A special gathering (*iwan*) was convened in the	Al-'Ayni, *'Iqd al-Juman*, 789a.
			Ibn Bahadur, 48b.

Dates	Ottoman	Mamluk	Purpose/details	Source
Was still present in the city when the king of Cyprus was brought to Cairo on 8 Shawwal 829/ August 12, 1426			Ottoman ambassador's honor. Gifts included nine slaves, a substantial amount of textiles, and furs. While this mission was in Cairo, the victorious Mamluk expedition came back from Cyprus. Janus, the King of Cyprus (1375–1432), was captured and brought to Cairo. When the prisoners were paraded through the streets of Cairo, the Ottoman envoy, along with other foreign dignitaries, witnessed the triumphant procession.	Ibn Hajar, *Inba'*, ed. Habashi, 3:369–70. Ibn Taghribirdi, *Nujum*, trans. Popper, 18:41–3. Al-Maqrizi, *Kitab al-Suluk*, 4/2:624–5.
Shawwal 830/ August 1427			The news of Murad's successful campaigns in Serbian and Hungarian lands arrived.	Al-Maqrizi, *Kitab al-Suluk*, 4/2:747–8. İnalcık, "Murad II," *İA*, 8:602.
Returned to Cairo on 2 Ra I 831/ December 21, 1427(?)[9]		Taghribirdi al-Hijazi al-Khas-saki al-Ashrafi	Apparently, the Mamluk sultan received information about a unified Crusader (?) attack on the Ottomans and offered an alliance to Murad II. Actually, by the time this envoy reached Murad II, his army had been defeated.	Al-'Ayni, *'Iqd al-Juman*, 793b. Ibn al-Sayrafi, *Nuzhat al-Nufus*, 3:128–9. Feridun, 1274, 1:195–7.

Appendix III

		This ambassador was well-treated by Murad II who honored the ambassador with garments from his own wardrobe.	Muhanna, "New Clothes," p. 191.
Arrived in Cairo in late JA 831/April 1428	Hoca Cemaleddin ibn Hasan	He returned with Murad II's letter dated 10 ZH 831/ September 20, 1428 that announced the capture of Güvercinlik and the ongoing campaign in Hungarian and Serbian territories. In this letter, Murad first offers thanks for Taghribardi's message and then describes his conquests.	
		To announce officially the capture of Güvercinlik.	Ibn Bahadur, 52b.
			Ibn Hajar, *Inba'*, ed. Habashi, 3:402
Given an audience on 2 Rajab 831/ April 17, 1428		This mission was honored in an impressive ceremony with other missions. The Ottoman sultan's gifts to the Mamluk sultan included fifty slaves, hunting	Ibn Taghribirdi, *Nujum*, trans. Popper, 18:55. Al-Maqrizi, *Kitab al-Suluk*, 4/2:776–7 (slightly misinformed).

Dates	Ottoman	Mamluk	Purpose/details	Source
			birds, furs, and European silk textiles for *mahmal*.	Ibn al-Sayrafi, *Nuzhat al-Nufus*, 3:131–2.
			(According to Ibn Hajar and Ibn Bahadur, the Ottoman ambassadors came to request permission for pilgrimage.)	Feridun, 1274, 1:197–8. (Mistitled as the Mamluk letter to the Ottoman court)
Two undated letters that were possibly exchanged in 831–2/1428–9	2> Saadeddin Ağa (only mentioned in Barsbay's response)	<1 Aqbugha Bey (only mentioned in Murad's letter)	Murad II returned this Mamluk ambassador with a letter describing how the Hungarian King Sigismund (1368–1437) had besieged Güvercinlik after the Ottomans had previously conquered it, and how Murad had recaptured the beleaguered city for a second time.	For Murad's letter, see Feridun, 1274, 1:201–2. For Barsbay's response, see Feridun, 1274, 1:202–3.
An undated Ottoman letter, tentatively dated 832–3/1428–30		Badr al-din Hashim (only mentioned in the Ottoman letter)	Tentatively, this text is considered to be the Ottoman response to a previous Mamluk letter that had been brought to Murad II by Amir Badr al-din Hashim.	BNF MS 4440, 42b–44a.

| Ra II 833/January 1430 | The letter discusses the Aqqoyunlu ruler 'Uthman ibn Qara Yuluk and his captured son, who the Ottomans sent back with this letter. According to this letter, this son was captured in Ruha. It also possibly refers to Habil bin 'Uthman, who was captured during the Mamluk siege of Amid in Shawwal 832/July 1429. Habil died in Rajab 832/April 1430 in a Mamluk prison despite his father's repeated attempts to save him.

However, Dr. Dekkiche, whose dissertation is on BNF MS 4440, raises some doubts about the recipient of this particular letter.

Both al-Maqrizi and Ibn Taghribirdi mention the arrival of news about the plague in Bursa | Ibn Taghribirdi, *Nujum*, trans. Popper, 18:69. |

Dates	Ottoman	Mamluk	Purpose/details	Source
Arrived in JU 833/ January–February 1430	1>	<2	in Ra II 833/January 1430. It is not clear, however, if this news came with a diplomatic mission (see below) or through other channels.	Al-Maqrizi, *Kitab al-Suluk*, 4/2:821–2.
Was present in the citadel, along with Qaraqoyunlu ambassadors, on 8 JU 833/February 2, 1430	Imaddedin Ivaz Bey (according to the letter in Feridun's collection)		To inform the Mamluk sultan Barsbay that Murad had signed a three-year truce with the "Franks." In Feridun's collection, two undated letters that were exchanged between Murad and Barsbay indeed deal with the truce that the Ottoman sultan signed with the Hungarians (İnalcık dates this truce to 831/1427–8).	Al-Maqrizi, *Kitab al-Suluk*, 4/2:823. Al-'Ayni, *'Iqd al-Juman*, 799b. Ibn Bahadur, 57a–b. Ibn Taghribirdi, *Nujum*, trans. Popper, 18:69. For undated letters, see Feridun, 1274, 1:203–5, 205–6. For the historical context surrounding the treaty, see İnalcık, "Murad II," *İA*, 6:803.
Probably arrived in Cairo on 29 Ra I 834/December 15, 1430	Emir Bedreddin Mahmud Bey		To announce the conquest of Thessalonica (5 Rajab 833/ March 30, 1430) and the suppression of Gjon Kastrioti's uprising in	Feridun, 1274, 1:198–200 (the undated letter mistakenly gives 5 Rajab 832—instead of 833—for the conquest of Thessalonica.)

Appendix III

Was given an audience in early Ra II 834/late December 1430		Kruje. Murad II also offers condolences for the death of Muhammad ibn Barsbay, Sultan Barsbay's eldest son who succumbed to plague on 26 JA 833/ March 22, 1430.	For the arrival of the Ottoman mission with splendid gifts, see al-ʿAyni, *ʿIqd al-Jumān*, 803b (especially for gifts). Ibn Bahadur, 61a. For the death of the Mamluk prince, see Ibn Hajar, *Inbāʾ*, ed. Habashi, 3:449.
Barsbay's letter was dated 12 Safar 837/ September 28, 1433	1> Cemaleddin Yahya (from Barsbay's letter)	To announce Barsbay's campaign to Aqqoyunlu territory. This letter also congratulates Murad for his success against the Hungarians. According to the letter, Barsbay returned from Amid to Cairo on 1 Muharram 837/August 18, 1433, which correlates with the Mamluk narratives of this Aqqoyunlu campaign. This letter is the first correspondence in which Barsbay addresses Murad II with *al-Maqarr al-Karīm*.	BNF MS 4440, 45b–47b. (In the manuscript, this letter is mistitled as Murad's letter to Barsbay. In fact, it is Barsbay's response to Murad's previous embassy headed by Cemaleddin Yahya.) For the Ottoman recognition of this Mamluk military campaign, see Neşri, ed. Öztürk, p. 288.

Dates	Ottoman	Mamluk	Purpose/details	Source
839/1435–6		✓	Barsbay sent a letter to request Murad II's support against the Timurid sovereign Shah Rukh.	Ibn Bahadur, 84b. For the disagreement and the escalating tension over the *kiswa* between Barsbay and Shah Rukh, see Ibn Taghribirdi, *Nujum*, trans. Popper, 18:68–9, 90, 117–18, 120, 124, 133–4. Dekkiche, "Le Caire," 1:82–94.
Probably arrived in Cairo in JU 840/ November–December 1436 with a letter dated mid-Safar 840/early September 1436	Mevlana Hüsameddin (a judge of Bursa)		To ask for the Mamluk sultan's assistance with a legal issue. According to the letter, Hacı Ömer b. Halil (also known as al-Khatib), who was a prominent merchant from Gallipoli, died in Tripoli. Mevlana Hüsameddin, a judge, who was married to this merchant's daughter, brought Murad's letter, and needed the	Feridun, 1274, 1:206. For the arrival of an Ottoman mission with gifts, Ibn Hajar, *Inba'*, ed. Habashi, 4:43.

JU 840/ November–December 1436	>	Mamluk sultan's assistance in securing his deceased father-in-law's remaining goods and revenues.	Ibn al-Sayrafi, *Nuzhat al-Nufus*, 3:376.
		See the next entry. Ottoman ambassadors arrived with a letter and gifts. No explanation is given by the sources.	
		For possible reasons, see both the previous and next entry.	
ZQ 840/May 1437	?	The Mamluk sultan Barsbay married the Ottoman princess, who was a grandchild of Bayezid I. After this marriage, the Mamluks captured Janibak al-Sufi, who had taken refuge in Murad II's court. This overlap may not be coincidental. Murad and Barsbay may have come to an agreement, even though no reference to such an agreement has been discovered.	Ibn Bahadur, 89b. Ibn Iyas, 2:172. For the death of this princess, see Ibn Iyas, 2:329. For information about the arrival of these two siblings in Mamluk lands, see Ibn Hajar, *Inba'*, ed. Habashi, 4:39–42.

Dates	Ottoman	Mamluk	Purpose/details	Source
13 ZH 841/June 7, 1438			Sultan Barsbay died and his son al-Malik al-'Aziz Yusuf took his place.	Ibn Taghribirdi, *Nujum*, trans. Popper, 18:155.
Tentatively dated to 842/1438–9	1> Emir Şemseddin Ahmed (only mentioned in the Mamluk letter in Feridun's collection).	<2	To congratulate Murad's success in Albania (against Yuvan) and in the surrounding region of Thessalonica. The Mamluk sultan, who may have been Barsbay's son Yusuf (although Feridun's collection lists Barsbay as the sender of this letter), also expresses his satisfaction with the agreement between Aqqoyunlu Hamza Bey and Murad II.	Feridun, 1274, 1:200–1. For Hamza's first recognition as the Aqqoyunlu leader by Barsbay's son Yusuf in Muharram 842/July 1438, see Ibn Taghribirdi, *Nujum*, trans. Popper, 19:7.
20 Ra I 842/September 10, 1438			Sultan Jaqmaq replaced Yusuf.	Ibn Taghribirdi, *Nujum*, trans. Popper, 19:23–4.
Tentatively dated to JU 842/October-November 1438		Sayf al-din Asandamir al-Khassaki al-Zahiri	The Mamluk sultan sent this ambassador to the Ottomans to declare that he had assumed power after Barsbay's death. For the reference to the Mamluk gifts, see the letter and also pp. 102–4.	Feridun, 1274, 1:207–8.

Arrived probably in ZQ 843/April 1440 and was received on 21 ZQ 843/April 24, 1440	1> Veled Bey, who returned with the accompanying Mamluk ambassador (see the next column)	<2 Ahmad ibn Inal al-Yusufi Zahiri	To congratulate Jaqmaq for his accession and to announce the Ottoman conquest of Smederova on 16 Ra I 843/August 27, 1439. His gifts included textiles, various types of fur, and 30 slaves.	For the arrival and the gifts of the Ottoman ambassador, see Ibn al-Sayrafi, *Nuzhat al-Nufus*, 4:176, 177.
Jaqmaq's response letter was composed on 20 ZH 843/May 23, 1440			This embassy arrived when the Dulkadirid ruler Nasir al-din Mehmed Bey was also present in Cairo.	Ibn Iyas, 2:223. For the undated Ottoman letter, see Feridun, 1274, 1:208–12.
Departed on an unknown date after 20 ZH 843/May 23, 1440			Jaqmaq responded to this announcement by sending valuable gifts and a letter with the Ottoman ambassador Veled Bey and another Mamluk ambassador, Ahmad ibn Inal.	For two versions of Jaqmaq's response, see BNF MS 4440, 202b–205a and Feridun, 1274, 1:212–14. For the Mamluk gifts, see Muhanna, "New Clothes," pp. 192–3. For the conquest of Semendire, see İnalcık, "Murad II," *DİA*, 31:168.
1442			The Dulkadirid leader Nasir al-din Mehmed Bey died. His son Suleyman Bey succeeded him.	

Dates	Ottoman	Mamluk	Purpose/details	Source
848/1444, although it is possible that this event took place earlier	>		Before launching an expedition against the Karamanids, Murad asked for the legal opinion of Egyptian scholars, which may indicate that the Mamluk court gave its consent to the expedition.	Uzunçarşılı, "Karamanoğulları Devri Vesikalarından Ibrahim Bey'in Karaman Imareti Vakfiyesi," *Belleten* 1 (1937), Appendix. Boyacıoğlu, "Osmanoğullarının Karamanoğlu İbrahim Bey Aleyhine Aldığı Fetvalar," in *Pax Ottomana: Studies in memoriam of Nejat Göyünç* (Ankara, 2001), pp. 641–59. İnalcık, "Murad II," *DİA*, 31:169.
JU 848/August–September 1444			Murad II stepped down from power in favor of his young son Mehmed II.	İnalcık, "Murad II," *DİA*, 31:169–70.
28 Rajab 848/November 10, 1444			The battle of Varna	Ibn Taghrībirdī, *Nujum*, trans. Popper, 19:96–7.
Sha'ban 848/November–December 1444			Tension between Shahrukh and Jaqmaq escalated. Shahrukh sent *kiswa*, yet the Cairene people publicly condemned the gesture.	
16 Shawwal 848/January 25, 1445			According to Ibn Taghrībirdī, the news of Varna reached to Cairo.	Ibn Taghrībirdī, *Hawadith ad-Duhur*, trans. Popper and ed. Fischel, p. 9. Ibn Taghrībirdī, *Hawadith*, ed. Izz al-din, 1:110–11.

APPENDIX III

Arrived between late Shawwal 848 and early 849/1445 According to al-ʿAyni, arrived or was given an audience on 22 ZH 848/April 1, 1445 (or in early 849/1445, according to Ibn Hajar)	Azeb Bey	To carry the news of Varna to Cairo. In addition to other valuable gifts such as slaves, Murad sent numerous war prisoners in their steel outgear to Cairo. The Mamluk sultan gave a notable reception to this mission and the prisoners. Some victory announcements were sent in the name of Murad II, while some were sent in the name of Mehmed II.	For the victory proclamation that was sent to Cairo in the name of Mehmed II, see BNF MS 4434, 133b-139a. The title also says that it was prepared by Molla Hüsrev during the lifetime of Murad II. Neşri, ed. Öztürk, 297, p. 298n3698. Hadidi, pp. 212–13. Konstantin Mihailovic, p. 81. Ibn Bahadur, 103a–b. Al-ʿAyni, ʿIqd al-Juman, 835a. Ibn Hajar, Inbaʾ, ed. Habashi, 4:234. Ibn Iyas, 2:245–7. Ibn al-Sayrafi, Nuzhat al-Nufus, 4:311–12. Ibn Taghribirdi, Hawadith ad-Duhur, trans. Popper and ed. Fischel, pp. 9–10.

Dates	Ottoman	Mamluk	Purpose/details	Source
3 Shawwal 849/ January 2, 1446	>	<	To announce Sultan Mehmed II's accession.	Ibn Iyas, 2:252. Ibn al-Sayrafi, *Nuzhat al-Nufus*, 4:324. Ibn Taghribirdi, *Hawadith ad-Duhur*, trans. Popper and ed. Fischel, p. 12. Ibn Taghribirdi, *Hawadith*, ed. Izz al-din, 1:123.
On an unknown date between 8 Safar 850/May 5, 1446 and JU-JA 850/ August 1446			Murad II was enthroned in Edirne for a second time.	İnalcık, "Murad II," *DİA*, 31:169–70.
25 ZH 850/March 13, 1447			Shahrukh died.	
18–21 Sha'ban 852/ October 17–20, 1448			The Second Battle of Kosova took place.	İnalcık, "Murad II," *DİA*, 31:170.
Left Cairo either on 1 Ra I 853/April 24 1449 or 4 JA 853/ July 25, 1449	(?)	<2 Qanim al-Tajir b. 'Abd Allah min	Qanim probably left Cairo in the company of Ottoman ambassadors. Although the sources make no reference to such ambassadors,	Ibn Taghribirdi, *Al-Manhal Al-Safi*, ed. Ahmad Yusuf al-Najati

APPENDIX III

Came back on 1 Safar or 18 Safar 854/March 16 or April 2, 1450	Safar Shah al-Mu'ayyadi	they might have come to Cairo to announce the Second Battle of Kosova. No further details about Qanim's mission to Edirne have come to light, except for the fact that he was given a robe of honor by Murad II.	(Cairo,1956-), 9:13–14. Ibn Taghribirdi, *Hawaditb*, ed. Izz al-din, 2:211. Ibn Taghribirdi, *Nujum*, trans. Popper, 19:117, 125.
		Shortly after his return to Cairo, Jaqmaq sent him to the Qaraqoyunlu ruler Jihan Shah as an envoy. Although not confirmed by sources, Qanim's consecutive missions to Edirne and Tabriz may have been related.	For Qanim's later mission to the Qaraqoyunlu court, see Ibn Taghribirdi, *Hawaditb*, ed. Izz al-din, 2:321.
Precise date unknown	V	This mission brought a letter to one of Murad's influential viziers, Saruca Paşa. Only the titulature and the introductory parts of the letter have survived.	BNF MS 4440, 55b-56a.
1 Muharram 855/ February 3, 1451		Murad II died and Mehmed II came to power.	İnalcık, "Murad II," *DİA*.

Dates	Ottoman	Mamluk	Purpose/details	Source
Departed on 15 Ra II 855/May 17, 1451	2>	<1 Amir Asanbay al-Jamali al-Zahiri.	To express Jaqmaq's condolences to Mehmed II for his father Murad's death.	Al-Biqa'i, *Tarikh al-Biqa'i*, 1:163, 165. Ibn Taghribirdi, *Hawadith*, ed. Izz al-din, 2:325, 342. Har-El, *Struggle*, p. 77.
Likely returned in ZQ 855/December 1451			Asanbay came back with Ottoman ambassadors that carried gifts and a formal announcement of Mehmed's enthronement.	
The Ottoman mission that returned with Asanbay was hosted at a banquet on 28 ZQ 855/December 22, 1451			The mission brought slaves and furs as gifts.	
The Ottoman embassy was granted an audience on 29 ZQ 855/December 23, 1451			They were hosted with the utmost generosity by the Mamluk sultan, who granted them 100 *dinars* daily and an additional 3,000 *dinars* for their return trip. Among the gifts they took back to Mehmed were swords belonging to the Prophet's family. These special gifts were stolen while the mission was still in Mamluk territory.	
Departed on 24 ZH 855/January 17, 1452				

15 ZH 855/ January 9, 1452		Sultan Muhammad ibn Baysunghur ibn Shahrukh died.	Beatrice Forbes Manz, *Power, Politics and Religion in Timurid Iran* (Cambridge: Cambridge University Press, 2007), p. xvii.
Undated, but likely departed in early 856/early 1452	2> <1 Yakhshi Beg (from Jaqmaq's letter)	Jaqmaq's undated letter makes reference to Mehmed's march to the East. This letter was likely sent either during or after Mehmed's first campaign to the Karamanid lands before the siege of Constantinople.	For Jaqmaq's letter, see Feridun, 1274, 1:265–6. For Mehmed's letter, see Feridun, 1274, 1:266–8. For a letter that is very similar to Mehmed's, see BNF MS 4434, 130b–133b. According to the title, this letter which is composed by Molla Hüsrev is from Murad II to the Mamluk sultan, possibly after the death of the Timurid sultan Shahrukh (d.1447).
Mehmed's letter, which was sent in response to Jaqmaq's letter, was dated 2 Safar 856/ February 23, 1452		Mehmed's response to Jaqmaq presents multiple problems for historians. It reiterates Mehmed's wish to maintain positive relations with Cairo, but also updates Jaqmaq about the death of Muhammad Juki (who, in fact, died in 848/1445). However, judging from its date, the letter may mention the death of Muhammad ibn Baysunghur,	

Dates	Ottoman	Mamluk	Purpose/details	Source
			Shahrukh's grandson and the ruler of Herat who had died two months before (instead of Muhammad Juki).	
			Besides this chronological discrepancy between the recorded date of composition and the contents of the letter, a very similar yet undated copy of this letter is also present in BNF MS 4434. In this source, the letter is introduced as Murad II's letter to the Mamluk sultan (rather than Mehmed II's). Moreover, this version talks about the death of Shahrukh, rather than any of his children or grandchildren, as is the case in Feridun's version.	
857/March 1453			Sultan Inal came to power.	Şehabettin Tekindağ, "Īnāl," *EI*², 3:1198.

APPENDIX III

20 JU 857/May 29, 1453	1> Celaled-din al-Kabuni	<2 Amir akhur-i thani Yarshbay al-Inali al-Mu'ayyadi	The conquest of Constantinople	For the arrival and departure of the Ottoman mission, see al-Biqa'i, *Tarikh al-Biqa'i*, 1:421–2; Ibn Taghribirdi, *Hawadith*, ed. Popper, 8[1]:195, 196, 197–8; Ibn Taghribirdi, *Hawadith*, ed. Izz al-din, 2:455–56; Ibn Taghribirdi, *Nujum*, trans. Popper, 22:38–9.[10]
Arrived on 23 Shawwal 857/ October 27, 1453 (five months after the conquest)			To announce the conquest of Constantinople.	
Was given an audience on 25 Shawwal 857/October 29, 1453			Gifts brought by the Ottoman envoy included silver and gold items, fur, and slaves, some of whom were from the notable figures in Constantinople. The *fathname* was composed by Molla Gürani. Sultan Inal hosted the Ottoman mission in the deserted mansion of Zayn al-din Yahya al-Ustadar.	For the undated Ottoman victory proclamation, see Feridun, 1274, 1:235–8.
Was given a robe by Inal before his departure on 10 ZQ 857/December 12, 1453				For a different version of this letter, see al-Biqa'i, *Tarikh al-Biqa'i*, 1:425–31 and BNF MS 4434, 139a-143a. This version may have reached Mamluk lands instead of Feridun's version.
Yarshbay left Cairo on 20 ZQ 857/ December 22, 1453 with a letter carrying the same date			The Mamluk sultan Inal sent two responses. The first one was sent with Amir Yarshbay, one of the leading members of Inal's administration, with gifts including rare ones such as balsam and elephants.	For the Mamluk sultan's response that was sent with Yarshbay, see

Dates	Ottoman	Mamluk	Purpose/details	Source
Celaleddin left Cairo on 22 ZQ 857/December 24, 1453 in the company of another Mamluk commander			The Mamluk sultan's second response was entrusted to the Ottoman ambassador Celaleddin, who left Cairo two days after Yarshbay and in the company of another Mamluk amir, Burunduk al-Ashrafi (?). It further stated that the gifts Mehmed had sent for Mecca and Medina had been entrusted to an ambassador, possibly called Hoca Zaytuni. They probably left after the Ottoman gifts for the Sharifs of Mecca and Medina left for their intended destination.	Feridun, 1274, 1:238–9. This letter lists Inal's gifts for Mehmed. The Mamluk ambassador's name is misspelled as "Barsbay." For a study of the gifts, see Muhanna, "New Clothes," p. 194. For another copy of this letter, see al-Biqa'i, *Tarikh al-Biqa'i*, 1:431–6. (According to al-Biqa'i, this letter was composed by Katib al-Sirr Mu'in al-din. 'Abd al-Latif b. al-'Ajami).
Yarshbay returned to Cairo on 6 Sha'ban 858/ August 1, 1454 with a letter dated 22 Ra II 858/April 21, 1454			For his return trip, Inal granted Celaleddin 2,000 *dinars* for his preparations and other gifts in addition to the letter.	For Inal's second letter that was entrusted to Celaleddin, see Feridun, 1274, 1:240–3. (It is mistakenly identified as a letter Mehmed sent to to the Sharif of Mecca via the Mamluk sultan.)[11] For an additional version of Inal's response, see BNF MS 4440, 157a–160a. This copy combines Inal's two

answers that are found in Feridun's collection (one to Yarshay and the other to Celaleddin). After this letter was prepared, Inal must have changed his mind and decided to send two separate letters with two separate individuals.

For a translation and analysis of these letters from Feridun's compilation, see Ateş, "Istanbulun fethine dair," *Tarih Dergisi* 4 (1952): 11–51.

For details of Yarshbay's stay in Constantinople, see Ibn Taghribirdi, *Hawadith*, ed. Izz al-din, 2:494.

For the letter Yarshbay brought back to Inal, see BNF MS 4440, 160a-161b.

1454 — Dulkadirid leader Suleyman Bey died. His son Malik Arslan succeeded him.

Dates	Ottoman	Mamluk	Purpose/details	Source
Safar 859/January–February 1455			A rumor spread that a relative of the Abbasid caliph sent a forged letter with the caliphal seal and requested gifts from Mehmed II. Mehmed was pleased to respond to the caliph's special request.	Al-Biqa'i, *Tarikh al-Biqa'i*, 2:79.
Arrived on 18 JU 860/April 24, 1456 with a letter dated 2 ZH 859/November 13, 1455 Was given an audience on 21 JU 860/April 27, 1456 Departed on 20 Rajab or 5 Sha'ban 860/June 24 or July 9, 1456 with the Mamluk ambassador Qanibay	1> Celaleddin al-Kabuni	<2 Qanibay al-Yusufi al-Mihmandar (the *muhtasib* of Cairo)	To announce the conquest of Serbia with accompanying gifts and prisoners of war. The letter also informs the Mamluk sultan about the approaching circumcision festival of Mehmed's princes. He was hosted in Amir Qaraja al-Zahiri's residence in close proximity to the Azhar mosque. Qanibay accompanied the Ottoman envoy to Istanbul. The Mamluk sultan's letter was composed by Katib al-Sirr Mu'in al-din 'Abd al-Latif b. al-'Ajami.	For the Ottoman letter, see BNF MS 4440, 78a-80a; Ibn Taghribirdi, *Hawadith*, ed. Popper, 8¹:256–63; Lugal and Erzi, "Fatih Sultan Mehmed'in Muhtelif Seferlerine Ait Fetihnameleri," pp. 169–73.[12] For an abbreviated version of this letter, see al-Biqa'i, *Tarikh al-Biqa'i*, 2:171–4. Ibn Taghribirdi, *Nujum*, trans. Popper, 22:57, 58. For an alternative explanation of the mission's delay, see Al-Biqa'i, *Tarikh al-Biqa'i*, 2:188–9.

Qanibay returned in Rajab 861/May 1457	Shortly before their departure, rumours spread that Mehmed II had died, which delayed the mission. Qanibay (d.ZQ 862/ September–October 1458) reported receiving the utmost hospitality in Constantinople. Following this envoy and after receiving the news that the Karamanids had attacked Mamluk territory, Inal also sent his armies to the Karamanids. According to Aşıkpaşazade, Mehmed logistically supported the Mamluk sultan's campaign to the Karamanid lands. However, no information about this collaboration has been found in the correspondence or in any other sources.	For Inal's response that was sent with Qanibay and dated early Rajab 860/June 1456, see BNF MS 4440, 80a–82b; Ibn Taghrībirdī, *Hawādith*, ed. Popper, 8¹:263–9. The version in BNF MS 4440 also lists Inal's gifts for Mehmed and his two princes, Mustafa and Bayezid. Ibn Iyas, 2:165, 332, 334. For Inal's campaign to the Karamanids, see Ibn Taghrībirdī, *Nujum*, trans. Popper, 22:58–9. Aşıkpaşazade, ed. Giese, p. 220.

Dates	Ottoman	Mamluk	Purpose/details	Source
15 JU 865/ February 26, 1461			Sultan Inal died.	Tekindağ, "İnal," EI^2, 3:1198.
19 Ramadan 865/ June 22, 1461			Sultan Khushqadam came to power.	P.M. Holt, "Khushkadam," EI^2, 5:73.
1460s	Bernedette Dei		Only Babinger mentions this envoy, and he does not footnote the information.	Babinger, "Fatih Sultan Mehmed ve İtalya," *Belleten* 17 (1953), p. 71.
865/1461– 872/1468	>	V	According to Aşıkpaşazade, after the conquest of Trebizond (865/1461), the Mamluk sultan did not send an envoy to Mehmed II to congratulate him. In the meantime, Mehmed II sent envoys and money to the Mamluk governors for the repair of water wells on the pilgrimage roads. While Aşıkpaşazade broadly dates this event to 863/1458–9, the Mamluk chronicler al-Biqa'i lists a similar incident among the events of ZH 865/September 1461.	For the incident after the conquest of Trebizond, see Aşıkpaşazade, ed. Giese, p. 221. For the other one, ibid, pp. 221–2. Al-Biqa'i, *Tarikh al-Biqa'i*, 3:364–5. Har-El dates this incident to 871/1466. See Har-El, *Struggle*, p. 87.

Appendix III

Ramadan 868/ May–June 1464 or Shaʻban 868–Shawwal 868/June–July 1464 (This list follows Ibn Taghribirdi's chronology)	Relying on Las Matrie's work, Tekindağ claims that Mehmed II was informed about a titulature that was accorded to him by the Mamluk sultan in a letter sent to Jean II de Lusignan (the king of Cyprus). Mehmed II was reportedly displeased with the title. So far, I have not found any evidence to support this argument. Sources that I have read so far narrate that the behavior of the Ottoman envoy and the inappropriate epithet in the Ottoman letter angered the Mamluk sultan in 1464.	Tekindağ, "Fatih Devrinde," p. 76. For the attempts of the king of Cyprus and the Master of the Hospitallers, who urged the Mamluk sultan to protect them against Mehmed's attacks, see al-Biqaʻi, *Tarikh al-Biqaʻi*, 1:422, 3:129. Ibn Iyas, 2:420, 421. Ibn Taghribirdi, *Hawadith*, ed. Popper, 8²:471–73, 477. Aşıkpaşazade, ed. Giese, pp. 222–3. For a detailed treatment of this mission by Ibn Taghribirdi, Ibn Iyas, and Aşıkpaşazade, pp. 119–22.
ZQ 868/July 1464	Karamanid leader İbrahim Bey died.	

Dates	Ottoman	Mamluk	Purpose/details	Source
Departed in JU 869/December 1464		Al-Sayyid al-Sharif Nur al-din ʿAli al-Kurdi	To offer an alliance against the Aqqoyunlus. Mehmed II did not receive him properly.	Aşıkpaşazade, ed. Giese, pp. 222–3. Ibn Iyas, 2:427, 434. Har-El, *Struggle*, p. 82.
Returned in Ra I–Safar 870/October 1465 with a letter composed on 10 ZQ 869/July 4, 1465				For the Ottoman response that was sent back with the same ambassador, see BNF MS 4440, 76b-78a.
Safar 870/October 1465			The Dulkadirid leader Malik Arslan was assassinated on the order of the Mamluk Sultan Khushqadam, and the struggle between the Mamluks and the Ottomans to control the Dulkadirid region intensified.	Ibn Iyas, 2:434–5. Venzke, "Mamluk-Dulqadir Iqta," p. 424.
Ra I 870/October–November 1465			One month after the death of the Dulkadirid ruler Malik Arslan, the Mamluk sultan Khushqadam appointed Shahbudaq to take his assassinated brother's place.	Ibn Iyas, 2:435–6. Venzke, "Mamluk-Dulqadir Iqta," p. 424.

An Ottoman ambassador arrived in JA 870/ January–February 1466	Four letters sent from Constantinople to Cairo, one possibly from Mahmud Paşa and the others from Mehmed II.	For Mehmed's letters, see Anonymous, *Fatih Devrine Ait Münşeât Mecmuası*, pp. 3–5 (dated Ra II 871/ November 1466), pp. 40–1 (dated 10 Ra II 870/November–December 1465 and mistakenly identified as Mehmed's letter to the Dulkadirids), pp. 66–8 (again dated Ra II 871/ November 1466).
The letter was dated 10 Ra II 870/ November 30, 1465	According to Ibn Iyas, Mehmed II asked Khushqadam to appoint Shahsuwar instead of Shahbudaq, a statement corroborated by his letters. When the Mehmed II sultan did not comply, Mehmed sent his troops to support his candidate.	For Mahmud Paşa's letter, ibid., pp. 64–5.
Another letter was dated Ra II 871/ November 1466	According to Ibn Iyas, this act marked the beginning of animosity between Cairo and Constantinople. (In 1466, Mehmed was preoccupied with his campaigns in Albania.)	Ibn Iyas, 2:436–7.

Dates	Ottoman	Mamluk	Purpose/details	Source
871–872/August 1466–July 1468			According to Tursun Bey and İbn Kemal, Mehmed II suddenly decided to march to Mamluk territory, supposedly to reconquer the frontier cities of Malatya and Darende, which had been lost in the aftermath of the Battle of Ankara. Then the Ottoman ruler changed his mind and decided to attack the Karamanid lands instead.	Tursun Bey, ed. Tulum, pp. 145–6. İbn Kemal, *TAO: VII. Defter*, p. 272.
Muharram–Ra I 872/August–October 1467			Shahsuwar defeated a Mamluk contingent. Many Mamluk commanders either died or were captured while Shahbudaq escaped.	Ibn Iyas, 2:451. Venzke, "Mamluk–Dulqadir Iqta," p. 425.
10 Ra I 872/ October 9, 1467			Sultan Khushqadam died while preparing a new army to fight Shahsuwar.	
6 Rajab 872/ January 31, 1468			Qaytbay came to power.	Carl Petry, *Twilight of Majesty*, p. 36.

872/1468 (?)	>	<	According to Aşıkpaşazade, after Qaytbay (r.872–901/1468–96) came to power, Mehmed sent a proper goodwill mission. Afterwards, Mehmed and Qaytbay came to an agreement about the Dulkadirid territory. No other source, however, mentions this agreement.	Aşıkpaşazade, ed. Giese, p. 223. For a detailed treatment of this alleged agreement and its later reversal, see pp. 127–9.
872–7/ 1466–72			Consecutive Mamluk campaigns to the Dulkadirid territory.	
Muharram 874/ July 1469	An Ottoman messenger who brought reports about Uzun Hasan's acquisitions on the Black Sea coast.		Petry's account does not clarify whether this messenger was a diplomatic representative or merely an agent of intelligence.	Petry, *Protectors*, pp. 46–7.

Dates	Ottoman	Mamluk	Purpose/details	Source
Arrived in Muharram-Safar 875/ July–August 1470	1>	<2	To announce Mehmed's recent success against the Venetians (in the conquest of Eğriboz).	For the Ottoman mission, see Ibn Iyas, 3:52.
			Shortly after this mission, a Mamluk mission visited Constantinople.	For the Mamluk mission, see Tursun Bey, ed. Tulum, p. 149; Tursun Bey, ed. İnalcık and Murphey, 131a.
			It is useful to note that the Ottomans were also engaged in suppressing the Karamanids at this time. Although no textual evidence has been found, the missions may have communicated about this issue.	For the statement about the Karamanids, see Ibn Kemal, *TAO: VII. Defter*, pp. 298–316.
Sent in Ra I 875/ September 1470		Shaykh 'Ala' al-din al-Husni	During his campaign to the Dulkadirids, Amir Yashbak sent envoys to the Aqqoyunlus, to the Ottomans, and to Prince Bayezid (the future Bayezid II), who was the Ottoman governor of Amasya at that time. The purpose of these missions was probably to assure these rulers that the march of the Mamluk army did not pose any threat to their lands.	Ibn Aja, ed. Tulaymat, p. 94. For the letters exchanged between Prince Bayezid and Yashbak (?), see Anonymous, *Fatih Devrine Ait Mün-şeât Mecmuası*, pp. 69–70, 70–1.[13]
Returned to Cairo either in ZH 876/ May–June 1472 or Safar 877/July 1472				For the return of 'Ala' al-din al-Husni, see Ibn Iyas, 3:75; Al-Jawhari al-Sayrafi, *Inba' al-Hasr bi-Abna' al-'Asr*, ed. Habashi, pp. 445–6.

>	According to Ibn Iyas, 'Ala' al-din, who was sent to Mehmed II, was angry at Amir Yashbak when he returned to Cairo. Ibn Aja corroborates Ibn Iyas' statements about a disagreement between Amir Yashbak and 'Ala' al-din regarding the latter's mission in Constantinople. For a detailed treatment of this incident, see Chapter 4.	Bernadette Martel-Thoumian, 'Les Dernières Batailles'. Har-El, *Struggle*, p. 96.
	Al-Sayyid Amir Jan was sent to Prince Bayezid. He returned with a letter dated JU 876/ October–November 1471.	
Ramadan 876/February 1472 (before Shaykh 'Ala' al-Din al-Husni, the previous Mamluk ambassador, returned to Cairo) >	An Ottoman ambassador brought presents to Cairo from Sultan Mehmed II while Amir Yashbak was still campaigning against Shahsuwar.	Ibn Iyas, 3, p. 69. Benjamin Arbel, 'Venetian Trade Letters in Fifteeenth-Century Acre', Asian and African Studies 22 (1988), pp. 236–37, 274–75, 286–87.

Dates	Ottoman	Mamluk	Purpose/details	Source
Ra I-Safar 877/ August 1472			Shahsuwar was executed in Cairo.	Venzke, "Mamluk-Dulqadir Iqta," p. 425.
An Ottoman ambassador arrived in ZQ 877/ March–April 1473	1> 3>	<2 Ibn Aja <4	A series of exchanges to build an alliance against the Aqqoyunlus. According to Ibn Iyas, an Ottoman envoy came to the camp of Amir Yashbak, who had left Cairo in Rajab 877/December 1472 to march on Uzun Hasan. The envoy brought his sultan's offer for help and alliance.	Ibn Iyas, 3:80, 86, 87. (From p. 80 onward, Ibn Iyas concentrates on Uzun Hasan.) Har-El, *Struggle*, pp. 97–8. For Uzun Hasan's letters that were sent to European courts but were seized by both the Ottomans and the Mamluks, see Ibn Iyas, 3:86–7; Petry, *Protectors*, p. 48; M.M. Ziyadeh, 203; Ziyade, *The Fall*, p. 6.
Returned to Mehmed II with Ibn Aja		Dawlatbay Hamam al-Ashrafi[14]	Yashbak sent the Ottoman envoy back with Ibn Aja, along with gifts and letters.	
Another Ottoman ambassador either arrived in ZH 877/ April–May 1473, or departed at this time after a banquet was given in his honor by Qaytbay			According to Ibn Iyas, another Ottoman envoy reached Cairo in ZH 877/April–May 1473. This envoy brought the captured	For the later Ottoman ambassador, see Ibn Shahin, *Nayl al-Amal*, 7:65. For an example of the close Mamluk supervision of Ottoman–Aqqoyunlu affairs, see Ibn Shahin,

Ibn Aja returned to Cairo in Safar 878/ July 1473	letters of Uzun Hasan to the European courts. In return, the Mamluk sultan sent Dawlatbay as an envoy.	*Nayl al-Amal*, 7:68 (a report on Murad Paşa's death at the hands of the Aqqoyunlu). For the return of Ibn Aja, see Ibn Shahin, *Nayl al-Amal*, 7:72.
16 Ra I 878/ August 11, 1473	The Battle of Otlukbeli (Başkent) between Mehmed II and Uzun Hasan.	
After the battle of Otlukbeli >	To announce the battle of Otlukbeli. According to İbn Kemal, Mehmed also sent the severed head of Mirza Zaynal, Uzun Hasan's oldest son, with this mission.[15]	İbn Kemal, *TAO: VII. Defter*, p. 366. For the arrival of this news in Cairo and Qaytbay's reaction, see Ibn Iyas, 3:91. For the close Mamluk involvement in Ottoman–Aqqoyunlu affairs, see Ibn Shahin, *Nayl al-Amal*, 7:83.
Was appointed or left Cairo in ZQ 878/April 1474	< Amir Yashbak al-Jamali	Most likely to congratulate Mehmed for his recent success over Uzun Hasan. Qaytbay had first appointed Barsbay al-Ashrafi to lead this	For the death of the first ambassador, see Ibn Iyas, 3:90, 91. For the selection of the new envoy, see Ibn Iyas, 3:94.

Dates	Ottoman	Mamluk	Purpose/details	Source
Returned in JU 879/September 1474			mission (RE 878/July 1473).[16] However, Barsbay died near Aleppo on his way to Constantinople. The sultan then chose Amir Almas from his own household after promoting him to the post of *Ustadar*. He later changed his mind, dismissed Almas, and appointed Yashbak al-Jamali. Both Ibn Shahin and Ibn Iyas claim that Qaytbay sent this envoy with valuable gifts, including an elephant and a giraffe. This statement is corroborated by Muali's account, although some details from the two lists do not match. According to Muali, among the many gifts brought by the Mamluk ambassador, there was a caravan of 800 camels loaded with wheat and oats. The convoy reached Aleppo in 40 days and	For the gifts sent by Qaytbay to Mehmed II, see Ibn Shahin, *Nayl al-Amal*, 7:89–90. Anhegger, "Mu'âli," p. 155. Har-El, *Struggle*, p. 99.

Muharram 879/ May–June 1474		Kayseri in seventy days, where they were welcomed by Mahmud Paşa (d.3 Ra I 879/July 18, 1474). In Constantinople, the envoy received a daily allocation of 300 *dinars*. I suspect this mission was the same one that departed from Cairo on 17 Muharram 879 (see below).	
		Mehmed's son Prince Mustafa died.	Anhegger, "Mu'âli," pp. 158–9. İbn Kemal, *TAO: VII. Defter*, p. 376.
Departed on 17 Muharram 879/ June 3, 1474	Asma-i Jundi (?)	To convey Qaytbay's condolences for Mustafa's death. No reference to this mission exists, however, in Mamluk sources. İbn Kemal records that many diplomatic missions arrived to convey their condolences, but he does not list the senders.	

Dates	Ottoman	Mamluk	Purpose/details	Source
			According to Muali, gifts included 40 Arabian horses, one horse from a rare species, and 400 camels loaded with goods from India. The mission was welcomed at the frontier by Prince Bayezid's men. The city was prepared before the entrance of the ambassador, and he presented his gifts to the dignitaries in the capital before seeing the sultan.	
Ra II 879/August 1474	>		Possibly to thank the Mamluk sultan for his condolence mission after Mustafa's death. He brought letters requesting the pardon of Inal al-Hakim, who had defied the sultan's authority. The sultan accepted this request. He also treated the Ottoman envoy very well and gave him robes of honor. After a stay in Cairo, the envoy then returned to his lands.	Ibn Iyas, 3:98. Ibn Shahin, *Nayl al-Amal*, 7:103.

The letter was dated ZH 881/ March 1477	∧	When the Karamanid ruler took refuge in Mamluk lands, Mehmed II sent this letter to the Mamluk sultan to request his return.	T.E.5848 Ibn Iyas, 3:130.
		Two months later in Safar 882, Ibn Iyas reports the arrival of an Ottoman envoy with a letter, but does not offer any information about its content.	
883–4/1478–80, tentatively dated Ra II 883/July 1478	∧ ∨	According to Aşıkpaşazade, Mehmed II sent an envoy to Cairo who was not treated well. The Mamluk sultan had appointed the *muhtasib* of Cairo to be his envoy to the Ottoman court. Supposedly, Mehmed II was deeply offended by the envoy's social status. (Also see p.129.)	Aşıkpaşazade, ed. Giese, p. 225. Ibn Shahin, *Nayl al-Amal*, 7:209.

Dates	Ottoman	Mamluk	Purpose/details	Source
			This event may have taken place on an earlier date, but it is useful to note that Ibn Shahin mentions the arrival and departure of an Ottoman ambassador during this time.	
4 Ra I 886/May 3, 1481			Mehmed II died.	Turan, "Bayezid II," *DİA*, 5:234.
23 Ra I 886/May 22, 148			Bayezid II took power.	Ibid., p. 235.
886/1481–2	>	∨	Qaytbay offered to mediate the Cem affair. Probably, envoys were exchanged, although this episode of Ottoman–Mamluk relations needs further investigation to establish its chronology.	Har-El, *Struggle*, p. 108ff. For a recent assessment of the Mamluk sultan's role in this affair, see Hatrox, "Qaytbay's Diplomatic Dilemma Concerning the Flight of Cem Sultan (1481–1482)."
888/1483–4			Before the Ottoman–Mamluk war, the battle for control of the Dulkadirid lands flared up again. Sources do not mention any diplomatic missions between the two capitals, though some may have been exchanged.	Hadidi, pp. 307–8, 311, 317–19.

Mid-Muharram 888/February 1483		Kasim Bey of the Karamanids died.	Uruç Bey, ed. Öztürk, p. 135.
1485–91		Ottoman–Mamluk War.	For a detailed chronology of the Ottoman–Mamluk war, see Har-El. For a more concise version, see Chapter 5 of this book.
Departed in Safar 890/February–March 1485	Amir Akhur-i Thani Janibak al-Habib al-Alay al-Inali[17]	To ameliorate the relationship between Constantinople and Cairo (see pp.1–2, 133–6, 139–41 for a detailed treatment of this mission).	Anonymous, *Tarib Al-i Osman*, TKSK Revan 1099, 100a. Anonymous, *Tarib-i Sultan Bayezid*, TKSK Revan 1272, 9b.
Was given an audience on 29 Safar 890/March 16, 1485		The missions were given an audience in Çöke Yaylası (Edirne) after the sun equinox on 29 Safar 890/March 16, 1485. (Bayezid had likely been there since 5 Shawwal 889.)	Anonymous, *Anonim Osmanlı Kroniği*, ed. Necdet Öztürk, p. 131. Bihişti, *Die Chronik*, pp. 103–6. Ibn Iyas, 3:215–17, 221.
Returned to Damascus on 23 Shawwal 890/November 2, 1485		Janibak returned to Cairo by land through Malatya.	Ibn al-Himsi, *Hawadith*, 1:303–4.
Departed for Cairo on 3 ZQ 890/			

Dates	Ottoman	Mamluk	Purpose/details	Source
November 11, 1485 and arrived in the same month			Soon after this embassy returned to Cairo, the war between the two powers resumed.	İbn Kemal, *TAO: VIII. Defter*, pp. 79–81. Uruç Bey, *The Frühosmanischen Jahrbücher*, p. 133. Uruç Bey, *Tevarih-i Al-i Osman*, Manisa Il Halk Kütüphanesi. Muradiye 5506/2, 75a–75b. Uruç Bey, ed. Öztürk, pp. 136–7. Al-Husayni, "Kitab Nafa'is al-Majalis al-Sultaniyya," pp. 133–4. Tursun Bey, ed. Tulum, p. 106. Mustafa Âli, *Künhü'l-Abbâr*, TTK, 2009, 176b.
890/1485 (?)	>		In 890/1485, before the Ottoman army marched to the south, Har-El claims: "Bayezid did not fail to present the Mamluks with an adequate causus belli justifying his war according to the legal	Har-El, *Struggle*, pp. 134–5.[18]

892/1486–7	Hersekzade Ahmed Paşa	precepts of Islam. He sent an envoy to Cairo with an official letter, reinforced by a fatwa from the ulama..." The Mamluk sultan hoped that Hersekzade, the captured Ottoman vizier, could mediate between the two sultans. See pp.141–3 for a detailed treatment of this incident.	Aşıkpaşazade, ed. Giese, p. 230. Ibn Iyas, 3:226, 237. For a detailed study of Hersekzade's stay in Mamluk lands, see Halil Ethem, "Hersekoğlu Ahmed Paşa'nin Esaretine dair Kahire'de bir Kitabe."
JA 894/May 1489	An envoy from Davud Paşa	Davud Paşa suggested to the Mamluk sultan that a truce may be possible if the ruler sent an envoy to the Ottoman sultan. Ottoman sources do not mention the incident.	Ibn Iyas, 3:266. For a detailed treatment of this mission and the Mamluk sultan's response, see p. 144.
Muharram 895/ November– December 1489		The wedding festival for Bayezid's three daughters.	Uruç Bey, ed. Öztürk, pp. 144–5.

Dates	Ottoman	Mamluk	Purpose/details	Source
22 JU 895/ April 13, 1490	An envoy from Molla ʿArab		He lobbied actively in the Ottoman capital for peace and communicated with Mamluk officials through his representatives.	Ibn Tulun, *Mufakahat*, ed. Muhammad Mustafa, 1:132. For Ottoman peace efforts, also see ibid., 1:122–3.
Arrived in Constantinople on 15 Shaʿban 895/July 4, 1490 (According to a version of Uruç Bey's chronicle, he arrived between the wedding festival of Bayezid's three daughters and the fire of Güngörmez)		< Mamay min Hudad al-Khassaki	To offer peace. Mamay arrived with a Dulkadirid envoy. Ibn al-Himsi states that, because Amir Mamay was sent to Constantinople while the Mamluk army under Azbak's command was pillaging the Karaman-Kayseri region (between Ra I 895 and ZH 895/ late January 1490 and October 1490), the ambassador was actually imprisoned in the Ottoman capital. (An anonymous Ottoman chronicler also states that the ambassador was not treated well.)	For the bad treatment of Mamay, see Ibn al-Himsi, *Hawadith*, 1:325; Anonymous, *Tarih-i Al-i Osman*, Revan 1099, 102a–b. Ibn Iyas, 3:273. For the allegedly generous treatment of the Mamluk ambassador, see Uruç Bey, ed. Öztürk, p. 145. (In contrast, the Manisa manuscript of Uruç Bey does not say anything about the way the Mamluk ambassador was treated. See Uruç Bey, *Tevarih-i Al-i Osman*, Muradiye 5506/2, 81b.)

Appendix III

Departed from Istanbul in the middle of Safar 896/December 1490	>	Mamay (?) Ali Çelebi	According to Uruç Bey, the Dulkadirid envoy was not treated well, but the Mamluk envoy enjoyed a particularly hospitable visit. (Other Ottoman sources are generally silent about the Mamluk ambassador's experience.) Uruç Bey claims that after the arrival of the envoy, the council (*divan*) gathered to discuss the war with the Mamluks and decided to sign for peace. After the *divan*, on 24 Sha'ban 895/July 13, 1490, an earthquake and the famous fire of Güngörmez took place. Ottoman sources claim that a Mamluk envoy arrived in Constantinople when Bayezid had just returned from a hunting party in Edirne.	For the alleged arrival of a Mamluk ambassador in Muharram 896/November–December 1490, see Anonymous, *Tarih-i Al-i Osman*, TKSK Revan 1099, 102b; Uruç, ed. Öztürk, p. 146.

Dates	Ottoman	Mamluk	Purpose/details	Source
Arrived in Damascus on 22 JU 896/ April 2, 1491			I think that this ambassador was Mamay, who had not been allowed to return to Cairo previously. When Bayezid decided to sign the peace treaty, he released Mamay and sent him, carrying lavish gifts, back with Ali Çelebi.	Hadidi, pp. 332–4. For the joint departure of the Ottoman and Mamluk ambassadors from İstanbul, see Uruç Bey, *Tevarih-i Al-i Osman*, Muradiye 5506/2, 83a; Uruç Bey, ed. Öztürk, p. 146.
Entered Cairo in JA 896/April–May 1491				Ibn Iyas, 3:281.
Attended the *mahmal*'s departure ceremony in Rajab 896/May–June 1491 and subsequently undertook his pilgrimage				Ibn Shahin, *Nayl al-Amal*, 8:226, 227, 228. Ibn al-Himsi, *Hawadith*, 1:325–6, 1:327.
For Ali Çelebi's return, see the next entry				For the allocations granted to the Ottoman ambassador by the Mamluks, see T.E.6944. (This undated document is tentatively placed here.)

Appendix III

Departed in Rajab 896/May–June 1491	(Ali Çelebi)	Janbulat (future Mamluk sultan)	Janbulat came to Ottoman lands with a returning Ottoman ambassador (probably Ali Çelebi). He also brought some Ottoman prisoners, including Mihaloğlu İskender Bey (released on 14 Sha'ban 896/June 22, 1491), that had been released by the Mamluk sultan as a sign of good will.[19]	Anonymous, *Tarih-i Al-i Osman*, Revan 1099, 102b–103a. Ibn Iyas, 3:282, 283. Ibn Tulun, *Mufakahat*, 1:147, 154. For the release of İskender Bey, see Ibn Shahin, *Nayl al-Amal*, 8:226. Ibn al-Himsi, *Hawadith*, 1:326, 327–38, 331.
Arrived to the Ottoman court on 7 ZH 896/ October 11, 1491				
Returned to Damascus in Ra I 897/January 1497			He was present during the *'id* and concluded the peace agreement before his departure.	For the arrival of these ambassadors in İstanbul, see Uruç, ed. Öztürk, p. 147. Uruç, *Die Frühosmanischen Jahrbücher des Urudsch*, p. 136. İbn Kemal, *TAO: VIII.Defter*, pp. 122–3.
Arrived in Safar or Ra I 899/December 1493–January 1494		Davud Paşa (the future Nişancı)	He was probably sent to inform about the Kırbova victory that took place on 27 ZH 898/ October 9, 1493 (Uruç dates the battle of Kırbova to 7 ZH 898/ September 19, 1493).	Ibn Iyas, 3:298. For the return trip of the Ottoman ambassador, Ibn al-Himsi, *Hawadith*, 1:347. For the date of the Battle of Kırbova, see Uruç, ed. Öztürk, p. 160.

Dates	Ottoman	Mamluk	Purpose/details	Source
Was appointed in Ra II 899/January 1494		Mamay min Hudad al-Khassaki	Probably to express Qaytbay's congratulations for the Kirbova victory.	Ibn al-Himsi, *Hawadith*, 1:356, 372–3.
Arrived in Damascus on his way to the Ottoman capital in Sha'ban 899/May–June 1494			Ibn al-Himsi gives a detailed description of Mamay's return to Cairo and the gifts he received. Uruç Bey also claims that this ambassador was hosted particularly well by Bayezid (along with ambassadors from the Polish king).	For the unusually detailed description of Mamay's preparations for departure, see Ibn Iyas, 3:299–300. İbn Kemal, *TAO: VIII.Defter*, p. 39. Uruç, ed. Öztürk, p. 163.
Entered Damascus on his return trip to Cairo in Safar 900/November 1494			When he returned to Damascus, Shaykh Badr al-din al-Jum'a accompanied him.	
Arrived in Cairo on 9 Ra I 900/December 8, 1494			When Mamay left Damascus for Cairo, Ibn al-Himsi joined his entourage.	

Appendix III

Was given an audience on 25 Ra II 900/January 23, 1495	>	Envoys from both Iraq and Ottoman lands were received together, but no further information is known.	Ibn al-Himsi, *Hawadith*, 1:376.
Arrived in Constantinople in Ramadan 900/June 1495	Shaykh 'Abd al-Mu'min al-'Ajami	The envoy took many gifts, such as fabrics and animals (including a giraffe, according to Uruç Bey, but a lion, a giraffe, a parrot, and colored mules according to Ibn Iyas), to the Ottoman capital.	For this embassy's arrival in Constantinople and their gifts, see Uruç, ed. Öztürk, p. 168. Ibn Iyas, 3:315–16.
Returned to Cairo in Muharram-Safar 901/October–November 1495		Ibn Iyas reports this envoy's return to Cairo. He brought the news that the Ottoman ruler was preparing his army for a campaign, but that he would not march on Mamluk lands. The Mamluk sultan was pleased with this news.	M.M.Ziyadeh, p. 210.[20] Ziyadeh, "The Fall," p. 13.
27 ZQ 901/ August 6–7, 1496		Qaytbay died and his son Muhammad al-Nasir succeeded him.	

Dates	Ottoman	Mamluk	Purpose/details	Source
903–4/1498–9	Kemal Reis		Kemal Reis transported pilgrims and gifts for the annual pilgrimage caravan to Mamluk lands. During his return trip, he was attacked by ships from Rhodes. After seizing the ships and numerous war prisoners, he presented them to Bayezid. See the next entry about Khayr Bey's mission.	İbn Kemal, *TAO: VIII.Defter*, pp. 169–79. Uruç, ed. Öztürk, pp. 183–4.
Was appointed in Muharram 903/ September 1497 Was given a robe of travel (*khil'a al-safar*) on 7 Rajab 903/March 1,1498 Left Cairo in Rajab 903/March 1498 Reached Constantinople at the end of ZQ 903/July 1498		Khayr Bey (the future Ottoman governor)	To announce Qaytbay's son Muhammad al-Nasir's enthronement to the Ottomans, and he also brought many gifts. According to Uruç Bey's unique account, Khayr Bey requested the hand of Bayezid's daughter on Sultan Muhammad ibn Qaytbay's behalf, and Bayezid agreed. By the time he returned from his mission, another sultan had taken the throne.	Hadidi, pp. 348–50. İbn Kemal, *TAO: VIII.Defter*, pp. 169–70. Ibn al-Himsi, *Hawadith*, 2:38, 72. Ibn Iyas, 3:377, 387, 410. For the marriage proposal of Qaytbay's son, Uruç Bey, ed. Öztürk, pp. 184–85.

APPENDIX III

Was present when Kemal Reis and Mihaloğlu presented their spoils to Bayezid at the end of ZQ 903/July 1498			
Returned from his mission on 11 or 15 Sha'ban 904/March 24 or 28, 1499			
903–4/1497–9		These years were marked by conflict between 'Ala' al-Dawla and the Mamluk regime.	Uruç, ed. Öztürk, p. 185.
17 Ra I 904/ November 2, 1498		Qansuh al-Ghawri al-Zahir took the throne.	
Sha'ban 904/ March–April 1499	∨ ∧	Ibn Iyas claims that Bayezid ordered the governor of Aleppo to dismiss Ibn Turgud (Turgudoğulları). It is not clear, however, whether this message	Ibn Iyas, 3:411. İbn Kemal, *TAO: VIII.Defter*, pp. 268–72.

260   THE OTTOMANS AND THE MAMLUKS

Dates	Ottoman	Mamluk	Purpose/details	Source
			was brought by Khayr Bey or another Ottoman ambassador. Likewise, according to Ibn Kemal, diplomatic missions may have been exchanged between capitals to discuss a matter regarding the Ramazanids, and he even suggests that this issue lingered until 916/1510.	
Appointed to this mission in Ra I 905/October 1499		Amir Qansuh al-Khazinadar	Bayezid was displeased when Qaytbay's son was deposed.	For Bayezid's disapproval regarding the execution of Qaytbay's son, see Ibn Iyas, 3:411.
Left Cairo or Damascus on 11 Sha'ban 905/ March 12, 1500			Ziyada claims that the new Mamluk sultan Qansuh al-Zahir sent an envoy to exonerate himself.	Ibn Iyas, 3:426, 4:9. Ibn al-Himsi, *Hawadith*, 2:95, 125–6.
Was hosted in Edirne between 18 Ra II and 10 JU 906/November 11 and December 2, 1500			Upon the order of Qansuh al-Zahir, the Mamluk ambassador took a large entourage and gifts to Ottoman lands. When he arrived in Ottoman lands, Bayezid was away on a campaign to Modon, Koron, and Anavarya.	İbn Kemal, *TAO: VIII.Defter*, p. 208. See the expenditure record found in the Başbakanlık Arşivi/İbnü'l-emin Hariciye 1 (the recording date of the document is 26 JU 906/January 17, 1501 and it was recorded by Zaim-i Ulufeciyan Ali Bey).

Appendix III

Returned to Cairo on 13 ZQ 906/May 31, 1501	After Bayezid returned on 22 Safar 906/September 17, 1500, he rested in Edirne for three months and accepted Qansuh there.	Ziyadeh, "the Fall," p. 13. Ziyadeh, p. 211. For the date of Bayezid's return from his campaign, see Uruç Bey, ed. Öztürk, p. 203.
	When Qansuh reached Cairo, Qansuh al-Ghawri had become sultan (see below for the list of Mamluk sultans).	
29 ZQ 905/ June 26, 1500	The rule of Qansuh al-Ghawri al-Zahir (who had sent the previous mission) ended.	
ZH 905/July 1500	Janbulat became the Mamluk sultan.	
JA 906/January 1501	Tumanbay became the Mamluk sultan.	
Ramadan 906/ March–April 1501	Qansuh al-Ghawri came to power in Cairo.	
Shawwal 906/April 1501	The insurgency of Dawlatbay and Sibay.	Ibn Iyas, 4:7.

Dates	Ottoman	Mamluk	Purpose/details	Source
			Although Petry dates this insurgency to 910/1504–5, Ibn Iyas first mentions it in Shawwal 906/April 1501.	Petry, *Protectors and Praetorians*, pp. 37–8.
			He recounts that Dawlatbay sought refuge in Ottoman territory and the Dulkadirid leader 'Ala' al-Dawla intervened in Cairo on behalf of this Mamluk commander.	
			The only documentary verifications for the missions, that were exchanged between Bayezid and Qansuh al-Ghawri concerning Dawlatbay, are available first in the letters found in Feridun's collections and then in the *İnamat Defteri*.	
			According to *İnamat Defteri*, Dawlatbay have been receiving allocations from Bayezid in Konya at least since 909/1503.	

			For these references, see below the embassies of Mamluk commanders Tanibay and Yunus.[21]
Arrived in Cairo in JA 908/ November–December 1502 with a letter dated mid-Safar 908/ mid-August 1502	1> Silahtarbaşı Haydar Ağa	<2 Hindubay al-Khassaki	Ibn al-Iyas, 4:46–7.
			Ibn al-Himsi, *Hawadith*, 2:164–5, 167–8.
			For the letter that Haydar Ağa presented to the Mamluk sultan, see Feridun, 1274, 1:347–9.
Departed in Rajab 908/December–January 1502 after a seventy-day stay with Hindubay		While the letter Haydar Ağa brought from Constantinople as well as the one he was given by Qansuh al-Ghawri clearly state that the primary purpose of this mission was to congratulate Qansuh on his accession to power, both letters also refer to the Safavids and other news that was confidentially entrusted to first Haydar Ağa and then to Hindubay (although Ottoman sources do not reference the Mamluk ambassador).	For the undated letter that Haydar Ağa presented to the Ottoman sultan after his return, see Feridun, 1274, 1:349–50.
			Hoca Saadeddin, *Tac al-Tevarih*, 1279, 2:127–8.
		Additionally, Hoca Saadeddin claims that Haydar Ağa brought Cem Sultan's daughter back from Cairo.	For a reference to Cem's daughter who stayed in Egypt, see İbn Kemal, *TAO: VIII.Defter*, p. 39 (No reference to a son).

Dates	Ottoman	Mamluk	Purpose/details	Source
Was given a robe of honor in Ramadan 908/February–March 1503		Tanibay al-Khazinadar (Teymin Bey, according to the *İnamat Defteri*)	Qansuh's letter to Haydar refers to an additional letter that was entrusted to Hindubay, but this letter has not been found.	Ibn al-Himsi, *Hawadith*, 2:170.
Left Cairo in Muharram 909/July 1503			Althought sources do not reveal the reason for Tanibay's mission, the timing of the mission suggests that he was sent to discuss an alliance against the Safavids.[23]	For the gifts and allocations given to the Mamluk ambassador in Constantinople, see Anonymous, *İnamat Defteri*, 9b, 10b.
Received gifts in Constantinople on 25 JU 909/November 15, 1503 the day of "the banquet"(?)			During his stay at the Ottoman court, he received at least two sets of gifts on two separate days. The itemized list of the second set details items intended for the Mamluk administrators in Cairo. It is not clear, however, which items were intended for the Mamluk sultan.	For multiple references to the allocations granted to Dawlatbay during his stay in Konya, see Anonymous, *İnamat Defteri*, 4b, 11a, and 11b.
Received a second set of gifts on 6 JA 909/November 25 1503[22]			The significant gift list in the Ottoman treasury book suggests that this embassy could have been a major mission that somehow went unnoticed by other sources.	For the reference to Cafer Çelebi, see Anonymous, *İnamat Defteri*, 12a. Ibn Iyas, 4:55, 63.

Appendix III

Returned to Cairo in ZQ 909/ April–May 1504		According to the *İnamat Defteri*, the letter that Bayezid sent with Tanibay to Qansuh was composed by the famous Tacizade Cafer Çelebi.	Anonymous, *İnamat Defteri*, 2b.
Received the allocation on 22 Muharram 909/ July 17, 1503	Arab Mehmed (?)	According to the *İnamat Defteri*, Bayezid allocated some money to be sent to Ahmed, the son of his brother Cem. Another entry from one day later notes a separate allocation to an individual called "Arab Mehmed." Perhaps this individual was entrusted with the allocation for Ahmed, who may still have been in Cairo. We know that Cem's daughter was brought back (see above for the relevant mission), but perhaps Haydar Ağa was not able to bring Cem's son.	
Safar 910/July–August 1504	Alaaddin (?)	A reference to a letter to Egypt, which could have been an intelligence or secret correspondence.	Anonymous, *İnamat Defteri*, 35b.

Dates	Ottoman	Mamluk	Purpose/details	Source
Yunus received gifts from Bayezid II on 8 Ra I 910/ August 19, 1504	1> 3> Sinan Bey	<2 Yunus al-Khassaki <4 Yunus and Sinan Bey	Bayezid sent this letter on behalf of Dawlatbay, who took refuge in Ottoman lands. It also addressed the Safavid issue. For earlier references to Dawlatbay in other Ottoman sources, see the embassy of Amir Tanibay.	For Bayezid's letter, see Feridun, 1274, 1:354–5. For the Mamluk response letter that was sent back with Sinan Bey, see Feridun, 1274, 1:355–6. For the gifts and allocations that were granted by Bayezid to Yunus al-Khassaki, see Anonymous, *İnamat Defteri*, 36a. For multiple references to the allocations that were granted to Dawlatbay during his stay in Konya, see Anonymous, *İnamat Defteri*, 4b, 11a, and 11b. Kopraman, "Osmanlı-Memluk," p. 482. Mutawalli, *Al-Fatkh Al-'Uthmani*, p. 44.

APPENDIX III 267

Rajab 912/November 1506		Dawlatbay was accepted by the Mamluk sultan in Cairo.	
Arrived in ZQ 912/ March 1507	>	An Ottoman envoy traveled to Mamluk lands. No further details are known.	Ibn Iyas, 4:107, 109, 118. Brummett, "Kemal Re'is and Ottoman Gunpowder Diplomacy," p. 5.
Mamluk preparations against the Safavids were possibly witnessed in Ra II 913/August–September 1507			
25 ZH 912/May 8, 1507	Yunus (?)	This individual could have been the same person who had already visited the Ottoman capital once in Ra I 910/August 1505.	Anonymous, *İnamat Defteri*, 102a.
Kemal Reis was entrusted with gifts and allocations by the Ottoman sultan, possibly on 10 Muharram 913/ May 22, 1507	Mevlana Alaaddin (?) and Kemal Reis, probably with the above-mentioned Mamluk	To bring artillery, canonry, and ship-building equipment. His mission was not only to dispel the Porruguese threat, but also to prevent the Mamluk sultan from negotiating with the Safavids.	For an extremely detailed list of allocations and gifts given to Kemal Reis to take to Egypt, see Anonymous, *İnamat Defteri*, 107b. For the reference to Mevlana Alaaddin, see Anonymous, *İnamat Defteri*, 108a.

Dates	Ottoman	Mamluk	Purpose/details	Source
Mevlana Alaaddin (?) was given an audience on 14 JU 913/September 21, 1507	ambassador Yunus		As Ibn Iyas' account reveals, there might have been an additional Ottoman ambassador who was given an audience a few days before Kemal Reis' audience. This ambassador might have been a certain Mevlana Alaadeddin who received an allocation from the Ottoman sultan on 21 Ra I 913.	Ibn Iyas, 4:109, 118, 119–20, 122. For the possible return date of Kemal Reis to the Ottoman lands, see Anonymous, *Inamat Defteri*, 107b, 108a.[24] Bostan, "Kemal Reis," pp. 226–7.
Kemal Reis was accepted by the Mamluk sultan on 19 JU 913/ September 26, 1507			These ambassadors were well-received by the Mamluk sultan and granted robes of honor. Their entourage received additional outfits with fur.	Brummett, "Kemal Re'is and Gunpowder Diplomacy."
Both were granted permission to leave on 11 JA 913/ October 18, 1507				
Probably arrived to Ottoman lands in Sha'ban 913/ December 1507				

Safar 915/ May–June 1509		Prince Korkud appeared in Dimyat.	Ibn al-Himsi, *Hawadith*, 2:193–4.
Was appointed in Muharram 915/ April–May 1509	'Allan al-Dawadar	When 'Allan was first appointed ambassador, he was tasked with delivering the Mamluk sultan's good will as the Ottoman sultan recovered from an illness. After Korkud's arrival, 'Allan's departure must have been delayed and the goal of his mission revised. Finally, 'Allan left Cairo with an impressive entourage, possibly by sea, since a Mamluk fleet was prepared for this purpose.	Ibn Iyas, 4:152, 156, 160, 184. For his stay in Constantinople, see Anonymous, *Inamat Defteri*, 179b, 180a, 180b. For Korkud's stay in Mamluk lands, see pp.169–72.
Left on 6 JU 915/ August 22, 1509			
Arrived in Constantinople (probably) on 9 Shawwal 915/January 20, 1510			
Was given an audience on 15 Shawwal 915/January 26, 1510		During his stay in Constantinople, he was treated very well and received valuable gifts for both himself and Qansuh al-Ghawri.	
Returned to Damascus on 19 Muharram 916/ April 28, 1510		One month after 'Allan's return to Cairo on 4 Ra II 916/July 11, 1510, Prince Korkud asked for the Mamluk sultan's permission	

Dates	Ottoman	Mamluk	Purpose/details	Source
Either left Damascus for Cairo or arrived in Cairo on 10 Ra I 916/ June 17, 1510			to return to his father's lands—an indication that 'Allan had negotiated successfully on the prince's behalf. 'Allan was also promoted soon after his return.	Ibn al-Himsi, *Hawadith*, 2:189–90.
Left Cairo on 12 ZH 915/March 23, 1510		Yunus al-Dawla al-'Adili	This envoy came to Edirne with a large entourage and reiterated the Mamluk sultan's request for help.	For the audience in Edirne, see Anonymous, *İnamat Defteri*, 200a.
Arrived in Ra I 916/June 1510			Yunus was probably in Istanbul when the news that Rhodes had attacked the Mamluk fleet in Ayas arrived.	For the return of Yunus, see Ibn Iyas, 4:196.
Was given an audience on 25 Ra I 916/July 2, 1510			According to Brummett, this attack was one of the topics the Ottoman sultan discussed with Yunus. Rhodes had incorrectly expected an allied Ottoman–Mamluk attack against the island. They were unaware that that the recent exchanges between the two capitals could have been about the Portuguese approach.	For the arrival of Ottoman aid, see Ibn Iyas, 4:201. Brummett, "Kemal Re'is and Gunpowder Diplomacy," p. 9. Brummett, "The Overrated Adversary," pp. 534–5.
Returned to Cairo in Rajab 916/ October 1510 with Bayezid's promise for aid				For Sultan Qansuh al-Ghawri's distress and initial reactions to the destruction of the Mamluk fleet, see Ibn Iyas 4:191–2, 195.

Appendix III

Was given an audience on 5 Ra II 916/July 12, 1510	Kasabay	Kasabay presented an undated letter to Bayezid that negotiated on Korkud's behalf.	For the audience and gifts that were given to Kasabay, see Anonymous, *İnamat Defteri*, 202b, 203a.
Was granted gifts on 5 JU 916/ August 10, 1510		The surviving copy of this letter is a Turkish text, possibly a translation of the original.	For the Turkish copy of this letter, see T.E.5464.
		The ambassador received multiple sets of gifts during the same month.	For Bayezid's undated response to this letter, see Feridun, 1274, 1:356–7.
		He returned with Bayezid's letter. In the copy that survives, no reference is made to an Ottoman ambassador returning with Kasabay.	
20 JU 916/ August 25, 1501	Kasım Bey	Bayezid sent some allocations to Korkud with Kasım Bey. It is unclear whether the prince was still in Cairo or had already left. It is also unclear whether Kasım Bey was an official ambassador or merely a messenger.	Anonymous, *İnamat Defteri*, 204a.

Dates	Ottoman	Mamluk	Purpose/details	Source
1 >	Necmeddin	< Baktay	According to Qansuh al-Ghawri's undated response, Necmeddin was sent again to discuss Korkud's case. Qansuh al-Ghawri sent him back with his own ambassador, Baktay al-Khassaki. Additional references to these individuals have not been found.	Feridun, 1274, 1, pp. 357–8.
Shawwal 916/ January 1511	An Ottoman ambassador and Selman Reis		In response to Qansuh al-Ghawri's request through Yunus (for his mission, see above), Ottoman aid arrived in Alexandria under the command of Selman and Ahmed Reis in Sha'ban 916/ November 1511. Parts of the fleet were transferred to Cairo in Shawwal 916/January 1511.	Ibn Iyas, 4:201.

Appendix III

16 ZQ 916/ February 14, 1511	>	(Same as above?)	According to Ibn Iyas, this ambassador was hosted exceptionally well. The letter he presented communicated the news of Kemal Reis' disappearance. The ambassador quickly returned with a Mamluk response.	Ibn Iyas, 4:202–3. For the death of Kemal Reis in Rajab 916/October 1510, Bostan, "Kemal Reis," p. 227.
7 Ra I 917/June 4, 1511 (from Khayr Bey's letter)	Hayreddin Ağa (from the letter)		This ambassador may have been Hayreddin Ağa, whose name was mentioned in Khayr Bey's letter (see below). He may have stopped in Aleppo on his return trip. Khayr Bey's letter (in Turkish) was sent to the Ottoman ruler with the knowledge of the Mamluk sultan. The letter raises the possibility of an alliance against the Safavids.	T.E.5483[26]

Dates	Ottoman	Mamluk	Purpose/details	Source
			Because of his unusual name by Mamluk conventions, this ambassador may have been an Ottoman who was sent back with Khayr Bey's letter.	
			(See above)	
7 Safar 918/April 24, 1512			Selim replaced his father Bayezid II.	Turan, "Bayezid II," *DİA*, 5:237.
Left for Constantinople in late Safar 918/April–May 1512		Hamid Maghribi	After the enthronement of Selim I, this envoy arrived to request aid.	Ibn Iyas, 4:285.
Returned to Cairo in Ramadan 918/November–December 1512				
5 Ra I 918/May 21, 1512			Bayezid II died on his way to Dimetoka.	Turan, "Bayezid II," *DİA*, 5:237.

Ra II 918/June– July 1512	>	Cairo hosted 14 foreign missions at once, including one from the Ottomans. The Ottoman mission announced that Selim had replaced his father Bayezid on the Ottoman throne.	Ibn Iyas, 4:268–9.
Ra II–JU 918/ June–August 1512		The news of Bayezid's death reached Cairo.	Ibn Iyas, 4:269–70.

Notes:

According to Fahir İz, Aşık Paşa (670/1272–733/1333) was sent as an envoy to Egypt. However, İz does not discuss who may have sent Aşık Paşa to Cairo.[27]

According to Wansbrough, the Mamluk ambassador, Taghribirdi was also sent to Bayezid II. However, he does not give the date of this mission.[28]

According to Hüseyin Hüsameddin, El-Hac Mustafa Çelebi, a prominent merchant who established pious endowments in Amasya, was sent by both Mehmed II and Bayezid II to Egypt as an ambassador. No additional information has been found concerning these missions.[29]

NOTES

Introduction

1. For the spelling of this name, see al-Maqrizi, *Durar al-'Uqud al-Farida fi Tarajim al-'Ayan al-Mufida*, ed. Mahmud Jalili, 4 vols. (Beyrout, 2002), 2:7–8.
2. See pp. 50–1, 78–9.
3. Ibn al-Furat, *Tarikh al-Duwal wa-l-Muluk*, ed. K. Zurayk and N. Izzedine (Beirut, 1936–42), 9:339.
4. See pp. 134–6, 139–41, 147, 153.
5. For the authoritative study on this war, see Shai Har-El, *Struggle for Domination in the Middle East: The Ottoman–Mamluk War, 1485–1491* (Leiden: E.J. Brill, 1995).
6. Author's translation. Al-Husayni, "Kitab Nafa'is al-Majalis al-Sultaniyya," in *Majalis al-Sultan al-Ghawri*, ed. 'Abd al-Wahhab 'Azzam (Cairo, 1941), pp. 133–4.
7. For imperial ideologies in diplomacy, see Anne F. Broadbridge, *Kingship and Ideology in the Islamic and Mongol Worlds* (Cambridge: Cambridge University Press, 2008), pp. 6–26. For the significance of diplomatic ceremonials in European context, see Garrett Mattingly, *Renaissance Diplomacy* (Boston: Houghton Mifflin, 1955); William Roosen, "Early Modern Diplomatic Ceremonial: A Systems Approach," *The Journal of Modern History* 52 (1980):452–76.
8. For an introduction to ceremonies in Islamic courts, see Paula Sanders and et al., "Marāsim," *EI*[2], 6:518–34; Paula Sanders et al., "Mawākib," *EI*[2], 6:849–67.

9. For example, Broadbridge, *Kingship*; Paula Sanders, *Ritual, Politics, and the City in Fatimid Cairo* (New York, NY: SUNY, 1994); Dominique Sourdel, "Questions de Cérémonial Abbaside," *Revue des Études Islamiques* (1960):121–48; Konrad Dilger, *Untersuchungen zur Geschichte des Osmanischen Hofzeremoniells in 15. und 16. Jahrhundert* (München: Dr. Rudolf Trofenik, 1967); Hakan Karateke, *Padişahım Çok Yaşa! Osmanlı Devletinin Son Yüzyılında Merasimler* (İstanbul: Kitab Yayınları, 2004); Karl Stowasser, "Manners and Customs at the Mamluk Court," *Muqarnas* 2 (1984):13–20. For an example from the Byzantine context, see Michael McCormick, "Analyzing Imperial Ceremonies," *Jahrbuch der Österreichischen Byzantinistik* 35 (1985):1–20.
10. For a recent criticism of the prevalent emphasis on the establishment of resident embassies in the West, see John Watkins, "Toward a New Diplomatic History of Medieval and Early Modern Europe," *Journal of Medieval and Early Modern Studies* 38 (2008):4–5.
11. For the term "courtly insults," see Sanjay Subrahmanyam, *Courtly Encounters: Translating Courtliness and Violence in Early Modern Eurasia* (Cambridge, MA: Harvard University Press, 2012), pp. 34–102.
12. For a similar emphasis on religion as the prime denominator in diplomatic relations of medieval and early-modern European powers, see Mattingly, *Renaissance Diplomacy*, p. 16. For a recent criticism of this emphasis, see Watkins, "Toward a New Diplomatic History," pp. 2–3.
13. This term is often misleadingy translated as holy war. T.M. Johnstone, "Ghazw," *EI*², 2:1055–6.
14. Johnstone, "Ghazw"; Emile Tyan, "Djihād," *EI*², 2:538–40. For a preliminary comparative study of nuances between the concepts of *ghaza* and *jihad* in Ottoman and Mamluk contexts, see Albrecht Fuess, "Ottoman Ghazwah and Mamluk Jihād: Two Arms on the Same Body?" in *Everything is on the Move: The "Mamluk Empire" as a Node in (Trans-) Regional Networks*, ed. Stefan Conermann (forthcoming). Also see Cemal Kafadar, *Between Two Worlds: The Construction of the Ottoman State* (Berkeley CA: University of California Press, 1995), pp. 79–80; Linda Darling, "Contested Territory: Ottoman Holy War in Comparative Context," *SI* 91 (2000):133–63; Colin Imber, "The Ottoman Dynastic Myth," *Turcica* 19 (1987):7–29. For the development of this particular rhetoric in diverse historical contexts, see Stephen Humphreys, "Ayyubids, Mamluks, and the Latin East in the Thirteenth Century," *MSR* 2 (1998):1–19; Carole Hillenbrand, *The Crusades: Islamic Perspectives* (New York, NY: Routledge, 1999); Kafadar, *Between Two Worlds*; Roy Parviz Mottahedeh and Ridwan al-Sayyid, "The Idea of *Jihād* in Islam Before the Crusades," in *The Crusades from the Perspective of Byzantium and the Muslim World*, ed. Angeliki E. Laiou and Roy Parviz Mottahedeh (Washington, WA: Dumbarton Oaks, 2001), pp. 23–9.
15. For example, Humphreys, "Ayyubids, Mamluks, and the Latin East"; Georg Christ, *Trading Conflicst: Venetian Merchants and Mamluk Officials in Late Medieval Alexandria* (Leiden: E.J. Brill, 2012), pp. 113–19; Maria Pia Pedani, "*Osmanlı Padişahının Adına*": *İstanbul'un Fethinden Girit Savaşı'na Venedik'e*

Gönderilen Osmanlılar, trans. Elis Yıldırım (Ankara: TTK, 2011); P. M. Holt, *Early Mamluk Diplomacy (1260–1290): Treaties of Baybars and Qalawun with Christian Rulers* (Leiden: E.J. Brill, 1995).

16. Adel Allouche, *The Origins and Development of the Ottoman-Safavid Conflict* (Berlin: Klaus Schwarz Verlag, 1983).
17. For the Mamluk sultans' image and sovereignty, see P.M. Holt, "The Position and Power of the Mamluk Sultan," *BSOAS* 38 (1975):237–49; Holt, "Some Observations on the 'Abbāsid Caliphate of Cairo," *BSOAS* 47 (1984):501–7; Holt, "The Structure of Government in the Mamluk Sultanate," in *The Eastern Mediterranean Lands in the Period of the Crusades*, ed. Holt (Warminster, 1977), pp. 44–61; Ulrich Haarmann, "Der Arabische Osten im späten Mittelalter 1250–1517," in *Geschicte der Arabischen Welt*, ed. Ulrich Haarmann (München, 1992), pp. 228–31; Broadbridge, *Kingship*, pp. 12–16.
18. Claude Cahen, "Ayyūbids," *EI* ^{2}, 1:797–808; Michael Chamberlain, "The Crusader Era and the Ayyūbid Dynasty," in *Cambridge History of Egypt*, ed. Carl F. Petry, vol.1 (Cambridge: Cambridge University Press, 1998), pp. 211–42; Stephen Humphreys, *From Saladin to the Mongols: The Ayyubids of Damascus* (New York, NY: SUNY, 1977).
19. Haarmann, "Der Arabische Osten," p. 220.
20. Ulrich Haarmann, "Regicide and the 'Law of the Turks'," in *Intellectual Studies on Islam: Essays in honor of Martin B. Dickson* (Salt Lake City, 1990), p. 130; P.M. Holt, "Succession in the Early Mamluk Sultanate," *Deutschen Orientalistentag* 16 (1985):146, 148.
21. Haarmann, "Regicide," p. 130.
22. Henning Sievert, *Der Herrscherwechsel im Mamlukensultanat* (Berlin: Klaus Schwarz Verlag, 2003).
23. Carl Petry, ed., *CHE*, p. 523.
24. Also see Amalia Levanoni, "The Mamluk Conception of the Sultanate," *IJMES* 26 (1994):373–92.
25. Haarmann, "Der Arabische Osten," p. 228; Albrecht Fuess, "Mamluk Politics," in *Ubi sumus? Quo vademus? Mamluk Studies – State of the Art*, ed. Stephan Conermann (Bonn: Bonn University Press, 2013), pp. 99–102.
26. Linda Northrup, "The Baḥrī Mamlūk Sultanate," in *CHE*, p. 249, 255; Northrup, *From Slave to Sultan: The Career of al-Manṣūr Qalāwūn and the Consolidation of Mamluk Rule in Egypt and Syria (678–689 A.H./1279–1290 A.D.)* (Stuttgart: F.Steiner, 1998), pp. 85–6, 118–21; Nasser O. Rabbat, *The Citadel of Cairo: A New Interpretation of Royal Mamlūk Architecture* (Leiden: E.J. Brill, 1995), p. 136.
27. For instance, Emmanuel Sivan, *L'Islam et la Croisade: Idéologie et Propagande dans les Réactions Musulmanes aux Croisades* (Paris, 1968), pp. 165–89; Holt, "Position and Power," pp. 246–7.
28. Reuven Amitai-Preiss, *Mongols and Mamluks: The Mamluk-Īlkhānid War, 1260–1281* (Cambridge: Cambridge University Press, 1995), pp. 157–78; Holt, *The Age of the Crusades*, pp. 96, 173–4; Peter Thorau, *The Lion of Egypt: Sultan*

Baybars I and the Near East in the Thirteenth Century, trans. P.M.Holt (London: Longman, 1992), pp. 135–40.
29. Al-'Umari, *Al-'Umarī's Bericht über Anatolien in seinem Werke: Masālik al-Abṣār fi Mamālik al-Amṣār: al-'Umari's Bericht über Anatolien*, ed. Franz Taeschner (Leipzig: 1929), pp. 12–13; Ibn Shaddad, *Tarikh al-Malik al-Zahir*, ed. Ahmad Hutayt (Wiesbaden: Franz Steiner Verlag, 1983), pp. 175–7.
30. Har-El, *Struggle*, pp. 27–54; Barbara Flemming, *Landschaftsgeschichte von Pamphylien, Pisidien und Lykien im Spätmittelalter* (Wiesbaden, 1964), pp. 34–66.
31. Neşri, *Kitâb-ı Cihan-nümâ: Neşrī Tarihi*, ed. Faik Reşit Unat and Mehmed A. Köymen (Ankara: TTK, 1949), pp. 41–3, 51; Neşri, *Ǧihānnümâ: Die altosmanische Chronik des Mevlānā Meḥemmed Neṣrī*, ed. Theodor Menzel and Franz Taeschner (Leipzig: Otto Harrosowitz, 1951), 1:15; Neşri, *Cihânnümâ*, ed. Necdet Öztürk (İstanbul: Çamlıca, 2008), p. 28. For the preoccupation of the fifteenth-century Anatolian residents (probably in Konya) with the Mamluk affairs, see also Osman Turan, ed., *İstanbul'un Fethinden Önce Yazılmış Tarihi Takvimler* (Ankara: TTK, 1954), pp. 12–27.
32. Al-'Umari, *Masālik*, ed. Taeschner, pp. 24–5.
33. For the Dulkadirids, Refet Yınanç, *Dulkadir Beyliği* (Ankara: TTK, 1989); Margaret Venzke, "The Case of a Dulgadir-Mamluk *Iqṭā'*,"*JESHO* (2000):399–474. For the Ramazanids, Faruk Sümer, "Ramazan-oğulları," *İA*, 9:612–20. Also see Broadbridge, *Kingship*, pp. 153–6.
34. See p. 93.
35. Venzke, "Dulgadir-Mamluk *Iqṭā'*," p. 339.
36. Faruk Sümer, "Ramazan-oğulları."
37. Amitai-Preiss, *Mongols and Mamluks*; Angus Donald Stewart, *The Armenian Kingdom and the Mamluks: War and Diplomacy during the Reigns of Het'um II (1289–1307)* (Leiden: E.J. Brill, 2001).
38. Holt, "Position and Power," pp. 246–7.
39. Peter W. Edbury, *The Kingdom of Cyprus and the Crusades, 1191–1374* (Cambridge: Cambridge University Press, 1991), pp. 161–8; Albrecht Fuess, *Verbranntes Ufer: Auswirkungen mamlukischer Seepolitik auf Beirut und die syro-palästinensische Küste (1250–1517)* (Leiden: E.J. Brill, 2001), pp. 24–51, 74–80; Mohamed Ouerfelli, "Les Relations entre le Royaume de Chypre et le Sultanat Mamelouk au XVe Siècle," *Le Moyen Âge* CX (2004):327–44; Hassanein Rabie, "Mamlūk Campaigns against Rhodes," in *The Islamic World: From Classical to Modern Times: Essays in Honor of Bernard Lewis*, ed. C.E. Bosworth et al. (Princeton, 1989), pp. 281–6; M. Mustafa Ziada, "The Mamluk Conquest of Cyprus in the Fifteenth Century: Part I," *Bulletin of the Faculty of Arts of the University of Egypt* 1 (1933):99–110; Ziada, "The Mamluk Conquest of Cyprus in the Fifteenth Century: Part II," *Bulletin of the Faculty of Arts of the University of Egypt* 2 (1934):37–58.
40. Broadbridge, *Kingship*.
41. For the title and its probably first usage by the Ayyubids, see Bernard Lewis, "Khādim al-Ḥaramayn," *EI*^{2}, 4:899–900. Holt, "The Structure of Govern-

ment," 44–6; Holt, "Some Observations"; Holt, "Position and Power," pp. 243–4. For *mahmal*, see J. Jomier, "Maḥmal" *EI²*, 6:44–6. For Mamluk monopoly on *mahmal* and for the precedence of the Mamluk litter, see Jacques Jomier, *Le Maḥmal et la Caravane Égyptienne des Pèlerins de la Mecque* (Cairo, 1953), pp. 3, 10, 31, 27–34.

42. Broadbridge, *Kingship*, p. 16; Jomier, *Le Maḥmal*, p. 50; Malika Dekkiche, "Le Caire: Carrefour des Ambassades," 2 vols. (PhD diss., Université de Liège, 2010–11), 1:74–82, 82–94 (for the incidents between the Mamluk sultan Barsbay and the Timurid sultan Shahrukh). For the Aqqoyunlu leader Uzun Hasan's attempts to send the cover of *mahmal* between 1469 and 1477, see John E. Woods, *The Aqquyunlu Clan, Confederation, Empire (Revised and Expanded)*, (Salt Lake City, UT: The University of Utah Press, 1999), pp. 107–8.
43. Holt, "Some Observations"; Holt, "Position and Power."
44. Haarmann, "Der Arabische Osten," pp. 229–30. For the continuing significance of the Abbasid caliphate at least for the eleventh and twelfth centuries, see Eric Hanne, *Putting the Caliph in His Place: Power, Authority, and the Late Abbasid Caliphate* (Madison, NJ: Farleigh Disckinson University Press, 2007), pp. 207–10. For Baybars' pledge of allegiance to the Abbasid caliph in the presence of the Mongol ambassadors, see Broadbridge, *Kingship*, pp. 52–4. Although Holt believes in the initial significance of the Abbasid caliphate to sanction the Mamluk regime, he does not say much about its continuing significance in the international arena. See Holt, "Structure," p. 45; Holt, "Some Observations."
45. Nasser Rabbat, "Mamluk Throne Halls: 'Qubba' or 'Iwān'," in "Pre-Modern Islamic Palaces," ed. Gülru Necipoğlu, special issue, *Ars Orientalis* 23 (1993):209.
46. Broadbridge, *Kingship*, p. 150.
47. For various Mamluk sultans who used this tactic, see Broadbridge, *Kingship*, pp. 42, 45, 47–8, 85, 183.
48. Sanjay Subrahmanyam, *The Career and Legend of Vasco de Gama* (Cambridge: Cambridge University Press, 1997), pp. 97–9; Haroon Khan Sherwani, *The Bahmanis of the Deccan* (New Delhi, 1985), pp. 62–3. For the Ottoman ruler Bayezid I requesting caliphal approval, see p. 79 and also Broadbridge, *Kingship*, p. 175.
49. Subrahmanyam, *Vasco de Gama*, pp. 94–112; Mohammad Habib and Khaliq Ahmad Nizami, *A Comprehensive History of India*, vol. 5 (New Delhi, 1970), pp. 492–93, 537–38, 557, 589; Sherwani, *The Bahmanis of Deccan*, pp. 62–3, 228–9; H.K. Sherwani, "Bahmanīs," *EI²*, 1:923–6.
50. For instance, Broadbridge, *Kingship*, pp. 149–50; Doris Behrens-Abouseif, "The Citadel of Cairo: Stage for Mamluk Ceremonial," *Annales Islamologiques* 24 (1988):32.
51. See al-Qalqashandi, *Subh al-A'sha fi Sina'at al-Insha'*, ed. Muhammad Husayn Shams al-din (Beyrout: Dar al-Kutub al-'Ilmiyya, 1987), 3:294. For a recent analysis of *tashrif*, see Finbarr Flood, *Objects of Translation: Material Culture and*

Medieval "Hindu-Muslim" Encounter (Princeton, NJ: Princeton University Press, 2009), pp. 75–7. For the gradually changing meaning of *tashrīf*, see Werner Diem, *Ehrendes Kleid und Ehrendes Wort: Studien zu Tašrīf in Mamlūkischer and Vormamlūkischer Zeit* (Würzburg: Ergon Verlag, 2002).

52. Broadbridge, *Kingship*, p. 150.
53. Jørgen S. Nielsen, *Secular Justice in an Islamic State: Maẓālim under the Baḥrī Mamlūks, 662/1264–789/1387* (Leiden, 1985); Albrecht Fuess, "Ẓulm by Maẓālim? The Political Implications of the Use of *Maẓālim* Jurisdiction by the Mamluk Sultan," *MSR* 13 (2009):121–47; Fuess, "Between *dihlīz* and *dār al-'adl*: Forms of Outdoor and Indoor Royal Representation at the Mamluk Court in Egypt," in *Court Cultures in Muslim World: Seventh to Nineteenth Centuries*, ed. Albrecht Fuess and Jan-Peter Hartung (London: Routledge, 2011), pp. 156–60; Behrens-Abouseif, "Citadel of Cairo," pp. 35–42; Nasser O.Rabbat, "The Ideological Significance of the *Dār al-Adl in the Medieval Islamic Orient*," *IJMES* 27 (1995):3–28; Holt, "Structure," pp. 50–1.
54. Jørgen S.Nielsen, "Maẓālim," *EI*^{2}, 7:933.
55. P.M. Holt, *The Age of the Crusades: the Near East from the Eleventh Century to 1517* (London: Longman, 1986), pp. 73, 144–5.
56. Doris Behrens-Abouseif, *Cairo of the Mamluks: A History of Architecture and its Culture* (London: I.B.Tauris, 2007), p. 27. For Rabbat's claim about the decreasing importance of this institution, see Rabbat, "The Ideological Significance," p. 18.
57. For architectural patronage, see Stephen Humphreys, "The Expressive Intent of the Mamluk Architecture of Cairo," *SI* 35 (1972):69–119; Rabbat, "Ideological Significance." For patronage of scholars and educational institutions, see Jonathan Berkey, *The Transmission of Knowledge in Medieval Cairo* (Princeton: Princeton University Press, 1992), pp. 128–60. For imperial charity and pious patronage, see Adam Sabra, *Poverty and Charity in Medieval Islam* (Cambridge: Cambridge University Press, 2000), pp. 69–100, pp. 52–8, 138; Behrens-Abouseif, *Cairo of the Mamluks*, pp. 9–13.
58. Berkey, *Transmission*, pp. 128–60.
59. Carl Petry, *The Civilian Elite of Cairo in the Later Middle Ages* (Princeton, NJ: Princeton University Press, 1981), pp. 139–40, 269–72; Leonor Fernandes, *The Evolution of a Sufi Institution in Mamluk Egypt: The Khanqah* (Berlin, 1988); Barbara Flemming, "Šerīf, Sultan Ġavrī, und die 'Perser'," *Islam* 45 (1969):81–93 (especially 84); Helena Hallenberg, "The Sultan Who Loved Sufis," *MSR* 4 (2000):147–66.
60. Jomier, *Le Maḥmal*, pp. 35–42; Boaz Shoshan, *Popular Culture in Medieval Cairo* (Cambridge: Cambridge University Press, 1993), pp. 70–6; Behrens-Abouseif, *Cairo of the Mamluks*, pp. 25–33.
61. For the Germiyanids, see Mustafa Çetin Varlık, *Germiyan-oğulları* (Ankara: Ankara Üniversitesi, 1974); Irene Mélikoff, "Germiyān-oghullari," *EI*^{2}, 2:989–90. For the Karamanids, Faruk Sümer, "Ḳaramān-oghullari," *EI*^{2}, 4:619–25; Şehabettin Tekindağ, "Karamanlılar," *İA*, 6:316–30.

62. For the transfer of the capital, see Halil İnalcık, "Bursa," *DİA*, 6:446. It is likely that this transfer of power from Bursa to Edirne was a gradual process and only finalized during the reign of Murad II (r.1421–51). Between 1402 and the 1420s, the two cities of Bursa and Edirne were used interchangeably depending on the political context, although Edirne increasingly gained attention. In 1432, when Bertrandon de la Broquière was visiting the Ottoman lands, Edirne was the capital. For a claim that Murad I made Edirne his capital, see Laonikos Chalkokondyles, *A Translation and Commentary of the "Demonstrations of Histories,"* trans. and ed. Nicolaos Nicoloudis (Athens, 1996), p. 125.
63. For religious motivations and also for the earlier Muslim attacks on the city, see J.H. Mordtmann, "Ḳusṭanṭīniyya," *EI*^{2}, 5:532.
64. Fuess, "Ottoman Ghazwah and Mamluk Jihād." For the Ottoman use of *ghazi* (champions of *ghaza*), see Irene Mélikoff, "Ghāzī," *EI*^{2}, 2:1043–5.
65. Halil İnalcık, "Osmanlılar'da saltanat veraseti usulü ve Türk hâkimiyet telâkkisiyle ilgisi," *Siyasal Bilgiler Fakültesi Dergisi* 14 (1956):69–94.
66. Woods, *Aqquyunlu.*
67. Faruk Sümer, *Kara Koyunlular* (Ankara: TTK, 1967); Faruk Sümer, "Ḳarā-ḳoyunlu," *EI*^{2}, 4:584.
68. Woods, *Aqquyunlu*, pp. 98–9; Matthew Melvin-Koushki, "The Delicate Art of Aggression: Uzun Hasan's *Fathnama* to Qaytbay of 1469," *Iranian Studies* 44 (2011):193–214.
69. Allouche, *Origins and Development*, pp. 10–11, 13–15; John Wansbrough, "A Mamluk Letter of 877/1473," *BSOAS* 24 (1961):200–13; Anthony Bryer, "Lodovico da Bologna and the Georgian and Anatolian Embassy of 1460–61," *Bedi Kartlisa, Revue de Kartvélologie* 19–20 (1965):179–98; Caterino Zeno, "Travels in Persia," in *A Narrative of Italian Travels in Persia in the Fifteenth and Sixteenth Centuries*, ed. and trans. Charles Gray (London: The Hakluyt Society, 1873), pp. 12–13; Jean Adorno, *Itinéraire d'Anselme Adorno en Terre Sainte (1470–71)*, trans. and ed. Jacques Heers and Georgette de Groer (Paris, 1978), pp. 3, 15.
70. Woods, *Aqquyunlu*, pp. 115–16. For Yaqub's involvement with the Mamluks, see J. Woods, "Turco-Iranica I: An Ottoman Intelligence Report on Late Fifteenth/Ninth Century Iranian Foreign Relations," *Journal of Near Eastern Studies* 38 (1979):1–9.
71. Allouche, *Origins and Development*, p. 91.
72. Ibid., p. 65.
73. Hugh Kennedy, *Muslim Spain and Portugal: A Political History of al-Andalus* (London: Pearson, 1996).
74. L.P. Harvey, *Muslims in Spain, 1500 to 1614* (Chicago, IL: Chicago University Press, 2005); Andrew Hess, "The Moriscos: An Ottoman Fifth Column in Sixteenth-Century Spain," *The American Historical Review* 74 (1968):1–25.
75. Subrahmanyam, *Vasco de Gama*, p. 248.
76. For the Hafsids and Nasrids, see p. 148.

77. For the commercial connections of Egypt with the rest of the world, see for instance Francisco Javier Apellániz Ruiz de Galarreta, *Pouvoir et Finance en Méditerranée pré-moderne: le deuxième État mamelouk et le commerce des épices (1382–1517)* (Barcelona: CSIC, 2009); Eliahu Ashtor, *The Levant Trade in the Later Middle Ages* (Princeton, NJ: Princeton University Press, 1983); Damien Coulon, *Barcelone et le grand commerce d'orient au moyen âge: un siècle de relations avec l'Egypte et la Syrie-Palestine, ca. 1330-ca. 1430* (Madrid, 2004); Steven Humphreys, "Egypt in the World System of the Later Middle Ages," in *CHE*, pp. 445–62; Subhi Labib, *Handelsgeschichte Ägyptens im Spätmittelalter, 1171–1517*, Vierteljahrschrift für Sozial- und Wirtschaftsgeschichte Beihefte 46 (Wiesbaden: F. Steiner, 1965). For trade relations between Anatolia and Egypt, see for instance, Kate Fleet, *European and Islamic Trade in the early Ottoman State: The Merchants of Genoa and Turkey* (Cambridge: Cambridge University Press, 1999), pp. 26, 37, 79, 82, 102, 141; Kate Fleet, "The Turkish Economy, 1071–1453" in *Cambridge History of Turkey*, ed. Kate Fleet, vol. 1 (Cambridge: Cambridge University Press, 2009), pp. 228–9; Halil İnalcık, "Bursa and the Commerce of the Levant," *JESHO* 3 (1960):131–47; Halil İnalcık, "Bursa: XV. Asır Sanayi ve Ticaret Tarihine Dair Vesikalar," *Belleten* 24 (1960):45–102; E.A. Zachariadou, *Trade and Crusade, Venetian Crete and the Emirates of Mentesche and Aydın 1300–1415* (Venice: Istituto Ellenico di Studi Bizantini e Postbizantini, 1983).

78. Richard T. Mortel, "Aspects of Mamlūk Relations with Jedda during the Fifteenth Century: The Case of Timrāz al-Mu'ayyadī," *Journal of Islamic Studies* 6 (1995):1–13; John Meloy, *Imperial Power and Maritime Power: Mecca and Cairo in the later Middle Ages* (Chicago, 2010), especially pp. 250–4.

79. P.M. Holt, *Early Mamluk Diplomacy (1260–1290): Treaties of Baybars and Qalawun with Christian Rulers* (Leiden: E.J. Brill, 1995).

80. For the significance of spice trade (especially pepper) from India both for the Mamluks and European merchants, see Apellániz Ruiz de Galarreta, *Pouvoir et Finance*. For slave trade between the Ottomans and the Mamluks, see Fleet, *European and Islamic Trade*, pp. 37, 41 and 141.

81. Fleet, *European and Islamic Trade*, p. 26.

82. Ibid., p. 102; Fleet, "The Turkish Economy," p. 249.

83. İnalcık, "Bursa and the Commerce," p. 147; Fleet, *European and Islamic Trade*, pp. 79, 131–2.

84. Fleet, "The Turkish Economy," pp. 249, 251.

85. Ibid., pp. 241, 251.

86. Ibid., p. 251.

87. Ibid.; Fleet, *European and Islamic Trade*, p. 71.

88. İnalcık, "Bursa and the Commerce"; İnalcık, "Bursa: Vesikalar"; Claude Cahen, *The Formation of Turkey: The Seljukid Sultanate of Rūm: Eleventh to Fourteenth Century*, trans. P.M. Holt (New York, NY: Longman, 2001), pp. 91–6. For the Ottoman hostel in Alexandria, see Bernhard von Breydenbach, *Bernhard von Breydenbach: Peregrinatio in Terram Sanctam*, ed. Isolde Mozer

(Berlin, 2010), p. 157; Olivia Remie Constable, *Housing the Stranger in the Mediterranean World* (Cambridge: Cambridge University Press, 2003), p. 273.
89. İnalcık, "Bursa and the Commerce"; İnalcık, "Bursa: Vesikalar."
90. For instance, for the role of Jewish merchants, see Halil İnalcık, "Jews in the Ottoman Economy and Finances, 1450–1500," in *The Islamic World from Classical to Modern Times*, pp. 513–50. For the role of Genoese merchants, Fleet, *European and Islamic Trade*, p. 37.
91. Coulon, *Barcelone et le grand commerce d'orient*.
92. Giovanni Curatola, "Venetian merchants and travellers in Alexandria," in *Alexandria, Real and Imagined*, ed. Anthony Hirst and Michael Silk (Aldershot, Hampshire: Ashgate, 2004), p. 191. For an overview of relations between Venice and the Mamluks, see Deborah Howard, "Venice and the Mamluks," in *Venice and the Islamic World*, ed. Stefano Carboni (New York, NY: Metropolitan Museum of Art, 2007), pp. 72–90.
93. For the dominant Genoese presence in the Black Sea region, see Fleet, "The Turkish Economy," p. 252.
94. For Venetian attempts to build alliances with the Portuguese although the Portuguese geographic explorations threatened Venetian interests in the Mediterranean, see Subrahmanyam, *Vasco de Gama*, pp. 184–9.
95. For the significance of the Ottomans and Mamluks for Dom Manuel's politics, see Subrahmanyam, *Vasco de Gama*, pp. 245–57.
96. Ibid., pp. 47–58.
97. Palmira Brummett, *Ottoman Seapower and Levantine Diplomacy in the Age of Discovery* (Albany: SUNY, 1994), pp. 111–16, 114–18.
98. Cyriac of Ancona, *Later Travels*, ed. and trans. by Edward W. Bodnar and Clive Foss (Cambridge, Massachusetts: The I Tatti Renaissance Library, 2003); Eve Borsook, "The Travels of Bernardo Michelozzi and Bonsignore Bonsignori in the Levant (1497–98)," *Journal of the Warburg and Courtauld Institutes* 36 (1973):145–97; Anne Wolff, "Merchants, pilgrims, and naturalists: Alexandria through European eyes from the fourteenth to the sixteenth century," in *Alexandria, Real and Imagined*, ed. Anthony Hirst and Michael Silk (Aldershot: Ashgate, 2004), pp. 200–1.
99. For this term, see Borsook, "Travels," p. 146.
100. Allouche, *Origins and Development*, pp. 20–9; Edbury, *Kingdom of Cyprus*, p. 168.
101. Allouche, *Origins and Development*, pp. 20–9.
102. For instance, for the Mamluk mistreatment of European and especially Venetian merchants, see Curatola, "Venetian merchants and travelers,"p. 191; Wansbrough, "A Mamluk Letter of 877/1473." For Mamluk documents of safe-conduct, see John Wansbrough, "The Safe-Conduct in Muslim Chancery Practice," *BSOAS* 34 (1971):20–35.
103. Har-El, *Struggle*. For a list of Şehabettin Tekindağ's old but useful articles, see Bibliography.

104. For different approaches to war in international relations, see Christer Jönsson and Martin Hall, *Essence of Diplomacy* (Houndmills: Palgrave Macmillan, 2005), pp. 16–17.
105. Giancarlo Casale, *The Ottoman Age of Exploration* (Oxford: Oxford University Press, 2010).
106. Har-El, *Struggle*; Muhammad Harb, "I.Selim'in Suriye ve Mısır Seferi Hakkında İbn İyās'da Mevcut Haberlerin Selimnamelerle Mukayesesi: XVI. Asır Osmanlı-Memluklu Kaynakları Hakkında Bir Tetkik" (PhD diss., İstanbul University, 1980); Ahmad Fu'ad Mutawalli, *Al-Fatkh al-'Uthmani li'l-Sham wa Misr wa Muqaddimatuhu min Waqi al-Wathaiq wa al-Masadir al-Turkiyah wa al-Arabiyah al-Muasirah* (Cairo, 1976); Şehabettin Tekindağ, "II. Bayezid Devrinde Çukurova'da Nüfuz Mücadelesi," *Belleten* 31 (1967):345–75; Şehabettin Tekindağ, "Fatih Devrinde Osmanlı Memluklü Münasebetleri," *İstanbul Üniversitesi Edebiyat Fakültesi* 30 (1976):73–99.

Chapter 1 The Tools of Diplomacy

1. In *Durar al-'Uqud*, al-Maqrizi claimed that he heard some of these phrases from Amir Husam al-din Hasan al-Kujkuni, who was among the confidants of Barquq and sent as an envoy to Bursa in 1392. However, the fifteenth-century Mamluk scholar Ibn Hajar claimed that these sentences were reported by the famous scholar Ibn Khaldun (d.1406). In this instance, Ibn Bahadur, who relied on both al-Maqrizi's and Ibn Hajar's works, follows Ibn Hajar's account. See al-Maqrizi, *Durar*, 1:445, 2:8; Ibn Hajar, *Inba' al-Ghumr bi-Abna al-'Umr*, ed. Hasan Habashi, 4 vols. (Cairo, 1969–98), 1:491–2. For the vocalization of both Amir al-Kujkuni and Ibn al-Sughayr's names, I follow the vocalizations in Mahmud Jalili's editions of al-Maqrizi's *Durar*.
2. Author's translation. Ibn Bahadur, *Waqai'i Turkman*, TKSK III. Ahmed 3057, 23b–25b.
3. For the symbolic importance of the diplomatic embassies, see Broadbridge, *Kingship*, pp. 16–26.
4. Ibn Taghribirdi, *History of Egypt: 1382–1469*, trans. W. Popper (Berkeley, CA: University of California Press, 1958), 18:11. Henceforth, Ibn Taghribirdi, *Nujum*, trans. Popper.
5. For non-verbal communication in diplomacy, see Jönsson and Hall, *Essence of Diplomacy*, pp. 84–8.
6. Behrens-Abouseif, "Citadel of Cairo," p. 29:
7. Gülru Necipoğlu, "An Outline of Shifting Paradigms in the Palatial Architecture of the Pre-Modern Islamic World," in "Pre-Modern Islamic Palaces," ed. Gülru Necipoğlu, special issue, *Ars Orientalis* 23 (1993):12–14.
8. Behrens-Abouseif, "Citadel of Cairo," pp. 29–30.
9. Ibid., pp. 26–30.

10. For the possible influence of other Islamic courts on the Ottoman ceremonial and organizational structure, see İsmail Hakkı Uzunçarşılı, *Osmanlı Devleti Teşkilatına Medhal* (Ankara: TTK, 1988). For Mehmed's inquiry about court etiquette in Akkoyunlu and Mamluk palaces, see Gülru Necipoğlu, *Architecture, Ceremonial, and Power: The Topkapı Palace in the Fifteenth and Sixteenth Centuries* (Cambridge, MA: MIT Press, 1991), pp. 15–16. Also see Pedani, *Osmanlı Padişahının Adına*, pp. 4–5.
11. Necipoğlu, "Shifting Paradigms," pp. 15–19; Necipoğlu, *Topkapı*, pp. 248–9.
12. Necipoğlu, *Topkapı*, pp. 19–20, 31, 91–110.
13. Ibid., pp. 248–9; Necipoğlu, "Shifting Paradigms," pp. 15–19; Gülru Necipoğlu, "Framing the Gaze in Ottoman, Safavid, Mughal Palaces," in "Pre-Modern Islamic Palaces," ed. Gülru Necipoğlu, special issue, *Ars Orientalis* 23 (1993):303–6.
14. Nizam al-Mulk, *The Book of Government*, trans. Hurbert Darke, 3rd ed. (London: Curzon, 2002), p. 98.
15. Al-Qalqashandi, *Subh al-A'sha*, 6:344–7.
16. Also see E.Kohlberg et al., "Safīr," *EI*[2], 8:811–5.
17. Pedani, *Osmanlı Padişahının Adına*, pp. 10, 34.
18. For an ambassador who was asked to translate the letter he brought from Ceylon(?), see al-Qalqashandi, *Subh al-A'sha*, 8:78–9.
19. Maria Pia Pedani-Fabris, "Ottoman Diplomats in the West: The Sultan's Ambassadors to the Republic of Venice," *Tarih İncelemeleri Dergisi* 11 (1996):187–212; Naimur Rahman Farooqi, *Mughal-Ottoman Relations: A Study of Political and Diplomatic Relations between Mughal India and the Ottoman Empire, 1555–1748*, IAD Oriental (Original) Series 32 (Delhi, 1989), p. 222.
20. Walther Björkman, *Beiträge zur Geschichte der Staatskanzlei im Islamischen Ägypten* (Hamburg, 1928), p. 45; al-Qalqashandi, *Subh al-A'sha*, 1:170.
21. For Şükrullah's multiple missions during Murad II's reign, see Şükrullah, *Behcetü't-Tevârîh*, ed. Nihal Atsız (İstanbul, 1947), p. 39. Also see Pedani, *Osmanlı Padişahının Adına*, pp. 4, 31–2. For the frequent appointments of Ibn Aja as a Mamluk ambassador, see Stephan Conermann, "Ibn Aǧās (st. 881/1476) 'Ta'rīḫ al-Amīr Yašbak aẓ-Ẓāhirī' – Biographie, Autobiographie, Tagebuch oder Chronik?" in *Die Mamlūken: Studien zu ihrer Geschichte und Kultur: Zum Gedenken an Ulrich Haarmann (1942–1999)*, ed. Stephan Conermann and Anja Pistor-Hatam (Hamburg, 2004), pp. 133–4. For other Mamluk quasi-diplomats, see Dekkiche, "Le Caire," 1:47; John Wansbrough, "A Mamluk Ambassador to Venice in 913/1507," *BSOAS* 26 (1963):503–30.
22. Bernard Lewis, "Elči," *EI*[2], 2:694; Mehmed İpşirli, "Elçi," *DİA*, 11:3–15.
23. For a similar correlation between the mission and the social status of an envoy, see Silvio A. Bedini, *The Pope's Elephant* (Manchester: Carcanet Press, 1997), 27; Pedani, *Osmanlı Padişahının Adına*, p. 39.
24. For example, for Azeb Bey's mission, see p. 38, 107.
25. For example, for Ali Çelebi's mission, see pp. 149–51.

26. The positions of ambassadors who were sent to Venice between 1453 and 1669 reinforce a similar impression. See Pedani, *Osmanlı Padişahının Adına*, p. 39. Although the Ottomans frequently sent people who occupied the position of *çavuş* to the European courts, they did not seem to follow the same practice for their ambassadors to the Mamluk court. For *çavuş*es in diplomatic tasks, see Pedani, *Osmanlı Padişahının Adına*, pp. 33–5. For the identity of agents sent to Italy by Bayezid II, see Nicolas Vatin, "Itinéraires d'Agents de la Porte en Italie," *Turcica* 19 (1987): 29–51.
27. Dekkiche, "Le Caire," 1:50; Donald P. Little, "Diplomatic Missions and Gifts Exchanged by Mamluks and Ilkhans," in *Beyond the Legacy of Genghiz Khan*, ed. Linda Komaroff (Leiden: E.J. Brill, 2006), p. 34.
28. Behrens-Abouseif, *Cairo of the Mamluks*, 10; Dekkiche, "Le Caire," 1:47–9. In the Ottoman–Mamluk context, some exceptional cases exist such as the missions of Ibn Aja, Nur al-din 'Ali al-Kurdi, and Shaykh 'Ala' al-din al-Husni. For a detailed list of names, see Appendix III.
29. Haarmann, "Der arabische Osten," pp. 231–3; Holt, *The Age of Crusades*, pp. 145–6.
30. Kristen Stilt, *Islamic Law in Action: Authority, Discretion, and Everyday Experiences in Mamluk Egypt* (Oxford: Oxford University Press, 2011), p. 71. Also see A.A. Duri et al., "Dīwān," *EI*^{2}, 2:323–37.
31. For an example from the Timurids, see Denis Sinor, "Diplomatic Practices in Medieval Inner Asia," in *The Islamic World from Classical to Modern Times*, p. 346.
32. Nizam al-Mulk, *The Book of Government*, p. 95. For the Mongol sensitivity about diplomatic immunity of ambassadors, see Sinor, "Diplomatic Practices," pp. 343–8. For the universality of diplomatic immunity, see Linda S. Frey and Marsha L. Frey, *History of Diplomatic Immunity* (Columbus, OH: Ohio State University Press, 1999).
33. Sinor, "Diplomatic Practices," pp. 346–7.
34. For Zeyneddin Sefer Şah, the Ottoman envoy who died on his way to Cairo from natural causes, see al-'Ayni, *'Iqd al-Juman*, Süleymaniye Carullah 1591, 612b. For Kasım Çavuş, who was robbed on his way to the Gonzagas in 1494, see Hans Joachim Kissling, *Sultan Bâyezîd II's Beziehungen zu Markgraf Francesco II. von Gonzaga* (München: Max Hueber Verlag, 1965), p. 40.
35. Dekkiche, "Le Caire," 1:62; Wansbrough, "A Mamluk Letter of 877/1473," p. 202.
36. Halil İnalcık, "Power Relationship between Russia, the Crimea and the Ottoman Empire as Reflected in Titulature," in *Passé Turco-Tatar Présent Sovietique*, ed. Ch. Lemercier-Quelquejay, G. Veinstein, S.E. Wimbush (Paris: EHESS, 1986), pp. 175–211. For the significance of imperial titulature in the representation of Roman emperors, see Janneke de Jong, "The Employment of Epithets in the Struggle for Power: A Case Study," ed. Olivier de Kleijn Hekster, Danielle Gerda Slootjes, in *Crises and the Roman Empire: Proceedings of the Seventh Workshop of the International Workshop of the International*

Network Impact of Empire (Impact of Empire, Volume 7) (Leiden: E.J. Brill, 2007), pp. 311–26.
37. Dekkiche, "Le Caire," 1:289.
38. Ibid.
39. Adrian Gully, *The Culture of Letter-Writing in Pre-Modern Islamic Society* (Edinburg: Edinburgh University Press, 2008), pp. 179–80. For diplomatic contacts between Mamluks and non-Muslim powers, see Holt, *Early Mamluk Diplomacy*; Mohamed Tahar Mansouri, *Recherches sur les Relations entre Byzance et L'Egypte (1259–1453) (d'apres les sources arabes)* (Tunis, 1992); Aziz Suryal Atiya, *Egypt and Aragon: Embassies and Diplomatic Correspondence between 1300 and 1330 A. D.* (Leipzig, 1938); Blochet, "Les Relations Diplomatiques des Hohenstaufen avec les Sultans d'Égypte," *Revue Historique* 80 (1902):51–64.
40. For external characteristics, see Dekkiche, "Le Caire," 1:292–345. For types of calligraphy, penmanship, and its hierarchical organization, see al-Qalqashandi, *Subh al-A'sha*, 3:1–220; Dekkiche, "Le Caire," 1:318–330. For papers, see Iraj Afshar, "Manuscript and Paper Sizes Cited in Persian and Arabic Texts," in *Essays in Honour of Salah al-din al-Munajjid* (London, 2002), pp. 659–73; Jonathan Bloom, *Paper before Print: The History and Impact of Paper in the Islamic World* (New Haven, CT: Yale University Press, 2001), pp. 50–3, 62. For ink and its various qualities, Dekkiche, "Le Caire," 1:330–3. For the role of ink color in diplomatic relations between Mamluks and Mongols, see Broadbridge, *Kingship*, pp. 20, 87–8, 92, 113, 135.
41. For paper sizes, see al-Qalqashandi, *Subh al-A'sha*, 6:180–6; Dekkiche, "Le Caire," 1:292–317.
42. Broadbridge, *Kingship*, p. 17.
43. Dekkiche, "Le Caire," 1:315.
44. In chronological order; BNF MS 4440, 50b-51a; Ibn Hijja, *Das Rauschgetränk der Stilkunst oder Qahwat al-Inšā'*, ed. Rudolf Veselý (Beirut: Klaus Schwarz Verlag, 2005), pp. 178, 183.
45. BNF MS 4440, 50b-51a; Ibn Hijja, *Qahwat*, ed. Veselý, p. 183.
46. For internal characteristics, see Dekkiche, "Le Caire," 1:345–93.
47. For a sample list of these sections based on Dekkiche's study, see Appendix I in this book. For an analysis of these sections, see Dekkiche, "Le Caire," 1:345–98; Gully, *Culture of Letter-Writing*, pp. 131–65.
48. Ibid.
49. For the general significance of introductions, see Gully, *Culture of Letter-Writing*, pp. 133–6, 166–96.
50. For an introduction to the scholarship on this topic, see G.L. Lewis, "Fatḥnāme," *EI*[2], 2:839–40; G.L. Lewis, "The Utility of Ottoman *Fethnames*," in *Historians of the Middle East*, ed. Bernard Lewis and P.M. Holt (London, 1962), pp. 192–6; Maria Pia Pedani-Fabris, "Ottoman Fetihnames: The Imperial Letters Announcing a Victory," *Tarih İncelemeleri Dergisi* 13 (1998):181–92; M.S Kütükoğlu, *Osmanlı Belgelerinin Dili* (İstanbul, 1994), pp. 159–60.

51. C.E. Bosworth, "Laḳab,"*EI*², 5:618–31; Dekkiche, "Le Caire," 1:359–77, 2:206–30; Gully, *Culture of Letter-Writing*, pp. 166–74. For sample studies on titulature, see İnalcık, "Power Relationship"; Gottfried Herrmann, "Zur Intitulatio Timuridscher Urkunden," *Zeitschrift der Deutschen Morgenländischen Gesellschaft Supplement II* (1972):498–521. For a discussion of *laqab* within the Mamluk domestic politics, see Amalia Levanoni, "The Sultan's *Laqab* – a Sign of a New Order in Mamluk Factionalism," in *Mamluks in Egyptian and Syrian Politics and Society*, ed. Michael Winter and Amalia Levanoni (Leiden: E.J. Brill, 2004), pp. 79–115. Also see Linda Northrup, *From Slave to Sultan* (Stuttgart: Franz Steiner Verlag, 1998), pp. 174–7. For multiple references to the appearance of titulature in epigraphy and architectural works, see Max Van Berchem, *Matériaux pour un Corpus Inscriptionum Arabicarum* (Paris, 1894).
52. For titulature in the Mamluk context, see al-Qalqashandi, *Subh al-A'sha*, 5:412–73, 6:1–174; Dekkiche, "Le Caire," 1:359–77, 2:206–30. For the Ottoman context, see Ahmed Feridun Bey, *Münşeat al-Salatin*, 2 vols. (İstanbul: 1274–5/1857–9), 1:1–14. Henceforth, Feridun, 1274.
53. Bosworth, "Laḳab."
54. See pp. 119–22.
55. For changes in the hierarchical organization of political powers from the Bahri to the Burji Mamluk regime, see Dekkiche, "Le Caire," 1:287–91.
56. See Appendix II.
57. Cihan Yüksel Muslu, "Attempting to Understand the Language of Diplomacy between the Ottomans and the Mamluks," *Archivum Ottomanicum* 30 *Archivum Ottomanicum* 30 (2013): 247–69.
58. For example, Broadbridge, *Kingship*, p. 17; Melvin-Koushki, "Fathnama," p. 198.
59. Gully, *Culture of Letter-Writing*, pp. 141, and also 32, 41, 142.
60. Ibid., p. 138.
61. See pp. 71–2, 111–13, 119.
62. See pp. 77, 182–3.
63. See pp. 91–2, 102–1.
64. Broadbridge, *Kingship*, p. 194. For Uzun Hasan's similar attack on Mamluk legitimacy, see Woods, *Aqquyunlu*, p. 116; Melvin-Koushki, "Fathnama," p. 196.
65. For example, Adel Allouche, "Tegüder's Ultimatum to Qalawun," *IJMES* 22 (1990):437–46; Melvin-Koushki, "Fathnama."
66. For earlier chancery manuals available in modern editions, see Anne Broadbridge, "Diplomatic Conventions in the Mamluk Sultanate," *Annales Islamologiques* 41 (2007):97–108; al-'Umari, *A Critical Edition of and Study on Ibn Faḍl Allāh's Manual of Secretaryship "Al-Ta'rīf Bi'l-Muṣṭalaḥ Al-Sharīf,"* ed. Samir Al-Droubi, 2 vols. (Al-Karak, 1992), 1:60–79.
67. C.E. Bosworth, "Al-Ḳalḳashandī," *EI*², 4:509; Broadbridge, "Diplomatic Conventions," pp. 104–7.
68. Bosworth, "Al-Ḳalḳashandī," p. 509.

69. For Şinasi Tekin's works, see the bibliography. Also see W. Björkman, "Die Anfänge der türkischen Briefsammlungen," in *Orientalia Suecana* 5 (1956):20–9; W. Björkman, "Eine türkische Briefsammlung aus dem 15. Jahrhundert," in *Documenta Islamica Inedita* (Berlin, 1952), pp. 189–96; Anonymous, *Fatih Devrine Ait Münşeat Mecmuası*, ed. Necdet Lugal and A.S. Erzi (İstanbul, 1956); H. İlaydın and A.S. Erzi, "XVI. Asra âid bir Münşeât Mecmuası," *Belleten* 21 (1957):221–52; A.S. Erzi, "Sarı Abdullah Efendi Münşeâtının Tavsîfi," *Belleten* 14 (1950):631–47.
70. J.H. Mordtman and V. Ménage, "Ferīdūn Beg," *EI²*, 2:881–2.
71. The earliest available code of legislation with a specific section called *Elçi Kanunnamesi* is that of Tevkii Abdurrahman Paşa, who put the document in writing in approximately 1676. Tevkii Abdurrahman Paşa, "Osmanlı Kanunnameleri," *Milli Tetebbular Mecmuası* 3 (1331/1912):497–544. Before this code, information about ceremonies, processions, and ambassadorial visits was scattered. For a recent and detailed analysis of these codes and similar texts, see Hakan Karateke, Introduction to *An Ottoman Protocol Register*, ed. Hakan Karateke (İstanbul: Royal Asiatic Society Books, 2007).
72. Karateke, Introduction.
73. For instance, Ibn Battuta, *Travels in Asia and Africa, 1325–1354*, trans. and ed. H.A.R. Gibb (New York, NY: R.M. McBride & Co, 1929).
74. For instance, Bertrandon de la Brocquière, *Bertrandon de la Broquière'in Denizaşırı Seyahati*, trans. İlhan Arda (İstanbul: Eren, 2000); ibid., *Le Voyage d'Outremer de Bertrandon de la Broquière*, ed. Charles Schefer (1892; repr., Frankfurt am Main, 1994); Cyriac of Ancona, *Later Travels*, trans. and ed. Edward W. Bodnar with Clive Foss (Cambridge, MA: Harvard University Press, 2003).
75. For instance, Johannes Schiltberger, *The Bondage and Travels of Johann Schiltberger: a Native of Bavaria, in Europe, Asia, and Africa, 1396–1427*, trans. J. Buchan Telfer (1879; repr., Elibron Classics, 2005); Johannes Schiltberger, *Als Sklave im Osmanischen Reich und bei den Tataren, 1394–1427* (Stuttgart: Thienemann, 1983).
76. For example, Tursun Bey, *The History of Mehmed the Conqueror*, ed. İnalcık and Murphey (Minneapolis, MN: Bibliotheca Islamica, 1978), pp. 25–6.
77. For instance, Esad Efendi, *Teşrifat-ı Kadime* (İstanbul, 1870); Aziz Berker, "Teşrifati Naim Efendi Tarihi," *Tarih Vesikaları* 3 (1949):69–80, 150–60, 230–40; Ali Seydi Bey, *Teşrifat ve Teşkilatımız*, ed. Niyazi Ahmet Banoğlu (İstanbul, 1973); Zarif Orgun, "Osmanlı İmparatorluğunda Kaptan Paşalara ve Donanmaya Yapılan Merasim," *Tarih Vesikaları* 2 (1941):135–44; Zarif Orgun, "Osmanlı İmparatorluğunda Tuğ ve Sancak," *Tarih Vesikaları* 4 (1941):245–55, 5 (1941):344–55; Zarif Orgun, "Osmanlı İmparatorluğunda Nâme ve Hediye Getiren Elçilere Yapılan Merasim," *Tarih Vesikaları* 5 (1942):407–13; Maria Pia Pedani, "The Sultan and the Venetian Bailo: Ceremonial Diplomatic Protocol in Istanbul," in *Diplomatisches Zeremoniell in*

Europa und im Mittleren Osten in der frühen Neuzeit, ed. R.Kauz et al. (Wien, 2009), pp. 287–99.

78. For a treatment of Ottoman–Mamluk correspondence in Feridun Bey's text, see Yüksel Muslu, "The Language of Diplomacy." Although Yınanç proves that the letters from the reigns of Osman, Orhan, and Murad are fictitious, I believe that, beginning with Bayezid I's reign, the letters exchanged between the Ottomans and Mamluks are relatively reliable. Also see Mükrimin Halil Yınanç, "Feridun Bey Münşeatı," *TOEM* 77 (1923):161–8, 78 (1924):37–46, 79:95–104, 81:216–26; Irène Beldiceanu-Steinherr, *Recherches sur les Actes des Règnes des Sultans Osman, Orkhan et Murad I* (Monaco, 1967); L. Fekete, "Das Fethnāme über die Schlacht bei Varna," *Byzantinoslavica* 15 (1953):258–70; Kurt Holter, "Studien zu Ahmed Ferîdûn's Münşe'at es-selâṭîn," *Mitteilungen des Österreichischen Instituts für Geschichtsforshung* 14 (1939):429–51; İlaydın and Erzi, "XVI. Asra Aid Bir Münşeat Mecmuası"; Hans Georg Majer, "Urkunden Fälschung im Osmanischen Reich," in *Living in the Ottoman Ecumenical Community: Essays in Honor of Suraiya Faroqhi*, ed. Suraiya Faroqhi, Vera Constantini, and Markus Koller (Leiden: E.J. Brill, 2008), pp. 45–70; Mordtman and Ménage, "Ferīdūn Beg"; Mordtman, "Feridun Bey," *İA*, 4:569–70; Abdülkadir Özcan, "Feridun Ahmed Bey," *DİA*, 12:396–7; J. Rypka, "Briefwechsel der Hohen Pforte mit den Krimchanen im II. Bande von Ferīdūns Münšeāt," in *Festschrift Georg Jacob*, ed. Theodor Menzel (Leipzig: Otto Harrassowitz, 1932), pp. 241–70; Halil Ethem, "Mısır Fethi Mukaddematına Aid Mühim bir Vesika," *TTEM* 96 (1328/1909):31–6; Ali Anooshahr, The *Ghazi Sultans and the Frontiers of Islam* (London: Routledge, 2009), pp. 120–3.

79. For instance, Ibn Taghribirdi, *Nujum*, trans. Popper, 18:27–8. For the public performance of some Mamluk letters which were claimed to be intended for other political rulers yet were never dispatched to the alleged destination, see Broadbridge, *Kingship*, p. 86.

80. Broadbridge, *Kingship*, p. 17; Dekkiche, "Le Caire," 1:423–34; P.M. Holt, "The Īlkhān Ahmad's Embassies to Qalāwūn: Two Contemporary Accounts," *BSOAS* 49 (1986):129.

81. For a comparison between a confidential and composition secretary and for *Katib al-insha*'s responsibilities, see Gully, *Culture of Letter-Writing*, pp. 94, 109–11.

82. Ibn Taghribirdi, *Nujum*, trans. Popper, 18:11. Parentheses in brackets are the author's insertions.

83. Ibid., pp. 44–5.

84. H.R. Roemer, "Inshā'," *EI* ^{2}, 3:1241–44.

85. Here the word "diplomatic" is used in the sense of anything originating from a bureaucratic chancery. See Colin Mitchell, "Safavid Imperial Tarassul and the Persian Inshā' Tradition," *Studia Iranica* 26 (1997), 178n13; W. Björkman et al., "Diplomatic," *EI* ^{2}, 1:301–16.

86. For the cross-fertilization between Arabic, Persian, and Ottoman composition practices, see Roemer, "Inshā'"; Bjorkman et al., "Diplomatic." For the influence

of Mamluk institutions on Ottoman ones, see Uzunçarşılı, *Medhal*. Although he does not discuss the influence of Mamluk chancery practices specifically, he suggests a general Mamluk influence, among others, on Ottoman institutions. This raises the possibility of an influence on the chancery practices.
87. See the following chapters and also Yüksel Muslu, "The Language of Diplomacy."
88. For a Turkish letter of the Mamluk governor Khayr Bey to the Ottoman ruler in 1511, see T.E.5483. Some later pieces of correspondence between Selim and Qansuh al-Ghawri was composed in Turkish, but these cases go beyond the scope of this study. Celia Kerslake, "The Correspondence between Selīm I and Ḳānṣūh al-Ġawrī," *Revue de Philologie Orientale* 30 (1980):219–34.
89. M. Becheneb, "Ibn al-Djazarī," *EI*², 3:753.
90. Taşköprülüzade, *Eş-Şeḳā'iḳu n-nu'mānīye fī 'Ulemā'i d-Devleti l-'Osmānīye*, ed. Ahmed Subhi Furat (İstanbul: Edebiyat Fakültesi, 1985), pp. 42–3.
91. Ibid.
92. J. Pedersen, "Ibn 'Arabshāh," *EI*², 3:711–12. For his service as Mehmed's head of the chancery, see Ibrahim bin Hasan al-Biqa'i, *'Inwan al-Zaman bi-Tarajim al-Shuyukh wa al-Aqran*, ed. Hasan Habashi (Cairo, 2001), 1:243. Parallel to Mamluk conventions, al-Biqa'i calls Ibn 'Arabshah as Mehmed I's *katib al-sirr*, instead of *nişancı*.
93. J.R. Walsh, "Gūrānī," *EI*², 2:1040–1.
94. For these letters, see pp. 111–13.
95. Anonymous, *İnamat Defteri*, 10a.
96. Ibrahim bin Hasan al-Biqa'i, *Izhar al-'Asr li-Asrar Ahl al-Asr: Tarikh al-Biqa'i*, ed. Muhammad Salim ibn Shadid 'Awfi (Jizah, 1992), 2:171; Ibn Taghribirdi, *Hawadith al-Duhur fi Mada al-Ayyam wa al-Sharq*, ed. Muhammad Kamal al-din' Izz al-din (Beirut, 1990), 2:579.
97. Ibn Iyas, 4:102.
98. I owe this possible interpretation to Anne Broadbridge's feedback.
99. For a sample of anthropological works, see Maurice Gaudelier, *The Enigma of Gift*, trans. Nora Scott (Chicago: Chicago University Press, 1999); Marcel Mauss, *The Gift: Forms and Functions of Exchange in Archaic Societies*, trans. Ian Cunnison (New York, NY: Norton, 1967); Annette Weiner, *Inalienable Possessions: The Paradox of Keeping-while-giving* (Berkeley, CA: University of California Press, 1992). For samples from European history, see Gadi Algazi, Valentin Groebner, and Bernhard Jussen, eds., *Negotiating the Gift: Pre-modern Figurations of Exchange* (Gottinger: Vandenhoeck & Ruprecht, 2003); Natalie Zemon Davis, *The Gift in Sixteenth-Century France* (Madison, WI: University of Wisconsin Press, 2000); Valentin Groebner, *Liquid Assets, Dangerous Gifts: Presents and Politics at the end of the Middle Ages*, trans. Pamela E. Selwyn (Philadelphia, PA: University of Philadelphia Press, 2002). From an Islamic context, see Flood, *Objects of Translation*, pp. 26–37; Linda Komaroff, ed., *Gifts of the Sultan: The Arts of Giving at the Islamic Courts* (Los Angeles, CA: Los Angeles County Museum of Art, 2011); Christian Windler, "Tribut und Gabe:

Mediterrane Diplomatie als Interkulturelle Kommunikation," *Saeculum* 51 (2000):24–56.
100. For Mamluk diplomatic gift-giving exercises and protocols, see Dekkiche, "Le Caire," 1:61–5; Broadbridge, *Kingship*, pp. 22–3.
101. Li Guo, "Gift-giving," *Encyclopaedia of the Qur'an* (Leiden: E.J. Brill, 2002), 2:313–14; Ahmad ibn al-Rashid ibn al-Zubayr, *Books of Gifts and Rarities: Kitab al-Hadaya wa al-Tuhaf*, trans. and ed. Ghada al-Hijjawi al-Qaddumi (Cambridge, MA: Distributed for the Center for Middle Eastern Studies of Harvard University, 1996), pp. 1–5.
102. Anonymous, *Kitab al-Hadaya wa al-Tuhaf*, ed. Muhammad Hamidullah (Kuwait: 1379/1959), pp. 127–8; Muhammad b. Hashim al-Khalidi, *Kitab al-Tuhaf wa-al-hadaya*, ed. Sami Dahhan (Cairo, 1956); Ibn al-Zubayr, *Books of Gifts and Rarities*, trans. and ed. al-Qaddumi.
103. Ibn al-Zubayr, *Books of Gifts and Rarities*, trans. and ed. al-Qaddumi, p. 6. For the diverse types of gifts and their hierarchical orders, see al-Qalqashandi, *Subh al-A'sha*, 4:53–7.
104. Abderrahmene El Moudden, "Sharifs and Padishahs: Moroccan-Ottoman Relations from the 16th through the 18th Centuries: Contribution to the Study of a Diplomatic Culture" (PhD diss., Princeton University, 1992), pp. 126–9.
105. F. Rosenthal et al., "Hiba," *EI*^{2}, 3:342–50; Y. Linant de Bellefonds, "Hiba," *EI*^{2}, 3:350–1.
106. El Moudden, "Sharifs and Padishahs," p. 127.
107. Uruç Bey, *Oruç Beğ Tarihi*, ed. Necdet Öztürk (İstanbul: Çamlıca, 2007), p. 43.
108. Ibid.
109. Aşıkpaşazade, *Die altosmanische Chronik des Āşıkpaşazāde*, ed. F. Giese (Leipzig: Otto Harrasowitz, 1929), pp. 52–3; El-Moudden, "Sharifs and Padishahs," 126–9; Maria Pia Pedani, "Sultans and Voivodas in the 16th C. Gifts and Insignia," *Uluslararası Sosyal Araştırmalar Dergisi* 1 (2007):196–7.
110. See Aşıkpaşazade, ed. Giese, pp. 52–3; İbn Kemal, *Tevārīḫ-i Āl-i Osmān: VIII. Defter*, ed. Ahmet Uğur (Ankara: TTK, 1997), p. 53.
111. Yazıcıoğlu Mehmed, *Muhammediye*, ed. Âmil Çelebioğlu, 2 vols. (İstanbul: Milli Eğitim Bakanlığı, 1996), 1:11; Neşri, ed. Öztürk, p. 207.
112. Neşri, ed. Öztürk, p. 207.
113. Ibid., p. 265.
114. İbn Kemal, *TAO: VIII.Defter*, p. 175.
115. C.E. Bosworth, "In'ām," *EI*^{2}, 3:1200–2.
116. El Moudden, "Sharifs and Padishahs," pp. 126–9; Mehmed İpşirli, "Osmanlı Devlet Teşkilatına Dair Bir Eser: Kavanin-i Osmani ve Rabita-i Asitane," *Tarih Enstitüsü Dergisi* 14 (1994):31.
117. Neşri, ed. Öztürk, p. 265.
118. F. Rosenthal et al., "Hiba"; Y. Linant de Bellefonds, "Hiba"; F. Rosenthal, "Rashwa," *EI*^{2}, 8:451. For a similar discussion about the blurred boundaries between gift-giving and bribery in European history, see Groebner, *Liquid Assets*.

119. Anthony Cutler, "Gifts and Gift Exchange as Aspects of the Byzantine, Arab, and Related Economies," *Dumbarton Oaks Papers* 55 (2001):248; Arjun Appadurai, Introduction to *The Social Life of Things*, ed. Arjun Appadurai (Cambridge: Cambridge University Press, 1986), pp. 11–13.
120. Al-Qalqashandi, *Subh Al-A'sha*, 9:246–50.
121. Cutler, "Gifts and Gift Exchange," pp. 247–8. For the importance of gift exchange at the Ottoman court, see Theodore Spandounes, *On the Origins of the Ottoman Emperors*, trans. and ed. Donald M. Nicol (Cambridge: Cambridge University Press, 2009), pp. 129–30; Pedani, *Osmanlı Padişahının Adına*, pp. 77–9. For European reactions to the Ottomans' emphasis on gift exchange, see Julian Raby, "The Serennisima and the Sublime Porte: Art in the Art of Diplomacy," in *Venice and the Islamic World*, pp. 100–2.
122. For the hidden meanings of gifts, see Broadbridge, *Kingship*, pp. 22–4, 36, 54, 88, 105–6.
123. Little, "Diplomatic Missions," pp. 33–4.
124. For the Ottoman ruler's attempt to display the Ottoman victory in the Balkans to the Dulkadirid ruler 'Ala' al-Dawla through spoils as diplomatic gifts, see Uruç, ed. Öztürk, p. 178.
125. Translation by the author. Neşri, ed. Öztürk, pp. 297, 298n3698. For this embassy, see p. 38, 107, 223 in this book.
126. In order to gain some special favors or stipulations from the Mamluk sultan, European consuls occasionally offered the release of Muslim prisoners. Although this exchange was not a typical gift, it can be considered as such. Christ, *Trading Conflicts*, p. 100.
127. Thomas Allsen, *The Royal Hunt in Eurasian History* (Philadelphia, PA: UPENN, 2006), pp. 58–70, 160–1.
128. For example, the Timurid court often sent valuable horses to the Chinese emperors of the Ming dynasty, due to the general low quality of Chinese horses. Ralph Kauz, "Gift Exchange between Iran, Central Asia, and China under the Ming dynasty, 1368–1644," in *Gifts of the Sultan*, pp. 116–17.
129. Kissling, *Sultan Bâyezîd II's Beziehungen*, pp. 4–7.
130. Ibid., p. 18; Franz Babinger, *Reliquienschacher am Osmanenhof im XV.Jahrhundert* (München, 1956); Halil İnalcık, "A Case Study in Renaissance Diplomacy: The Agreement between Innocent VIII and Bāyezīd II on Djem Sultan," *Journal of Turkish Studies* 3 (1979):215, 216.
131. For a general treatment of Ottoman–Mamluk gift exchanges, see Cüneyt Kanat, "Osmanlı ve Memlûk Devletleri'nin Birbirlerine Gönderdiği Armağanlar," in *Uluslararası Osmanlı Tarihi Sempozyumu (8–10 Nisan 1999) Bildirileri*, ed. Turan Gökçe (İzmir, 2000), pp. 35–52; Elias Muhanna, "The Sultan's New Clothes: Ottoman-Mamluk Gift Exchange in the Fifteenth Century," *Muqarnas* 27 (2010):189–207.
132. For a horse that the Mamluk sultan sent to Mehmed II, see Ibn Aja, *Ta'rikh Al-Amir Yashbak al-Zahiri*, ed. Abd al-qadir Ahmad Tulaymat (Cairo, 1974), p. 94.

133. See the cited paragraph from Neşri's chronicle on p. 38.
134. For weaponry as gifts that indicate animosity, see Broadbridge, *Kingship*, pp. 36, 88.
135. Halil İnalcık, "The Ottoman State: Economy and Society, 1300–1600," in *An Economic and Social History of the Ottoman Empire 1300–1914*, ed. Halil İnalcık and Donald Quataert (Cambridge: Cambridge University Press, 1994), pp. 58–61. For a possible symbolic meaning of silver cups, see Pedani, "Sultans and Voivoda," p. 197.
136. Kanat, "Armağanlar," pp. 48–9.
137. For the report that the Ottomans sent Hungarian slaves to the Mamluk sultan, see Felix Fabri, *Voyage en Egypte de Félix Fabri, 1483* (Cairo, 1975), 2:86a–86 (432–33), 3:172b (914).
138. Kanat, "Armağanlar," pp. 48–9.
139. Ibid.
140. Feridun, 1274, 1:214, pp. 238–9. For reference to the Mamluk gift of balsam to the "Grand Turc", see Felix Fabri, *Voyage*, 1:79b (393–5).
141. Julian Raby and Ünsal Yücel, "Chinese Porcelain at the Ottoman Court," in *Chinese Ceramics in the Topkapı Saray Museum: A Complete Catalogue*, ed. Regina Krahl (London: Sotheby's, 1986), 1:29–30. For porcelain from the Mamluk sultans to European courts, see John Wansbrough, "A Mamlūk Commercial Treaty Concluded with the Republic of Florence," in *Documents from Islamic Chanceries*, ed. S.M. Stern (Columbia, SC: University of South Carolina Press, 1965), p. 40; Howard, "Venice and the Mamluks," in *Venice and the Islamic World*, p. 84.
142. Feridun, 1274, 1:208, 214, 238–9; 'Abd al-Basit ibn Khalil ibn Shahin, *Nayl al-Amal fi Zayl al-Duwal*, ed. Abd al-Salam Tadmuri (Beirut, 2002), 7:89–90.
143. Uruç, ed. Öztürk, 168 and Ibn Iyas, 3:315–16 (same occasion); Ibn Shahin, *Nayl al-Amal*, 7:89–90.
144. Bihişti, *Die Chronik des Ahmed Sinân Čelebi Genannt Bihišti*, ed. Brigitte Moser (München: Dr. Dr.Rudolf Trofenik, 1980), p. 104; Ibn Iyas, 3:315–16.
145. Ibn Iyas, 3:315–16.
146. Feridun, 1274, 1:238–9; Ibn Iyas, 3:315–16. Some of these animals could be zebras.
147. For the symbolic significance of a menagerie for sovereignty in Eurasia, see Allsen, *The Royal Hunt*, pp. 203–4. For a parallel example, see Bedini, *The Pope's Elephant*, pp. 45–6, 83. For the Safavid ambassador bringing leopards to the Mamluk sultan, see Domenico Trevisan, *La Relation de l'Ambassade de Domenico Trevisan auprès du Soudan l'Égypte*, ed. C. Schefer (1884; repr., Frankfurt am Main, 1995), p. 200.
148. Feridun, 1274, 1:208. For the ceremonial usage of animals in the Ottoman court, see Necipoğlu, *Topkapı*, pp. 44, 53, 61, 90, 92, 206.
149. Little, "Diplomatic Missions," p. 42.
150. For a recent treatment of this particular exchange, see Melvin-Koushki, "*Fathnama*," pp. 193–4 and especially 194n3. For his interpretation, he

primarily refers to my dissertation, yet gives further examples supporting this interpretation.
151. Melvin-Koushki, "Fathnama," 194n3.
152. See pp. 130–1, 177–8. Also see Cihan Yüksel Muslu, "Ottoman–Mamluk Relations: Diplomacy and Perceptions," (PhD diss., Harvard University, 2007), p. 187; Elias Muhanna, "New Clothes," p. 198; Ibn Iyas, 4:462–3, 5:60–1; Yınanç, *Dulkadir Beyliği*, pp. 50–1; J.H. Mordtmann, "Dhu'l-Kadr," *EI*^{2}, 2:239–40.
153. Davis, *The Gift*, p. 5, quoting Annette Weiner, *Women of Value, Men of Renown: New Perspectives in Trobriand Exchange* (Austin, TX: Texas UP, 1976): "Exchange is an ongoing process wherein the donor and the recipient may continually reevaluate the other's and their own current condition."
154. For robes of honor in general, see N.A. Stillmann, "Khil'a," *EI*^{2}, 5:6–7; Diem, *Ehrendes Kleid*; Steward Gordon, ed., *Robes and Honor: The Medieval World of Investiture*, (New York, NY: Palgrave, 2001); Flood, *Object of Translations*, pp. 61–87; Monika Springberg-Hinsen, *Die Ḥila: Studien zur Geschichte des geschenkten Gewandes im Islamischen Kulturkreis* (Würzburg: Ergon, 2000). For a brief treatment of the robes in Mamluk context, see Carl F. Petry, "Robing Ceremonials in Late Mamluk Egypt: Hallowed Traditions, Shifting Protocols," in *Robes and Honor*; Broadbridge, *Kingship*, pp. 22–3.
155. See pp. 9–10.
156. Avinoam Shalem, "Performance of the Object," in *Gifts of the Sultan*, p. 113; L.A. Mayer, *Mamluk Costume: A Survey* (Geneva, 1952), pp. 56–64; J.M. Rogers, Hülya Tezcan, and Selma Delibaş, *The Topkapı Saray Museum: Costumes, Embroideries, and Other Textiles* (Boston, MA: 1986), pp. 37–8. Similar to robes, banners also signified a hierarchical relationship between the donor and the recipient. Although they never appeared in an Ottoman–Mamluk context, the Mamluks frequently sent banners to their vassals and governors. Broadbridge, *Kingship*, p. 22.
157. Linda Komaroff, "The Art of the Art of Giving at the Islamic Courts," in *Gifts of the Sultan*, p. 14, 28n4. For the robe of travel (*khil'a al-safar*) that an ambassador might receive from his own sovereign at the time of his appointment to the diplomatic mission, see Dekkiche, "Le Caire," 1:62–3; Diem, *Ehrendes Kleid*, pp. 74–5. For samples from Ottoman–Mamluk context, see the missions of Tanibay al-Khazinadar in 1503 and Khayr Bey in 1497 in Appendix III.
158. See p. 114, 141, 158, 170.
159. For the Ottoman ambassador who did not receive a robe of honor, see pp. 120–1.
160. For a similar interpretation from the Anatolian Seljuks, see Mehmet Ersan, "Türkiye Selçuklularında Hediye ve Hediyeleşme," *Tarih İncelemeleri Dergisi* 14 (1999):65–79; Mehmet Ersan, "Türkiye Selçuklularında Hediye ve Hediyeleşme II," *Tarih İncelemeleri Dergisi* 15 (2000):95–104.
161. Anonymous, *16. Asırda Yazılmış Grekçe Anonim Osmanlı Tarihi*, trans. and ed. Şerif Baştav (Ankara: Ankara Üniversitesi, 1973), p. 103; Chalkokondyles, *A*

Translation and Commentary, p. 235. For a similar exchange between Timur and the Mamluk sultan Faraj, Broadbridge, *Kingship*, pp. 195–6.
162. For a fuller treatment of Amir al-Kujkuni's mission, see p. 1 and 78–9.
163. See pp. 101–2.
164. Ibn Taghribirdi, *Nujum*, trans. Popper, 18:127.
165. Anonymous, *Grekçe Osmanlı Tarihi*, p. 187.
166. For Sultan Barquq's routine distribution of his clothes, see Leonardo Frescobaldi, Giorgio Gucci, and Simone Sigole, *Visit to Holy Places of Egypt, Sinai, Palestine, and Syria in 1384* (Jerusalem, 1948), pp. 172–3.
167. For parallel evidence, see Allsen, "Robing in the Mongolian Empire," in *Robes and Honor*, pp. 308–9.
168. Anthony Cutler, "The Emperor's Old Clothes: Actual and Virtual Vesting and the Transmission of Power in Byzantium and Islam," in *Byzance et le Monde Extérieur*, ed. M. Balard and J.-M. Spieser (Paris: Publications de la Sorbonne, 2005); Flood, *Objects of Translation*, pp. 77–8.
169. Jamal J. Elias, "The Sufi Robe (Khirqa) as a Vehicle of Spiritual Authority," in *Robes and Honor*, pp. 275–89; Cutler, "The Emperor's Old Clothes."
170. Paula Sanders, "Robes of Honor in Fatimid Society," in *Robes and Honor*, pp. 226–7.
171. Flood, *Objects of Translation*, p. 78; Stillmann, "<u>Khil</u>'a."
172. For a fuller treatment of this mission, see pp. 98–9.
173. Franz Babinger, *Mehmed the Conqueror and His Time*, trans. Ralph Manheim (Princeton, NJ: Princeton University Press, 1992), p. 371. For a recent study of the treaty, Diana Gilliland Wright and Pierre A. Mackay, "When the Serenissima and the *Gran* Turco Made Love: The Peace Treaty of 1478," Study Veneziani 3 (2007):261–77.
174. Babinger, *Mehmed the Conqueror*, p. 371; Pedani, *Osmanlı Padişahının Adına*, p. 92.
175. For an earlier example from the Mamluk context, see Broadbridge, *Kingship*, p. 61.
176. Komaroff, "The Art of the Art of Giving," in *Gifts of the Sultan*, p. 41.
177. For a scene of Murad I's gift redistribution, see p. 70.
178. Ibn Hajar, *Inba'*, ed. Habashi, 3:98. Also see ibid., 3:78, 88.
179. Shalem, "Afterlife and Circulation of Objects," in *Gifts of the Sultan*, pp. 92–3. For regifting the gifts to other sovereigns and the value of provenance, see Anthony Cutler, "Significant Gifts: Patterns of Exchange in Late Antique, Byzantine, and early Islamic Diplomacy," *Journal of Medieval and Early Modern Studies* 38 (2008):91–3; Anthony Cutler, "The Enduring Present: Gifts in Medieval Islam and Byzantium," in *Gifts of the Sultan*, pp. 79–92, particularly p. 68. For Bayezid II's regifting of an Italian textile to the Mamluk sultan Qansuh al-Ghawri, see Raby, "The Serenissima and the Sublime Porte," pp. 101–2.
180. For a brief introduction to the Safavid manuscripts sent to the Ottomans, see Lale Uluç, "Gifted Manuscripts from the Safavids to the Ottomans," in *Gifts of*

the Sultan, p. 144. For the multi-volume Qur'an sent by the Ilkhanid ruler to the Mamluk sultan, see Broadbridge, *Kingship*, pp. 105–6.
181. See pp. 74–5, 103–4, 196.
182. For a general desciption of these ceremonies, in addition to previously cited sources see Dilger, *Osmanischen Hofzeremoniells*, pp. 52–62; İ.H. Uzunçarşılı, *Osmanlı Devletinin Merkez ve Bahriye Teşkilatı* (Ankara: TTK, 1988), pp. 268–325.
183. Al-Qalqashandi, *Subh al-A'sha*, 4:60. For a translation of this passage, see Holt, *Early Mamluk Diplomacy*, pp. 6–7. For a Mamluk mission's arrival and transfer to the Ottoman capital in 1474, see Robert Anhegger, "Mu'âli'nin Hünkârnâmesi," *Tarih Dergisi* 1 (1949):159. Also see Pedani, *Osmanlı Padişahının Adına*, p. 16.
184. Anhegger, "Mu'âli," p. 159.
185. Uzunçarşılı, *Merkez ve Bahriye Teşkilatı*, pp. 276–7.
186. Broadbridge, *Kingship*, p. 21.
187. Al-Qalqashandi, *Subh al-A'sha*, 4:60. For the escort's changing role and function depending on the mission in Mamluk conventions, see Broadbridge, *Kingship*, pp. 20–1.
188. Stowasser, "Manners," p. 15.
189. Ibid.
190. The lodgings of non-Muslim European missions are not treated here because the issue does not have a direct bearing on Ottoman–Mamluk relations.
191. Al-Qalqashandi, *Subh al-A'sha*, 4:60.
192. Ibid.; Stowasser, "Manners," p. 15.
193. See p. 229.
194. Similar to the Mamluk capital, Venice and Genoa had resident consuls in Constantinople. The residences of these consuls often served as lodgings for the ambassadors sent by their sovereigns. İpşirli, "Kavanin-i Osmani," p. 31.
195. Semavi Eyice, "Elçi Hanı," *DİA*, 11:15–18.
196. Mübahat Kütükoğlu, "XVIII. Yüzyılda Osmanlı Devletinde Fevkalade Elçilerin Ağırlanması," *Türk Kültürü Araştırmaları* 27 (1989):203–6.
197. Bertrandon de la Brocquière, *Denizaşırı Seyahati*, p. 236.
198. For instance, see pp. 1–2, 162, 260–1, 270.
199. Mübahat Kütükoğlu, "Lütfi Paşa Âsafnâmesi," in *Bekir Kütükoğlu'na Armağan* (İstanbul: Edebiyat Fakültesi, 1991), p. 79. For a similar interpretation for the housings of Ilkhanid and Timurid embassies in Mamluk lands, see Broadbridge, *Kingship*, p. 21.
200. Karateke, Introduction, pp. 19–20.
201. Susan A. Skilliter, "An Ambassador's *tayin*: Edward Barton's Ration on the Eğri Campaign, 1596," *Turcica* 25 (1993):153–65; Şerafettin Turan, "1560 Tarihinde Bir İran Elçilik Hey'eti Masraf Defteri," *Ankara Üniversitesi Dil ve Tarih–Coğrafya Fakültesi Dergisi* 12 (1964):273–94.
202. For the Mamluk practice, see Broadbridge, *Kingship*, p. 21. For the provisions given by the Mamluk sultan to the Venetian ambassador in 1512, see Trevisan,

La Relation, pp. 181–2. For the provisions given to the Ottoman ambassador by the Mamluk sultan in 1491 (tentatively), see T.E.6944.
203. Faik Reşit Unat, *Osmanlı Sefirleri ve Sefaretnameleri*, ed. Bekir Sıtkı Baykal (Ankara: TTK, 1987), pp. 14–7. For the date of 1538, see Uzunçarşılı, *Merkez ve Bahriye Teşkilatı*, pp. 276–7. He refers to Hammer for this information. For two different Mamluk ambassadors who received allocation by the Ottoman court long before 1538, see Anhegger, "Mu'âli," p. 155, Başbakanlık Arşivi/ İbnü'l-emin Hariciye 1.
204. For evidence in Mamluk practices, see Christ, *Trading Conflicts*, pp. 51, 149–50. For the courtesy visits that the Mamluk ambassadors paid in Constantinople in 1474, see Anhegger, "Mu'âli," p. 159.
205. Christ, *Trading Conflicts*, pp. 149–50.
206. Ibid. For additional evidence, see Wansbrough, "A Mamluk Ambassador to Venice"; Joos van Ghistele, *Le Voyage en Egypte de Joos van Ghistele, 1482–83*, ed. Renée Bauwens-Préaux (Cairo, 1976), pp. 138 [16], 140 [22]; Adorno, *Itinéraire*, pp. 209–11. For a similarly influential role that the dragomans played in the Ottoman sultans' relations with European powers, see Pedani, *Osmanlı Padişahının Adına*, pp. 35–8.
207. Sultan Barsbay kept the ambassadors waiting until a Mamluk victory procession arrived. Ibn Taghribirdi, *Nujum*, trans. Popper, 18:42. For an example from the Ottoman context, see İbn Kemal, *TAO: VIII.Defter*, pp. 169–70.
208. For an attempt by the ambassadors of the King of Naples and Cyprus to increase the size of their parade and entourage in order to impress the observers and the Mamluk court, see Joos van Ghistele, *Le Voyage*, p. 147 [41]. For similar attempts of Ottoman ambassadors to Venice, see Pedani, *Osmanlı Padişahının Adına*, pp. 46–7; Antonio Fabris, "From Adrianople to Constantinople: Venetian–Ottoman Diplomatic Missions, 1360–1453," *Mediterranean Historical Review* 7 (1992):171.
209. For a brief overview of Mamluk ceremonials in the city and citadel, see Behrens-Abouseif, *Cairo of the Mamluks*, pp. 25–33.
210. Based on the account of Brancaccini, who received an audience from the Mamluk Sultan Barsbay in 1422, see Wiet, *Cairo: City of Art and Commerce*, trans. Seymour Feiler (Norman: University of Oklahoma Press, 1964), pp. 144–5; Trevisan, *La Relation*, pp. 182–3.
211. Doris Behrens-Abouseif, "The Façade of the Aqmar Mosque in the context of Fatimid Ceremonial," *Muqarnas* 9 (1992):33–5. For the history of this tradition, see ibid., pp. 34–5; Necipoğlu, "Framing the Gaze," pp. 319–20n5 and n9.
212. Rabbat, *Citadel*, pp. 140, 156; Behrens-Abouseif, "Citadel of Cairo," pp. 71–2, 79.
213. Behrens-Abouseif, "Citadel of Cairo," pp. 66–8.
214. For Barquq's successors who also made their own changes to ceremonials, see ibid., pp. 41, 49, 50, 52, 56–7, 58.
215. Ibid., 29ff. For various references to the ceremonial, administrative, and legal changes Barquq promulgated, see Nielsen, *Secular Justice*, pp. 40, 45, 51–2, 55, 61, 90; Rabbat, *Citadel*, pp. 139, 151, 233, 245, 275, 293–4.

216. Behrens-Abouseif, "Citadel of Cairo," p. 41.
217. Ibid. For night sessions, also see Broadbridge, *Kingship*, pp. 39, 43.
218. Behrens-Abouseif, "Citadel of Cairo," pp. 35–45; Rabbat, *Citadel*, pp. 244–63.
219. Behrens-Abouseif, "Citadel of Cairo," p. 41; Behrens-Abouseif, *Cairo of the Mamluks*, p. 27; Linda Darling, "Circle of Justice," *MSR* 10 (2006):14; Nielsen, *Secular Justice*, pp. 51–2, 61.
220. For other spatial changes brought about by other Mamluk sultans, see Behrens-Abouseif, "Citadel of Cairo"; Behrens-Abouseif, *Cairo of the Mamluks*, pp. 25–6.
221. Behrens-Abouseif, *Cairo of the Mamluks*, p. 63. For an Ottoman mission that was given an audience in this square, see p. 98 in this book.
222. Rabbat, "Ideological Significance." For other halls, see Behrens-Abouseif, "Citadel of Cairo," pp. 40–1; Behrens-Abouseif, *Cairo of the Mamluks*, pp. 25, 27.
223. For the specific sitting position of the Sultan, see Jean Thenaud, *Le Voyage d'Outremer* (1884; repr., Paris: Frankfurt am Main, 1995), p. 45; Arnold von Harff, *The Pilgrimage of Arnold von Harff*, trans. Malcolm Letts (London: Hakluyt Society, 1946), pp. 106–7.
224. Behrens-Abouseif, "Citadel of Cairo," pp. 42–5; Rabbat, *Citadel*, pp. 253–5. For the significance of the seating arrangements in the Fatimid court, see Sanders et al., "Marāsim," p. 519.
225. Stowasser, "Manners," p. 15. Joos van Ghistele, *Le Voyage*, p. 140 [22].
226. Behrens-Abouseif, "Citadel of Cairo," pp. 42–5. For the common usage of this practice in most courts, see Broadbridge, *Kingship*, p. 24.
227. For instance, based on the Florentine traveler Brancacci, see Wiet, *Cairo: City of Art and Commerce*, pp. 144–5. For other descriptions, see Joos van Ghistele, *Le Voyage*, pp. 148 [42]–149 [46]; Thenaud, *Le Voyage d'Outremer*, pp. 44–5; Trevisan, *La Relation*, p. 183.
228. Behrens-Abouseif, "Citadel of Cairo," pp. 42–5. For some cases when they were instructed or expected to kiss the ground three to four times, see Joos van Ghistele, *Le Voyage*, pp. 140 [23]; 148 [43]; 149 [45]; Thenaud, *Le Voyage d'Outremer*, p. 45. For an instance during which they were forced to kiss the ground more than four times, see Wiet, *Cairo: City of Art and Commerce*, pp. 146–7. For a modified version of this practice, Broadbridge, *Kingship*, p. 37.
229. Ayalon, "Dawādār," *EI*[2], 2:172; Haarmann, "Der arabische Osten," pp. 231–2.
230. Trevisan claims he gave the letter to the Mihmandar who extended it to the sultan. Trevisan, *La Relation*, p. 185.
231. For a general summary of this ceremony, see Holt, *Early Mamluk Diplomacy*, pp. 6–7; Stowasser, "Manners," pp. 15–16.
232. Behrens, "Citadel of Cairo," pp. 44–5. For the roles of these figures in an ambassadorial audience, see Joos van Ghistele, *Le Voyage*, pp. 148 [44]–149 [45].
233. According to Trevisan's account, the Doge's gifts to the citadel were sent before Trevisan's audience and the gifts were present in the audience hall until the end of his audience. Trevisan, *La Relation*, pp. 186–8.
234. Behrens-Abouseif, "Citadel," p. 45. For an incidence where the sultan did not attend the banquet, see Wiet, *Cairo: City of Art and Commerce*, p. 147.

235. Broadbridge, *Kingship*, p. 22.
236. For a rare example when the Mamluk sultan gave the ambassador his response during the audience, see Joos van Ghistele, *Le Voyage*, p. 149 [45].
237. Behrens-Abouseif, "Citadel of Cairo," p. 45.
238. Wiet, *Cairo: City of Art and Commerce*, p. 146.
239. Joos van Ghistele, *Le Voyage*, p. 149 [45].
240. Al-Maqrizi, *Durar*, ed. Jalili, 1:451: "... houses were constructed from wood." I thank Professor Gülru Necipoğlu for this possible reading. It is also possible that this statement is about the general architectural style in Bursa (rather than the palace's).
241. For al-Kujkuni's description of a banquet Bayezid attended, see al-Maqrizi, *Durar*, ed. Jalili, 1:451–2. For a mid-fifteenth century pictorial depiction of an ambassadorial audience in Bayezid I's court, see Necipoğlu, *Topkapı*, p. 18.
242. For Ibn al-Sughayr, see Doris Behrens-Abouseif, *Fatḥ Allāh and Abū Zakariyya: Physicians under the Mamluks* (Cairo: Institut Français d'Archéologie Orientale, 1987), pp. 6–7. She spells Ibn al-Saghir.
243. Al-Maqrizi, *Durar*, ed. Jalili, 1:451.
244. Jere L. Bacharach, "Circassian Monetary Policy: Copper," *JESHO* 19 (1976):268; Bacharach, "Circassian Monetary Policy: Silver," *The Numismatic Chronicle* 7th Series, XI (1971); Labib, "Handelsgeschichte Ägyptens im Spätmittelalter, 1171–1517"; Warren C. Shultz, "The Monetary History of Egypt, 642–1517," in *CHE*; Boaz Shoshan, "From Silver to Copper: Monetary Change in Fifteenth Century Egypt," *SI* 56 (1982):97–116.
245. Al-Maqrizi, *Durar*, ed. Jalili, 1:451; Ibn Hajar, *Inba'*, ed. Habashi, 2:226.
246. For the transfer of the capital, see p. 11, 281n62.
247. For ceremonials in Edirne, see Bertrandon de la Broquière, *Denizaşırı Seyahat*, pp. 242–50; Cyriac of Ancona, *Later Travels*, pp. 35–6; Konstantin Mihailovich, *Memoirs of a Janissary*, trans. Benjamin Stolz (Ann Arbor, MI: University of Michigan, 1975), pp. 29, 195. For ceremonials in İstanbul before 1478, see Doukas, *Decline and Fall of Byzantium*, trans. Henry J. Magoulias (Detroit, MI: Wayne State University Press, 1975), pp. 150–1, 158, 161, 169, 186–7; Kritovoulos, *History of Mehmed the Conqueror*, trans. Charles T. Riggs (Princeton: Princeton University Press, 1954), pp. 22–3. Also see Necipoğlu, *Topkapı*, pp. 15–22 (and her bibliography).
248. Bertrandon de la Broquière, *Denizaşırı Seyahat*, p. 242; Spandounes, *On the Origins*, p. 113. We do not know if this practice went back as early as the days in Bursa.
249. Spandounes, *On the Origins*, p. 130.
250. Karateke, *Padişahım Çok Yaşa*, p. 123.
251. Ibid.; İpşirli, "Kavanin-i Osmani," p. 17.
252. Bertrandon de la Broquière, *Denizaşırı Seyahat*, p. 242.
253. Ibid., pp. 242–43; Spandounes, *On the Origins*, p. 123.
254. Necipoğlu, *Topkapı*, p. 83.
255. For the colonnaded hall in Edirne, see ibid., p. 17. For the portico, ibid., p. 18.

256. Bertrandon de la Broquière, *Denizaşırı Seyahat*, p. 244.
257. For the elevated dais, see ibid., p. 244. For the carpet example, see Cyriac of Ancona, *Later Travels*, p. 35.
258. For a unique reference to Prince Mehmed's presence during his father Murad II's peace negotiations with the Hungarian diplomatic mission, see Cyriac of Ancona, *Later Travels*, p. 35.
259. Bertrandon de la Broquière, *Denizaşırı Seyahat*, p. 254. For this rule in the Ottoman court, see Spandounes, *On the Origins*, p. 123; Doukas, *Decline*, pp. 250, 251. According to Ibn Taghribirdi, this practice of kissing the hand substituted the kissing the ground for a brief period during Sultan Barsbay's reign. Then, Barsbay reinstituted the old practice, with some amendments in its form. Ibn Taghribirdi, *Nujum*, trans. Popper, 18:4–5.
260. Bertrandon de la Broquière, *Denizaşırı Seyahat*, pp. 245–6. Despite the evidence from the narrative accounts, miniatures that depicted the late sixteenth-century ambassadorial audiences or illustrated earlier scenes in retrospect do not often picture ambassadors in seated positions.
261. Ibid., p. 246.
262. Cyriac of Ancona, *Later Travels*, pp. 35–6; Doukas, *Decline*, p. 250.
263. Based on Promontorio, who described an audience of Mehmed II in the Topkapı Palace before 1475, see Necipoğlu, *Topkapı*, pp. 18–9.
264. For this transformational phase, see ibid., pp. 15–22.
265. Ibid., p. 21.
266. Necipoğlu, "Framing the Gaze," p. 303.
267. Necipoğlu, *Topkapı*, p. 21.
268. Ibid., pp. 15–16.
269. Ibid., pp. 32–4. Uzunçarşılı claims this kiosk-tower was first constructed by Murad III, yet Necipoğlu thinks that a tower used for these purposes had already existed in Mehmed II's time. İsmail Hakkı Uzunçarşılı, *Osmanlı Devletinin Saray Teşkilatı* (Ankara: TTK, 1945), p. 25.
270. For the miniature, see Necipoğlu, *Topkapı*, p. 36.
271. Ibid., pp. 218–42. For some rulers who held special sessions in these shore pavilions for diplomatic missions, ibid., pp. 238–9.
272. This menagerie might have been outside of the Topkapı Palace. Borsook, "Travels," 160.
273. For the entire paragraph, see Necipoğlu, *Topkapı*, 61.
274. Ibid., pp. 58–9.
275. Necipoğlu, "Framing the Gaze," pp. 303–6. For the quotation, see ibid., p. 318.
276. Tevkii Abdurrahman Paşa, "Osmanlı Kanunnameleri," p. 513.
277. Ibid.
278. Necipoğlu, *Topkapı*, p. 61. For the earlier signs of this change, see pp. 53–4 in this book.
279. Ibid.
280. For the ceremony in Chamber of Petitions, see ibid., pp. 96–110.

281. Ibid., pp. 96–7. For the historical precedence of this practice, see Sanders et al., "Marāsim," pp. 522, 524.
282. Spandounes, *On the Origins*, p. 129.
283. Tevkii Abdurrahman Paşa, "Osmanlı Kanunnameleri," p. 514.
284. Bertrandon de la Broquière, *Denizaşırı Seyahat*, p. 245. For Bertrandon de la Broquière's description of the Karamanid court and ceremony, see Bertrandon de la Broquière, *Denizaşırı Seyahat*, pp. 185–7. According to Bertrandon de la Broquière, the Karamanid ruler was accepting gifts in the same manner as in the 1430s.
285. Necipoğlu, *Topkapı*, pp. 96–7.
286. Ibid., p. 98; Dilger, *Osmanischen Hofzeremoniells*, p. 56; Pedani, *Osmanlı Padişahının Adına*, p. 5.
287. Orgun, "Osmanlı İmparatorluğunda Nâme ve Hediye Getiren Elçilere Yapılan Merasim," p. 408.
288. Bertrandon de la Broquière, *Denizaşırı Seyahat*, pp. 247–8; Spandounes, *On the Origins*, p. 123. Spandounes does not say anything about these later visits, but states that the affair was handled by the paşas.
289. Bertrandon de la Broquière, *Denizaşırı Seyahat*, pp. 248–9.
290. For example, Barquq instituted a yearly celebration of the Prophet's birthday (*mawlid*), while the celebration of the birthday of Sayyida Nafisa was first inaugurated by Qaytbay. Behrens-Abouseif, *Cairo of the Mamluks*, pp. 30, 56.
291. Ibid., pp. 28–31.
292. For a description of the sultan's attendance to the annual opening of the Nilometer in 1470–71, see Adorne, *Itinéraire d'Anselme Adorno*, pp. 205–7.
293. For ambassadors being exposed to additional ceremonies in other historical contexts, see Broadbridge, *Kingship*, pp. 24, 111–12.
294. See p. 115, 150–1.
295. For the significance of victory processions in other historical periods, see Michael McCormick, *Eternal Victory: Triumphal Leadership in Late Antiquity, Byzantium and the Early Medieval West* (Cambridge: Cambridge University Press, 1986), pp. 189–231; Mary Beard, *The Roman Triumph* (Cambridge, MA: Belknap, 2007).
296. T.E.3739.
297. See the following chapters and also the Appendix.
298. Ibn Taghribirdi, *Nujum*, trans. Popper, 18:42.
299. Behrens-Abouseif, "Citadel of Cairo," p. 50.
300. Ibid., p. 69.
301. Fuess, "Between *dihlīz* and *dār al-'adl*." For general references to *dihlīz*, Peter Alford Andrews, *Felt Tents and Pavilions: The Nomadic Tradition and its Interaction with Princely Tentage* (London: Melisende, 1991), 2:825–6, 829.
302. Fuess, "Between *dihlīz* and *dār al-'adl*," 150–3.
303. For the appearances of the Mamluk sultans in the city, see Behrens-Abouseif, *Cairo of the Mamluks*, pp. 28–32 and Joos van Ghistele, *Le Voyage*, p. 146 [38];

for the Mamluk sultan's actual participation in and overseeing of construction work, see ibid., pp. 31–3.
304. For Mamluk emphasis, see Albrecht Fuess, "Sultans with Horns: About the Political Significance of Headgear in the Mamluk Empire," *MSR* 12 (2008):71–94.
305. For Sultan Inal's time with the Ottoman ambassador, see Ibn Taghribirdi, *Hawadith*, ed. 'Izz al-din, 2:454. For Qaytbay's tour of Cairo with the Ottoman ambassador in 1493–4, see pp. 157–8; Ibn Iyas, 3:298.
306. Nurhan Atasoy, "Processions and Protocol in Ottoman İstanbul," in *The Sultan's Procession: The Swedish Embassy to Sultan Mehmed IV in 1657–1658 and the Ralamn Paintings*, ed. by Karen Adahl (İstanbul: Swedish Research Institute, 2006), pp. 168–95; Zeynep Tarım-Ertuğ, "Osmanlılar'da Teşrifat," in *Türk Dünyası Kültür Atlası* (İstanbul, 1999), pp. 428–77.
307. For the Mamluk ambassador's presence at Prince Bayezid's wedding to the Germiyanid princess, see pp. 69–70, 306n27. Likewise, many dignitaries were invited to Prince Mehmed (the future Mehmed II)'s wedding with the Dulkadirid princess, although no reference was made to the Mamluk ambassador. For the circumcision festival of the Princes Cem and Bayezid in 1455–6, see Chapter 4.
308. For example, Esin Atıl, ed. *Levni and Surname: The Story of an Eighteenth-Century Ottoman Festival* (İstanbul: Koçbank, 1999).
309. Sanders et al., "Mawākib," p. 858.
310. Doukas, *Decline*, pp. 241–2.
311. For a detailed treatment of this procession, see pp. 160–1.
312. For the ceremonial departure of the Ottoman ruler Mehmed IV from his capital to Edirne that went unnoticed by the Ottoman sources yet survived only in a foreign diplomat's paintings, see Karin Adahl, ed. *The Sultan's Procession: The Swedish Embassy to Sultan Mehmed IV in 1657–1658 and the Ralamn Paintings* (İstanbul: Swedish Research Institute, 2006). For a discussion of this possibility from the Byzantine context, see McCormick, "Analyzing Imperial Ceremonies," p. 9.
313. For example, Pedani, *Osmanlı Padişahının Adına*, pp. 81–2.
314. For a parallel example, see Anonymous, *Grekçe Osmanlı Tarihi*, p. 101.
315. For an Ottoman example from 1495, see Nebi Bozkurt and Kemal Beydilli, "Sefaretname," *DİA*, 36:290.
316. For the survival of a fourteenth century poetry collection from Anatolia thanks to a member of a British diplomatic mission to Constantinople, see Abdülkerim Özaydın and Hatice Tören, "Kadı Burhaneddin," *DİA*, 24:75.
317. For samples of ambassadorial accounts from Mamluk sources, see Ibn Aja, ed. Tulaymat; al-Maqrizi, *Durar*, ed. Jalili, 1:439–53. Also see Pedani, *Osmanlı Padişahının Adına*, pp. 37–8.
318. Taşköprülüzade, *Eş-Şekā'iku*, p. 94.
319. Şükrullah, *Behcetü't-Tevârîh*, ed. Nihal Atsız, p. 51.
320. Kafadar, *Between Two Worlds*, pp. 96, 122.

Chapter 2 Perceptions in Transformation (c.1350–1402)

1. For the transfer of the Ottoman capital, see p. 11, 281n62.
2. For the efforts of earlier Mamluk sultans and governors to establish a solid and coherent northern border in Syria, see Reuven Amitai-Preiss, "Northern Syria between the Mongols and Mamluks: Political Boundary, Military Frontier, and Ethnic Affinities," in *Frontiers in Question: Eurasian Borderlands, 700–1700*, ed. Daniel Power and Naomi Standen (New York, NY: St. Martin's Press, 1999), pp. 128–52.
3. Quoted in p. 23.
4. Abdülaziz al-Alevi, "Ibn Fazlullah el-Ömeri," *DİA*, 19:483–4.
5. For the Ottomans, see al-'Umari, *Masālik*, ed. Taeschner, 22, pp. 41–2. For the Germiyanids, see ibid., pp. 22, 34–7. For the Karamanids, see ibid., pp. 24–7, 30, 48–9. For the place of the Germiyanids in early Ottoman history, see Rudi Paul Lindner, *Explorations in Ottoman Prehistory* (Ann Arbor, MI: University of Michigan Press, 2007), pp. 57–80; İsenbike Togan, "Beylikler Devri Anadolu Tarihinde Yöntem Sorunları: Germiyan'dan Örnekler," in *Şinasi Tekin'in Anısına: Uygurlardan Osmanlıya* (İstanbul: Simurg, 2005), pp. 704–20; İsenbike Togan, "Türkler'de Devlet Oluşum Modelleri: Osmanlılar'da ve Timurlular'da," in *Prof.Dr. İsmail Aka Armağanı*, ed. Nejdet Bilgi (İzmir, 1999), p. 79.
6. For the relationship between the Mamluks and the Karamanids, see pp. 6–8, 11.
7. For the document of investiture to the Karamanids, see al-'Umari, *Masālik*, ed. Taeschner, pp. 24–7. For the status of the Germiyanids, see al-'Umari, *Masālik*, ed. Taeschner, pp. 34–7. For a discussion of this title, see Paul Wittek, "Le Sultan de Rûm," *Annuaire de l'Institut de Philologie et d'Histoire Orientales et Slaves* 6 (1938):361–90.
8. The exact location of this place is not known. Al-'Umari identifies Qawaya (or Qawiya) as a place between Samsun and Sinop that neighbored the lands of the lords of Kastamonu. Al-'Umari, *Masālik*, ed. Taeschner, p. 41. Both Samir al-Droubi and Lindner identify this location as modern Geyve in the Sakarya (Sangarius) Valley, west of Kastamonu. See al-'Umari, *Al-Ta'rīf*, 1:125n11; Lindner, *Explorations in Ottoman Prehistory*, pp. 46, 63, 106–7. Kazim Dilcimen argues that this location was possibly Bafra or Ünye along the Black Sea coast. Kazim Dilcimen, *Canik Beyleri*, (Samsun, 1940), pp. 60–3.
9. Al-'Umari, *Masālik*, ed. Taeschner, p. 22.
10. Ibid., pp. 41–2.
11. Al-'Umari, *Al-Ta'rīf*, 2:51–3.
12. Ibid., 2:53n14–15.
13. For translations I generally use the renderings that Ann Broadbridge suggests in her book. If I prefer an alternate wording, I explain my choice in the footnotes.

14. This stressed 'y' indicated a higher rank than the title of *al-majlis al-sami* with a single y. See Bosworth, "Laķab."
15. Al-Qalqashandi, *Subḥ al-A'sha*, 5:465. For the hierarchical ranking of the titulature, see Appendix II.
16. Ibid., 5:422. For the usage of this adjective (*al-amiri*) as a part of Mamluk sultans' epithets, see John Wansbrough, "Venice and Florence in the Mamluk Commercial Privileges," *BSOAS* 28 (1965):497.
17. Ibid.
18. For both *al-Maqarr* and *al-Majlis*, Broadbridge uses "The Seat." To differentiate between the two, I use "His Residence" for *al-Maqarr*. Broadbridge, *Kingship*, p. 139.
19. Al-'Umari, *Al-Ta'rīf*, 1:52. For the Artuqids, see Claude Cahen, "Artuqids," *EI*², 1:662–7; Fuad Köprülü, "Artuklular," *İA*, 1:617–18; Coşkun Alptekin, "Artuklular," *DİA*, 3:415–18. For a discussion of the Artuqid position caught between the Mamluks and the Mongol rulers, see Broadbridge, *Kingship*, pp. 151–6.
20. P. Balog, "Pious Invocations Probably used as Titles of Office or as Honorific Titles in Umayyad and Abbāsid Times," in *Studies in Memory of Gaston Wiet*, ed. Myriam Rosen-Ayalon (Jerusalem: The Hebrew University of Jerusalem, 1977). Balog calls these formulas pious invocations.
21. In addition to this formula, al-'Umari gave a second alternative for addressing the Germiyanids. The alternative (*al-Janab al-Karim al-Amir*) still ranked higher than *al-Majlis al-Samiyy*. The only similarity between the alternative address for the Germiyanids and the one for the Ottomans would be the epithet of *Amir*. Al-'Umari, *Al-Ta'rīf*, 2:52, 53.
22. A. Ayalon, "Malik," *EI*², 6:261–2; al-Qalqashandi, *Subḥ al-A'sha*, 5:420, 422; Hasan Al-Basha, *Al-Alqab al-Islamiyya* (Iskandariyya: Dar al-Nahda al-Arabiyya, 1978), pp. 496–506.
23. The titulature that al-'Umari gave for the Karamanids ranked between those for the Mamluk governors and the Germiyanids: "Adam Allah Ta'ala Ni'ma al-Majlis al-'Ali..." (May God Almighty prolong the prosperity of His Exalted Seat...). The titulature *al-Majlis* with the adjective *al-'Ali* was ranked more highly than *al-Majlis al-Samiyy*. See al-'Umari, *Al-Ta'rīf*, 1:55.
24. Ibn Nazir al-Jaysh, *Kitāb Tatqīf Al-Ta'rīf Bi'l-Muṣṭalaḥ Al-Šarīf*, ed. Rudolf Veselý (Cairo: Institut Français d'Archéologie Orientale du Caire, 1987). For the author's life, see Veselý, Introduction to *Kitāb Tatqīf Al-Ta'rīf Bi'l-Muṣṭalaḥ Al-Šarīf*; C.E. Bosworth, "Ibn Nāẓir al-Djaysh," *EI*², 12 (Supp.):395.
25. Ibn Nazir al-Jaysh, *Kitāb Tatqīf*, p. 52.
26. Ibid.
27. Ottoman chroniclers first mentioned the arrival of a Mamluk envoy for the circumcision festival of Yakub and Bayezid (the future Bayezid I), the two sons of Murad I. The circumcision took place after the battle of Sırpsındığı in 1371. Hadidi, *Tevârih-i Âl-i Osman*, ed. Necdet Öztürk (İstanbul: Edebiyat Fakültesi, 1991), pp. 90–2; Müneccimbaşı, *Jami' al-Duwal*, Süleymaniye Esad

Efendi 2103, 688a. Scholars present two conflicting opinions about the first Ottoman mission to Cairo. Björkman, who cites al-Maqrizi as his source, writes that in June 15, 1366 an ambassador from Orhan (A'rdkhan Malik al-Rum Ibn 'Othman) brought the news that his navy could aid the Mamluk campaign in Cyprus. Al-'Ayni and Ibn Iyas both identified this mission as an Ottoman one. Recently, Har-El follows Björkman's argument and designates this envoy as the first-known Ottoman envoy to Cairo. Assuming that al-Maqrizi and al-'Ayni confused Murad I with his predecessor and father Orhan, who died in the 1350s, Har-El changes the ruler's name to Murad I, who was the Ottoman ruler in 1366. Citing Al-Qalqashandi's work, Tekindağ presents an alternative opinion and argues that this Orhan was not the Ottoman ruler who was the father of Murad I. This Orhan, Tekindağ claims, was the ruler of Menteşeoğulları. From its inception onward, the principality of Menteşe was a maritime power located along the shores of southwestern Anatolia. Moreover, in 1366 (when Orhan's envoy visited Cairo), the principality of Menteşeoğulları was involved in naval warfare against Rhodes and Cyprus. Tekindağ's argument makes sense because in 1366 the Ottomans were probably not in a position to offer naval support to the Mamluks, despite the fact that they had recently acquired the lands and the navy of Karesioğulları, another seafaring principality in western Anatolia. It is possible that the diplomatic mission in 1366, which Björkman claims was the first Ottoman embassy to Cairo, was not sent by the Ottoman ruler Murad I. However, the revision of Björkman's argument does not mean that the Ottomans did not exchange missions with the Mamluks during those years. For primary sources, see al-'Ayni, *'Iqd al-Juman*, 548a; Ibn Iyas, 2:33, 38; al-Maqrizi, *Kitab al-Suluk li-Ma'rifa al-Duwal al-Muluk*, ed. Sa'id 'Abd al-Fattah 'Ashur (Cairo: Dar al-Kutub, 1970), 3:121. See Walther Björkman,"Die Frühesten Turkisch-Ägyptischen Beziehungen im 14. Jahrhundert, in *Mélanges Fuad Köprülü* (İstanbul: Dil ve Tarih-Coğrafya Fakültesi, 1953), pp. 57–63; Har-El, *Struggle*, p. 66; Tekindağ, "Fatih Devrinde," p. 73. For information about Orhan of the Menteşeoğulları, see Erdoğan Merçil, "Menteshe-Oghulları," *EI*[2], 6:1018–19; Paul Wittek, *Menteşe Beyliği: 13–15. Asırda Garbī Küçük Asya Tarihine Ait Tetkik*, trans. Orhan Şaik Gökyay (Ankara: Türk Tarih Kurumu, 1986).

28. Varlık, *Germiyan-oğulları*, pp. 57–60.
29. Aşıkpaşazade, ed. Giese, pp. 52–5; Aşıkpaşazade, *Tevārīḫ-i Āl-i Osmāndan Āşık paşazāde Ta'rīḫi*, ed. Âli Bey (İstanbul, 1332/1914), pp. 57–8; Aşıkpaşazade, *Osmanoğulları'nın Tarihi*, ed. Kemal Yavuz and Yekta Saraç (İstanbul, 2003), pp. 385–6.
30. Aşıkpaşazade, ed. Giese, pp. 52–5; Aşıkpaşazade, ed. Âli Bey, pp. 57–8; Aşıkpaşazade, *Osmanoğulları'nın Tarihi*, pp. 385–6; Hadidi, ed. Öztürk, pp. 93–8; Müneccimbaşı, *Jami' al-Duwal*, 688b; Neşri, ed. Unat and Köymen, p. 205.
31. Aşıkpaşazade, ed. Giese, p. 53.

32. For the significance of the Germiyanids in early Ottoman history, see Lindner, *Explorations in Ottoman Prehistory*, pp. 57–80; see Togan, "Germiyan'dan Örnekler," pp. 704–20.
33. See pp. 58–61.
34. For examples from a parallel historical context, see the circumcision of and wedding festivities for the son of the Mamluk sultan Baybars in 1264 and 1276. Broadbridge, *Kingship*, pp. 56, 61.
35. Müneccimbaşı, *Jami' al-Duwal*, 688b. This detail was only given by Müneccimbaşı. Other chroniclers said that the gifts Evranos brought were distributed among other envoys.
36. For a discussion of this practice, see p. 44. For similar practices in the Mamluk context, see Broadbridge, *Kingship*, p. 61.
37. For the political ramifications of this marriage, see İ.H. Uzunçarşılı, "Karamanoğulları Devri Vesikalarından İbrahim Bey'in Karaman İmareti Vakfiyesi," *Belleten* 1 (1937):111–12; İ. H. Uzunçarşılı, "Osmanlı Tarihine Ait Bazı Yanlışlıkların Tashihi," *Belleten* 31 (1957): 178–81.
38. Lindner, "Anatolia, 1300–1451," in *Cambridge History of Turkey*, ed. Kate Fleet, vol.1 (Cambridge: Cambridge University Press, 2009), p. 114; Sümer, "Ḳaramān-oghullari" EI^2, 4:619–25.
39. İnalcık, "Murad I," *DİA*, 31:160.
40. Author's translation. Neşri, ed. Menzel and Taeschner, 1:59, 2:91; Neşri, ed. Unat and Köymen, 217–19; Neşri, ed. Öztürk, 100–1.
41. Müneccimbaşı, *Jami' al-Duwal*, 689a.
42. Broadbridge, *Kingship*, pp. 172–3. Broadbridge suggests that these embassies were exchanged to discuss both sovereigns' concerns about Timur, who had wreaked havoc in Iraq and Eastern Anatolia in 1384. For a detail concerning this particular embassy, please see pp. 194–5 in this book. I owe the suggestion for a possible change of Mamluk policy toward the Karamanids and the manifestation of this change in Barquq's response to Murad to Prof. Jane Hathaway.
43. Neşri, ed. Menzel and Taeschner, 1:65, 2:101; ibid., ed. Unat and Köymen, p. 239; ibid., ed. Öztürk, p. 109. Neşri said "Yazıcıoğlun (the son of Yazıcı)" came back that year from Egypt. This name was used for the two sons of Yazıcı Salih (Yazıcıoğlu Mehmed and Ahmed Bican). However, Neşri was probably referring to their father Yazıcı Salih because the year 1388 was too early for either of the two brothers to have become envoys. Yazıcıoğlu Mehmed, the elder of the two brothers, died in 1451. Ahmed Bican died after 1466.
44. Bursalı Mehmed Tahir, *Osmanlı Müellifleri* (İstanbul, 1914–24) 1:195, 3:307–9. He does not cite his source for this information.
45. See Neşri, ed. Öztürk, p. 109. For this theory concerning Timur, see Broadbridge, *Kingship*, pp. 172–3.
46. Hatice Aynur, " Yazidji Ṣāliḥ b. Suleymān," EI^2, 12:834–5; Björkman, "Die Frühesten Turkish-Ägyptischen Beziehungen"; Âmil Çelebioğlu, "Ahmed Bican," *DİA*, 2:49–51; Yazıcıoğlu Mehmed, *Muhammediye*, ed. Çelebioğlu;

Âmil Çelebioğlu and Kemal Eraslan, "Yazıcı-oğlu," *İA*, 13:365–8; Bursalı Mehmed Tahir, *Osmanlı Müellifleri* (İstanbul, 1914–24), 1:195, 3:307–9.

47. Şehabettin Tekindağ, *Berkuk Devrinde Memlûk Sultanlığı* (İstanbul: Edebiyat Fakültesi, 1961), pp. 115–16.
48. For another of the many Turkish-speaking poets, authors, scholars, and Sufis who benefitted from Barquq's generosity, see Mustafa Erkan, "Darīr," *DİA*, 8:498–9; Gottfried Hagen, "Some Considerations about the Terğüme-i Ḍarir ve Taqdimetü z̧-Ẓahīr Based on Manuscripts in German Libraries," *Journal of Turkish Studies* 26 (2002):323–37. Studies suggest that al-Darir had a significant impact on the transformation of Mamluk Turkish into Oghuz Turkish.
49. Amil Çelebioğlu, "Yazıcı Salih ve Şemsiyyesi," *Atatürk Üniversitesi İslami İlimler Fakültesi Dergisi* 1 (1976):171–218.
50. For other works of Yazıcı Salih, see ibid.; Çelebioğlu, "Ahmed Bican."
51. Ahmed Tevhid, "İlk Altı Padişahımızıñ Bursa'da Kâ'in Türbeleri: Ḥüdāvendigâr Sulṭān Murad Ḫān'ıñ Türbesi," *TOEM* 13–18 (1328):1048–1049; E.H. Ayverdi, *İstanbul Mi'mârî Çağının Menşe'i: Osmanlı Mi'mârîsinin İlk Devri* (İstanbul, 1966), 292–3; İ.H. Uzunçarşılı, "Murad I," *İA*, 8:595; Fehmi Ethem Karatay, *Topkapı Sarayı Müzesi Kütüphanesi Arapça Yazmalar Kataloğu* (İstanbul: Topkapı Sarayı Müzesi, 1962), vol.1, # 168. For the most detailed information on these items, see Ahmed Tevhid's article, where he also includes Barquq's endowment inscription in the Qur'an.
52. Anonymous, *Byzantium, Europe, and the Early Ottoman Sultans, 1373–1513: An Anonymous Greek Chronicle of the Seventeenth Century*, trans. and ed. Marios Philippides (New Rochelle, New York, NY: Caratzas, 1990), pp. 31–2. For a slightly different version of the same anecdote, see Chalkokondyles, *A Translation and Commentary*, p. 325.
53. Anonymous, *Grekçe Osmanlı Tarihi*, p. 105.
54. Manuel Palaeologus, *The Letters of Manuel II Palaeologus*, trans. and ed. George T. Dennis (Washington, D.C., WA: Dumbarton Oaks, 1977), pp. 50–1.
55. Ibid.
56. For a manifestation of Barquq's awareness, see the quotation from Ibn Bahadur on p. 23.
57. Al-Qalqashandi, *Subh al-A'sha*, 5:348–9.
58. Ibid., 5:350. For a fuller treatment of al-Qalqashandi's comments on the Ottomans, see p. 87. For al-'Umari's focus on the Germiyanid's outfits, see al-'Umari, *Masalik*, ed. Taeschner, pp. 34–7.
59. Ibid., 8:15–16.
60. Al-Qalqashandi, *Subh al-A'sha*, 6:122–3. It is not very clear who al-Qalqashandi meant by the rulers of Hind. At least three political powers could be candidates for this address: the Delhi Sultanate, the Malwa Sultanate, and the Bahmani Sultanate. The rulers of all three powers exchanged letters with the Mamluk sultans. In BNF MS 4440, two letters were exchanged with the sultans of Delhi. Unfortunately, the surviving sections of these letters do

not include titulature. In the same manuscript, two more letters were available and were exchanged between the Mamluk Sultan Qaytbay and the sultan of Malwa, who was addressed by *al-Maqam al-'Ali*, a title that ranked slightly lower than *al-Maqam al-Ashraf*. For an assessment of these two letters, see Ahmad Darrag, "Risalatan bayn Sultan Malwa wa al-Ashraf Qaytbay," *Majalla Ma'had al-Mahtutat al-'Arabiyya* 4 (1958):97–123. For a general assessment of Burji Mamluk diplomatic relations in light of the letters in BNF MS 4440, see Frédérick Bauden, "Les Relations Diplomatiques entre les Sultans Mamlouks Circassiens et les autres Pouvoirs du Dār al-Islām," *Annales Islamologiques* 41 (2007):1–31.

61. Al-Qalqashandi, *Subh al-A'sha*, 6:126. For translation, see Wansbrough, "A Mamluk Ambassador to Venice," pp. 524 (arabic text) and 530; Wansbrough, "Safe-Conduct," pp. 22 (arabic text) and 23. Broadbridge prefers "His Dignity."
62. Al-Qalqashandi, *Subh al-A'sha*, 6:122–3.
63. Feridun, 1274, 1:116–17, pp. 117–18.
64. Ibn al-Furat, *Tarikh*, 9:38, 50.
65. Feridun, 1274, 1:118.
66. The titulature in the introductory parts of both letters were either confused, miscopied, or heavily editorialized. The addresses that should have belonged to the Mamluk sultans came up in the letter to the Ottoman court and vice versa. However, the rest of the letters are helpful.
67. For the translation, see Wansbrough, "A Mamluk Letter of 877/1473," p. 211.
68. Yınanç disagrees with this conclusion and claims that the Mamluk sultan Barquq was suggesting that Bayezid attack Qadı Burhan al-din. Halil Yınanç, "Bayezid I," *İA*, 2:374.
69. For the relationship between Barquq and al-Kujkuni, see Ibn Taghribirdi, *Nujum*, trans. Popper, 13:64–7, 122, 123, 14:100.
70. For a treatment of this particular exchange, see Diem, *Ehrendes Kleid*, pp. 49–50.
71. Ibn Qadi Shuhba, *Tarikh Ibn Qadi Shuhba*, 1:471, 476; Ibn al-Furat, *Tarikh*, 9:339, 347.
72. For earlier references to al-Kujkuni's embassy, see pp. 1, 50–1.
73. Harb, "I.Selim'in Suriye ve Mısır Seferi," p. 4; Har-El, *Struggle*, pp. 66–7; Tekindağ, *Berkuk Devrinde*, pp. 102–3. For the primary sources referring to this mission, see pp. 197–9 in this book.
74. P.Wittek, "Le Sultan de Rûm."
75. For a selective analysis of al-Kujkuni's and Ibn al-Sughayr's comments, see p. 1, 50–1.
76. These events are narrated by at least three Mamluk authors: first, by al-Maqrizi, who Ibn Hajar named as his source; second, by Ibn Hajar; and third, by Ibn Bahadur, who identified himself as a student of Ibn Hajar and al-'Ayni. While narrating these sections, the last two authors (Ibn Hajar and Ibn Bahadur) abbreviated and edited significantly those events in al-Maqrizi's work. Therefore, my treatment relies on al-Maqrizi's account. His was the most detailed version of these events that were recounted to al-Maqrizi

directly by al-Kujkuni and Ibn Sughayr. Ibn Hajar, *Inba'*, ed. Habashi, 1:453, 1:491–92; 2:225–8, 2:255; al-Maqrizi, *Durar*, ed. Jalili, 1:451–3. For Ibn Hajar's direct reference to al-Maqrizi, see Ibn Hajar, *Inba'*, ed. Habashi, 2:226.

77. For this practice, see p. 10. For Bayezid and *mazalim*, see Ibn Hajar, *Inba'*, ed. Habashi, 2:227.
78. See 197–9 in this book.
79. Al-Maqrizi, *Durar*, ed. Jalili, 1:444.
80. For Shams al-din al-Jazari, see p. 35.
81. For the important networks between the Mamluk military class and scholars, see Berkey, *Transmission of Knowledge*.
82. Broadbridge, *Kingship*, pp. 180–1; J.M. Smith Jr., "DJalāyir," *EI*[2], 2:401. For a relatively unknown yet very detailed biography of the Jalayirid ruler Ahmad, see al-Maqrizi, *Durar*, ed. Jalili, 1:228–43.
83. Broadbridge, *Kingship*, pp. 188–9; Sümer, *Kara Koyunlular*, pp. 60–3. For Ahmad and Qara Yusuf's final attempts to seek refuge in Mamluk lands in 1405, see Broadbridge, pp. 196–7; Sümer, *Karakoyunlular*, pp. 63–8.
84. Broadbridge, *Kingship*, p. 188.
85. Ibn al-Furat, *Tarikh*, 9:456.
86. Aziz Suryal Atiya, *The Crusade of Nicopolis* (London, 1934); Aziz Suryal Atiya, "Nīkbūlī," *EI*[2], 8:35–36; Şehabettin Tekindağ, "Niğbolu," *İA*, 9:247–53. Particularly for the captives fell to the Ottomans during the battle, see Atiya, *The Crusade of Nicopolis*, pp. 95–7.
87. For instance, al-'Ayni, *'Iqd al-Juman*, 614a–b; Ibn al-Furat, *Tarikh*, 9:465–466; Ibn Qadi Shuhba, *Tarikh Ibn Qāḍī Šuhba*, 1:607, 15.
88. Al-'Ayni, *'Iqd al-Juman*, 615b.
89. The exact number of slaves has not been established. Ibn al-Furat, *Tarikh*, 9:464–6; Emmanuel Piloti, *Traité* d'Emmanuel Piloti sur la Passage en Terre Sainte, ed. Hermann Dopp (Louvain, 1958), p. 229; Johannes Schiltberger, *Als Sklave im Osmanischen Reich*, p. 50.
90. Piloti, *Traité*, p. 229.
91. For a discussion of this practice of sending items that were not readily available to the recipient, see pp. 39–40.
92. Holt, "Position and Power," p. 246. For the definition of *jihad* as a defensive war, see Fuess, "Ottoman Ghazwah and Mamluk Jihād."
93. See p. 23, 285n1.
94. Johannes Schiltberger, *Als Sklave im Osmanischen Reich*, pp. 74–5. For two conflicting presentation of Bayezid's policies towards the residents of the Mamluk territories, see İbn Kemal, *Tevârih-i Âl-i Osman: IV.Defter*, ed. Koji Imazawa (Ankara: TTK, 2000), pp. 365–9; Ibn Hajar, *Inba'*, ed. Habashi, 2:255.
95. Venzke, "Dulkadir-Mamluk Iqṭā'," p. 420.
96. Broadbridge, *Kingship*, p. 188.
97. Venzke, "Dulkadir-Mamluk Iqṭā'," p. 467.
98. Yınanç, "Bayezid I," p. 382.

99. Ibn Iyas, 2:633.
100. Ibn Taghribirdi, *Nujum*, trans. Popper, 14:33–4.
101. Ahmedi, *İskender-nāme: İnceleme, Tıpkıbasım*, ed. İsmail Ünver (Ankara: Türk Tarih Kurumu, 1983); ibid., *Tevārīḫ-i Mülūk-i Āl-i Osmān Ġazv-i İşān Bā Küffār*, ed. Kemal Sılay (Harvard Üniversitesi: Yakın Doğu Dilleri ve Medeniyetleri Bölümü, 2004).
102. For the date of this work's completion, see Pal Fodor, "Aḥmedī's Dāsitān as a Source of Early Ottoman History," *Acta Orientalia Academiae Scientiarum Hung* 38 (1984):43.
103. For example, Anonymous, *Anonim Osmanlı Kroniği*, ed. Necdet Öztürk (İstanbul: Türk Dünyası Araştırmaları Vakfı, 2000), pp. 35–9.
104. Not every chronicler considered this campaign to be a mistake. For instance, Anonymous, *Tevārīḫ Āl-i Osmān: F. Giese Neşri*, ed. Nihat Azamat (İstanbul: Edebiyat Fakültesi Basımevi, 1992), p. 37.
105. Ahmedi, *Tevārīḫ*, ed. Sılay, pp. 21 and 47–8.
106. Broadbridge, *Kingship*, pp. 198–200.

Chapter 3 From Titulature to Geopolitical Affairs: An Age of Negotiations (1413–1451)

1. For Barsbay's reign, see Ahmad Darrag, *L'Égypte sous le Règne de Barsbay* (Damas: Institut Français de Damas, 1961). For a parallel increase in references to ideological supremacy in the correspondence between Barsbay and Shahrukh, see Dekkiche, "Le Caire," 1:73–4.
2. For a parallel increase in references to ideological supremacy in the correspondence between Barsbay and Shahrukh, see Dekkiche, "Le Caire," 1:73–4.
3. Al-Qalqashandi, *Subh al-A'sha*, 8:224–6, 232.
4. BNF MS 4440, 50b–51a. The compiler of this manuscript either copied this letter from the writings of Shams al-din al-'Umari, who, according to Björkmann, became the head of the Mamluk chancery during Faraj's second sultanate, or it was composed by Shams al-din al-'Umari himself. If it was composed by Shams al-din al-'Umari, the letter was likely sent sometime between 808/1405 and 811/1409. See Björkmann, *Staatskanzlei*, p. 70. However, in his list of *kuttab al-sirr* from the Burji reign, Bernadette Martel-Thoumian did not include this person. See Bernadette Martel-Thoumian, *Les Civils et l'Administration dans L'État Militaire Mamlūk (IXe/XVe Siècle)* (Damas: Institut Francais de Damas, 1991), pp. 455–8.
5. Feridun, 1274, 1:117.
6. BNF MS 4440, 50b–51a.
7. Ibn Taghribirdi, *Nujum*, trans. Popper, 14:215.

8. Ibn al-Hijja, *Qahwat*, ed. Veselý, 179; BNF MS 4440, 42b–44a. For a closer study of this work and author, see Rudolf Veselý, "Eine Stillkunstschrift oder eine Urkundensammlung? Das Qahwat al-inšā' des Abū Bakr Ibn Ḥidjdja al-Ḥamawī," in *Threefold Wisdom: Islam, the Arab World, and Africa*, ed. Hulec and Mendel (Prague, 1993), pp. 237–47.
9. BNF MS 4440, 45b–47b. This letter is mistitled in the manuscript as one sent from Murad to Barsbay.
10. Al-Sahmawi, *Al-Thaghr al-Basim fi Sinaʿat al-Katib wa al-Katim*, ed. Ashraf Muhammad Anas and Husayn Nassar (Cairo, 2009), 1:518–19. For an alternate yet very similar titulature and salutatio for Murad II, see al-Sahmawi, *Al-Thaghr*, 2:784. Suggested translation: "The Noble and Elevated Residence, Grand, Sapient, Just, Fighting in the name of God, Supported (by God), Aid, Nourishment, Leader, [...], Might of Islam and the Muslims, Lord of Amirs in the World, Leader of the Soldiers, Preparer of Empires, Builder of Kingdoms, Commander of the Armies of the Unitarians, Support of the Islamic Community, Nourishment (or Aid) of the religion, Support of Kings and Sultans, Support of the Commander of the Faithful." For some of these renderings and others, see Broadbridge, *Kingship*, pp. 113, 141; Wansbrough, "Venice and Florence in the Mamluk Commercial Privileges," pp. 497 (Arabic text) and 509.
11. Ibid., 2:784.
12. For Timurid and Ilkhanid titles, see al-Sahmawi, *Al-Thaghr*, 1:516–17.
13. Feridun, 1274, 1:164–5.
14. Ibid., 1:197, pp. 202–3, 207.
15. Wansbrough translates this epithet as "Champion of kings and sultans" in a series of titles used for Sultan Qaytbay by the Mamluk chancery. Wansbrough, "Venice and Florence in Mamluk Commercial Privileges," p. 509.
16. Feridun, 1274, 1:207, 212.
17. Ibid., 1:207. Broadbridge translates this term as "Victorious One of Islamic Holy Fighters." Broadbridge, *Kingship*, p. 141.
18. Ibn Hijja, *Qahwa*, ed. Veselý, pp. 178–83, 287–90. For a closer study of these letters, see Rudolf Veselý, "Ein Kapitel aus den osmanischen-mamlukischen Beziehungen Meḥemmed Çelebi und al-Muʾayyad Shaykh," in *Armağan: Festschrift für Andreas Tietze* (Praha: Enigma, 1994), pp. 241–69.
19. Ibn Hijja, *Qahwa*, ed. Veselý, pp. 183–7, 287–90; Feridun, 1274, 1:164–5.
20. For Mehmed I, see İnalcık, "Mehmed I," *DİA*, 28:391–4. For al-Muʾayyad Shaykh's reign, see P.M. Holt, "al-Muʾayyad Shaykh," *EI*[2], 7:271–2; Kâzım Yaşar Kopraman, *Mısır Memlükleri Tarihi: Sultan Al-Malik Al-Muʾayyad Şeyh Al-Mahmûdî Devri* (Ankara: Kültür Bakanlığı Yayınları, 1989).
21. For a complete list of these letters, see Appendix III.
22. For instance, see the victory proclamation that al-Muʾayyad Shaykh sent to Mehmed after the Mamluk campaign to the Karamanid lands. Ibn Hijja, *Qahwa*, ed. Veselý, pp. 287–90.

23. Feridun, 1274, 1:145. The titulature in this and the following letter is probably mixed up or edited by either Feridun or later copyists.
24. Ibid., 1:145–6.
25. For the Ottoman embassy, see Ibn Bahadur, 46b; al-Maqrizi, *Kitab al-Suluk*, 4/2:656. For the elimination of these two princes, see İnalcık, "Murad II," *DİA*, 31:165–6.
26. For the executions of sultans or candidates for sultanate, see Haarmann, "Regicide and the 'Law of the Turks'." For a rare example of fratricide during the Burji period, see Sievert, *Der Herrscherwechsel*, p. 28.
27. Al-Maqrizi, *Durar*, ed. Jalili, 1:442–3.
28. Al-Maqrizi, *Kitab al-Suluk*, 4/2:625–6, 634.
29. Ibn Bahadur, 46b; al-Maqrizi, *Kitab al-Suluk*, 4/2:656.
30. Feridun, 1274, 1:145. For the contextualization, see İnalcık, "Mehmed I," *DİA*, 28:391–2.
31. For the contextualization, see İnalcık, "Mehmed I," *DİA*, 28:391–2. For an alternate contextualization, see in this book pp. 202–3.
32. Feridun, 1274, 1:145–6. Tekindağ claims that the Mamluk sultan intervened on behalf of the Karamanid ruler Mehmed Bey and his son Mustafa, who were captured by Mehmed I. Upon Mamluk intervention, Mehmed pardoned the Karamanid ruler and returned Konya to him. Tekindağ, "Karamanlılar," p. 324.
33. For the historical context, see Faruk Sümer, "Ḳaramān-oghullari," *EI*[2]; Tekindağ, "Karamanlılar," p. 324; Kopraman, *Sultan Al-Malik Al-Mu'ayyad Şeyh Al-Mahmûdî Devri*, pp. 177–8, 188–9.
34. Ibn Taghribirdi, *Nujum*, trans. Popper, 14:62–75.
35. Ibn Hijja, *Qahwa*, ed. Veselý, pp. 287–90.
36. Feridun, 1274, 1:165–6.
37. For a complete list of these letters, see Appendix III.
38. For Murad's specific request to spread the news to the Sharifs of Mecca and Medina, see Feridun, 1274, 1:196.
39. For this promotion, see Yüksel Muslu, "The Language of Diplomacy."
40. For these campaigns, see Albrecht Fuess, *Verbranntes Ufer: Auswirkungen mamlukischer Seepolitik auf Beirut und die syro-palästinensische Küste (1250–1517)* (Leiden: E.J. Brill, 2001), pp. 24–51, 74–80; Albrecht Fuess, "Rotting Ships and Razed Harbors: The Naval Policy of the Mamluks," *MSR* 5 (2001):49–60; Louis Cheikho, "Un Dernier Echo des Croisades," *Melanges de la Faculte Orientale* 1 (1909):303–75; Darrag, *L'Égypte sous le Règne de Barsbay*, pp. 239–69; Ziada, "The Mamluk Conquest of Cyprus in the Fifteenth Century: Part I" and "The Mamluk Conquest of Cyprus in the Fifteenth Century: Part I"; M.M. Ziada and John La Monte, "Bedr ed din Al-'Aini's Account of the Conquest of Cyprus 1424–26," *Annuaire de l'Institut de philologie et d'histoire orientales et slaves* 7 (1939):241–64; Ouerfelli, "Les Relations entre le Royaume de Chypre et le Sultanat Mamelouk."
41. Behrens, "Citadel of Cairo," pp. 41, 49, 51, 52.

42. Ibn Taghribirdi, *Nujum*, trans. Popper, 18:42; al-'Ayni, *'Iqd al-Juman*, 787a, 789a; Ibn Bahadur, 48b, 49a; M.M. Ziada, "The Mamluk Conquest of Cyprus: Part 1," p. 104; Ziyada, "The Fall of the Mamluks 1516–1517," *Majallat Kulliyat al-Adab* 6 (1942):4; M. Mustafa Ziyada, "Nihayat Salatin Al-Mamalik," *Egyptian Historical Review* 4 (1951):200. The manuscript of al-'Ayni, which is used in this study, mentions only the arrival of the Ottoman envoys and the gifts they brought, but does not say anything about the ceremony in which the Ottoman envoy participated.
43. See pp. 212–3.
44. Reuven Amitai-Preiss, "Mamluk Perceptions of the Mongol-Frankish Rapprochment," *Mediterranean Historical Review* 7 (1992):50–65; Steward, *The Armenian Kingdom and The Mamluks*, pp. 43, 187.
45. Kopraman, *Al-Muayyad Şeyh al-Mahmudi Devri*, pp. 199–204.
46. BNF MS 4440, 45b–47b. This letter is mistitled as one from Murad to Barsbay.
47. Gaston Wiet, "Barsbāy," *EI*^{2}, 1:1053; see Woods, *Aqquyunlu*, p. 52.
48. BNF MS 4440, 47a.
49. For at least two more letters exchanged between Murad and Barsbay concerning the affairs of the Aqqoyunlus, see BNF MS 4440, 42b–44a (undated, tentatively dated to July 1429–April 1430); Feridun, 1274, 1:200–201 (Undated, tentatively dated to 1438). For a study of these issues, see Woods, *Aqquyunlu*, pp. 67–71.
50. See pp. 83–4.
51. Al-'Ayni, *'Iqd al-Juman*, 793b.
52. For the significance of this gesture, see pp. 43–4. For the letter that Murad trusted to Taghribirdi, see Feridun, 1274, 1:195–7. For the gifts that Murad gave the ambassador, see Muhanna, "New Clothes," p. 191. For the symbolic significance of giving hats, see Pedani, "Sultans and Voivodas," p. 198.
53. For the letter this ambassador brought, see Feridun, 1274, 1:197–8. This letter is mistakenly titled as a Mamluk letter to the Ottoman court.
54. Ibn Bahadur, 52b; Ibn Hajar, *Inba'*, ed. Habashi, 3:402; Ibn Taghribirdi, *Nujum*, trans. Popper, 18:55; al-Maqrizi, *Kitab al-Suluk*, 4/2:776–7. This *maydan* or square of Nasiriyya is probably Rumayla square at the foot of the citadel and was renovated by Sultan Qalawun al-Nasir. Also called a hippodrome in modern studies, it was occasionally used for large processions and events. Behrens-Abouseif, *Cairo of the Mamluks*, p. 63.
55. Ibn Bahadur, 52b. Ibn Bahadur and other Mamluk chroniclers do not say anything about the content of the letter or the mission, but the dates and types of gifts suggest that this envoy was sent for the conquest of Güvercinlik.
56. Ziyada, "The Fall of the Mamlūks 1516–1517," p. 2; Ziyada, "Nihāyāt Salāṭīn Al-Mamālik," p. 200.
57. For sending textiles for *mahmal*, see p. 9.
58. For a detailed treatment of these incidents between 1424 and 1435, see Dekkiche, "Le Caire," 1:82–94.

59. Feridun, 1274, 1:203–6. These two letters are undated. For the arrival of this particular mission, see al-Maqrizi, *Kitab al-Suluk*, 4/2:823. According to İnalcık, this treaty was signed in 1428–9. İnalcık, "Murad II," *İA*, 8:603.
60. For the first one, see al-'Ayni, *'Iqd al-Juman*, 759b; for the second, Feridun, 1274, 1:207. Al-'Ayni uses this title as early as for Mehmed I.
61. According to Ibn Taghribirdi, Shahzada. See Ibn Tagrhribirdi, *Nujum*, trans. Popper, 22:127. Ibn Bahadur, 70b–71, 88b. Sara, the name of the princess, comes from Ibn Bahadur. Al-'Ayni gives a shortened version of the story which mentions only the prince, not the princess. Al-'Ayni, *'Iqd al-Juman*, 814a. Uzunçarşılı uses Ibn Taghribirdi and Ibn Iyas, both of whom wrote their accounts much later. İ.H. Uzunçarşılı, "Memluk Sultanları Yanına İltica Etmiş Olan Osmanlı Hanedanına Mensub Şehzadeler," *Belleten* 17 (1953):519–35; Gaston Wiet, "Deux Princes Ottomans à la Cour d'Égypte," *Bulletin de l'Institue d'Égypte* 20 (1938):137–50.
62. For a treatment of this campaign to the Aqqoyunlus, see Chapter 3.
63. For the princess' death, see Ibn Taghribirdi, *Nujum*, trans. Popper, 22:127. For both of their deaths and a version of their stories, see Ibn Taghribirdi, *Hawadith*, ed. 'Izz al-din, 2:559, 560–1.
64. Ibn Bahadur, 89b, 90b–91a; Aşıkpaşazade, ed. Âli, p. 246.
65. For a detailed treatment of these incidents between 1424 and 1435, see Dekkiche, "Le Caire," 1:82–94. Ibn Bahadur, 57a, 97a–b, 101b.
66. Ibn Taghribirdi, *Nujum*, trans.Popper, 18:127.
67. For an analysis of this gesture, see p. 42.
68. Ibn Bahadur, 84b.
69. For the problems Shahrukh experienced during these years, see Beatrice Manz, "Sh̲āh Rukh b. Tīmūr," *EI*^{2}, 9:197–8.
70. Dekkiche, "Le Caire," 1:91–2 (especially n.269). However, later in 1444, the same issue caused tension between these rulers as well. See Ibn Taghribirdi, *Nujum*, trans. Popper, 19:96–7.
71. Feridun, 1274, 1:207–8.
72. Ibid., 1:207.
73. Ibid., 1:208.
74. Ibid., 1:214.
75. Hilal al-Sabi, *Rusum Dar al-Khilafah*, p. 73; Hilal al-Sabi, *Rusum Dar al-Khilafah: The Etiquette, Protocol and Diplomacy of the Abbasid Caliphate in Baghdad*, ed. Mikhail Awad (Baghdad: Al-Aini Press, 1964), pp. 90–1.
76. Feridun Bey's compilation consists of 37 letters exchanged between the Ottomans and the Mamluks (until 1517). Of these, only three (including the one above) contain itemized lists of gifts sent by the Mamluks to the Ottomans. See Feridun, 1274, 1:145; 1:212–14; 235–8.
77. BNF MS 4440, 44a–45a.
78. Ibn Taghribirdi, *Nujum*, trans. Popper, 19:78.
79. Ibid., 19:81–2.

80. For instance, Ibn al-Hijja, *Qahwa*, ed. Veselý, pp. 178–183; Feridun, 1274, 1:164–5.
81. Feridun, 1274, 1:206, 207–8.
82. For Bayezid I's alms, see Ş. Tufan Buzpınar and Mustafa S. Küçükaşcı, "Haremeyn," *DİA*, 16:157. For Mehmed I, see Aşıkpaşazade, ed. Giese, p. 194; Neşri, ed. Unat and Köymen, pp. 551, 679–81. For Murad II, see Aşıkpaşazade, ed. Giese, 194, 210; İ.H. Uzunçarşılı, "Sultan II.Murad'ın Vasiyetnamesi," *Vakıflar Dergisi* 4 (1958):2, 4; Mustafa Güler, *Osmanlı Devleti'nde Harameyn Vakıfları (XVI.–XVII. Yüzyıllar)* (İstanbul, 2002), p. 101. Also see Suraiya Faroqhi, *Pilgrims and Sultans: The Hajj under the Ottomans* (London: I.B. Tauris, 1994), pp. 76–7. This discussion does not include the donations or endowments of individuals (including the prominent members of Ottoman military and administrative class) who lived in Ottoman lands.
83. For a recent treatment of "pious gifts," see Sheila Blair, "On Giving to Shrines: 'Generosity is a Quality of the People of Paradise,'" in *Gifts of the Sultan*, pp. 51–75.
84. Feridun, 1274, 1:207:"Malja' al-fuqara wa al-masakin."
85. Dekkiche, "Le Caire," 1:74–82. For a detailed discussion of these incidents between Shahrukh and the Mamluk sultans between 1424 and 1435, see Dekkiche, "Le Caire," 1:82–94. For an incident concerning *kiswa* that took place between the Mongol ruler Abu Sa'id and the Mamluk sultan al-Nasir Muhammad, see Charles Melville, "The Year of Elephant," *Studia Iranica* 21 (1992):197–207.
86. For Uzun Hasan's attempts to send the cover of *mahmal*, see Woods, *Aqquyunlu*, pp. 107–8; Jomier, *Le Maḥmal*, pp. 50–3.
87. İnalcık, "Murad II," *İA*, 8:608.
88. Uzunçarşılı, "Karamanoğulları Devri Vesikalarından," p. 129. The photographs attached to the article are readable copies of the actual documents. Unfortunately, Uzunçarşılı does not give the number of the documents in the Archives of Topkapı Sarayı. For a recent translation of these documents to Turkish, see Boyacıoğlu, "Osmanoğullarının Karamanoğlu İbrahim Bey Aleyhine Aldığı Fetvalar," in *Pax Ottomana: Studies in memoriam of Nejat Göyünç* (Ankara, 2001), pp. 641–59.
89. Ibid.
90. İnalcık, "Murad II," *İA*, 8:608.
91. For the announcement of victory that was composed by Molla Hüsrev, see BNF MS 4344, 133b–139a. For versions sent to other rulers, see Adnan Erzi, "Türkiye Kütüphanelerinden Notlar ve Vesikalar II," *Belleten* 14 (1950):595–647; Fekete, "Das Fethnāme über die Schlacht bei Varna."
92. For a complete list of references, see p. 223. Although Neşri claims that Azeb Bey was sent by Murad II, Mehmed II was still the official Ottoman ruler at the time of this mission. For Neşri's passage about this mission, see p. 38.
93. Ibid., 1:123. For other correspondence exchanged between Jaqmaq and Mehmed II, see Feridun, 1274, 1:265–6, 266–8. These letters present some

discrepancy between their contents and their composition dates. For the confusion surrounding these letters, see pp. 223–5 in this book.
94. Ibn Taghribirdi, *Hawadith*, ed. 'Izz al-din, 1:211.
95. Ibid., 2:321.
96. Ibn Taghribirdi, *Nujum*, trans. Popper, 19:232–3.
97. Uzunçarşılı, "Sultan II.Murad'ın Vasiyetnamesi," pp. 2, 4.

Chapter 4   Imperial Ambition Resurrected (1453–1481)

1. Ibn Taghribirdi, *Hawadith*, ed. 'Izz al-din, 2:325.
2. For further details, see p. 226.
3. For the transformation of Ottoman institutions and its public image during Mehmed's reign, see for instance Necipoğlu, *Topkapı*, pp. 10–13, 15–22; Raby, "The Serennisima and the Sublime Porte," p. 107; Julian Raby, "A Sultan of Paradox," *Oxford Art Journal* 5 (1982):3, 7–9.
4. For a detailed list of Mamluk sources discussing this mission, see pp. 229–31.
5. Ibn Taghribirdi, *Hawadith*, ed. 'Izz al-din, 2:453.
6. Al-Biqa'i, *Tarikh al-Biqa'i*, 1:379.
7. Ibid., 1:421–2.
8. For *hawsh*, see Behrens-Abouseif, "Citadel of Cairo," pp. 51–2; Rabbat, *Citadel*, pp. 274–7.
9. Al-Biqa'i, *Tarikh al-Biqa'i*, 1:422.
10. Ibn Taghribirdi, *Hawadith*, ed. 'Izz al-din, 2:454.
11. For the first variant, see Feridun, 1274, 1:235–8; for the second, see al-Biqa'i, *Tarikh al-Biqa'i*, 1:425–31 and BNF MS 4434, 139a-143a.
12. On other occasions where multiple copies of a letter have been available, the differences have never been as dramatic as they are in this case. For similar copies of the same diplomatic correspondence in Ottoman and Mamluk sources, see BNF MS 4440, 202b-205a and Feridun, 1274, 1:212–14; al-Biqa'i, *Tarikh al-Biqa'i*, 1:431–36 and Feridun, 1274, 1:238–9; BNF MS 4440, 78a–80a and Necati Lugal and Adnan Erzi, "Fâtih Sultan Mehmed'in Muhtelif Seferlerine Ait Fetih-nâmeleri," *İstanbul Enstitüsü Dergisi* II (1956):169–73.
13. For these adjectives, see Feridun, 1274, 1:236: "*Al-Malik al-Altaf al-Sultan al-Ashraf al-'Abawi al-'Atifi...*" For the significance of adjectives such as "paternal" (or "fatherly") or "brotherly" in Mamluk diplomatic conventions, see Broadbridge, *Kingship*, pp. 113–14.
14. For a Turkish translation of these letters, see Ahmed Ateş, "İstanbul'un Fethine Dair Fatih Sultan Mehmed Tarafından Gönderilen Mektublar ve Bunlara Gelen Cevablar," *Tarih Dergisi* 7 (1952):11–51.
15. Holt, "Power and Position."

16. I owe this alternative explanation to Christopher Markiewicz (University of Chicago)'s careful comments.
17. Ibn Taghribirdi, *Hawadith*, ed. 'Izz al-din, 2:455.
18. Ibid., 2:456.
19. For Inal's first response, see Feridun, 1274, 1:238–9; al-Biqa'i, *Tarikh al-Biqa'i*, 1:431–6; BNF MS 4440, 157a–160a. For clarifications concerning these letters, see Appendix III.
20. Ibn Taghribirdi, *Hawadith*, ed.'Izz al-din, 2:456.
21. BNF MS 4440, 157a–160a; Feridun, 1274, 1:240–3. For clarifications concerning these letters, see in this book pp. 230–1.
22. BNF MS 4440, 157a–160a; Feridun, 1274, 1:238–9.
23. BNF MS 4440, 157a.
24. For Yarshbay's return and robe, see Ibn Taghribirdi, *Hawadith*, ed.'Izz al-din, 2:494.
25. For Ibn Taghribirdi's claim that Inal did not listen to the Karamanid complaints, see Ibn Taghribirdi, *Hawadith*, ed.'Izz al-din, 2:516. Based on an edition of Ibn Iyas, Tekindağ claimed that İbrahim Bey complained that Mehmed was protecting the Orthodox subjects under his sovereignty. However, the Mamluk sources I checked (Ibn Taghribirdi and Ibn Iyas) did not mention the content of the complaint. See Tekindağ, "Fatih Devrinde," p. 75; Tekindağ, "Karamanlılar," p. 326.
26. For multiple variants of these letters, see pp. 232–3. Al-Biqa'i mistakenly reported that this mission came to announce the conquests of Kefe (1475) and Trebizond (1461). Al-Biqa'i, *Tarikh al-Biqa'i*, 2:169–74.
27. Ibn Taghribirdi, *Hawadith*, ed.'Izz al-din, 2:574.
28. Ibid.; Ibn Taghribirdi, *Hawadith*, ed. Popper, 8^1:256–7.
29. Ibn Taghribirdi, *Hawadith*, ed. 'Izz al-din, 2:575–9; Ibn Taghribirdi, *Hawadith*, ed. Popper, 8^1:256–63; BNF MS 4440, 78a-82b; Lugal and Erzi, "Fâtih Sultan Mehmed'in Muhtelif Seferlerine Ait Fetih-nâmeleri," pp. 170–3.
30. Ibn Iyas, 2:349.
31. For an alternative explanation for the delay of this mission's departure and the false rumor concerning Mehmed's health, see al-Biqa'i, *Tarikh al-Biqa'i*, 2:188–9.
32. Ibn Taghribirdi, *Hawadith*, ed. Popper, 8^1:263–9; Ibn Taghribirdi, *Hawadith*, ed. 'Izz al-din, 2:579–84; BNF MS 4440, 80a-82b.
33. For the unique gift list, see BNF MS 4440, 82b. This list is the only description of Mamluk gifts to the Ottoman court that survived in a Mamluk compilation of letters (rather than in chronicles and Ottoman collections).
34. Ibn Iyas, 2:340.
35. Ibn Taghribirdi, *Hawadith*, ed.'Izz al-din, 2:590, 594. Ibn Taghribirdi did not state exactly when this news arrived in Cairo.
36. For the relationship of Sultan Inal and the Karamanid İbrahim Bey, see Dekkiche, "Le Caire," 1:196–212.

37. Aşıkpaşazade, ed. Giese, p. 220; Şehabettin Tekindağ, "Fâtih'le Çağdaş bir Memlûklu Sultanı: Aynal el-Ecrûd," *Tarih Dergisi* 23 (1969):40.
38. For the claim that this destruction in Karamanid territories was criticized in Cairo, see Tekindağ, "Fatih ile Çağdaş," p. 40.
39. Tekindağ, "Fatih ile Çağdaş"; Tekindağ, "Karamanlılar," p. 326. For additional relevant works of Tekindağ, see the Bibliography.
40. For the relationship between Inal and the Aqqoyunlu leaders, see Woods, *The Aqquyunlu*, pp. 97, 106. For Inal's problems with the Qaraqoyunlus, see Dekkiche, "Le Caire," 1:161–78.
41. Aşıkpaşazade, ed. Giese, p. 220. This section (pp. 220–36) is devoted to Ottoman–Mamluk relations. It was probably added by another individual during or after the Ottoman–Mamluk war (1485–91).
42. Author's translation. Ibid., p. 221.
43. Woods, *Aqquyunlu*, pp. 93–100.
44. Tekindağ, "Fatih ile Çağdaş," p. 40.
45. Aşıkpaşazade, ed. Giese, pp. 220–1.
46. Şevket Pamuk, "Appendix: Money in the Ottoman Empire, 1326–1914," in *An Economic and Social History of the Ottoman Empire 1300–1914*, ed. Halil İnalcık and Donald Quataert (Cambridge: Cambridge University Press, 1994), p. 954; Barbara Flemming, "The Reign of Murad II: A Survey (I)," *Anatolica* 20 (1994):252. According to recent studies, Ottoman mints had produced Venetian gold ducats during the first half of the fifteenth century. Nevertheless, the first official Ottoman gold coins were struck under Mehmed II.
47. Halil Ethem, *Meskukat-ı Osmaniyye*, Müze-yi Hümayun Meskukat-i Kadime-i Islamiyye Kataloğu 6 (Konstantiniyya, 1334/1915), 81; İsmail Galib, *Takvim-i Meskukat-ı Osmaniyye* (Konstantiniyye, 1307/1890), 41. Two separate catalogues display what is probably the same coin. The coin is dated 1470: "*Sultan al-Barrayn ve Khaqan al-Bahrayn al-Sultan i. al-Sultan Mehmed i. Murad Han Khallada Allahu Sultanahu.*"
48. Halil Ethem, *Meskukat-ı Osmaniyye*, p. 80; İsmail Galib, *Takvim-i Meskukat*, p. 40. These coins are dated 1478. The titles on the coins reads: "*Darib al-Nadr Sahib al-Izz wa al-Nasr fī al-Barr wa al-Bahr Sultan Mehmed i. Murad Khan 'Azza Nasruhu.*"
49. Süha Umur, *Osmanlı Padişah Tuğraları* (İstanbul: Cem Yayınevi, 1980), pp. 44–7; 106; 109–17. The earliest surviving example of "Victorious! (*Muzaffer!*)" in the royal insignia dates to 1426, although there is an example from 1427 without it. During Mehmed's reign, every example after 1475 has "Victorious Forever (*Muzaffer Daima*)!"
50. Aşıkpaşazade, ed. Giese, pp. 222–3. Aşıkpaşazade dated this event to 1459–60, as opposed to Ibn Taghribirdi, who dated it to 1464. Despite the difference between the two authors' chronologies, these two events must be the same because the details of the events are almost identical. In general, Ibn Taghribirdi's chronology appears more accurate.

51. Ibid., pp. 221–2. For the issue regarding the repair of water wells along the pilgrimage route, also see pp. 234–5 in this book.
52. Ibid. If this event took place in 1464, the Mamluk sultan during this incident must have been Khushqadam, who came to the throne in 1461. Italics belong to the author.
53. For a recent treatment of this same incident, see Kristof D'Hulster, "Fixed Rules to Changing Games?" (paper presented at the *Mamluk Cairo: A Crossroad for Embassies*, University of Liège, September 6–8, 2012.)
54. Ibn Taghribirdi, *Hawadith*, ed. Popper, 8^2:471–3, 477; Ibn Iyas, 2:420–1.
55. Ibn Iyas, 2:420.
56. Behrens, *Cairo of the Mamluks*, pp. 27, 28.
57. Ibn Taghribirdi, *Hawadith*, ed. Popper, 8^2:472–3.
58. For this garment, see Mayer, *Mamluk Costume*, p. 24.
59. Ibn Taghribirdi, *Hawadith*, ed. Popper, 8^2:473. However, it sounds too daring for the ambassador not to follow the Mamluk Sultan's order.
60. Ibn Iyas, 2:427.
61. Ibid. For Uzun Hasan's later disapproval of the Karamanid princes' removal from the Aqqoyunlu to the Ottoman court, see ibid., 2:426.
62. Ibid. For the problems concerning Gerger, see Woods, *Aqquyunlu*, pp. 106–7.
63. Ibn Iyas, 2:426.
64. Ibid., 2:427, 434.
65. Aşıkpaşazade, ed. Giese, p. 223. Author's translation.
66. For instance, see Ahmed Akgündüz, *Osmanlı Kanunnâmeleri ve Hukuki Tahlilleri*, Vol. 1 (İstanbul, 1990).
67. Holt, "Position and Power," p. 247.
68. Ibn Iyas, 2:429.
69. Ibid., 2:427, 434.
70. BNF MS 4440, 76b–78a. For the editorialized titulature of Mamluk sultans, see pp. 88–90 in this book.
71. Aşıkpaşazade, ed. Giese, p. 221; Ibn Taghribirdi, *Nujum*, trans. Popper, 23:66, 114. Aşıkpaşazade dated this incident incorrectly to 1457–8 rather than 1467–8. Malik Arslan was assassinated in 1465–6. In fact, after the assassination, the sword of Malik Arslan was sent to Cairo. Venzke, "Mamluk-Dulqadir Iqta," p. 424.
72. Anonymous, *Fatih Devrine Ait Münşeât Mecmuası*, pp. 40–1.
73. Ibid., pp. 3–5, 66–8. For the close involvement of the Grand Vizier Mahmud Pasa in Dulkadirid affairs, see ibid., pp. 64–5; Stavrides, *The Sultan of Viziers*, pp. 342–3.
74. Tursun Bey, *Târîh Ebü'l-Feth*, ed. Mertol Tulum (İstanbul: İstanbul Fetih Cemiyeti, 1977), pp. 145–6; İbn Kemal, *Tevârih-i Âl-i Osman: VII. Defter*, ed. Şerafettin Turan (Ankara: TTK, 1991), p. 272.
75. Ibn Iyas, 2:436–7.
76. Aşıkpaşazade, ed. Giese, pp. 221–2. Tekindağ believes the pilgrim to be Molla Gürani. Neither Ahmet Ateş nor J.R.Walsh discusses this possibility. See Ateş,

"Mollā Gūrānī (1416–1488)," *İA*, 8:407; R.C. Repp, *The Müfti of İstanbul: A Study in the Development of the Ottoman Learned Hierarchy* (London: Ithaca Press, 1986), pp. 166–74; Tekindağ, "Fatih Devrinde," p. 77; Walsh, "Gūrānī."

77. Al-Biqaʻi, *Tarikh al-Biqaʻi*, 3:364–5.
78. Additionally, al-Biqaʻi also recounted in two separate incidents that the people of Cyprus and Rhodes implored the Mamluk sultan to prevent the Ottomans from attacking their islands. The Ottomans, by the same token, expected that the Mamluk sultan would aid them in any conflict with these islands. These claims have not been substantiated by any other primary source. In the light of Mehmed's campaigns to Rhodes, however, they seem possible and deserve further investigation. Al-Biqaʻi, *Tarikh al-Biqaʻi*, 1:422, 3:129.
79. Aşıkpaşazade, ed. Giese, pp. 221–2.
80. Suraiya Faroqhi, *Pilgrims and Sultans*, pp. 28–9. For instance, Barsbay's refusal to accept Shahrukh's offer to send *kiswa*, see Dekkiche, "Le Caire," 1:82–94.
81. Ibn Iyas, 3:19; Woods, *Aqquyunlu*, pp. 100–8.
82. For these missions, see pp. 238–41.
83. For Amir Yashbak min Mahdi's campaigns between 1470 and 1480, see Bernadette Martel Thoumian, "Les Dernières Batailles du Grand Émir Yašbak min Mahdī," in *War and Society in the Eastern Mediterranean, 7th–15th Centuries*, ed. Yaacov Lev (Leiden: E.J. Brill, 1997), pp. 301–42.
84. Ibn Iyas, 3:73–4.
85. For these missions, see Appendix III.
86. Aşıkpaşazade, ed. Giese, p. 223.
87. Ibn Aja, ed. Tulaymat, p. 142.
88. Ibn Iyas, 3:75.
89. İbn Kemal provides a second and alternative explanation stating that Mehmed ceased supporting Shahsuwar because he was angered by the independent decisions of his so-called vassal. İbn Kemal, *TAO: VII.Defter*, pp. 391–7.
90. Har-El, *Struggle*, pp. 81–102. Har-El believes that Mehmed II consented to both the Mamluk expedition and the execution of Shahsuwar. I am not completely convinced of this.
91. For ʻAlaʼ al-Dawla seeking refuge in Ottoman lands, see İbn Kemal, *TAO: VII. Defter*, pp. 396–7. For a more detailed account about how Mehmed II sent ʻAlaʼ al-Dawla back with Ottoman troops, how ʻAlaʼ al-Dawla and these troops were defeated, and how the severed heads of Ottoman captives were taken back to Cairo, see Aşıkpaşazade, ed. Giese, p. 224. For an alternative treatment of ʻAlaʼ al-Dawla's whereabouts during the 1470s, see Venzke, "Dulkadir-Mamluk Iqṭāʻ," pp. 427–8.
92. Aşıkpaşazade believed that this event happened in 1479–80.
93. Aşıkpaşazade, ed. Giese, p. 225. It is important to remember that the only *muhtasib* who was known to be sent to the Ottoman court was Amir Qanibay who was sent by Sultan Inal in 1456, whereas Aşıkpaşazade placed the sending of a *muhtasib* in 1470s. Either these two cases are separate or Aşıkpaşazade made a mistake. Further evidence is needed to resolve this issue.

NOTES TO PAGES 130–137 323

94. For the deteriorating relationship between Uzun Hasan and Qaytbay, see Woods, *Aqquyunlu*, pp. 107–8; Melvin-Koushki, "*Fathnama.*"
95. For the alliance between the two, see Ibn Aja, ed. Tulaymat, p. 146; Bernadette Martel-Thoumian, "Les Dernières Batailles," p. 325.
96. For the correspondence exchanged between Yashbak and the Ottomans, see pp. 241–2.
97. Martel-Thoumian, "Les Dernières Batailles," pp. 321–7; Woods, Aqquyunlu, pp. 116–17.
98. For Abu Sa'id's head, see Melvin-Koushki, "Fathnama." For his ideological challenges, see Woods, *Aqquyunlu*, pp. 100–6, 107–8 (for *mahmal*).
99. İbn Kemal, *TAO: VII.Defter*, p. 366.
100. Anhegger, "Mu'âli," p. 155.
101. For further details concerning this mission, see Anhegger, "Mu'âli."
102. Anhegger, "Mu'âli," pp. 158–9.
103. Ibn Iyas, 3:98.
104. T.E.5848. It is likely that the letter was sent by an Ottoman governor or another high-ranking administrator rather than by Mehmed.
105. Ibn Iyas, 3:130.
106. For a discussion of Mehmed's last campaign, see Cihan Yüksel Muslu, "Ottoman–Mamluk Relations and the Complex Image of Bāyezīd II," in *Conquête Ottomane de l'Égypte (1517): Arrière-plan, impact, échos*, ed. Benjamin Lellouch and Nicolas Michel (Leiden: E.J. Brill, 2013), pp. 70–2.
107. For a similar claim of Angiolello, see Colin Imber, *The Ottoman Empire 1300–1481* (İstanbul, 1990), p. 252.

Chapter 5 From Captivity Narratives to a Peace Treaty: A New Era of Image-Building (1481–1491)

1. Al-Husayni, "Kitab Nafa'is al-Majalis al-Sultaniyya," pp. 133–4.
2. See pp. 1–2.
3. For this war, see Har-El, *Struggle*.
4. For various versions of this episode in 1460s, see pp. 126–7.
5. For different approaches to war in international relations, see Jönsson and Hall, *Essence of Diplomacy*, pp. 16–7.
6. For previous cases of Ottoman family members seeking refuge in Mamluk lands, see Wiet, "Deux Princes Ottomans à la Cour d'Égypte"; Uzunçarşılı, "Memluk Sultanları Yanına İltica Etmiş"; also see pp. 101–2 in this book.
7. For different approaches in Ottoman sources, see Yüksel Muslu, "Ottoman–Mamluk Relations," p. 61n40.

8. It is unclear if he was accompanied by any Mamluk contingents in this battle. For a recent discussion of this issue, see Ralph S. Hattox, "Qaytbay's Diplomatic Dilemma Concerning the Flight of Cem Sultan," *MSR* 6 (2002):177–90.
9. Nicolas Vatin, *Sultan Djem* (Ankara: TTK, 1997), pp. 65–9. It is likely that he was poisoned by his brother's agents.
10. Kenneth M. Setton, *The Papacy and the Levant, 1204–1571* (Philadelphia: American Philosophical Society, 1978), 2:407n90; İnalcık, "A Case Study in Renaissance Diplomacy," pp. 211–12. Qaytbay's attempts to interfere in these negotiations might have attracted Bayezid's anger. For Mamluk Sultan's possible negotiation with Bayezid concerning Cem, see T.E.5690.
11. Tursun Bey, ed. Tulum, p. 196; Tursun Bey, ed. İnalcık and Murphy, p. 65; İbn Kemal, *TAO: VIII. Defter*, pp. 83–4. The name of the Ottoman ambassador was recorded only in Tursun Bey's account.
12. Ibn Iyas, 3:215–17.
13. Ibid., 3:202–3; İbn Kemal, *TAO: VIII.Defter*, pp. 81–5.
14. İbn Kemal defined this meeting as an "invitation" from the Ottoman Sultan. İbn Kemal, *TAO: VIII. Defter*, pp. 35–7.
15. Ibid., pp. 115–16. In his comprehensive study, Har-El suggested that Bayezid half-heartedly "consented" to send reinforcements, and that 'Ala' al-Dawla successfully convinced Bayezid to help him. Har-El, *Struggle*, pp. 124–5.
16. For Bayezid's years in Amasya, see Petra Kappert, *Die Osmanischen Prinzen und ihre Residenz Amasya in 15. Und 16. Jahrhundert* (Leiden: Nederlands Instituut voor het Nabije Oosten, 1976).
17. Venzke, "The Case of a Dulgadir-Mamluk *Iqṭāʿ*," pp. 427–8. She makes valuable and corrective suggestions about the marriage networks between the Ottomans and the Dulkadirids. For a discussion of Prince Bayezid's exposure to the affairs of the Dulkadirids in Amasya, see Har-El, *Struggle*, pp. 94–6; Anonymous, *Fatih Devrine Ait Münşeât Mecmuası*, pp. 69–70, 70–1.
18. For 'Ala' al-Dawla's reign, Venzke, "The Case of a Dulgadir-Mamluk *Iqṭāʿ*," pp. 427–33. Venzke offers a different chronology for these events during 'Ala' al-Dawla's reign. She does not agree that Selim was the grandson of 'Ala' al-Dawla.
19. W. Barthold and C.E. Bosworth, "Shīrwān Shāh," *EI*[2], 9:488–9.
20. İbn Kemal, *TAO: VIII. Defter*, pp. 79–81. Sources generally confused this earlier ceremony with the later one at which Janibak was accepted. For instance, see Mustafa Âli, *Künhü'l-Ahbâr: Dördüncü Rükn*, Tıpkı Basım, (Ankara: TTK, 2009), 176b.
21. İbn Kemal, *TAO: VIII. Defter*, p. 84.
22. Mustafa Âli, *Künhü'l-Ahbâr*, TTK, 176b.
23. İbn Kemal, *TAO: VIII.Defter*, pp. 94–5; Bihiştî, *Die Chronik*, ed. Moser, pp. 103–6. İbn Kemal mentioned only the Mamluk, Bahmani, and Hungarian ambassadors.
24. For the dating of these ceremonies, see Lütfi Paşa, *Lütfi Paşa ve Tevârih-i Âl-i Osman*, ed. Kayhan Atik (Ankara: Kültür Bakanlığı, 2001), p. 190.

He mentioned that a solar eclipse delayed the start of the audiences. For the solar eclipse, see NASA, "Five Millenium Catalog of Solar Eclipses: 1401 to 1500," http://eclipse.gsfc.nasa.gov/SEcat5/SE1401-1500.html (Accessed on May 8, 2013).
25. For the seating plan, see Bihişti, *Die Chronik*, ed. Moser, p. 105.
26. For the only reference to this gift, see ibid., p. 104.
27. Ibid., pp. 104–5 (24r).
28. Ibn Iyas, 3:215.
29. Ibid., 3:221.
30. Ibid., 3:221, 226.
31. Ibid., 3:226. According to Ibn Iyas, he might have been captured in one of the battles that took place before March 15.
32. Har-El, *Struggle*, p. 147.
33. For Hersekzade's captivity in Mamluk lands, see Halil Ethem, "Hersekoğlu Ahmed Paşa'nin Esaretine da'ir Kahire'de bir Kitabe," *TOEM* 28 and 29 (1330/1911):200–22, 272–94.
34. Aşıkpaşazade, ed. Âli, 231: "Hakaretle"; Aşıkpaşazade, ed. Giese, p. 228.
35. Ibn Iyas, 3:237.
36. Aşıkpaşazade, ed. Âli, 233–5; Aşıkpaşazade, ed. Giese, pp. 229–31.
37. Different reports described Hersekzade's entrance into the Ottoman system. One version stated that the young prince traveled to Constantinople after a disagreement with his older brother (who had seized the inheritance of their father, the Duke of Herzegovina) before voluntarily offering his services to Mehmed. For this version, see H. Šabanović, "Hersek-zade," *EI*[2], 3:340–2; Heath W. Lowry, *Hersekzāde Ahmed Paşa: An Ottoman Statesman's Career and Pious Endowments* (İstanbul: Bahçeşehir University Press, 2011), p. 3 (based on Šabanović). For the sources and studies that considered Hersekzade to be a typical recruit of the *devşirme* system (rather than a volunteer), see Hedda Reindl, *Männer um Bāyezīd: Eine Prosopographische Studie über die Epoche Bāyezīd II (1481–1512)* (Berlin: Klaus Schwarz Verlag, 1983), pp. 129–47. Particularly for her rejection of Sabanovic's thesis, see p.129n3. One suggestion stipulated that his father sent him to Constantinople during his lifetime.
38. For a sample of 'Ala' al-Dawla's correspondence with Bayezid before 1488, see T.E.6385. For 'Ala' al-Dawla's presence in the Mamluk encampment during this war, see T.E.12105.
39. Har-El, *Struggle*, p. 191. For the later improvement of his career, see Reindl, *Männer um Bāyezīd*, p. 154.
40. Ibn Iyas, 3:266.
41. Ibid.
42. For similar attempts by other intermediaries in other historical contexts, probably with the Ottoman sultan's initiation, see Pedani, *Osmanlı Padişahının Adına*, p. 21.
43. Venzke, "Dulkadir-Mamluk Iqṭā," pp. 429–33.
44. Ibn Iyas, 3:266.

45. Ibid., 3:268; Ibn al-Himsi, *Hawadith al-Zaman wa Wafayat al-Shuyukh wa al-Aqran*, ed. Tadmuri (Beirut, 1991), 1:316.
46. For a reference to this wedding, see Uruç, ed. Öztürk, pp. 144–5.
47. For a similar argument about the general role of public celebrations on rulers' image, see Sanders et al., "Mawākib," p. 858.
48. For Qaytbay's strict economic measures, see Ibn Iyas, 3:330–1.
49. Ibid., 3:271.
50. Carl Petry, *Protectors and Praetorians? The Last Mamlūk Sultans and Egypt's Waning as a Great Power*, (Albany: SUNY, 1994), p. 18.
51. For intermittent references to this military maneuver, see Ibn Iyas, 3:269–76.
52. Carl F. Petry, *Twillight of Majesty: The Reigns of Mamlūk Sultans al-Ashraf Qāytbāy and Qānṣūh al-Ghawrī in Egypt* (Seattle, 1993), p. 95.
53. Ibn al-Himsi, *Hawadith*, 1:325.
54. For Mamay's mission, see pp. 252–4.
55. See pp. 122–3.
56. There was another contemporary figure called Molla Arab (d.1531). For distinguishing between the two, see John Curry, *The Transformation of Muslim Mystical Thought in the Ottoman Empire* (Edinburgh: Edinburgh University Press, 2010), pp. 273–5, 287–8.
57. Repp, *The Müfti*, p. 128.
58. İdris-i Bitlisi, *Tercüme-i Heşt Behişt li-Sadi*, TKSK Bağdad 196, 198b; Hoca Saadeddin, *Tac al-Tevarih* (İstanbul, 1279–80/1863–4), 2:67; Hoca Saadeddin, *Tacü't-Tevarih*, ed. Parmaksızoğlu (Ankara: Kültür Bakanlığı, 1979), 3:268–71; Ibn Tulun, *Mufakahat-ul-Hillan fi Hawadith-iz-zaman*, ed. Muḥammad Mustafa (Cairo: Ministry of Culture, 1962), 1:132; Mustafa Âli, *Künhü'l-Ahbâr*, TTK, 183a-184a; Mustafa Âli, *Kayseri Raşid Efendi Kütüphanesindeki 901 ve 920 no.'lu nüshalara gore Kitābü't-tārīḫ-i Künḫü'l- Aḫbār*, ed. Ahmed Uğur, Ahmed Gül, Mustafa Çuhadar, İbrahim Hakkı Çuhadar (Kayseri: Erciyes Üniversitesi Yayınları, 1997-), 2:862–5; Müneccimbaşı, *Saha'if al-Ahbar* (İstanbul, 1285/1868–69), 3:416.
59. Author's translation. Bihişti, *Die Chronik*, ed. Moser, p. 34v. For the completion date of his chronicle, see ibid., p. 12.
60. Uruç, ed. Öztürk, p. 145.
61. For an abbreviated list of such disasters, see Uruç, ed. Öztürk, pp. 237–9.
62. Mustafa Âli, *Künhü'l- Ahbâr*, ed. Uğur, Gül, Çuhadar, and Çuhadar, 2:863–4.
63. For gifts, see Bihişti, *Die Chronik*, ed. Moser, 35r; İdris-i Bitlisi, *Tercüme-i Heşt Behişt li-Sadi*, TKSK Bağdad 196, 199b. For later chroniclers who adopted this account, see Mustafa Âli, *Künhü'l-Ahbâr*, Süleymaniye Fatih 4225, 162a; Müneccimbaşı, *Saha'if al-Ahbar*, 3:415–16. For secondary literature, see Har-El, *Struggle for Domination*, pp. 205–6.
64. Har-El, *Struggle*, pp. 205–6; A. Hess, *The Forgotten Frontier: A History of the Sixteenth Century Ibero-African Frontier* (Chicago, II: University of Chicago Press, 1978), p. 60.

65. Maribel Fierro, "The Almohads (524–668/1130–1269) and the Ḥafṣids (627–932/1229–1526)," in *The New Cambridge History of Islam*, ed. Maribel Fierro (Cambridge: Cambridge University Press, 2010), 2:82; H.R. Idris, "Ḥafṣids," *EI*², 3:66–9.
66. Bihişti, *Die Chronik*, ed. Moser, 35r.
67. With the exception of Aşıkpaşazade, who discussed Bayezid's peace attempts in a vague and inconclusive manner. Aşıkpaşazade, ed. Giese, p. 227.
68. Mustafa Âli, *Künhü'l- Ahbār*, Süleymaniye Fatih 4225, 162a: "...ulema, ümera, nudema, ve vükela..."
69. Taşköprülüzade, *Eş-Şeḳā'iḳu n-Numānīye*, p. 309. For Ali Çelebi's background, see Yusuf Küçükdağ, "Osmanlı-Memlûklü Barışını Yapan Osmanlı Diplomatı Şeyh Ali Çelebi'nin Kimliği Hakkında," *S.Ü. Fen-Edebiyat Fakültesi Edebiyat Dergisi* 5 (1990):213–16.
70. Ibn Iyas, 3:281–2.
71. Bihişti, *Die Chronik*, ed. Moser, pp. 131–3; Aşıkpaşazade, ed. Giese, p. 234; Aşıkpaşazade, ed. Âli, 240; İbn Kemal, *TAO: VIII Defter*, pp. 122–3. For the allegedly humble (almost apologetic) attitude of Qaytbay, see Hadidi, ed. Öztürk, pp. 332–3; Anonymous, *Tarih-i Sultan Bayezid*, TKSK Revan 1272, 17a. Researchers attribute the manuscript of Revan 1272 to Matrakçı Nasuh (d.1564). For a recent edition of this work, see Matrakçı Nasuh, *Tarih-i Sultan Bayezid*, ed. Reha Bilge and Mertol Tulum (İstanbul, 2012).
72. Ibn Iyas, 3:273, 275.
73. Ibn al-Himsi, *Hawadith*, 1:325.
74. Ibid., 1:327; Ibn Iyas, 3:282.
75. For Maqam Ibrahim, see M.J. Kister, "Maḳām Ibrāhīm," *EI*², 6:104–7; Wensick and Jomier, "Ka'ba," *EI*², 4:317–18. This spot was a small building with a dome in the vicinity of Ka'ba. The Prophet Abraham was believed to have stood on this spot while overseeing the construction of Ka'ba.
76. Ibn al-Himsi, *Hawadith*, 1:325–7; Ibn Iyas, 3:281. Ibn Iyas did not give a date, but the ceremony of palanquin generally took place on a Monday or a Thursday or immediately after the middle of the month of Rajab. Shoshan, *Popular Culture*, p. 70.
77. Ibn al-Himsi, *Hawadith*, 1:327.
78. Ibid. For a possible report from Ali Çelebi concerning the allocations that were granted to the Ottoman mission during their stay, see T.E.6944. However, this undated document may have also belonged to a later mission.
79. Har-El, *Struggle*, p. 213.
80. For the sense of relief, see Ibn al-Himsi, *Hawadith*, 1:331; Aşıkpaşazade, ed. Giese, p. 234.
81. Uruç, ed. Öztürk, p. 146; İbn Kemal, *TAO: VIII Defter*, p. 123; Anonymous, *Tarih-i Al-i Osman*, TKSK Revan 1099, 102b-103a, Anonymous, *Tarih-i Sultan Bayezid*, 17a.
82. Hoca Saadeddin, ed. Parmaksızoğlu, 3:270–71; Anonymous, *Tarih-i Sultan Bayezid*, 17a.

83. For his release, see Ibn Shahin, *Nayl al-Amal*, 8:226; Ibn Iyas, 3:282; Ibn al-Himsi, *Hawadith*, 1:327 (especially for the date of his release). I accept Ibn al-Himsi's date and assume that Mihaloğlu was released only after Qaytbay received the Ottoman peace delegation. Some Ottoman sources, however, suggested that the Mamluk sultan initiated peace only after releasing Mihaloğlu. This claim fits well with the Ottoman sources' general narrative that implied Qaytbay's submission and desperation to sign for peace. See Anonymous, *Tarih-i Sultan Bayezid*, 16b; İbn Kemal, *TAO: VIII Defter*, p. 117. For miscellaneous information about Mihaloğlu's captivity, see Ibn Iyas, 3:270.
84. Anonymous, *Tarih-i Sultan Bayezid*, 16b; İbn Kemal, *TAO: VIII Defter*, p. 117.
85. Al-Husayni, "Kitab Nafa'is al-Majalis al-Sultaniyya," p. 134. The author began with, "When Sultan Qaytbay captured Iskandar Paşa..."
86. Winter, "Attitudes toward the Ottomans in the Egyptian Historiography during Ottoman Rule," in *The Historiography of Islamic Egypt (c.950–1800)*, ed. Kennedy (Leiden: E.J. Brill, 2001), pp. 198–9; Ulrich Haarmann, "Ideology and History, Identity and Alterity: The Arab Image of the Turks from the Abbasids to Modern Egypt," *IJMES* 20 (1988):183–6.
87. For the identity of this author, see Barbara Flemming, "Šerīf, Sultan Ġavrī, und die 'Perser'," *Islam* 45 (1969):81–93.
88. Author's translation. İbn Kemal, *TAO: VIII.Defter*, p. 83: "*Ḥāḳān-ı 'aṣrla sultān-ı Mıṣr arasında vāḳi' olan esbāb-ı vaḥşeti, bu 'ālī nesille ol bed-aṣıl ortasında vuḳu' bulan mūcibāt-ı 'adāveti beyān eyler.*"
89. Tursun Bey, ed. Tulum, p. 204: "*Ne şahenşahsın devletlü sultan/Ki kulun olsa cayiz Mısr'a sultan.*"
90. Ibid., p. 209: "*Kula kul ile muamele itti.*" It is also possible that Tursun Bey might have been trying to defend the Ottoman ruler from criticism he received for not leading his army in person.
91. On the other hand, we cannot definitively answer the question of whether individuals such as Davud Paşa were secretly trusted by one of the sovereigns with the task of facilitating or easing communications.
92. For example, Ibn Iyas, 3:278–9; Petry, *Protectors and Praetorians*, pp. 102–31.

Chapter 6 From Warfare to Alliance: The Intricacies of Imperial Diplomacy (1491–1512)

1. İbn Kemal, *TAO: VIII.Defter*, pp. 136–7; Sydney Nettleton Fisher, *The Foreign Relations of Turkey 1481–1512*, Illinois Studies in the Social Sciences 30 (Urbana, Il: University of Illinois Press, 1948), p. 34.
2. For his first diplomatic mission to the Gonzagas of Mantua, see Kissling, *Sultan Bâyezîd II's Beziehungen*, p. 51.

3. Mehmed Süreyya believes that he became a *Tuğrakeş* in 1494. If so, Paşa went to Egypt shortly before this time. Reindl, *Männer um Bāyezīd*, pp. 177–89; Mehmed Süreyya, *Sicill-i Osmani* (İstanbul, 1311/1893), 2:324. Probably not a *paşa* yet, a title which individuals generally received when they were appointed to the vizierate.
4. İbn Kemal, *TAO: VIII.Defter*, pp. 243–4.
5. For this building, see Amy Whittier Newhall, "The Patronage of the Mamluk Sultan Qa'it Bay," (PhD diss., Harvard University, 1987), pp. 268–9.
6. Ibn Iyas, 3:298. For this ambassador's stay in Damascus, see Ibn al-Himsi, *Hawadith*, 1:347.
7. Ibn Iyas recorded that this embassy was the last one Qaytbay dispatched to the Ottomans. However, Qaytbay sent another mission a year later. See pp. 158–8, 257.
8. He was next in line for the position of *dawadar*, whose significant role in Mamluk ceremonies is highlighted in Chapter 1. Also see Ayalon, "Dawādār."
9. Ibn Iyas, 3:353.
10. For a comparison between the treatment given to Mamay and the Apulien and Polish ambassadors who simultanously arrived in Constantinople, see İbn Kemal, *TAO: VIII.Defter*, p. 140. For the political context that surrounded the Polish and Apulien missions, see Fisher, *Foreign Relations*, pp. 34, 48–9.
11. For possible identifications of this particular building (Qubbat al-Fadawiyyah), see Newhall, "The Patronage of the Mamluk Sultan Qa'it Bay," pp. 68–9. For a chronological list of those patronized by Qaytbay, see ibid., pp. 264–5. For a general reference to Qaytbay's patronage, Ibn Iyas, 3:329.
12. For Qaytbay, see Hallenberg, "The Sultan Who Loved Sufis." For Bayezid, see H.J. Kissling, "Aus der Geschichte des Chalvetijje-Ordens," *Zeitschrift der Deutschen Morgenländischen Gesellschaft* 28 (1953):233–89.
13. For these gifts, see p. 257.
14. This menagerie might have been outside of the Topkapı Palace. Borsook, "Travels," p. 160.
15. Ibn Iyas, 3:315–16; Petry, *Twillight of Majesty*, p. 102. For Qaytbay's and the Venetians' continuing concern about an Ottoman attack, see Fisher, *Foreign Relations*, p. 45.
16. Jean-Claude Garcin, "The Regime of the Circassian Mamlūks," in *CHE*, p. 297. Also see Ibn Iyas, 3:372.
17. Ibn Iyas, 3:353.
18. İdris Bostan, "Kemal Reis," *DİA*, 25:227; also see pp. 258 in Appendix III.
19. For Barak Reis, another seaman who was sent to Italy by Bayezid for secret missions, see the relevant works of Şerafettin Turan and V.L. Ménage in the selected bibliography.
20. H.J. Kissling, "Betrachtungen über die Flottenpolitik Sultan Bâyezîds II," *Saeculum* 20 (1969):35–43.
21. T. E. 6938; T.E.12301.

22. İbn Kemal, *TAO: VIII.Defter*, pp. 169–70; Nicholas Vatin, *L'Ordre de Saint-Jean-de-Jérusalem, l'Empire Ottoman et la Méditerranée Orientale entre les Deux Sieges de Rhodes* (Paris: Peeters, 1994), pp. 238, 464–5; Bostan, "Kemal Reis," p. 227. İbn Kemal mentioned that the famous "Santurluogli" was among the captives. For the identity of this individual, see Vatin, ibid. 464–5. Relying on Vatin's detailed study of various individuals with the same family name of Centurione, I conclude that this "Santurlioglu" probably was Nicola Centurione and was probably ransomed by his family in 1500. Relying on European sources, Fisher says that Kemal Reis captured a Portuguese ship and impaled its crew. He does not say anything about the Hospitallers of St. John. Fisher, *Foreign Relations*, p. 58n66.
23. The following studies give diverse and complimentary details about Khayr Bey's mission and this particular procession in Constantinople. Kâzım Yaşar Kopraman, "Osmanlı-Memlûk Münâsebetleri," in *Türkler* (Ankara, 2002), 9:482; Hadidi, ed. Öztürk, pp. 348–50; Ibn al-Himsi, *Hawadith*, 2:38, 72; İbn Kemal, *TAO: VIII. Defter*, pp. 169–70; Mutawalli, *Al-Fatkh Al-Uthmani*, p. 40; Uruç, ed. Öztürk, pp. 183–4; Ziyada, "The Fall of the Mamluks 1516–1517," p. 10; Ziyada, "Nihayat Salatin Al-Mamalik," p. 210.
24. For Malkoçoğlu, see Gary Leiser, "Malḳoč-oghullari," *EI^2*, 12 (Supp.):578–9.
25. For correspondence between Khayr Bey and Ottoman officials both before and after 1517, see for example T.E.5483, 5552, 5594/1, 5594/2, 5594/3, 7143. For a detailed study of these and other letters between Khayr Bey and the Ottoman officials, see Mutawalli, *Al-Fatkh Al-Uthmani*.
26. For the disappointment of Bayezid, see Ibn Iyas, 3:411.
27. For the only reference to this marriage alliance, see Uruç, ed. Öztürk, pp. 184–5.
28. For a detailed list of references, see pp. 260–1.
29. BA İbnü'l-Emin, Hariciye 1. Although the document did not specify whether the prices were for silver (*akçe*) or gold coins (*sultani*), they were probably for silver. See Pamuk, "Money in the Ottoman Empire," p. 950.
30. Janbulat had been sent to the Ottoman capital to procure the final version of the peace treaty in 1491.
31. Al-Qalqashandi, *Subh al-A'sha*, 5:466–8; al-Sahmawi, *Al-Thaghr*, 1:521–2.
32. T.E.9504. Tentatively, I think that this piece belonged to a letter from Qansuh al-Ghawri to Bayezid II, due to the address "His Brother."
33. A preliminary study of the titulature between Qansuh al-Ghawri and Selim (as preserved in Feridun Bey's collection) presents a similarly confusing picture because both the previous conventions of titulature (such as *al-Maqarr*) and others (such as *al-Hadra* or *al-Majlis*) were simultaneously used by both sides. Likewise, a dated letter of Qansuh al-Ghawri in Ottoman archives (T.E.12282) reveals that the Mamluk sultan addressed Selim with *al-Maqam al-'Ali* (instead of *al-Hadra* or *al-Majlis*) and refered to him as "Our Son," as Selim was younger than the Mamluk sultan. A detailed analysis of these letters awaits a separate study. For T.E.12282, see Halil Ethem, ""Mısır Fethi Mukaddematına Aid Mühim bir Vesika." Also see Kerslake, "The Correspondence."

34. Bosworth, "Laḳab."
35. For the earliest reference to the Safavid penetration into Mamluk territory, see Ibn Iyas, 4:39; Ibn al-Himsi, *Hawadith*, 2:158; Allouche, *Origins and Development*, pp. 81–2.
36. Feridun, 1274, 1:347–9.
37. Ibid., 1:349–50.
38. For Cem's daughter, see İbn Kemal, *TAO: VIII.Defter*, 39; Hoca Saadeddin, *Tac al-Tevarih*, 2:127–8.
39. Carl Petry, ed., *CHE*, 527.
40. Ibn al-Himsi, *Hawadith*, 2:164–5, 167–8.
41. Hoca Saadeddin, *Tac al-Tevarih*, 2:127–8. Hoca Saadeddin was the only chronicler who claimed that Haydar Ağa returned with Cem's daughter. A book of allocations (*İnamat Defteri*) that started with the year 1503–4 had multiple references to the allocations and gifts that were granted to the Ottoman princess by Bayezid between 1504 and 1513. Unfortunately it did not give any information about the whereabouts of the princess. We do not know whether Hoca Saadeddin's information was accurate. For allocations granted by Bayezid to Cem's daughter, see Anonymous, *İnamat Defteri*, 1b, 4a, ff.
42. Petry, *Protectors and Praetorians*, pp. 37–8. In 1503–4 Sibay, the Mamluk governor of Aleppo, and Dawlatbay had joined forces in an attempt to depose Qansuh al-Ghawri, or at least to seize control of the Syrian provinces of his empire. Although Petry, who primarily focuses on Sibay, dates this event to 1504–5, Ibn Iyas first mentioned Dawlatbay's refuge in April 1501. The references in *İnamat Defteri* indicated that Dawlatbay may have been receiving allocations from Bayezid in Konya since at least 1503, if not before. See Ibn Iyas, 4:7; Anonymous, *İnamat Defteri*, 4b, 11a (to Konya), and 11b. In November 1506, Dawlatbay was accepted by the Mamluk sultan in Cairo.
43. Feridun, 1274, 1:354–5.
44. Ibid., 1:355–6.
45. See pp. 13–4.
46. For a general discussion, see Jean-Louis Bacqué-Grammont and Anne Krœll, *Mamlouks, Ottomans et Portugais en Mer Rouge: L'Affaire de Djedda en 1517* (Cairo: Institut Français d'Archéologie Orientale, 1988).
47. Ibn Iyas, 4:83. After this first reference to a campaign to "India" to curtail "the Franks," the volume made multiple references to similar attempts, the preparation of a navy, the construction or renovation of castles along the shores, and both land and naval military maneuvers along the coasts of "India," eastern Africa, and Hijaz.
48. It has also been argued that Qansuh al-Ghawri demanded maritime help from Bayezid in order to respond to these requests from the Sultan of Gujarat. İdris Bostan, "Selman Reis," *DİA*, 36:444; Fuess, *Verbranntes Ufer*, pp. 57–8.
49. Ibn Iyas, 4:107, 118–19.
50. Ibid., 4:109, 119–20. For further references in Ottoman sources concerning Kemal Reis's mission, see pp. 258, 268–9 in this book.

51. Ibid., 4:121–2.
52. Ibid., 4:119.
53. For the first reference to this address, see p. 164.
54. For a recent study of Prince Korkud, see Nabil Sirri al-Tikriti, "Şehzade Korkud and the Articulation of Early 16th Century Ottoman Religious İdentity," (PhD diss., Chicago University, 2004).
55. Fisher, *Foreign Relations*, pp. 105–6; Ibn Iyas, 4:152.
56. Ayalon, "Dawādār"; Haarmann, "Der Arabische Osten," pp. 231–2. A number of last Mamluk sultans rose to the sultanate from this position.
57. Ibn Iyas, 4:152. Until p. 182, Ibn Iyas frequently mentioned Korkud and his public appearances in Cairo.
58. Ibid., 4:157. For the expression "in gala," see Mayer, *Mamluk Costumes*, pp. 79–80.
59. Ibn Iyas, 4:154, 157.
60. T. E.5464/1: "*Emr iyledük yarāğin gördiler fāḫir ḫilatlar virüp ināmāt-ı celīle ettükten soñra...*"
61. Palmira Brummett, "Kemal Re'is and Ottoman Gunpowder Diplomacy," *Studies on Ottoman Diplomatic History* 5 (1990):1–17.
62. Anonymous, *İnamat Defteri*, 178b, 179a–b, 180a, 180b.
63. Ibn Iyas, 4:184. For allocations that Bayezid sent to Korkud with 'Allan, see Anonymous, *İnamat Defteri*, 180b.
64. Ibn Iyas, 4:184.
65. Ibid., 4:186.
66. For the long peace process between the Ottomans and the Venetians, see Fisher, *Foreign Relations*, pp. 67–89.
67. For the details concerning these missions, see pp. 270–1.
68. For activities of this individual (called Mahmud Bey by Brummett), see Ibn Iyas, 4:129, 130, 139, 142, 156, 160, 163, 164, 165, 183, 191–2 (his death). I was not able to find much information about this individual's background. Palmira Brummett, "The Overrated Adversary: Rhodes and Ottoman Naval Power," *The Historical Journal* 36 (1993):533.
69. Ibid., 4:164–5. While Ibn Iyas generically called them "Franks," Fuess claims that the success of the Mamluk fleet was against pirates. Fuess, *Verbranntes Ufer*, p. 57.
70. Ibn Iyas, 4:164–5.
71. Ibid., 4:191. Ibn Iyas uses the generic term "the Franks" for the attackers. Brummett, "Kemal Re'is and Ottoman Gunpowder Diplomacy," p. 8; Brummett, "The Overrated Adversary," p. 534–5.
72. T.E.5464; Feridun, 1274, 1:356–7, 1:357–8.
73. Feridun, 1274, 1:358.
74. Ibn Iyas, 4:191.
75. İdris Bostan, *Beylikten İmparatorluğa Osmanlı Denizciliği* (İstanbul: Kitab Yayınevi, 2006), p. 25; Bostan, "Selman Reis," *DİA*, 36:444–6; Svat Soucek, "Selmān Re'īs," *EI*^{2}, 9:135–6; Ibn Iyas, 4:201.

76. Ibn Iyas, 4:202–3.
77. For the disappearance of Kemal Reis, see Brummett, "Kemal Re'is and Ottoman Gunpowder Diplomacy," p. 9; Bostan, "Kemal Reis," p. 227.
78. Ibn Iyas, 4:202–3.
79. For negative comments of Mamluk chronicler Ibn Taghribirdi concerning the Ottoman correspondence, see p. 36.
80. For the capture of these Safavid messengers, see Ibn Iyas, 4:191. It is not clear whether this al-Bira is the town in modern-day Lebanon or one in modern-day Turkey in the vicinity of Şanlıurfa.
81. Ibid., 4:205.
82. Fisher, *Foreign Relations*, pp. 64–89.
83. Ibn Iyas, 4:118–19. For an earlier reference to this visit, see pp. 167–8 and 267–8 in this book.
84. Ibid., 4:201.
85. T.E.5483.
86. Ibn Iyas, 4:268–9.
87. For a different interpretation of this particular occasion, Behrens-Abouseif, "Citadel of Cairo," 69–70.
88. Ibn Iyas, 4:269–70.
89. For the continuing Mamluk dominance of at least the Ramazanids, see ibid., 4:193. For the continuing Ottoman resentment over their inability to subdue the Ramazanids, see İbn Kemal, *TAO: VIII.Defter*, pp. 268–72. In 1485, the Ramazanid ruler who fought on the side of the Mamluks was captured by the Ottomans. Sümer, "Ramazan-oğulları," p. 617. For Turgudoğulları, see Ibn Iyas, 3:411; İbn Kemal, *TAO: VIII.Defter*, pp. 268–72. Also see, Faruk Sümer, "Turgutlular," *DİA*, 12:420–1.
90. For the drastic contrast between the gifts for to a Mamluk ambassador and those for a Hungarian one in 1503–4, see Anonymous, *İnamat Defteri*, 8b, 9b, 10b. For this particular embassy headed by Amir Tanibey (Taymin Bey in the Ottoman source), we have only the dates of departure and arrival in the Mamluk sources. The significant gift list in the Ottoman treasury book suggests that this embassy could be a major one, yet somehow went unnoticed by others. For details, see pp. 264–5.
91. These conclusions are based on a preliminary study by İnamat Defteri. For other scholarly works on this particular source, see Mustafa Açıkgöz, "II.Bayezid Devri İnamat Defteri" (Master's Thesis, Marmara Üniversitesi Sosyal Bilimler Enstitüsü, 1996); Ömer Lutfi Barkan, "Osmanlı Saraylarına Ait Muhasebe Defterleri," *Belgeler* 9 (1979):296–380; İsmail Erünsal, "II.Bayezid Devrine Ait Bir İnamat Defteri," *Tarih Enstitüsü Dergisi* 10–11 (1979–80):303–41; Hilal Kazan, *XVI. Asırda Sarayın Sanatı Himayesi* (İstanbul: İSAR, 2010).
92. Kafadar, *Between Two Worlds*, p. 97.
93. For the significance of the Mamluks in the Ottoman historiography during Bayezid's reign, see Yüksel-Muslu, "Ottoman–Mamluk Relations."

94. Except for a possible promotion of Ottoman titulature in Mamluk correspondence during Qansuh al-Ghawri's reign. See p. 163.
95. For the embassy of Shaykh 'Abd al-Mu'min al-'Ajami, see pp. 158–9, 257.

Conclusion

1. Allouche, *Origins and Development*, p. 114. Based on the fact that Qansuh al-Ghawri accepted these refugees, Allouche claims that he supported Ahmed in the Ottoman succession struggle. This is not necessarily the case. For Korkud's case, see pp. 168–72 in this book.
2. Selim first eliminated Prince Korkud. Then he defeated Ahmed, another brother of his, definitively on April 15, 1514. Halil İnalcık, "Selīm I," *EI*², 9:127–31; Bacqué-Grammont and Krœll, *Mamlouks, Ottomans et Portugais en Mer Rouge*, p. 5; Ibn al-Himsi, *Hawadith*, 2:258.
3. Kerslake, "The Correspondence."
4. Allouche, *Origins and Development*, pp. 122–3. Venzke, "Dulgadir-Mamluk *Iqṭā'*," pp. 432–4; Yınanç, *Dulkadir Beyliği*, pp. 95–9. For the pact of non-aggression between Shah Isma'il and 'Ala' al-Dawla, Venzke, "Dulgadir-Mamluk *Iqṭā'*," p. 431.
5. Allouche, *Origins and Development*, pp. 124–5.
6. İnalcık thinks that Selim felt threated from the rear by the Mamluks and Dulkadirids while he marched to the Safavid territory. İnalcık, "Selīm I."
7. Ibn Iyas, 4:462, 463, and 467. For Selim's accompanying letter, see Feridun, 1274, 1:411–13. For diverse interpretations of this message, see Allouche, *Origins and Development*, pp. 124–5; Michael Winter, "Ottoman Occupation," in *CHE*, pp. 495–6; see Kerslake, "The Correspondence," pp. 211–12.
8. For a chronology and treatment of these exchanges, see Kerslake, "The Correspondence."
9. For a possible attempt to justify Bayezid II's failed attacks to Mamluk territory, see Yüksel Muslu, "Ottoman–Mamluk Relations."
10. Benjamin Lellouch and Nicolas Michel, "Introduction: Les échelles de l'événement," in *Conquête Ottomane de l'Égypte*, pp. 1–51; Feridun M. Emecen, *Yavuz Sultan Selim* (İstanbul, 2010), p. 193; Haarmann, "Der Arabische Osten," p. 251.
11. Yüksel Muslu, "Ottoman–Mamluk Relations," pp. 70–2.
12. T.E.1037.
13. For contradictory presentations of a single event in Ottoman and Mamluk sources, see pp. 119–22.
14. See p. 76. For al-Sahmawi's classification of titles, see Appendix II.
15. P.A. Andrews, "Miẓalla," *EI*², 7:191–5; Paula Sanders et al., "Marāsim," pp. 521, 522. For this item in Mamluk-Mongol diplomatic exchanges, see Broadbridge, *Kingship*, pp. 43, 108.

Notes to Pages 181–185

16. For examples from other historical contexts that emphasize the changing nature of ceremonials, see Sabine MacCormack, *Art and Ceremony in Late Antiquity* (Berkeley: University of California Press, 1981), pp. 13, 35 (for instance); Mc Cormick, "Analyzing Imperial Ceremonies"; Michael McCormick, *Eternal Victory: Triumphal Leadership in Late Antiquity, Byzantium and the Early Medieval West* (Cambridge: Cambridge University Press, 1986), 131ff.
17. See pp. 88–90, 94–5, and Yuksel Muslu, "Language of Diplomacy."
18. For the appellations of the Karamanids in a Mamluk letter dating 1458, see BNF MS 4440, 194b.
19. See pp. 119–20.
20. For Barquq and Murad I's correspondence, see pp. 71–2; for Mehmed II and Inal's correspondence, see p. 112; for Mehmed II and Khushqadam's correspondence (in a negative way, because Mehmed dismissed the fact that Khushqadam was his senior), see p. 119.
21. See p. 119.
22. For the use of this rhetoric in a letter between the Timurids and the Mamluks, see BNF MS 4440, 44b.
23. For the idea of cross-fertilization of diplomatic and ceremonial practices in the Mediterranean basin, see Marius Canard, "Le Cérémonial Fatimite et le Cérémonial Byzantin: Essai de Comparaison," *Byzantion* 21 (1951):355–420; John Wansbrough, *Lingua Franca in the Mediterranean* (Richmond, Surrey: Curzon Press, 1996).
24. For this comparative perspective, see Necipoğlu, "Shifting Palatine Paradigms"; Necipoğlu, *Topkapı*, pp. 242–58; Necipoğlu, "Framing the Gaze"; Fuess, "Between dihlīz and dār al-adl," pp. 163–4.
25. Necipoğlu, *Topkapı*, pp. 21–2. For an alternative approach to the idea of Ottoman imperial seclusion, see Ebru Boyar and Kate Fleet, *A Social History of Ottoman Istanbul* (Cambridge: Cambridge University Press, 2010), pp. 28–72.
26. See p. 79.
27. For a discussion of close connections between the dynastic lineage and the political legitimacy of Ottoman ruler, see Hakan Karateke, "Legitimizing the Ottoman Sultanate: A Framework for Historical Analysis," in *Legitimizing the Order: the Ottoman Rhetoric of State Power*, ed. Hakan T. Karateke and Maurus Reinkowski (Leiden: E.J. Brill, 2005), pp. 13–55.
28. See pp. 91–2.
29. For Murad II's requesting the legal opinions of Mamluk scholars against the Karamanids, see 106–7.
30. See pp. 112, 134–6, 154.
31. Broadbridge, *Kingship*, 194–5. For other occurrences of this trope in diverse historical contexts, ibid., 40–1, 62–3.
32. See pp. 102–3.
33. Sievert, *Der Herrscherwechsel*, pp. 82–3.
34. See pp. 161–2.

35. For old but very useful studies of this conquest's significance, see Andrew C. Hess, "The Evolution of the Ottoman Seaborne Empire in the Age of the Oceanic Discoveries," *American Historical Review* 75 (1970):1892–1919; Andrew C. Hess, "The Ottoman Conquest of Egypt (1517) and the Beginning of the Sixteenth Century-World War," *IJMES* 4 (1973):55–76.
36. For a recent treatment of this territory in the fifteenth-century, see Julien Loiseau, "De l'Asie centrale à l'Égypte: le siècle turc," in *Histoire du Monde au XVe siècle*, ed. Patrick Boucheron, Julien Loiseau, Pierre Monnet, Yann Potin (Paris, 2009), pp. 33–51.
37. Barbara Flemming, "Literary Activities in Mamluk Halls and Barracks," in *Studies in Memory of Gaston Wiet*, ed. Myriam Rosen-Ayalon (Jerusalem, 1977), pp. 252–60; Fikret Turan, "The Mamluks and Their Acceptance of Oghuz Turkish as a Literary Language: Political Maneuver or Cultural Aspiration," *Turcologica* 69 (2007):37–47; Erkan, "Darīr"; Gottfried Hagen, "Some Considerations"; Zuhal Kültüral and Latif Beyreli, *Şerîfî Şehnâme Çevirisi*, 4 vols. (Ankara: TDK, 1999); Mehmet Yalçın, *The Dīvan of Qânsûh al-Ghûrî* (İstanbul: Bay, 2002); A. Bodrogligeti, "Notes on the Turkish Literature at the Mameluke Court," *Acta Orientalia Academiae Scientiarum Hungaricae* 14 (1962):273–82. Although from a different geographical and historical context, the Mughal rulers Babur's and Humayun's autobiographies, which were composed in Caghatayish Turkish, can also be considered in this group.
38. For broad comments on Mamluk literary patronage, see Flemming, "Literary Activities," p. 251; Behrens-Abouseif, *Cairo of the Mamluks*, pp. 4–6.

Appendix I   The Anatomy of a Typical Letter (Diacriticals are Used)

1. Dekkiche, 1:345–93. For sample readings and translations of Mamluk correspondence and documents, for instance see Hans Ernst, *Die Mamlukischen Sultansurkenden des Sinai-Klosters* (Wiesbaden, 1960); Wansbrough, "A Mamluk Letter of 877/1473"; Wansbrough, "A Mamluk Ambassador to Venice"; Wansbrough, "Safe-Conduct"; Wansbrough, "Venice and Florence in the Mamluk Commercial Privileges"; Holt, *Early Mamluk Diplomacy*; D.S. Richards, "A Late Mamluk Document Concerning Frankish Commercial Practice at Tripoli," *BSOAS* 62 (1999):21–35. For Ottoman diplomatics, for instance see Kütükoğlu, *Osmanlı Belgelerinin Dili*; Jan Reychman and Ananiasz Zajaczkowski, *Handbook of Ottoman Turkish Diplomatics* (Mouton, 1968); Valeri Stojanow, *Die Entstehung und Entwicklung der Osmanischen-Türkischen Paläographie und Diplomatic: mit einer Bibliographie* (Berlin, 1983). For sample readings and translations of Ottoman correspondence and documents, for instance see Klaus Schwarz, *Osmanische Sultansurkunden des Sinai-Klosters in türkischer Sprache*

(Freiburg, 1970); Dariusz Kolodziejczyk, *Ottoman–Polish Diplomatic Relations (15th–18th Century): an Annotated Edition of Ahdnames and Other Documents* (Leiden: E.J. Brill, 2000); Josef Matuz, *Das Kanzleiwesen Sultan Süleymans des Prächtigen* (Wiesbaden, 1974). For sample works on the diplomatics of other Islamic powers, see Horst-Adolf, *Beiträge zur ayyubidschen Diplomatik* (Freiburg, 1968); Mehmet Şefik Keçik, *Briefe und Urkunden aus der Kanzlei Uzun Hasans: Ein Beitrag zur Geschichte Ost-Anatoliens in 15 Jahrhundert* (Freiburg, 1975); Heribert Busse, *Untersuchungen zum Islamischen Kanzleiwesen* (Cairo, 1959). This list presents only preliminary suggestions.

Appendix II   Titulature (Diacriticals are Used)

1. Al-Qalqashandi, *Subh*, 5:466–8; Bosworth, "Laḳab."

Appendix III   Missions and Envoys

1. For a very brief list of Ottoman-Mamluk exchanges, see Joseph von Hammer-Purgstall, *Geschichte des Osmanischen Reiches* (Pest, 1833), 9:303 and 326.
2. For the controversy surrounding this mission, see p. 306n27.
3. Ahmed Tevhid, "İlk Altı Padişahımızıñ Bursa'da Kâ'in Türbeleri: Ḥüdāvendigâr Sulṭān Murad Ḫān'ıñ Türbesi," TOEM 13–18 (1328):1048–1049; E.H. Ayverdi, İstanbul Mi'mârî Çağının Menşe'i: Osmanlı Mi'mârîsinin İlk Devri (İstanbul, 1966), 292–3; İ.H. Uzunçarşılı, "Murad I," İA, 8:595; Fehmi Ethem Karatay, Topkapı Sarayı Müzesi Kütüphanesi Arapça Yazmalar Kataloğu (İstanbul: Topkapı Sarayı Müzesi, 1962), vol.1, # 168. For the most detailed information on these items, see Ahmed Tevhid's article, where he also includes Barquq's endowment inscription in the Qur'an.
4. For an alternative explanation, see Yınanç, "Bayezid I," p. 374.
5. Following the account of Ibn Iyas, both Shefer and Behrens-Abouseif believe that Ibn al-Sughayr, who went to the Ottoman court with al-Kujkuni, died during his return trip. Doris Behrens-Abouseif, *Fatḥ Allāh and Abū Zakariyya: Physicians under the Mamluks*, Supplément aux Annales Islamologiques 10 (Cairo: Institut Français d'Archéologie Orientale, 1987), p. 7; Shefer, "Physician in Mamluk and Ottoman Courts," pp. 118–19. However, al-Maqrizi includes a biography of Ibn al-Sughayr and says that the doctor died in 823/1420. In contrast, Ibn Hajar claims that Ibn al-Sughayr died while he was accompanying the Mamluk Sultan Barquq on his campaign in Syria, one year after his return from the Ottoman court in 796/1394. Ibn Hajar, *Al-Durar al-Kamina*, 3:151–2.

Because of his personal relationship with Ibn al-Sughayr, al-Maqrizi's account is more credible. See al-Maqrizi, *Durar*, ed. Jalili, 3:439–40.

6. The chronicle of Ibn Iyas was composed later than the other sources cited in this entry. For this particular entry, earlier sources are taken as the main references.
7. Ahmed Tevhid, "Yıldırım Sultan Bayezid Han-ı Evvel Devrinde Mısır'a Sefaretle Gönderilen Sefer Şah'ın Vefatı," *TOEM* 13–18(1331):1031–2.
8. For the date of this correspondence, see p. 312n4.
9. I think this letter is miscopied. The date on the letter should be 10 ZH 830, not 831.
10. Here, Ibn Taghribirdi also says that he includes copies of both Mehmed's letter and Inal's letter in his *Hawadith*. Today's editions, however, do not contain the letters.
11. Elias Muhanna identifies this text as the letter of the Sharif of Mecca to Mehmed II. Further analysis is needed to reach a conclusion. Muhanna, "New Clothes," p. 194.
12. Tekindağ has information about the gifts that the parties exchanged. See, Tekindağ, "Fatih Devrinde," p. 76.
13. Despite the date on the second letter (896/1491), the editors Lugal and Erzi claim that this document was incorrectly dated and that this correspondence took place durign Bayezid's years in Amasya. Although their argument is tentatively accepted, these letters deserve further investigation.
14. For Dawlatbay's career, see Ibn Iyas, 2:361, 471.
15. According to Anhegger, the head was sent to Mehmed's son Cem. Anhegger, "Mu'âli," p. 154. No reference to this incident exists in Mamluk sources.
16. Accoring to Ibn Shahin, Barsbay was appointed before the Battle of Otlukbeli. Ibn Shahin, *Nayl al-Amal*, 7:73.
17. For Janibak's death on Muharram 893/December 1487, see Ibn Iyas, 3:246.
18. I could not find this envoy in the sources that I examined.
19. For Mihaloğlu İskender's release, see pp. 150, 152–3.
20. M.M. Ziyadeh claims that the Mamluk ambassador went to Napoli with the Ottoman ambassador, but he does not footnote that information in the Arabic version of his article. In the English version, he cites Ibn Iyas and a foreign source. Ibn Iyas does not say anything about Napoli.
21. Whether this "Yunus" (or others mentioned in this list among Mamluk ambassadors) could be Amir Yunus who was appointed as the chief dragoman in 1514 remains open to study. Wansbrough, "A Mamluk Ambassador to Venice," p. 513.
22. On the exact same date, a poet called Mehmed was given an award for a poem he composed for the letter that was going to be sent to the Mamluk court. However, the entry is very cryptic. This issue needs further investigation. See Anonymous, *İnamat Defteri*, 10a (dated 6 JA 909/November 26, 1503).
23. Ibn Tulun mentions Amir Azbak al-Khazinadar who entered Damascus in 8 Safar 909/August 2, 1503 on his way to the Ottoman court with gifts and

company. Further studies needed to identify this mission. Ibn Tulun, *Mufakahat*, 1:268–9.
24. According to *İnamat Defteri*, on 22 Sha'ban 913/December 22, 1507, a certain Kemal returned all the goods and allocations back to the treasury. I suspect this Kemal was Kemal Reis.
25. A possibility exists that a *qadi* named Ali was also among the Ottoman representatives sent to Cairo. This person was probably the same one who negotiated the peace treaty as the envoy of the Ottoman ruler.
26. Mutawalli, *Al-Fatkh Al-'Uthmani*, pp. 45–6.
27. Fahir İz, "'Aşık Paşa," *EI*[2], 1:698–9.
28. Wansbrough, "A Mamluk Ambassador to Venice," p. 510.
29. Abdizade Hüseyin Hüsameddin, *Amasya Tarihi* (İstanbul, 1328/1927), 1:109.

SELECTED BIBLIOGRAPHY

Abbreviations

B.A. – Başbakanlık Archive
BNF – Bibliotheque Nationale Français
BSOAS – Bulletin of the School of Oriental and African Studies
CHE – Carl Petry, ed. Cambridge History of Egypt. Vol.1 (Cambridge: Cambridge University Press, 1998).
DİA – Türkiye Diyanet Vakfı İslâm Ansiklopedisi (İstanbul: Türkiye Diyanet Vakfı Ansiklopedisi, 1988).
EI^2 – The Encyclopaedia of Islam. New Edition (Leiden: E.J. Brill, 1960).
Gifts of the Sultan – Linda Komaroff, ed. Gifts of the Sultan: The Arts of Giving at the Islamic Courts (Los Angeles, CA: Los Angeles County Museum of Art, 2011).
İA – İslâm Ansiklopedisi: İslâm Âlemi Tarih, Coğrafya, Etnografya ve Biyografya Lûgati (İstanbul: Millî Eğitim Basımevi, 1950–88).
IJMES – International Journal of Middle East Studies
İnamat Defteri – Anonymous. İnamat Defteri. İstanbul Büyükşehir Belediyesi Atatürk Kitaplığı (Taksim, İstanbul) Muallim Cevdet 71.
JESHO – Journal of Economic and Social History of the Orient
MSR – Mamluk Studies Review
Robes and Honor – Gordon, Stewart, ed. Robes and Honor: The Medieval World of Investiture (New York, NY: Palgrave, 2001).
SI – Studia Islamica
Süleymaniye – Süleymaniye Manuscript Library
T.E. – Document in Topkapı Palace Archive
TKSK – Topkapı Palace Library
TOEM – Tarih-i Osmani Encümeni Mecmuası, continued as Türk Tarih Encümeni Mecmuası (İstanbul, 1326–39/1910–21).
TTEM – Türk Tarih Encümeni Mecmuası (İstanbul, 1922–31).
TTK – Türk Tarih Kurumu (Publications of Turkish Historical Society).

Cited Archival Documents

B.A., İbnü'l-emin Hariciye 1
T.E.1037
T.E.3739
T.E.5464
T.E.5483
T.E.5552
T.E.5594/1,2,3
T.E.5690
T.E.5848
T.E.6385
T.E.6938
T.E.6944
T.E.7143
T.E.9504
T.E.12105
T.E.12282
T.E.12301

Other Primary Sources (Including Unpublished Manuscripts)

Adorno, Jean. *Itinéraire d'Anselme Adorno en Terre Sainte (1470–71)*. Translated and edited by Jacques Heers and Georgette de Groer (Paris, 1978).
Ahmedi.
(1) *İskender-nāme: İnceleme, Tıpkıbasım*. Edited by İsmail Ünver (Ankara: TTK, 1983).
(2) *Tevārīḫ-i Mülūk-i Āl-i Osmān Ġazv-i İşān Bā Küffār*. Edited by Kemal Sılay. (Harvard Üniversitesi: Yakın Doğu Dilleri ve Medeniyetleri Bölümü, 2004).
Âli, Mustafa.
(1) *Künhü'l-Ahbar*. Süleymaniye Fatih 4225.
(2) *Kayseri Raşid Efendi Kütüphanesindeki 901 ve 920 no.'lu nüshalara gore Kitābü't-tārīḫ-i Künhü'l-Ahbār*. Edited by Ahmed Uğur, Ahmed Gül, Mustafa Çuhadar, İbrahim Hakkı Çuhadar (Kayseri: Erciyes Üniversitesi Yayınları, 1997).
(3) *Künhü'l-Ahbâr: Dördüncü Rükn*. Tıpkı Basım (Ankara: TTK, 2009).
Ali, Seydi Bey. *Teşrifat ve Teşkilatımız*. Edited by Niyazi Ahmet Banoğlu (İstanbul, 1973).
Anhegger, Robert. "Mu'âli'nin Hünkârnâmesi." *Tarih Dergisi* 1 (1949):145–65.
Anonymous, *Anonim Osmanlı Kroniği (1299–1512)*. Edited by Necdet Öztürk (İstanbul: Türk Dünyası Araştırmaları Vakfı, 2000).
——— BNF MS 4440.
——— BNF MS 4434.

———— *Byzantium, Europe, and the Early Ottoman Sultans, 1373—1513:An Anonymous Greek Chronicle of the Seventeenth Century.* Translated and edited by Marios Philippides (New Rochelle, NY: Caratzas, 1990).
———— *İnamat Defteri.* İstanbul Büyükşehir Belediyesi Atatürk Kitaplığı (Taksim, İstanbul) Muallim Cevdet 71.
———— *Fatih Devrine Ait Münşeât Mecmuası.* Edited by N. Lugal and A.S. Erzi (İstanbul: İstanbul Enstitüsü Yayınları, 1956).
———— *Gazavât-ı Sultân Murâd b. Mehemmed Hân: İzladi ve Varna Savaşları (1443—1444) üzerinde Anonim Gazavâtnâme.* Edited by Halil İnalcık and Mevlûd Oğuz (Ankara: TTK, 1978).
———— *Kitab al-Hadaya wa al-Tuhaf.* Edited by Muhammad Hamidullah (Kuwait, 1379/1959).
———— *Onaltıncı Asırda Yazılmış Grekçe Anonim Osmanlı Tarihi.* Translated and edited by Şerif Baştav (Ankara: Ankara Üniversitesi, 1973).
———— *Osmanlı Devlet Düzenine Ait Metinler I: Kitâb-ı Müstetâb.* Edited by Yaşar Yücel (Ankara, 1974).
———— *Tarih-i Al-i Osman.* TKSK, Revan 1099.
———— *Tarih-i Sultan Bayezid.* TKSK, Revan 1272 (Also see under Matrakçı Nasuh).
———— *Tevārīḫ Āl-i Osmān: Giese Neşri.* Edited by Nihat Azamat (İstanbul: Edebiyat Fakültesi Basımevi, 1992).
Aşıkpaşazade.
(1) *Die altosmanische Chronik des Āşıkpaşazāde.* Edited by F. Giese (Leipzig: Otto Harrasowitz, 1929).
(2) *Tevārīḫ-i Āl-i Osmāndan Āşıkpaşazāde Ta'rīḫj.* Edited by Ālī Bey (İstanbul, 1332/1914).
(3) *Osmanoğulları'nın Tarihi.* Edited by Kemal Yavuz and Yekta Saraç (İstanbul, 2003).
Al-'Ayni. *Iqd al-Juman fi Tarikh Ahl al-Zaman.* Süleymaniye Carullah Efendi 1591.
Bihişti, Ahmed Sinan Çelebi. *Die Chronik des Ahmed Sinân Čelebi Genannt Bihišti: Eine Quelle zur Geschichte des osmanischen Reiches unter Sultan Bāyezid II.* Edited by Brigitte Moser (Münich: Dr. Rudolf Trofenik, 1980).
Al-Biqa'i, Ibrahim bin Hasan. *Izhar al-'Asr li-Asrar Ahl al-Asr: Tarikh al-Biqa'i.* Edited by Muhammad Salim ibn Shadid 'Awfi. 3 vols. (Jizah, 1992).
———— *'Inwan al-Zaman bi-Tarajim al-Shuyukh wa al-Aqran.* Edited by Hasan Habashi. 5 vols. (Cairo, 2001).
Breydenbach, Bernhard von. *Bernhard von Breydenbach: Peregrinatio in Terram Sanctam.* Edited by Isolde Mozer (Berlin, 2010).
Brocquière, Bertrandon de la.
(1) *Le Voyage d'Outremer de Bertrandon de la Broquière.* Edited by Charles Schefer (1892. Reprint, Frankfurt am Main, 1994).
(2) *Bertrandon de la Broquière'in Denizaşırı Seyahati.* Translated by İlhan Arda. Edited by Charles Schefer (İstanbul: Eren, 2000).
Chalkokondyles, Laonikos. *A Translation and Commentary of the "Demonstrations of Histories."* Translated and edited by Nicolaos Nicoloudis (Athens, 1996).
Cyriac of Ancona. *Later Travels.* Edited and translated by Edward W. Bodnar and Clive Foss (Cambridge, MA: The I Tatti Renaissance Library, 2003).

Doukas. *Decline and Fall of Byzantium.* Translated by Henry J. Magoulias (Detroit, MI: Wayne State University Press, 1975).
Ernst, Hans, ed. *Die Mamlukischen Sultansurkunden des Sinai-Klosters* (Wiesbaden, 1960).
Esad Efendi. *Teşrifat-ı Kadime* (İstanbul, 1287/1870).
——— *Osmanlılarda Töre ve Törenler: Teşrifāt-ı Kadīme.* Edited by Yavuz Ercan (İstanbul, 1979).
Fabri, Felix. *Voyage en Egypte de Félix Fabri, 1483* (Cairo, 1975).
Feridun Bey, Ahmed. ed. *Münşeat al-Salatin*, 2 vols. (İstanbul, 1274–5/1857–9).
Frescobaldi, Leonardo, Giorgio Gucci, and Simone Sigole. *Visit to Holy Places of Egypt, Sinai, Palestine, and Syria in 1384* (Jerusalem, 1948).
Ghistele, Joos van. *Le Voyage en Egypte de Joos van Ghistele, 1482–83.* Edited by Renée Bauwens-Préaux (Cairo, 1976).
Hadidi. *Tevârih-i Âl-i Osman.* Edited by Necdet Öztürk (İstanbul: Edebiyat Fakültesi, 1991).
Harff, Arnold von. *The Pilgrimage of Arnold von Harff: Knight from Cologne, through Italy, Syria, Egypt, Arabia, Ethiopia, Nubia, Palestine, Turkey, France and Spain, which he accomplished in the years 1496 to1499.* Translated by Malcolm Letts (London: Hakluyt Society, 1946).
Hoca Saadeddin.
(1) *Tac al-Tevarih.* Vols. 2 (İstanbul, 1279–80/1863–4).
(2) *Tacü't-Tevarih.* Edited by İsmet Parmaksızoğlu (Ankara: Kültür Bakanlığı, 1979).
Al-Husayni, Husayn b. Muhammad. "Kitab Nafa'is al-Majalis al-Sultaniyya fī Haqa'iq al-Asrar al-Qur'aniyya." In *Majalis al-Sultan al-Ghawri.* Edited by Abd al-Wahhab Azzam (Cairo, 1941).
Ibn Aja.
(1) *Tarikh Al-Amir Yashbak Al-Zahir.* Edited by Abd al-qadir Ahmad Tulaymat (Cairo, 1974).
(2) Conermann, Stephan. "Ibn Ağās (st. 881/1476) 'Ta'rīḫ al-Amīr Yašbak aẓ-Ẓāhirī" – Biographie, Autobiographie, Tagebuch oder Chronik?" In *Die Mamlūken: Studien zu ihrer Geschichte und Kultur: Zum Gedenken an Ulrich Haarmann,* edited by Stephan Conermann and Anja Pistor-Hatam (Hamburg: EB-Verlag, 2003), pp. 123–78.
Ibn Bahadur. *Waqai'i Turkman.* TKSK, III.Ahmed 3057.
Ibn Battuta, Abu 'Abd Allah Muhammad. *The Travels of Ibn Battuta.* Edited by H.A. R. Gibb. 2 vols. (London, 1956–61)
Ibn al-Furat. *Tarikh al-Duwal wa-l-Muluk.* Edited by Costi K. Zurayk and Nejla Izzeddin. Vols. 8 and 9 (Beirut, 1936–42).
Ibn Hajar al-'Asqalani. *Inba' al-Ghumr bi-Abna al-'Umr.* Edited by Hasan Habashi. 4 vols. (Cairo, 1969–98).
Ibn Hijja. *Das Rauschgetränk der Stilkunst oder Qahwat al-Inšā'.* Edited by Rudolf Veselý (Beirut: Klaus Schwarz Verlag, 2005).
Ibn al-Himsi. *Hawadith al-Zaman wa Wafayat al-Shuyukh wa al-Aqran.* Edited by 'Umar 'Abd al-Salam Tadmuri. 3 vols. (Beirut, 1991).
Ibn Iyas. *Bada'i' al-Zuhur fī Waqa'i' al-Duhur.* Edited by Muhammad Mustafa. 5 vols. (Cairo, 1982).

İbn Kemal. *Tevârih-i Âl-i Osman: IV. Defter.* Edited by Koji Imazawa (Ankara: TTK, 2000).
———. *Tevârih-i Âl-i Osman: VII. Defter.* Edited by Şerafettin Turan (Ankara: TTK, 1991).
———. *Tevârîh-i Âl-i Osman: VIII. Defter.* Edited by Ahmed Uğur (Ankara: TTK, 1997).
Ibn Nazir al-Jaysh. *Kitāb Tatqīf Al-Ta'rīf Bi'l-Musṭalaḥ Al-Šarīf.* Edited by Rudolf Veselý. Textes Arabes et Études Islamiques 27 (Cairo: Institut Français d'Archéologie Orientale du Caire, 1987).
Ibn Qadi Shuhba, Abu Bakr b. Ahmad. *Tarih Ibn Qadi Shuhba.* Edited by Adnan Darwich, 3 vols. (Damas, 1977).
Ibn al-Sayrafi, *Nuzhat al-Nufus wa-al-abdan fi Tawarikh al-Zaman.* Edited by Hasan Habashi, 4 vols. (Cairo, 1970–94).
Ibn Shaddad, 'Izz al-din Muhammad b. 'Ali b. Ibrahim. *Tarikh al-Malik al-Zahir.* Edited by Ahmad Hutayt (Wiesbaden: Franz Steiner Verlag, 1983).
Ibn Shahin, 'Abd al-Basit ibn Khalil. *Nayl al-Amal fi Zayl al-Duwal.* Edited by Abd al-Salam Tadmuri. 9 vols. (Beirut, 2002).
Ibn Taghribirdi. *Extracts from Abû'l-Maḥâsin Ibn Taghrî Birdî's Chronicle entitled Ḥawâdith Ad-Duhûr fî Madâ'l-Ayyâm wash-Shuhûr.* Edited by William Popper. University of California Publications in Semitic Philology. 2 vols (8^1 and 8^2) (Los Angeles and Berkeley, CA: California University Press, 1942).
———. *Hawadith al-Duhur fi Mada al-Ayyam wa al-Sharq.* Edited by Muhammad Kamal al-din Izz al-din. 2 vols. (Beirut, 1990).
———. *History of Egypt (845–854 A.H., A.D. 1441–1450): An Extract from Ibn Taghribirdi's Chronicle, Entitled Ḥawādith ad-Duhūr.* Translated by William Popper and prepared by Walther J. Fischel (Berkeley, CA: California University Press, 1967).
———. *History of Egypt, 1382–1469 A.D.* Translated by William Popper (Berkeley, CA: California University Press, 1954).
———. *Al-Manhal Al-Safi.* Edited by Ahmad Yusuf al-Najati (Cairo, 1956).
Ibn Tulun. *Mufakahat-ul-Hillan fi Hawadith-iz-zaman.* Edited by Muhammad Mustafa. 2 vols. (Cairo, 1962).
Ibn al-Zubayr, Ahmad ibn al-Rashid. *Books of gifts and rarities: Kitāb al-Hadāyā wa al-Tuḥaf.* Translated and edited by Ghada al-Hijjawi al-Qaddumi (Cambridge, MA: Distributed for the Center for Middle Eastern Studies of Harvard University, 1996).
İdris-i Bitlisi. *Tercüme-i Heşt Behişt li-Sadi.* TKSK, Bağdad 196.
İpşirli, Mehmed. "Osmanlı Devlet Teşkilatına Dair Bir Eser: Kavanin-i Osmani ve Rabita-I Asitane." *Tarih Enstitüsü Dergisi* 14 (1994):9–35.
Al-Khalidi, Muhammad b. Hashim. *Kitab al Tuhaf wa-al-hadaya.* Edited by Sami Dahhan (Cairo, 1956).
Karateke, Hakan, ed. *An Ottoman Protocol Register* (Istanbul: Royal Asiatic Society Books, 2007).
Kritovoulos. *History of Mehmed the Conqueror.* Translated by Charles T. Riggs (Princeton, NJ: Princeton University Press, 1954).
Lugal, Necati and Adnan Erzi. "Fâtih Sultan Mehmed'in Muhtelif Seferlerine Ait Fetih-nâmeleri." *İstanbul Enstitüsü Dergisi* 2 (1956):169–82.

Lütfi Paşa. *Lütfi Paşa ve Tevârih-i Âl-i Osman.* Edited by Kayhan Atik (Ankara: Kültür Bakanlığı, 2001).
——— "Lütfi Paşa Âsafnâmesi." In *Bekir Kütükoğlu'na Armağan*, edited by Mübahat Kütükoğlu (İstanbul: Edebiyat Fakültesi, 1991), 49–99.
Al-Maqrizi, Taqi al-din 'Ali Ibn Ahmad. *Durar al-'Uqud al-Farida fi Taragim al-Ayan al-Mufida.* Edited by Mahmoud al-Jalili. 4 vols. (Beyrout, 2002).
——— *Kitab al-Suluk li-Ma'rifa al-Duwal al-Muluk.* Edited by Sa'id 'Abd al-Fattah 'Ashur. 4 vols. (Cairo, 1970).
Mihailovich, Konstantin. *Memoirs of Janissary.* Translated by Benjamin Stolz. Michigan Slavic Translations (Ann Arbor, MI: Michigan University Press, 1975).
Müneccimbaşı. *Jami' al-Duwal.* Vol.3. Süleymaniye Esad Efendi 2103.
——— *Saha'if al-Ahbar fi Veka'i' al-Asar. 3 vols. (İstanbul, 1285/1868–9).*
Nasuh, Matrakçı. *Tarih-i Sultan Bayezid.* Edited by Reha Bilge and Mertol Tulum (İstanbul, 2012).
Neşri, Mehmed.
(1) *Kitâb-ı Cihan-nümâ: Neşrī Tarihi.* Edited by Faik Reşit Unat and Mehmed A. Köymen (Ankara: TTK, 1949).
(2) *Ğihānnümâ: Die altosmanische Chronik des Mevlānā Meḥemmed Neşrī.* Edited by Theodor Menzel and Franz Taeschner (Leipzig: Otto Harrosowitz, 1951).
(3) *Cihânnümâ.* Edited by Necdet Öztürk (İstanbul: Çamlıca, 2008).
Nizam al-Mulk. *The Book of Government or Rules for Kings: The Siyar al-Muluk or Siyat-nama of Nizam al-Mulk.* Translated by Hurbert Darke. 3rd ed. (London: Curzon, 2002).
Palaeologus, Manuel. *The Letters of Manuel II Palaeologus.* Translated and edited by George T. Dennis (Washington, D.C., WA: Dumbarton Oaks, 1977).
Piloti, Emmanuel. *Traité d'Emmanuel Piloti sur la Passage en Terre Sainte.* Edited by Hermann Dopp. (Louvain, 1958).
Al-Qalqashandi, Ahmad b. 'Ali. *Subh al-A'sha fi Sina'at al-Insha'.* Edited by Muhammad Husayn Shams al-din. 14 vols. (Beyrout, 1987).
Al-Sabi', Hilal.
(1) *Rusum Dar al-Khilafah: The Rules and Regulations of the 'Abbasid Court.* Translated by Elie A. Salem (Beirut: American University of Beirut, 1977).
(2) *Rusum Dar al-Khilafah: The Etiquette, Protocol and Diplomacy of the 'Abbasid Caliphate in Baghdad.* Edited by Mikhail 'Awad (Baghdad, 1964).
Al-Sahmawi. *Al-Thaghr al-Basim fi Sina'at al-Katib wa al-Katim.* Edited by Ashraf Muhammad Anas and Husayn Nassar (Cairo, 2009).
Schiltberger, Johannes.
(1) *The Bondage and Travels of Johann Schiltberger, a Native of Bavaria, in Europe, Asia, and Africa, 1396–1427.* Translated by J. Buchan Telfer (1879. Reprint, Elibron Classics, 2005).
(2) *Als Sklave im Osmanischen Reich und bei den Tataren, 1394–1427.* Edited by Ulrich Schlemmer (Stuttgart: Thienemann, Edition Erdmann, 1983).
Schwarz, Klaus. *Osmanische Sultansurkunden des Sinai-Klosters in türkischer Sprache* (Freiburg: Klaus Schwarz Verlag, 1970).
Spandounes, Theodore. *On the Origins of the Ottoman Emperors.* Translated and edited by Donald M. Nichol (Cambridge: Cambridge University Press, 1997).

Şerifi. *Şerîfî Şehnâme Çevirisi.* Edited by Zuhal Kültüral and Latif Beyreli. 4 vols. (Ankara: TDK, 1999).
Şükrullah. *Behcetü't-Tevârîh.* Edited by Nihal Atsız (İstanbul, 1947).
Taşköprülüzade. *Eş-Şekā'iķu n-Nu'mānīye fī 'Ulemā'i d-Devleti l-'Osmānīye.* Edited by Ahmed Subhi Furat (İstanbul: Edebiyat Fakültesi Basımevi, 1985).
Tekin, Şinasi. "Fatih Sultan Mehmed Devrine Âit Bir İnşâ Mecmuası." *Journal of Turkish Studies* 20 (1996):267–311.
───── "İkinci Bayezid Devrine Ait Bir Mecmua." *Journal of Turkish Studies* 3 (1979):343–83.
───── *Menāhicü'l İnşâ: Yahyā bin Meḥmed al-Kātib'in 15. Yy.dan Kalma En Eski Osmanlıca İnşâ Kitabı.* Cambridge, 1971.
Tevkii Abdurrahman Paşa, "Osmanlı Kanunnameleri." *Milli Tetebbular Mecmuası* 3 (1331/1912):497–544.
Thenaud, Jean. *Le Voyage d'Outremer.* Edited by Charles Schefer (1884. Reprint, Frankfurt am Main, 1995).
Trevisan, Domenico. *La Relation de l'Ambassade de Domenico Trevisan aupres du Soudan l'Egypte.* Edited by Charles Schefer (1884. Reprint, Frankfurt am Main, 1995).
Tursun Beg.
  (1) *Târîh Ebü'l-Feth.* Edited by Mertol Tulum (İstanbul: İstanbul Fetih Cemiyeti, 1977).
  (2) *The History of Mehmed the Conqueror.* Edited by Halil İnalcık and Rhoads Murphey (Minneapolis, MN: Bibliotheca Islamica, 1978).
Al-'Umari, Ahmad b. Fadl Allah. *Al-'Umarī's Bericht über Anatolien in seinem Werke: Masālik al-Abṣār fi Mamālik al-Amṣār: al-'Umari's Bericht über Anatolien.* Edited by Franz Taeschner (Leipzig, 1929).
───── *A Critical Edition of and Study on Ibn Faḍl Allāh's Manual of Secretaryship "Al-Ta'rīf Bi'l-Musṭalaḥ Al-Sharīf."* Edited by Samir Al-Droubi. 2 vols. (Al-Karak, 1413/1992).
Uruç ibn Adil,
  (1) *Tevarih-i Al-i 'Osman.* Manisa İl Halk Library Muradiye 5506/2.
  (2) *Die Frühosmanischen Jahrbücher des Urudsch: Nach den Handschriften zu Oxford und Cambridge erstmals herausgegeben und eingeleitet.* Edited by Franz Babinger (Hannover: Orient-Buchhandlung Heinz Lafaire, 1925).
  (3) *Oruç Beğ Tarihi.* Edited by Necdet Öztürk (İstanbul: Çamlıca, 2007).
Yazıcıoğlu Mehmed. *Muhammediye.* Edited by Âmil Çelebioğlu. 2 vols. (İstanbul: Milli Eğitim Bakanlığı, 1996).
Zeno, Caterino. *A Narrative of Italian Travels in Persia in the Fifteenth and Sixteenth Centuries.* Edited by Charles Grey (London: Hakluyt Society, 1873).

Modern studies

Açıkgöz, Mustafa. "II.Bayezid Devri İnamat Defteri." Master's Thesis, Marmara Üniversitesi Sosyal Bilimler Enstitüsü, 1996.
Adahl, Karin ed. *The Sultan's Procession: The Swedish Embassy to Sultan Mehmed IV in 1657–1658 and the Ralamn Paintings* (Istanbul: Swedish Research Institute, 2006).

Selected Bibliography

Afshar, Iraj. "Manuscript and Paper Sizes Cited in Persian and Arabic Texts." In *Essays in Honour of Salah al-din al-Munajjid* (London, 2002), 659–73.
Akgündüz, Ahmed. *Osmanlı Kanunnâmeleri ve Hukuki Tahlilleri.* Vol.1 (İstanbul, 1990).
Al-Alevi, Abdülaziz. "Ibn Fazlullah el-Ömeri." *DİA* 19:483–4.
Algazi, Gadi, Valentin Groebner, and Bernhard Jussen, eds. *Negotiating the Gift: Premodern Figurations of Exchange* (Göttinger: Vandenhoeck & Ruprecht, 2003).
Allouche, Adel. *The Origins and Development of the Ottoman-Safavid Conflict* (Berlin: Klaus Schwarz Verlag, 1983).
——— "Tegüder's Ultimatum to Qalawun." *IJMES* 22 (1990):437–46.
Allsen, Thomas T. "Robing in the Mongolian Empire." In *Robes and Honor*, 305–15.
——— *The Royal Hunt in Eurasian History* (Philadelphia, PA: University of Pennsylvania Press, 2006).
Alptekin, Coşkun. "Artuklular." *DİA* 3:415–18.
Amitai-Preiss, Reuven. "Mamluk Perceptions of the Mongol-Frankish Rapprochment." *Mediterranean Historical Review* 7 (1992):50–65.
——— "Northern Syria between the Mongols and Mamluks: Political Boundary, Military Frontier, and Ethnic Affinities." In *Frontiers in Question: Eurasian Borderlands, 700–1700*, edited by Daniel Power and Naomi Standen (New York, NY: St.Martin's Press, 1999), pp. 128–52.
——— *Mongols and Mamluks: The Mamluk-Īlkhānid War* (Cambridge: Cambridge University Press, 1995).
Andrews, Peter Alford. *Felt Tents and Pavilions: The Nomadic Tradition and its Interaction with Princely Tentage* (London: Melisende, 1991).
——— "Miẓalla." *EI*[2] 7:191–5.
Anooshahr, Ali. *The Ghazi Sultans and the Frontiers of Islam* (London: Routledge, 2009).
Apellániz Ruiz de Galarreta, Francisco Javier. *Pouvoir et Finance en Méditerranée prémoderne: le deuxième État mamelouk et le commerce des épices (1382–1517)* (Barcelona: CSIC, 2009).
Appadurai, Arjun. Introduction to *The Social Life of Things*. Edited by Arjun Appadurai (Cambridge: Cambridge University Press, 1986).
Arbel, Benjamin. "Venetian Trade Letters in Fifteeenth-Century Acre." *Asian and African Studies* 22 (1988):277–88.
Ashtor, E. *The Levant Trade in the Later Middle Ages* (Princeton, NJ: Princeton University Press, 1983).
Atasoy, Nurhan. "Processions and Protocol in Ottoman Istanbul." In *The Sultan's Procession: The Swedish Embassy to Sultan Mehmed IV in 1657–1658 and the Ralamn Paintings*, edited by Karen Adahl (Istanbul: Swedish Research Institute, 2006), pp. 168–95.
Ateş, Ahmet. "İstanbul'un Fethine Dair Fatih Sultan Mehmed Tarafından Gönderilen Mektublar ve Bunlara Gelen Cevablar." *Tarih Dergisi* 7 (1952):11–51.
——— "Mollā Gürānī (1416–1488)." *İA* 8:406–8.
Atıl, Esin. ed. *Levni and Surname: The Story of an Eighteenth-century Ottoman Festival* (İstanbul: Koçbank, 1999).
Atiya, Aziz Suryal. *The Crusade of Nicopolis* (London, 1934).
——— *Egypt and Aragon: Embassies and Diplomatic Correspondence between 1300 and 1330 A.D.* (Leipzig, 1938).

——— "Nīkbūlī." *EI*² 8:35–6.
Ayalon, A. "Malik." *EI*² 6:261–2.
——— "Dawādār." *EI*² 2:172.
Aynur, Hatice. "Yazidji Ṣāliḥ b. Suleymān." *EI*² 12:834–35.
Ayverdi, E.H. *İstanbul Mi'mârî Çağının Menşe'i: Osmanlı Mi'mârîsinin İlk Devri.* (İstanbul, 1966).
Babinger, Franz. "Fatih Sultan Mehmed ve İtalya." *Belleten* 17 (1953):41–82.
——— *Mehmed the Conqueror and His Time.* Translated by Ralph Manheim (Princeton, NJ: Princeton University Press, 1992).
——— *Reliquienschacher am Osmanenhof im XV.Jahrhundert* (München, 1956).
Bacharach, Jere L. "Circassian Monetary Policy: Copper." *JESHO* 19 (1976):32–47.
——— "Circassian Monetary Policy: Silver." *The Numismatic Chronicle* 7th Series, XI (1971):267–81.
Bacqué-Grammont, Jean-Louis, and Anne Krœll. *Mamlouks, Ottomans et Portugais en Mer Rouge: L'Affaire de Djedda en 1517.* Supplément aux Annales Islamologiques 12 (Cairo: Institut Français d'Archéologie Orientale, 1988).
Balog, Paul. "Pious Invocations Probably Used as Titles of Office or as Honorific Titles in Umayyad and 'Abbāsid Times." In *Studies in Memory of Gastow Wiet*, edited by Myriam Rosen-Ayalon (Jerusalem: The Hebrew University of Jerusalem, 1977), pp. 61–8.
Barkan, Ömer Lutfi. "Osmanlı Saraylarına Ait Muhasebe Defterleri." *Belgeler* 9 (1979):296–380.
Barthold, W. and C.E. Bosworth, "Shīrwān Shāh." *EI*² 9:488–9.
Al-Basha, Hasan. *Al-Alqab al-Islamiyya* (Iskandariyya, 1978).
Bauden, Frédérick. "Les Relations Diplomatiques entre les Sultans Mamlouks Circassiens et les autres Pouvoirs du Dār al-Islām" *Annales Islamologiques* 41 (2007):1–31.
Beard, Mary. *The Roman Triumph* (Cambridge, MA: Belknap, 2007).
Becheneb, M. "Ibn al-Djazarī." *EI*² 3:753.
Bedini, Silvio A. *The Pope's Elephant* (Manchester: Carcanet Press, 1997).
Behrens-Abouseif, Doris. *Cairo of the Mamluks: A History of Architecture and its Culture* (London: I.B.Tauris, 2007).
——— "The Citadel of Cairo: Stage for Mamluk Ceremonial." *Annales Islamologiques* 24 (1988):25–79.
——— "The façade of the Aqmar Mosque in the context of Fatimid Ceremonial." *Muqarnas* 9 (1992):29–38.
——— *Fatḥ Allāh and Abū Zakariyya: Physicians under the Mamluks.* Supplément aux Annales Islamologiques 10 (Cairo: Institut Français d'Archéologie Orientale, 1987).
Beldiceanu-Steinherr, Irène. *Recherches sur les Actes des Règnes des Sultans Osman, Orkhan et Murad I* (Monaco, 1967).
Berker, Aziz. "Teşrifati Naim Efendi Tarihi." *Tarih Vesikaları* 3 (1949):69–80, 150–60, 230–40.
Berkey, Jonathan P. *The Transmission of Knowledge in Medieval Cairo.* (Princeton: Princeton University Press, 1992).
Björkman, Walther. *Beiträge zur Geschichte der Staatskanzlei im Islamischen Ägypten* (Hamburg, 1928).

––––––– "Die Anfänge der türkischen Briefsammlungen." *Orientalia Suecana* 5 (1956):20–9.
––––––– "Eine türkische Briefsammlung aus dem 15. Jahrhundert." In *Documenta Islamica Inedita* (Berlin, 1952), pp. 189–96.
––––––– "Die Frühesten Turkish-Ägyptischen Beziehungen im 14. Jahrhundert." In *Mélanges Fuad Köprülü* (İstanbul: Dil ve Tarih-Coğrafya Fakültesi, 1953), pp. 57–63.
Björkman, W., G.S. Colin, H. Busse, J.Reychmann. "Diplomatic." *EI*² 1:301–16.
Blair, Sheila. "On Giving to Shrines: 'Generosity is a Quality of the People of Paradise'." In *Gifts of the Sultan*, pp. 51–75.
Blochet, E. "Les Relations Diplomatiques des Hohenstaufen avec les Sultans d'Égypte." *Revue Historique* 80 (1902):51–64.
Bloom, Jonathan. *Paper Before Print: The History and Impact of Paper in the Islamic World* (New Haven, CI: Yale University Press, 2001).
Bodrogligeti, A. "Notes on the Turkish Literature at the Mameluke Court." *Acta Orientalia Academiae Scientiarum Hungaricae* 14 (1962):273–82.
Borsook, Eve. "The Travels of Bernardo Michelozzi and Bonsignore Bonsignori in the Levant (1497–98)." *Journal of the Warburg and Courtauld Institutes* 36 (1973):145–97.
Bostan, Idris. *Beylikten İmparatorluğa Osmanlı Denizciliği* (İstanbul: Kitab Yayınevi, 2006).
––––––– "Kemal Reis." *DİA* 25:226–7.
––––––– "Selman Reis." *DİA* 36:444–6.
Bosworth, C.E. "Ibn Nāẓir al-Djaysh." *EI*² 12 (Suppl.):395.
––––––– "In'ām." *EI*² 3:1200–2.
––––––– "Al-Ḳalḳashandī." *EI*² 4:509.
––––––– "Laḳab."*EI*² 5:618–31.
Boyacıoğlu, Ramazan. "Osmanoğullarının Karamanoğlu Ibrahim Bey Aleyhine Aldığı Fetvalar." In *Pax Ottomana: Studies in Memoriam Prof. Dr. Nejat Göyünç*, edited by Kemal Çiçek (Haarlem: Sota, 2001), pp. 641–59.
Boyar, Ebru, and Kate Fleet. *A Social History of Ottoman Istanbul* (Cambridge: Cambridge University Press, 2010).
Bozkurt, Nebi, and Kemal Beydilli. "Sefaretname." *DİA* 36:288–94.
Broadbridge, Anne F. "Diplomatic Conventions in the Mamluk Sultanate." *Annales Islamologiques* 41 (2007):97–119.
––––––– *Kingship and Ideology in the Islamic and Mongol Worlds* (Cambridge: Cambridge University Press, 2008).
Brummett, Palmira. "Kemal Re'is and Ottoman Gunpowder Diplomacy." *Studies on Ottoman Diplomatic History* 5 (1990):1–17.
––––––– *Ottoman Seapower and Levantine Diplomacy in the Age of Discovery* (Albany, NY: SUNY, 1994).
––––––– "The Overrated Adversary: Rhodes and Ottoman Naval Power." *The Historical Journal* 36 (1993):517–41.
Buzpınar, Ş. Tufan, and Mustafa S. Küçükaşcı. "Haremeyn." *DİA* 16:153–7.
Bryer, Anthony. "Lodovico da Bologna and the Georgian and Anatolian Embassy of 1460–61." *Bedi Kartlisa, Revue de Kartvélologie* 19–20 (1965):179–98.
Cahen, Claude. "Artuqids" *EI*² 1:662–7.

——— "Ayyūbids," *EI*² 1:797–808.
——— *The Formation of Turkey: The Seljukid Sultanate of Rūm: Eleventh to Fourteenth Century.* Translated by P.M.Holt (New York: Longman, 2001).
Canard, Marius. "Le Cérémonial Fatimite et le Cérémonial Byzantin: Essai de Comparaison." *Byzantion* 21 (1951):355–420.
Casale, Giancarlo. *The Ottoman Age of Exploration* (Oxford: Oxford University Press, 2010).
Chamberlain, Michael. "The Crusader Era and the Ayyūbid Dynasty." In *CHE*, pp. 211–42.
Cheikho, Louis. "Un Dernier Echo des Croisades." *Mélange de la Faculté Orientale* 1 (1909):303–75.
Christ, Georg. *Trading Conflicst: Venetian Merchants and Mamluk Officials in Late Medieval Alexandria* (Leiden: E.J. Brill, 2012).
Conermann, Stephan. "Ibn Ağās (st.881/1476) 'Ta'rīḫ Al-Amīr Yašbak aẓ-Ẓāhirī' – Biographie, Autobiographie, Tagebuch oder Chronik?" In *Die Mamlūken: Studien zu ihrer Geschicte und Kultur: Zum Gedenken an Ulrich Haarmann (1942–1999),* edited by Stephan Conermann and Anja Pistor-Hatam (Hamburg, 2004), pp. 123–179.
Constable, Olivia Remie. *Housing the Stranger in the Mediterranean World* (Cambridge: Cambridge University Press, 2003).
Coulon, Damien. *Barcelone et le grand commerce d'orient au moyen âge: un siècle de relations avec l'Egypte et la Syrie-Palestine, ca. 1330-ca. 1430* (Madrid, 2004).
Curatola, Giovanni. "Venetian Merchants and Travellers in Alexandria." In *Alexandria, Real and Imagined,* edited by Anthony Hirst and Michael Silk (Aldershot, Hampshire: Ashgate, 2004), p. 185–98.
Curry, John J. *The Transformation of Muslim Mystical Thought in the Ottoman Empire* (Edinburgh: Edinburg University Press, 2010).
Cutler, Anthony. "The Emperor's Old Clothes: Actual and virtual vesting and the transmission of power in Byzantium and Islam." In *Byzance et le Monde Extérieur,* edited by M. Balard and J.-M. Spieser (Paris: Publications de la Sorbonne, 2005), pp. 195–211.
——— "The Enduring Present: Gifts in Medieval Islam and Byzantium." In *Gifts of the Sultan,* pp. 79–92.
——— "Gifts and Gift Exchange as Aspects of the Byzantine, Arab, and Related Economies." *Dumbarton Oaks Papers* 55 (2001):247–78.
——— "Significant Gifts: Patterns of Exchange in Late Antique, Byzantine, and early Islamic Diplomacy." *Journal of Medieval and Early Modern Studies* 38 (2008):81–102.
Çelebioğlu, Âmil. "Ahmed Bican." *DİA* 2:49–51.
———"Yazıcı Salih ve Şemsiyyesi." *Atatürk Üniversitesi İslami İlimler Fakültesi Dergisi* 1 (1976):171–218.
Çelebioğlu, Âmil, and Kemal Eraslan. "Yazıcı-oğlu." *İA* 13:365–8.
Darling, Linda. "Circle of Justice." *MSR* 10 (2006):1–17.
——— "Contested Territory: Ottoman Holy War in Comparative Context." *SI* 91 (2000):133–63.
Darrag, Ahmad. *L'Égypte sous le Règne de Barsbay* (Damas: Institut Français de Damas, 1961).

―――― "Risalatan bayn Sultan Malwa wa al-Ashraf Qaytbay." *Majalla Ma'had al-Mahtutat al-'Arabiyya* 4 (1958):97–123.
Davis, Natalie Zemon. *The Gift in Sixteenth-Century France* (Madison, WI: University of Wisconsin Press, 2000).
Dekkiche, Malika. "Le Caire: Carrefour des Ambassades." PhD diss., Université de Liège, 2011.
D'Hulster, Kristof. "Fixed Rules to Changing Games?" Paper presented at the *Mamluk Cairo: A Crossroad for Embassies*, University of Liège, September 6–8, 2012.
Diem, Werner. *Ehrendes Kleid und Ehrendes Wort: Studien zu Tašrīf in Mamlūkischer and Vormamlūkischer Zeit* (Würzburg: Ergon Verlag, 2002).
Dilcimen, Kazim. *Canik Beyleri* (Samsun, 1940).
Dilger, K. *Untersuchungen zur Geschicte des Osmanischen Hofzeremoniells in 15. und 16. Jahrhundert* (München: Dr. Rudolf Trofenik, 1967).
Duri, A.A., H.L. Gottschalk, G.S. Colin, A.K.S. Lampton, and A.S. Bazmee Ansari, "Dīwān." *EI* ^{2} 2:323–37.
Edbury, Peter W. *The Kingdom of Cyprus and the Crusades, 1191–1374* (Cambridge: Cambridge University Press, 1991).
Eldem, Halil Ethem. "Hersekoğlu Ahmed Paşa'nin Esaretine da'ir Kahire'de bir Kitabe." *TOEM* 28 and 29 (1330/1911):200–22 and 272–294.
―――― *Meskukat-ı 'Osmaniyye*. Müze-yi Hümayun Meskukat-i Kadime-i İslamiyye Kataloğu 6 (Konstantiniyya: Mahmut Bey Matbaası, 1334/1915).
―――― "Mısır Fethi Mukaddematına Aid Mühim Bir Vesika." *TTEM* 96 (1328/1909):30–6.
Elias, Jamal J. "The Sufi Robe (Khirqa) as a Vehicle of Spiritual Authority." In *Robes and Honor*, pp. 275–89.
Emecen, Feridun M. *Yavuz Sultan Selim* (Istanbul, 2010).
Erkan, Mustafa. "Darīr." *DİA* 8:498–9.
Ersan, Mehmet. "Türkiye Selçuklularında Hediye ve Hediyeleşme." *Tarih İncelemeleri Dergisi* 14 (1999):65–79.
―――― "Türkiye Selçuklularında Hediye ve Hediyeleşme II." *Tarih İncelemeleri Dergisi* 15 (2000):95–104.
Erünsal, İsmail. "II.Bayezid Devrine Ait Bir İnamat Defteri." *Tarih Enstitüsü Dergisi* 10–11 (1979–80):303–41.
Erzi, Adnan. "Sarı Abdullah Efendi Münşeâtının Tavsîfi." *Belleten* 14 (1950):631–47.
―――― "Türkiye Kütüphanelerinden Notlar ve Vesikalar II." *Belleten* 14 (1950):595–647.
Eyice, Semavi. "Elçi Hanı." *DİA* 11:15–18.
Fabris, Antonio. "From Adrianople to Constantinople: Venetian–Ottoman Diplomatic Missions, 1360–1453." *Mediterranean Historical Review* 7 (1992):154–200.
Farooqi, Naimur Rahman. *Mughal-Ottoman Relations: A Study of Political and Diplomatic Relations between Mughal India and Ottoman Empire, 1555–1748*. IAD Oriental (Original) Series 32 (Delhi, 1989).
Faroqhi, Suraiya. *Pilgrims and Sultans: The Hajj under the Ottomans* (London: I.B. Tauris, 1994).
Fekete, L. "Das Fethnāme über die Schlacht bei Varna." *Byzantinoslavica* 15 (1953):258–70.

Fernandes, Leonor. *The Evolution of a Sufi Institution in Mamluk Egypt: The Khanqah* (Berlin, 1988).

Fierro, Maribel. "The Almohads (524–668/1130–1269) and the Ḥafṣids (627–932/1229–1526)." In *The New Cambridge History of Islam*, edited by Maribel Fierro (Cambridge: Cambridge University Press, 2010), 2:66–106.

Fisher, Sydney Nettleton. *The Foreign Relations of Turkey 1481–1512*. Illinois Studies in the Social Sciences 30 (Urbana: University of Illinois Press, 1948).

Fleet, Kate. *European and Islamic Trade in the early Ottoman State: The Merchants of Genoa and Turkey* (Cambridge: Cambridge University Press, 1999).

———. "The Turkish Economy, 1071–1453." In *Cambridge History of Turkey*, edited by Kate Fleet (Cambridge: Cambridge University Press, 2009), 1:227–66.

Flemming, Barbara. *Landschaftsgeschichte vom Pampylien, Pisidien, und Lykien im Spätmittelalter*. Abhandlungen für die Kunde des Morgenlandes, 35 (Wiesbaden: Deutsche Morgenländische Gesellschaft, 1964).

———. "Literary Activities in Mamluk Halls and Barracks." In *Studies in Gaston Wiet*, edited by Myriam Rosen-Ayalon (Jerusalem, 1977), pp. 249–60.

———. "The Reign of Murad II: A Survey (I)." *Anatolica* 20 (1994):249–67.

———. "Šerīf, Sultan Ġavrī, und die 'Perser'." *Islam* 45 (1969):81–93.

Flood, Finbarr. *Objects of Translation: Material Culture and Medieval "Hindu-Muslim" Encounter* (Princeton, NJ: Princeton University Press, 2009).

Fodor, Pal. "Aḥmedī's Dāsitān as a Source of Early Ottoman History." *Acta Orientalia Academiae Scientiarum Hungaria* 38 (1984):41–54.

Frey, Linda S., and Marsha L. Frey. *History of Diplomatic Immunity* (Columbus, OH: Ohio State University Press, 1999).

Fuess, Albrecht. "Between *dihlīz* and *dār al-'adl*: Forms of Outdoor and Indoor Royal Representation at the Mamluk Court in Egypt." In *Court Cultures in Muslim World: Seventh to Nineteenth Centuries*, edited by Albrecht Fuess and Jan-Peter Hartung (London: Routledge, 2011), pp. 149–68.

———. "Mamluk Politics." In *Ubi sumus? Quo vademus? Mamluk Studies – State of the Art*, edited by Stephan Conermann (Bonn: Bonn University Press, 2013), pp. 95–119.

———. "Ottoman Ghazwah and Mamluk "Ottoman Ghazwah and Mamluk Jihād: Two Arms on the Same Body?" In *Everything is on the Move: The "Mamluk Empire" as a Node in (Trans-) Regional Networks*, edited by Stefan Conermann (forthcoming).

———. "Rotting Ships and Razed Harbors: The Naval Policy of the Mamluks." *MSR* 5 (2001):49–60.

———. "Sultans with Horns: About the Political Significance of Headgear in the Mamluk Empire." *MSR* 12 (2008):71–94.

———. *Verbranntes Ufer: Auswirkungen mamlukischer Seepolitik auf Beirut und die syropalästinensiche Küste (1250–1517)* (Leiden: E.J. Brill, 2001).

———. "Ẓulm by Maẓālim? The Political Implications of the Use of Maẓālim Jurisdiction by the Mamluk Sultan." *MSR* 13 (2009):121–47.

Galib, İsmail. *Takvim-i Meskukat-ı 'Osmaniyye* (Konstantiniyye, 1307/1390).

Garcin, Jean-Claude. "The Regime of the Circassian Mamlūks." In *CHE*, pp. 290–318.

Gaudelier, Maurice. *The Enigma of Gift*. Translated by Nora Scott (Chicago: Chicago University Press, 1999).

Gordon, Stewart, ed. *Robes and Honor: The Medieval World of Investiture* (New York, NY: Palgrave, 2001).
Groebner, Valentin. *Liquid Assets, Dangerous Gifts: Presents and Politics at the end of the Middle Ages.* Translated by Pamela E. Selwyn (Philadelphia, MN: University of Philadelphia Press, 2002).
Güler, Mustafa. *Osmanlı Devleti'nde Harameyn Vakıfları (XVI.-XVII. Yüzyıllar)* (İstanbul, 2002).
Gully, Adrian. *The Culture of Letter-Writing in Pre-Modern Islamic Society* (Edinburg: Edinburgh University Press, 2008).
Guo, Li. "Gift-giving." *Encyclopaedia of the Qur'an* (Leiden: E.J. Brill, 2002), 2:313–4.
Haarmann, Ulrich. "Der Arabische Osten im späten Mittelalter 1250–1517." In *Geschicte der Arabischen Welt*, edited by Ulrich Haarmann (München, 1992), pp. 217–63.
―――― "Ideology and History, Identity and Alterity: The Arab Image of the Turks from the Abbasids to Modern Egypt." *IJMES* 20 (1988):175–96.
―――― "The Mamlūk System of Rule in the Eyes of Western Travelers." *MSR* 5 (2001):1–24.
―――― "Regicide and the 'Law of the Turks'." In *Intellectual Studies on Islam: Essays in honor of Martin B. Dickson* (Salt Lake City, UT, 1990), pp. 127–35.
Habib, Mohammad, and Khaliq Ahmad Nizami. *A Comprehensive History of India.* Vol. 5 (New Delhi, 1970).
Hagen, Gottfried. "Some Considerations about the Terğüme-i Ḍarir ve Taqdimetü ẓ-Ẓahīr Based on Manuscripts in German Libraries." *Journal of Turkish Studies* 26 (2002):323–37.
Halil Ethem. See Eldem.
Hallenberg, Helena. "The Sultan Who Loved Sufis." *MSR* 4 (2000):147–66.
Hammer-Purgstall, Joseph von. *Geschichte des Osmanischen Reiches.* (Pest, 1833).
Hanne, Eric. *Putting the Caliph in His Place: Power, Authority, and the Late Abbasid Caliphate* (Madison, NJ: Farleigh Disckinson University Press, 2007).
Harb, Muhammad. "I.Selim'in Suriye ve Mısır Seferi Hakkında İbn İyās'da Mevcut Haberlerin Selimnamelerle Mukayesesi: XVI. Asır Osmanlı-Memluklu Kaynakları Hakkında Bir Tetkik." PhD diss., İstanbul Üniversitesi, 1980.
Har-El, Shai. *Struggle for Domination in the Middle East: The Ottoman-Mamluk War 1485–1491* (Leiden: E.J. Brill, 1995).
Harvey, L.P. *Muslims in Spain, 1500 to 1614* (Chicago, II: Chicago University Press, 2005).
Hattox, Ralph S. "Qaytbay's Diplomatic Dilemma Concerning the Flight of Cem Sultan (1481–1482)." *MSR* 6 (2002):177–90.
Hein, Horst-Adolf. *Beiträge zur ayyubidschen Diplomatik* (Freiburg, 1968).
Herrmann, Gottfried. "Zur Intitulatio Timuridscher Urkunden." *Zeitschrift der Deutschen Morgenländischen Gesellschaft, Supplement II* (1972):498–521.
Hess, Andrew C. "The Evolution of the Ottoman Seaborne Empire in the Age of the Oceanic Discoveries." *American Historical Review* 75 (1970):1892–919.
―――― *The Forgotten Frontier: A History of the Sixteenth Century Ibero-African Frontier* (Chicago, II: University of Chicago Press, 1978).
―――― "The Moriscos: An Ottoman Fifth Column in Sixteenth-Century Spain." *The American Historical Review* 74 (1968):1–25.

———— "The Ottoman Conquest of Egypt (1517) and the Beginning of the Sixteenth Century-World War." *IJMES* 4 (1973):55–76.
Hillenbrand, C. *The Crusades: Islamic Perspectives* (New York, NY: Routledge, 1999).
Holt, P.M. *The Age of the Crusades: The Near East from the Eleventh Century to 1517* (Essex: Longman, 1986).
———— *Early Mamluk Diplomacy (1260–1290):Treaties of Baybars and Qalāwūn with Christian Rulers* (Leiden: E.J. Brill, 1995).
———— "The Īlkhān Aḥmad's Embassies to Qalāwūn: Two Contemporary Accounts." *BSOAS* 49 (1986):128–32.
———— "Khushḳadam." EI^2 5:73.
———— "Al-Mu'ayyad Shaykh." EI^2 7:271–2.
———— "The Position and Power of the Mamluk Sultan." *BSOAS* 38 (1975):237–49.
———— "Some Observations on the 'Abbāsid Caliphate of Cairo." *BSOAS* 47 (1984):501–7.
———— "The Structure of Government in the Mamluk Sultanate." In *The Eastern Mediterranean Lands in the Period of the Crusades,* edited by (Holt, Warminster, 1977), pp. 44–61.
———— "Succession in the Early Mamluk Sultanate." *Deutschen Orientalistentag* 16 (1985):144–8.
Holter, Kurt. "Studien zu Aḥmed Ferîdûn's Münše'at es-selâṭîn." *Mitteilungen des Österreichischen Instituts für Geschichtsforshung* 14 (1939):429–51.
Howard, Deborah. "Venice and the Mamluks." In *Venice and the Islamic World,* edited by Stefano Carboni (New York, NY: Metropolitan Museum of Art, 2007), pp. 72–90.
Humphreys, Steven. "Ayyubids, Mamluks, and the Latin East in the Thirteenth Century." *MSR* 2 (1998):1–19.
———— "Egypt in the World System of the Later Middle Ages." In *CHE*, pp. 445–62.
———— "The Expressive Intent of the Mamluk Architecture of Cairo." *SI* 35 (1972):69–119.
———— *From Saladin to the Mongols: The Ayyubids of Damascus* (New York, NY: SUNY, 1977).
Hüsameddin, Abdizade Hüseyin. *Amasya Tarihi* (İstanbul, 1328/1927).
Idris, H.R. "Ḥafṣids." EI^2 3:66–9.
İlaydın, Hikmet and Adnan Sadık Erzi, "XVI. Asra Aid Bir Münşeat Mecmuası." *Belleten* 21 (1957):221–52.
Imber, Colin. "The Ottoman Dynastic Myth." *Turcica* 19 (1987):7–29.
———— *The Ottoman Empire 1300–1481* (İstanbul, 1990).
İnalcık, Halil. "Osmanlılar'da saltanat veraseti usulü ve Türk hâkimiyet telâkkisiyle ilgisi." *Siyasal Bilgiler Fakültesi Dergisi* 14 (1956):69–94.
———— "Bursa." *DİA* 6:445–9.
———— "Bursa and the Commerce of the Levant." *JESHO* 3 (1960):131–47.
———— "Bursa: XV.Asır Sanayi ve Ticarat Tarihine Dair Vesikalar." *Belleten* 24 (1960):45–102.
———— "A Case Study in Renaissance Diplomacy: The Agreement between Innocent VIII and Bāyezīd II on Djem Sultan." *Journal of Turkish Studies* 3 (1979):209–30.

———. "Jews in the Ottoman Economy and Finances, 1450–1500." In *The Islamic World from Classical to Modern Times: Essasys in Honor of Bernard Lewis*, edited by C.E.Bosworth, Charles Issawi, Roger Savory, and A.L. Udovitch (Princeton, NJ: Darwin Press, 1988), pp. 513–50.
———. "Mehmed I." *DİA* 28:391–4.
———. "Murad I." *DİA* 31:156–64.
———. "Murad II." *İA* 8:598–615.
———. "Murad II." *DİA* 31:164–72.
———. "The Ottoman State: Economy and Society, 1300–1600." In *An Economic and Social History of the Ottoman Empire 1300–1914*, edited by Halil İnalcık and Donald Quataert (Cambridge: Cambridge University Press, 1994), pp. 9–380.
———. "Power Relationship between Russia, the Crimea and the Ottoman Empire as Reflected in Titulature." In *Passé Turco-Tatar Présent Sovietique*, edited by Ch. Lemercier-Quelquejay, G. Veinstein, S.E. Wimbush (Paris: Éditions de l'École des Hautes Études en Sciences Sociales, 1986), pp. 175–211.
———. "Selīm I." *EI*² 9:127–31.
İpşirli, Mehmed. "Elçi." *DİA* 11:3–15.
İz, Fahir. "'Aşık Paşa." *EI*² 1:698–9.
Johnstone, T.M. "Ghazw." *EI*² 2:1055–6.
Jomier, J. "Maḥmal." *EI*² 6:44–6.
———. *Le Maḥmal et la Caravane Égyptienne des Pèlerins de la Mecque* (Cairo, 1953).
Jong, Janneke de. "The Employment of Epithets in the Struggle for Power: A Case Study." In *Crises and the Roman Empire: Proceedings of the Seventh Workshop of the International Workshop of the International Network Impact of Empire (Impact of Empire, Volume 7)*, edited by Olivier de Kleijn Hekster and Danielle Gerda Slootjes (Leiden: E.J. Brill, 2007), pp. 311–26.
Jönsson, Christer, and Martin Hall. *Essence of Diplomacy* (Houndmills: Palgrave Macmillan, 2005).
Kafadar, Cemal. *Between Two Worlds: The Construction of the Ottoman State* (Berkeley, CA: University of California Press, 1995).
Kanat, Cüneyt. "Osmanlı ve Memlûk Devletleri'nin Birbirlerine Gönderdiği Armağanlar." In *Uluslararası Osmanlı Tarihi Sempozyumu (8–10 Nisan 1999) Bildirileri*, edited by Turan Gökçe (İzmir, 2000), pp. 35–52.
Kappert, Petra. *Die Osmanischen Prinzen und ihre Residenz Amasya in 15. und 16. Jahrhundert* (Leiden, 1976).
Karatay, Fehmi Ethem. *Topkapı Sarayı Müzesi Kütüphanesi Arapça Yazmalar Kataloğu* (Istanbul: Topkapı Sarayı Müzesi, 1962). Vol.1.
Karateke, Hakan T. "Legitimizing the Ottoman Sultanate: A Framework for Historical Analysis." In *Legitimizing the Order: The Ottoman Rhetoric of State Power*, edited by Hakan T. Karateke and Maurus Reinkowski (Leiden: E.J. Brill, 2005), pp. 13–55.
———. *Padişahım Çok Yaşa! Osmanlı Devletinin Son Yüz Yılında Merasimler* (İstanbul: Kitab Yayınları, 2004).
Kauz, Ralph. "Gift Exchange between Iran, Central Asia, and China under the Ming dynasty, 1368–1644." In *Gifts of the Sultan*, pp. 115–23.
Kazan, Hilal. *XVI. Asırda Sarayın Sanatı Himayesi* (İstanbul: İSAR, 2010).
Keçik, Mehmet Şefik. *Briefe und Urkunden aus der Kanzlei Uzun Hasans: Ein Beitrag zur Geschichte Ost-Anatoliens in 15 Jahrhundert* (Freiburg, 1975).

Kennedy, Hugh. *Muslim Spain and Portugal: A Political History of al-Andalus* (London: Pearson, 1996).
Kerslake, Celia. "The Correspondence between Selīm I and Ḳānṣūh al-Ġawrī." *Revue de Philologie Orientale* 30 (1980):219–34.
Kissling, Hans Joachim. "Aus der Geschichte des Chalvetijje-Ordens." *Zeitschrift der Deutschen Morgenländischen Gesellschaft* 28 (1953):233–89.
——— "Betrachtungen über die Flottenpolitik Sultan Bâyezîds II." *Saeculum* 20 (1969):35–43.
——— *Sultan Bâyezîd II's Beziehungen zu Markgraf Francesco II. von Gonzaga* (München: Max Hueber Verlag, 1965).
Kister, M.J. "Maḳām Ibrāhīm." *EI*^{2} 6:104–7.
Kohlberg, E., A. Ayalon, M.J. Viguera, K.A. Nizami. "Safīr." *EI*^{2} 8:811–15.
Kolodziejczyk, Dariusz. *Ottoman-Polish Diplomatic Relations (15th–18th Century):an Annotated Edition of Ahdnames and Other Documents* (Leiden: E.J. Brill, 2000).
Komaroff, Linda. "The Art of the Art of Giving at the Islamic Courts." In *Gifts of the Sultan*, pp. 17–33.
Kopraman, Kâzım Yaşar. *Mısır Memlükleri Tarihi: Sultan Al-Malik Al-Mu'ayyad Şeyh Al-Mahmûdî Devri (1412–1421)* (Ankara: Kültür Bakanlığı Yayınları, 1989).
——— "Osmanlı-Memlûk Münâsebetleri." In *Türkler*, 9:470–85 (Ankara, 2002).
Köprülü, Fuad. "Artuklular." *İA* 1:617–18.
Küçükdağ, Yusuf. "Osmanlı-Memlûklü Barışını Yapan Osmanlı Diplomatı 'Şeyh Ali Çelebi'nin Kimliği Hakkında." *S.Ü. Fen-Edebiyat Fakültesi Edebiyat Dergisi* 5 (1990):213–16.
Kütükoğlu, Mübahat S. *Osmanlı Belgelerinin Dili* (İstanbul, 1994).
——— "XVIII. Yüzyılda Osmanlı Devletinde Fevkalade Elçilerin Ağırlanması." *Türk Kültürü Araştırmaları* 27(1989):199–231.
Labib, S. "Handelsgeschichte Ägyptens im Spätmittelalter, 1171–1517." *Vierteljahrschift für Sozial- und Wirtschaftsgeschichte Beihefte* 46 (1965).
Leiser, Gary. "Malḳoč-oghullari." *EI*^{2} 12 (Supp.):578–9.
Levanoni, Amalia. "The Mamluk Conception of the Sultanate." *IJMES* 26 (1994):373–92.
——— "The Sultan's *Laqab* –a Sign of a New Order in Mamluk Factionalim." In *Mamluks in Egyptian and Syrian Politics and Society*, edited by Michael Winter and Amalia Levanoni (Leiden: E.J. Brill, 2004), pp. 79–115.
Lowry, Heath. *Hersekzâde Ahmed Paşa: An Ottoman Statesman's Career and Pious Endowments* (İstanbul: Bahçeşehir University Press, 2011).
Lewis, Bernard. "Elči." *EI*^{2} 2:694.
——— "Khādim al-Ḥaramayn." *EI*^{2} 4:899–900.
Lewis, G.L. "Fatḥnāme." *EI*^{2} 2:839–40.
——— "The Utility of Ottoman *Fethnames*." In *Historians of the Middle East*, edited by Bernard Lewis and P.M. Holt (London, 1962), pp. 192–6.
Linant de Bellefonds, Y. "Hiba." *EI*^{2} 3:350–1.
Lindner, Rudi Paul. "Anatolia, 1300–1451." In *Cambridge History of Turkey*, edited by Kate Fleet (Cambridge: Cambridge University Press, 2009), pp. 102–38.
——— *Explorations in Ottoman Prehistory* (Ann Arbor, MI: University of Michigan Press, 2007).

Little, Donald P. "Diplomatic Missions and Gifts Exchanged by Mamluks and Ilkhans." In *Beyond the Legacy of Genghiz Khan*, edited by Linda Komaroff (Leiden: E.J. Brill, 2006), pp. 30–43.
Loiseau, Julien. "De l'Asie centrale à l'Égypte: le siècle turc." In *Histoire du Monde au XVe siècle*, edited by Patrick Boucheron, Julien Loiseau, Pierre Monnet, and Yann Potin (Paris, 2009), pp. 33–51.
MacCormack, Sabine. *Art and Ceremony in Late Antiquity* (Berkeley, CA: University of California Press, 1981).
Majer, Georg. "Urkunden Fälschung im Osmanischen Reich." In *Living in the Ottoman Ecumenical Community: Essays in Honor of Suraiya Faroqhi*, edited by Suraiya Faroqhi, Vera Constantini, and Markus Koller (Leiden: E.J. Brill, 2008), pp. 45–70.
Mansouri, Mohamed Tahar. *Recherches sur les Relations entre Byzance et L'Egypte (1259–1453) (d'apres les sources arabes)* (Tunis, 1992).
Manz, Beatrice. *Power, Politics and Religion in Timurid Iran* (Cambridge: Cambridge University Press, 2007).
———. "Shāh Rukh b. Tīmūr." *EI*² 9:197–8.
Martel-Thoumian, Bernadette. *Les Civils et l'Administration dans L'État Militaire Mamlūk (IXe/XVe Siècle)* (Damas: Institut Français de Damas, 1991).
———. "Les Dernières Batailles du Grand Émir Yašbak min Mahdī." In *War and Society in the Eastern Mediterranean, 7th–15th Centuries*, edited by Ed. Yaacov Lev, (Leiden: E.J. Brill, 2001), pp. 301–43.
Mattingly, Garrett. *Renaissance Diplomacy* (Boston: Houghton Mifflin, 1955).
Matuz, Josef. *Das Kanzleiwesen Sultan Süleymans des Prächtigen* (Wiesbaden, 1974).
Mauss, Marcel. *The Gift: Forms and Functions of Exchange in Archaic Societies*. Translated by Ian Cunnison (New York, NI: Norton, 1967).
Mayer, L.A. *Mamluk Costume* (Geneva, 1952).
McCormick, Michael. "Analyzing Imperial Ceremonies." *Jahrbuch der österreichischen Byzantinistik* 35 (1985):1–20.
———. *Eternal Victory: Triumphal Rulership in Late Antiquity, Byzantium, and the Early Medieval West* (Cambridge: Cambridge University Press, 1986).
Mélikoff, Irene. "Germiyān-oghulları." *EI*² 2:989–90.
———. "Ghāzī." *EI*² 2:1043–5.
Meloy, John. *Imperial Power and Maritime Power: Mecca and Cairo in the later Middle Ages*. Chicago, 2010.
Melville, Charles. "'The Year of the Elephant': Mamluk-Mongol Rivalry in the Hejaz in the Reign of Abū Saʿīd." *Studia Iranica* 21 (1992):197–207.
Melvin-Koushki, Matthew. "The Delicate Art of Aggression: Uzun Hasan's *Fathnama* to Qaytbay of 1469." *Iranian Studies* 44 (2011):193–214.
Menage, V.L. "The Mission of an Ottoman Secret Agent in France in 1486." *Journal of the Royal Asiatic Society* (1965): 112–32.
Merçil, Erdoğan. "Menteshe-Oghulları." *EI*² 6:1018–19.
Mitchell, Colin. "Safavid Imperial Tarassul and the Persian Inshāʾ Tradition." *Studia Iranica* 26 (1997):173–209.
Mordtmann, J.H. "Dhu'l-Ḳadr." *EI*² 2:239–40.
———. "Feridun Bey." *İA* 4:569–70.
———. "Ḳusṭanṭīniyya." *EI*² 5:532–4.
——— and V.L. Ménage. "Ferīdūn Beg." *EI*² 2:881–2.

Mortel, Richard T. "Aspects of Mamlūk Relations with Jedda during the Fifteenth Century: The Case of Timrāz al-Mu'ayyadī." *Journal of Islamic Studies* 6 (1995):1–13.
Mottahedeh, Roy Parviz, and Ridwan al-Sayyid. "The Idea of *Jihād* in Islam Before the Crusades." In *The Crusades from the Perspective of Byzantium and the Muslim World*, edited by Angeliki E. Laiou and Roy Parviz Mottahedeh, (Washington, WA: Dumbarton Oaks, 2001), pp. 23–9.
El Moudden, Abderrahmane. "Sharifs and Padishahs: Moroccan–Ottoman Relations from the 16th through the 18th Centuries: Contribution to the Study of a Diplomatic Culture." PhD diss., Princeton University, 1992.
Muhanna, Elias. "The Sultan's New Clothes: Ottoman–Mamluk Gift Exchange in the Fifteenth Century." *Muqarnas* 27 (2010):189–207.
Mutawalli, Ahmad Fu'ad. *Al-Fatkh Al-'Uthmani li'l-Sham wa Misr wa Muqaddimatuhu min Waqi' al-Watha'iq wa Al-Masadir Al-Turkiyah wa Al-'Arabiyah Al-Mu'asirah* (Cairo, 1976).
Mükrimin Halil. See Yınanç.
Necipoğlu, Gülru. *Architecture, Ceremonial, and Power: The Topkapı Palace in the Fifteenth and Sixteenth Centuries* (Cambridge, MA: MIT Press, 1992).
———. "Framing the Gaze in Ottoman, Safavid, Mughal Palaces." In "Pre-Modern Islamic Palaces," ed. Gülru Necipoğlu. Special issue, *Ars Orientalis* 23 (1993):303–42.
———. "An Outline of Shifting Paradigms in the Palatial Architecture of the Pre-Modern Islamic World." In "Pre-Modern Islamic Palaces," ed. Gülru Necipoğlu. Special issue, *Ars Orientalis* 23 (1993):3–27.
Newhall, Amy Whittier. "The Patronage of the Mamluk Sultan Qa'it Bay." PhD diss., Harvard University, 1987.
Nielsen, Jørgen S. "Maẓālim." *EI*[2] 7:933.
——— *Secular Justice in an Islamic State: Maẓālim under the Baḥrī Mamlūks, 662/1264–789/138.* (Leiden, 1985).
Northrup, Linda S. "The Baḥrī Mamlūk Sultanate, 1250–1390." In *CHE*, pp. 242–90.
——— *From Slave to Sultan: The Career of al-Mansụ̄r Qalāwūn and the Consolidation of Mamluk Rule in Egypt and Syria (678–689 A.H./1279–1290 A.D.)* (Stuttgart: F. Steiner, 1998).
Orgun, Zarif. "Osmanlı İmparatorluğunda Kaptan Paşalara ve Donanmaya Yapılan Merasim." *Tarih Vesikaları* 2 (1941):135–44.
——— "Osmanlı İmparatorluğunda Nâme ve Hediye Getiren Elçilere Yapılan Merasim." *Tarih Vesikaları* 5 (1942):407–13.
——— "Osmanlı İmparatorluğunda Tuğ ve Sancak." *Tarih Vesikaları* 4 (1941):245–5 and 5 (1941):344–55.
Ouerfelli, Mohamed. "Les Relations entre le Royaume de Chypre et le Sultanat Mamelouk au XVe Siècle." *Le Moyen Âge* CX (2004):327–44.
Özaydın, Abdülkerim, and Hatice Tören. "Kadı Burhaneddin." *DİA* 24:75.
Özcan, Abdülkadir. "Feridun Ahmed Bey." *DİA* 12:396–7.
Pamuk, Şevket. "Appendix: Money in the Ottoman Empire, 1326–1914." In *An Economic and Social History of the Ottoman Empire 1300–1914*, edited by Halil İnalcık and Donald Quataert (Cambridge: Cambridge University Press, 1994), pp. 947–81.

Pedani-Fabris, Maria Pia. "Ottoman Diplomats in the West: The Sultan's Ambassadors to the Republic of Venice." *Tarih Incelemeleri Dergisi* 11 (1996):187–202.

———. "Ottoman Fetihnames: The Imperial Letters Announcing a Victory." *Tarih İncelemeleri Dergisi* 13 (1998):181–92.

Pedani, Maria Pia. *"Osmanlı Padişahının Adına": İstanbul'un Fethinden Girit Savaşı'na Venedik'e Gönderilen Osmanlılar*. Translated by Elis Yıldırım (Ankara: TTK, 2011).

———. "The Sultan and the Venetian Bailo: Ceremonial Diplomatic Protocol in Istanbul." In *Diplomatisches Zeremoniell in Europa und im Mittleren Osten in der frühen Neuzeit*, edited by R. Kauz, G. Rota, J. Paul Niederkorn (Wien, 2009), pp. 287–99.

———. "Sultans and Voivodas in the 16th C. Gifts and Insignia." *Uluslararası Sosyal Araştırmalar Dergisi* 1 (2007):193–209.

Pedersen, J."Ibn 'Arabshāh." *EI*^{2} 3:711–12.

Petry, C.F. *The Civilian Elite of Cairo in the Later Middle Ages* (Princeton, NJ: Princeton University Press, 1981).

———. *Protectors or Praetorians? The Last mamluk Sultans and Egypt's Waning as a Great Power* (New York, NY: State University of New York Press, 1994).

———. "Robing Ceremonials in Late Mamlūk Egypt: Hallowing Traditions, Shifting Protocols." In *Robes and Honor*, pp. 353–79.

———. *Twillight of Majesty: The Reigns of the Mamlūk Sultans al-Ashraf Qāytbāy and Qānṣūh al-Ghawrī in Egypt* (Seattle, 1993).

Rabbat, Nasser O. *The Citadel of Cairo: A New Interpretation of Royal Mamlūk Architecture* (Leiden: E.J. Brill, 1995).

———. "The Ideological Significance of the Dār al-Adl in the Medieval Islamic Orient." *IJMES* 27 (1995):3–28.

———. "Mamluk Throne Halls: 'Qubba' or 'Iwān'." In "Pre-Modern Islamic Palaces," ed. Gülru Necipoğlu. Special issue, *Ars Orientalis* 23 (1993):201–19.

Rabie, Hassanein. "Mamlūk Campaigns against Rhodes." In *The Islamic World: From Classical to Modern Times: Essays in Honor of Bernard Lewis*, edited by C.E. Bosworth, Charles Issawi, Roger Savory, and A.L. Udovitch (Princeton, NJ: 1989), pp. 281–86.

Raby, Julian. "The Serenissima and the Sublime Porte: Art in the Art of Diplomacy." In *Venice and the Islamic World*, edited by Stefano Carboni (New York, NY: Metropolitan Museum of Art, 2007), pp. 90–120.

———. "A Sultan of Paradox: Mehmed the Conqueror as a Patron of the Arts." *Oxford Art Journal* 5 (1982):3–8.

——— and Ünsal Yücel. "Chinese Porcelain at the Ottoman Court." In *Chinese Ceramics in the Topkapı Saray Museum: A Complete Catalogue*, edited by Regina Krahl (London: Sotheby's, 1986), pp. 27–55.

Reindl, Hedda. *Männer um Bāyezīd: Eine Prosopographische Studie über die Epoche Bāyezīd II (1481–1512)* (Berlin: Klaus Schwarz Verlag, 1983).

Repp, R.C. *The Müfti of İstanbul: A Study in the Development of the Ottoman Learned Hierarchy* (London: Ithaca Press, 1986).

Reychman, Jan, and Andrew Ehrenkreutz, Ananiasz Zajackowski. *Handbook of Ottoman Turkish Diplomatics* (The Hague: Mouton, 1968).

Richards, D. S. "A Late Mamluk Document Concerning Frankish Commercial Practice at Tripoli," *BSOAS* 62 (1999):21–35.
Roemer, H.R. "Inshā'." *EI*² 3:1241–4.
Rogers, J.M., Hülya Tezcan, and Selma Delibaş. *The Topkapı Saray Museum: Costumes, Embroideries, and Other Textiles* (Boston, MA: 1986).
Roosen, William. "Early Modern Diplomatic Ceremonial: A Systems Approach."*The Journal of Modern History* 52 (1980):452–76.
Rosenthal, F. "Rashwa." *EI*² 8:451.
Rosenthal, F, C. Bosworth, J. Wansbrough, H. Busse, and B. Spuler. "Hiba." *EI*² 3:342–50.
Rypka, Jan. "Briefwechsel der Hohen Pforte mit den Krimchanen im II.Bande von Ferīdūns Münšeāt." In *Festschrift Georg Jacob*, edited by Theodor Menzel (Leipzig: Otto Harrassowitz, 1932), pp. 241–70.
Šabanović, H. "Hersek-zade." *EI*² 3:340–2.
Sabra, Adam. *Poverty and Charity in Medieval Islam* (Cambridge: Cambridge University Press, 2000).
Sanders, Paula. *Ritual, Politics, and the City in Fatimid Cairo* (New York, NY: SUNY, 1994).
———. "Robes of Honor in Fatimid Society." In *Robes and Honor*, pp. 225–41.
Sanders, P., Paul Chalmeta, A.K.S. Lambton, A.H.De Groot, J.Burton-Page. "Marāsim." *EI*² 6:518–34.
———. Paul Chalmeta, A.K.S. Lambton, Ö.Nutku, J. Burton-Page. "Mawākib." *EI*² 6:849–67.
Schultz, Warren C. "The Monetary History of Egypt, 642–1517." In *CHE*, 318–39.
Schwarz, Klaus. *Osmanischen Sultansurkunden des Sinai-Klosters in türkischer Sprache* (Freiburg, 1970).
Setton, Kenneth M. *The Papacy and the Levant, 1204–1571*. 4 vols. (Philadelphia: American Philosophical Society, 1978).
Shalem, Avinoam. "Afterlife and Circulation of Objects." In *Gifts of the Sultan*, pp. 92–95.
———. "Performance of the Object." In *Gifts of the Sultan*, pp. 111–15.
Sherwani, H.K. *The Bahmanis of Deccan* (New Delhi, 1985).
———. "Bahmanīs." *EI*² 1:923–6.
Shoshan, Boaz. "From Silver to Copper: Monetary Change in Fifteenth Century Egypt." *Studia Islamica* 56 (1982):97–116.
———. *Popular Culture in Medieval Cairo* (Cambridge: Cambridge University Press, 1993).
Sievert, Henning. *Der Herrscherwechsel im Mamlukensultanat* (Berlin: Klaus Schwarz Verlag, 2003).
Sinor, Denis. "Diplomatic Practices in Medieval Inner Asia." In *The Islamic World from Classical to Modern Times: Essays in Honor of Bernard Lewis*, edited by C.E. Bosworth, Charles Issawi, Roger Savory, and A.L. Udovitch (Princeton, NJ: 1989), pp. 281–6.
Sivan, Emmanuel. *L'Islam et la Croisade: Idéologie et Propagande dans les Réactions Musulmanes aux Croisades* (Paris, 1968).
Skilliter, Susan A. "An Ambassador's *ta'yin*: Edward Barton's Ration on the Eğri Campaign, 1596." *Turcica* 25 (1993):153–65.
Smith Jr., J.M. "DJalāyir." *EI*² 2:401.

Soucek, Svat. "Selmān Re'īs." *EI* ² 9:135–6.
Sourdel, Dominique. "Questions de Cérémonial Abbaside." *Revue des Études Islamiques* 1960:121–48.
Springberg-Hinsen, Monika. *Die Ḫil'a: Studien zur Geschichte des geschenkten Gewandes im Islamischen Kulturkreis* (Würzburg: Ergon, 2000).
Stavrides, Theoharis. *The Sultan of Vezirs: The Life and times of the Ottoman Grand Vezir Mahmud Pasha Angelovic* (Leiden: E.J.Brill, 2001).
Stern, S.M. ed. *Documents from Islamic Chanceries* (Columbia: University of South Carolina Press, 1970).
Steward, Angus Donald. *The Armenian Kingdom and the Mamluks: War and Diplomacy during the Reigns of Het'um II (1289-1307)* (Leiden: E.J. Brill, 2001).
Stillmann, N.A. "Khil'a." *EI* ² 5:6–7.
Stilt, Kristen. *Islamic Law in Action: Authority, Discretion, and Everyday Experiences in Mamluk Egypt* (Oxford: Oxford University Press, 2011).
Stojanow, Valeri. *Die Entstehung und Entwicklung der Osmanischen-Türkischen Paläographie und Diplomatic: mit einer Bibliographie* (Berlin: Klaus Schwarz Verlag, 1983).
Stowasser, Karl. "Manners and Customs at the Mamluk Court." *Muqarnas* 2 (1984):13–20.
Subrahmanyam, Sanjay. *The Career and Legend of Vasco de Gama* (Cambridge: Cambridge University Press, 1997).
——— *Courtly Encounters: Translating Courtliness and Violence in Early Modern Eurasia* (Cambridge, MA: Harvard University Press, 2012).
Sümer, Faruk. *Kara Koyunlular.* Ankara: TTK, 1967.
——— "Ḳarā-ḳoyunlu." *EI* ² 4:584–8.
——— "Ḳaramān-oghullari." *EI* ² 4:619–25.
——— "Ramazan-oğulları." *İA* 9:612–20.
——— "Turgutlular." *DİA* 12:420–1.
Süreyya, Mehmed. *Sicill-i 'Osmani.* 5 vols. (İstanbul, 1311/1893).
Tahir, Bursalı Mehmed. *Osmanlı Müellifleri.* 3 vols. (Istanbul, 1914–24).
Tarım-Ertuğ, Zeynep. "Osmanlılar'da Teşrifat." In *Türk Dünyası Kültür Atlası* (İstanbul, 1999), pp. 428–77.
Tekindağ, Şehabettin. *Berkuk devrinde Memluk Sultanlığı: XIV. Yüzyıl Mısır Tarihine Dair Araştırmalar* (İstanbul: İstanbul Edebiyat Fakültesi Matbaası, 1961).
——— "Fatih Devrinde Osmanlı Memluklü Münasebetleri." *İstanbul Üniversitesi Edebiyat Fakültesi Tarih Dergisi* 30 (1976):73–99.
——— "Fatih ile Çağdaş bir Memluklü Sultanı: Aynal el-Ecrûd." *Tarih Dergisi* 23 (1969):35–50.
——— "İnāl." *EI* ² 3:1198.
——— "Karamanlılar." *İA* 6:316–30.
——— "Karamanlılar'ın Gorigos Seferi (1367)." *İstanbul Üniversitesi Edebiyat Fakültesi Tarih Dergisi* 6 (1954):161–72.
——— "Memluk Sultanlığı Tarihine Toplu Bir Bakış." *İstanbul Üniversitesi Edebiyat Fakültesi Tarih Dergisi* 25 (1971):1–39.
——— "Niğbolu." *İA* 9:247–53.
——— "Son Osmanlı-Karaman Münasebetleri Hakkında Araştırmalar. " *İstanbul Üniversitesi Edebiyat Fakültesi Tarih Dergisi* 18 (1962–3):43–76.

——— "Süveyş'de Türkler ve Selman Reis'in Arizası." *Belgelerle Türk Tarihi* 9 (1968):77–80.
——— "II.Bayezid Devrinde Çukurova'da Nüfuz Mücadelesi." *Belleten* 31 (1967):345–75.
——— "XVI. Asrın Sonunda Memluk Ordusu." *İstanbul Üniversitesi Edebiyat Fakültesi Tarih Dergisi* 11 (1960):85–95.
Tevhid, Ahmed. "İlk Altı Padişahımızıñ Bursa'da Kâ'in Türbeleri: Hüdâvendigâr Sulṭān Murad Ḫān'ıñ Türbesi." *TOEM* 13–18 (1328):1047–51.
——— "Yıldırım Sulṭān Bāyezīd Ḫān-ı Evvel Devrinde Mışır'a Sefāretle Gönderilen Sefer Şah'ıñ Vefātı." *TOEM* 13–18 (1331):1031–2.
Thorau, Peter. *The Lion of Egypt: Sultan Baybars I and the Near East in the Thirteenth Century*. Translated by P.M.Holt (London: Longman, 1992).
Al-Tikriti, Nabil. "The Ḥajj as Justifiable Self-Exile: Şehzade Korkud's *Wasīlat al-Aḥbāb* (915–916/1509–1510)." *Al-Masāq* 17 (2005):125–46.
——— "Kalam in the Service of State: Apostasy and the Defining of Ottoman Islamic Identity." In *Legitimizing the Order: The Ottoman Rhetoric of State Power*, edited by Hakan K. Karateke and Maurus Reinkowski (Leiden: E.J. Brill, 2005), pp. 131–51.
——— "Şehzade Korkud and the Articulation of Early 16th Century Ottoman Religious Identity." PhD diss., Chicago University, 2004.
Togan, İsenbike. "Beylikler Devri Anadolu Tarihinde Yöntem Sorunları: Germiyan'dan Örnekler." In *Şinasi Tekin'in Anısına: Uygurlardan Osmanlıya* (İstanbul: Simurg, 2005), pp. 704–20.
——— "Türkler'de Devlet Oluşum Modelleri: Osmanlılar'da ve Timurlular'da." In *İsmail Aka Armağanı* (İzmir, 1999), pp. 71–84.
Turan, Fikret. "The Mamluks and Their Acceptance of Oghuz Turkish as a Literary Language: Political Maneuver or Cultural Aspiration." *Turcologica* 69 (2007):37–47.
Turan, Osman. *İstanbul'un Fethinden Önce Yazılmış Tarihi Takvimler* (Ankara: TTK, 1954).
Turan, Şerafettin. "1560 Tarihinde Bir İran Elçilik Hey'eti Masraf Defteri." *Ankara Üniversitesi Dil ve Tarih –Coğrafya Fakültesi Dergisi* 12 (1964):273–94.
——— "Barak Reis'in Şehzade Cem Meselesiyle İlgili Olarak Savoie'ya Gönderilmesi." *Belleten* 26 (1962): 539–55.
——— "Bayezid II." *DİA* 5:234–8.
Tyan, Emile. "Djihād." *EI*^{2} 2:538–40.
Uluç, Lale. "Gifted Manuscripts from the Safavids to the Ottomans." In *Gifts of the Sultan*, pp. 144–9.
Umur, Süha. *Osmanlı Padişah Tuğraları* (İstanbul: Cem Yayınevi, 1980).
Unat, Faik Reşit. *Osmanlı Sefirleri ve Sefaretnameleri*. Edited by Bekir Sıtkı Baykal, 2nd ed. (Ankara: TTK, 1987).
Uzunçarşılı, İsmail Hakkı. "Karamanoğulları Devri Vesikalarından İbrahim Bey'in Karaman İmareti Vakfiyesi." *Belleten* 1 (1937):56–164.
——— "Murad I." *İA* 8:587–99.
——— "Memluk Sultanları Yanına İltica Etmiş Olan Osmanlı Hanedanına Mensub Şehzadeler." *Belleten* 17 (1953):519–35.
——— *Osmanli Devleti Teşkilatına Medhal* (Ankara: TTK, 1988).
——— *Osmanlı Devletinin Merkez ve Bahriye Teşkilatı* (Ankara: TTK, 1988).

―――― *Osmanlı Devletinin Saray Teşkilatı* (Ankara: TTK, 1945).
―――― "Osmanlı Tarihine Ait Bazı Yanlışlıkların Tashihi." *Belleten* 31 (1957):178–81.
―――― "Sultan II.Murad'ın Vasiyetnamesi." *Vakıflar Dergisi* 4 (1958):1–17.
Walsh, J. "Gūrānī, Sharaf al-Dīn." *EI*² 2:1040–1.
Wansbrough, John. "Faradj." *EI*² 2:781–2.
―――― *Lingua Franca in the Mediterranean* (Richmond, Surrey: Curzon Press, 1996).
―――― "A Mamluk Ambassador to Venice." *BSOAS* 26 (1963):503–30.
―――― "A Mamlūk Commercial Treaty Concluded with the Republic of Florence." In *Documents from Islamic* Chanceries, edited by S.M. Stern (Columbia, SC: University of South Carolina Press, 1965), pp. 39–81.
―――― "A Mamluk Letter of 877/1473." *BSOAS* 24 (1961):200–13.
―――― "The Safe-Conduct in Muslim Chancery Practice." *BSOAS* 34 (1971):20–35.
―――― "Venice and Florence in the Mamluk Commercial Privileges." *BSOAS* 28 (1965):483–523.
Watkins, John. "Toward a New Diplomatic History of Medieval and Early Modern Europe." *Journal of Medieval and Early Modern Studies* 38 (2008):1–14.
Weiner, Annette. *Inalienable Possessions: The Paradox of Keeping-while-giving* (Berkeley: University of California Press, 1992).
Wensick and Jomier. "Ka'ba." *EI*² 4:317–18.
Wiet, Gaston. "Barsbay." *EI*² 1:1053.
―――― *Cairo: City of Art and Commerce*. Translated by Seymour Feiler (Norman: University of Oklahoma Press, 1964).
―――― "Deux Princes Ottomans à la Cour d'Égypte." *Bulletin de l'Institue d'Égypte* 20 (1938):137–50.
Windler, Christian. "Tribut und Gabe: Mediterrane Diplomatie als Interkulturelle Kommunikation." *Saeculum* 51 (2000):24–56.
Winter, Michael. "Attitudes toward the Ottomans in the Egyptian Historiography during Ottoman Rule." In *The Historiography of Islamic Egypt (C.950–1800)*, edited by H. Kennedy (Leiden: Brill, 2001), pp. 195–210.
Wittek, Paul. *Menteşe Beyliği: 13.–15. Asırda Garbî Küçük Asya Tarihine Ait Tetkik*. Translated by Orhan Şaik Gökyay (Ankara: TTK, 1986).
―――― "Le Sultan de Rûm." *Annuaire de l'Institut de Philologie et d'Histoire Orientales et Slaves* 6 (1938):361–90.
Wolff, Anne. "Merchants, Pilgrims, and Naturalists: Alexandria through European Eyes from the Fourteenth to the Sixteenth Century." In *Alexandria, Real and Imagined*, edited by Anthony Hirst and Michael Silk (Aldershot: Ashgate, 2004), pp. 199–225.
Woods, John E.*The Aqquyunlu Clan, Confederation, Empire (Revised and Expanded)* (Salt Lake City, UT: The University of Utah Press, 1999).
―――― "Turco-Iranica I: An Ottoman Intelligence Report on Late Fifteenth/Ninth Century Iranian Foreign Relations." *Journal of Near Eastern Studies* 38 (1979):1–9.
Wright, Diana Gilliland, and Pierre A.Mackay. "When the Serenissima and the *Gran Turco* Made Love: The Peace Treaty of 1478." *Study Veneziani* 3 (2007):261–77.
Varlık, Mustafa Çetin. *Germiyan-oğulları* (Ankara: Atatürk Üniversitesi Yayınları, 1974).
Van Berchem, Max. *Matériaux pour un Corpus Inscriptionum Arabicarum* (Paris, 1894).
Vatin, Nicholas. "Itinéraires d'Agents de la Porte en Italie." *Turcica* 19 (1987): 29–51.

―― *L'Ordre de Saint-Jean-de-Jérusalem, l'Empire Ottoman et la Méditerranée Orientale entre les Deux Sieges de Rhodes* (Paris: Peeters, 1994).

―― *Sultan Djem* (Ankara: TTK, 1997).

Venzke, Margaret L. "The Case of a Dulgadir-Mamluk *Iqṭāʿ*: A Reassessment of the Dulgadir Principality and Its Positions within the Ottoman-Mamluk Rivalry." *JESHO* 43 (2000):399–474.

Veselý, Rudolf. "Ein Briefwechsel zwischen Ägypten und den Qaramaniden im 14. Jahrhundert." *Asian and African Studies* 9 (2000):36–44.

―― "Ein Kapitel aus dem osmanisch-mamlukischen Beziehungen, Meḥemmed Çelebi und Muʾayyad Shaykh." In *Armağan: Festschrift für Andreas Tietze* (Prague: Enigma, 1994), pp. 241–59.

―― "Eine Stilkunstschrift oder Eine Urkunden Sammlung? Das Qahwat al-inšāʾ des Abū Bakr Ibn Ḥidjdja al-Ḥamawī." In *Threefold Wisdom: Islam, the Arab World and Africa: Papers in Honour of Ivan Hrbek*, edited by Otakar Hulec and Milos Mendel (Prague, 1993), pp. 237–48.

Yalçın, Mehmet. *The Dīvan of Qânsûh al-Ghûrî=Kansu Gavri Divanı* (İstanbul: Bay, 2002).

Yınanç, Mükrimin Halil. "Bayezid I." *İA* 2:369–92.

―― "Feridun Bey Münşeatı." *TOEM* 77 (1923):161–8, 78 (1924):37–46, 79:95–104, 81:216–26.

Yınanc, Refet. *Dulkadir Beyliği* (Ankara: TTK, 1989).

Yüksel Muslu, Cihan. "Attempting to Understand the Language of Diplomacy between the Ottomans and the Mamluks." *Archivum Ottomanicum* 30 (2013): 247–69.

―― "Ottoman-Mamluk Relations and the Complex Image of Bāyezīd II." In *Conquête Ottomane de l'Égypte (1517): Arrière-plan, impact, échos*, edited by Benjamin Lellouch and Nicolas Michel (Leiden: E.J. Brill, 2013), pp. 51–79.

―― "Ottoman-Mamluk Relations: Diplomacy and Perceptions." PhD diss., Harvard University, 2007.

Zachariadou, E.A. *Trade and Crusade, Venetian Crete and the Emirates of Menteshe and Aydın 1300–1415*. Venice: Istituto Ellenico di Studi Bizantini e Postbizantini, 1983.

Ziyada (or Ziada), M. Mustafa. "The Fall of the Mamlūks 1516–1517." *Majallat Kulliyat al-Adab* 6 (1942):1–40.

―― "The Mamluk Conquest of Cyprus in the Fifteenth Century." *Bulletin of the Faculty of Arts of the University of Egypt* 1 (1933):99–110 and 2 (1934):37–58.

―― "Nihayat Salatin Al-Mamalik." *Egyptian Historical Review* 4 (1951):197–228.

Ziada, M.M. and John La Monte, "Bedr ed din Al-ʿAini's Account of the Conquest of Cyprus 1424–26." *Annuaire de l'Institut de philologie et d'histoire orientales et slaves* 7 (1939):241–64.

INDEX

'Abd al-Mu'min al-'Ajami, Shaykh (Mamluk ambassador to the Ottoman court in 1495), 158–9
Abu Sa'id (Timurid ruler, r.1451–69), 13; his head, 41 and 131
Adana, 8, 116, 152; keys, 150; Ottoman defeat outside of, 141; Ağaçayırı, battle of (1488), 143–44
Ahmad the Jalayirid, 80
Ahmed Bey (Karamanid ruler, r.1464–69), 123–5, 132
Ahmed Bican (d. ca.1466), 74
Ahmed, Emir (ambassador to the Mamluk court in 1401), 83
Ahmed i. Bayezid II, 176
Ahmed Paşa, Hersekzade: captivity, 141–3, 152–3; 154, 173
Ahmed Paşa, Karaca (Ottoman ambassador to the Mamluk court in 1515), 177–8
Ahmedi (d.1413), 84–85
Aid, Ottoman maritime, 17, 21, 171, 172; 175
'Ala' al-dawla (Dulkadirid ruler, r.1480–1515): receiving robe from Mehmed II, 129; 138–9, 143–6, 166–8, 177
'Ala' al-din al-Husni (ambassador to the Ottoman court in 1470–2), 129

Albania (or Albanians), 94, 194, 220, 237
Aleppo, 5, 10, 126, 131, 136, 147, 160, 161, 173
Ali i. Shahsuwar, 177
Ali Çelebi (Ottoman ambassador to the Mamluk court in 1491), 149–51
'Allan, Amir (Mamluk ambassador to the Ottoman court in 1509–11), 168–71, 269–70
Amasya, 83, 132, 136, 138, 149
Ambassador: allocation for Mamluk ambassadors in the Ottoman court, 173–4; allocation for Prince Korkud, 170; allocation (stipend) for, 47, 104–5, 109, 131; arrival of, 45; audience, Mamluk, 49–50, passim; audience, Ottoman, 50–58; departure of, 61–2; as gifts, 73–4; lodging of, 16, 45–46; lodging of (Mamluk), 45–6; lodging of (Ottoman), 46; precedence (ambassadorial), 70, 140–1; return of, 61–3; seating arrangements in Cairo, 50, 121; seating arrangements in Ottoman capitals, 53, 55–56, 69, 70, 140; selection of, 25–28; shift in

selection of, 157–161, 185–6; status, social of, 27, 130, 168, 185; surveillance of, 46–7, 146; treatment of Muslim vs. non-Muslim, 55–56
Animals (in diplomacy, as gifts, other than horses), 38, 40, 113, 140, 159, 257
Ankara, the battle of (1402), 20, 50, 75, 79, 85, 93, 118, 125
Antalya: trade, 16
Antep, 8
Appearance of the Mamluk sultans: 59–60, 111, 158. Also see seclusion of Ottoman sultans.
Aqbay al-Tawil (Mamluk ambassador to the Ottoman court in 1512), 176
Aqqoyunlus, 12, 13, 41, 54, 96–97, 110, 116, 117, 122–3; Yashbak min Mahdi's campaigns and the Ottoman campaign, 130–2; 139
Aragon, 14, 17
Armenia, Kingdom of, 8; Prince, 82
Artuqids, 67–8
Aşıkpaşazade, 69, 117–124, 126–7, 128–9, 129–20, 142
Atabak (atabeg), 6
Attack, Ottoman on Mamluk territory, 82–83, 134–56, 179–80
Audience (ambassadorial), Mamluk, 49–50, passim; Ottoman, 50–58
Aybak al-Turkmani (Mamluk sultan, r.1250–7), 5
'Ayn al-Jalut, battle of (1260), 6
Ayyubids, 5–6, 10, 24, 82
Azbak, Amir, 146
Azeb Bey (Ottoman ambassador to the Mamluk court in 1444), 38, 107, 317n92.

Bahmanis, 9; Bahmani mission stopped in Jidda, 137–9, 139–40
Bahri period, 5, 27, 48, 59, 64; transition to Burji period, 64

Balsam (in diplomacy, as gift), 40, 229, 295n140
Banquet, 10; for Cem in Cairo, 137; for Korkud in Cairo, 169; in Mamluk ceremonial, 50, 59; in Ottoman ceremonial, 51, 53, 56; Ottoman for Mamluk ambassadors, 71; Mamluk for Ottoman ambassadors, 81, 82, 95, 165
Barquq (Mamluk sultan, r.1382–9 and 1390–9), 1, 42, 50, 83, 84; comment on Ottomans, 23; exchanges with Bayezid, 75–77, 78–9 (Amir al-Kujkuni), 80, 81–2; exchanges with Murad I, 71–3, 74–5; role in Mamluk ceremonials, 48–9
Barsbay (Mamluk sultan, r.1422–38), 20, 34, 40, 42, 86, 92, 99–100, 179; accession, 91; addressing Murad II, 89, 90, 94–5; interest in ceremonials, 59; campaign to Aqqoyunlus, 96–7; campaign to Cyprus, 95–6; marriage to the Ottoman princess, 100; offer of alliance to Murad II, 97–99; refugees, 100–1; Shahrukh, 101–2; succession after, 102–3
Baybars (Mamluk sultan, r.1260–77): campaign to Anatolia, 6–7, 11, 78
Bayezid I (Ottoman ruler, r.1389–1402), 1, 66, 88, 93, 97, 107, 118, 125, 179, 184; attack on Mamluk territory, 82–4; comment (Ahmedi), 84–5; comment (Mamluk sources), 1, 23, 51, 71, 75–6; correspondence with Barquq, 76–7; impact on Ottoman-Mamluk relationship, 65; Mamluk ambassador Amir al-Kujkuni, 78–9; al-Maqrizi on, 92; marriage to the Germiyanid princess, 69–71; Nicopolis, battle and embassy of, 79–82;

Index

al-Qalqashandi on, 75–6, 87; role in Ottoman ceremonials, 75–6, 79; Shams al-din al-Jazari, 35, 80; Timur, 42, 75
Bayezid II (Ottoman ruler, r.1481–1512), 1–2, 17–8, 21, 27, 36, 39, 42, 46, 133, 134–56, 156–76; campaign in Anatolia in 1481–2, 138–9; council in Beşiktaş, 147–9; governor in Amasya, 131–2; marriage to the Dulkadirid princess, 138–9
Bedreddin, Şeyh, 74, 83–4
Behisni, 7
Beşiktaş, 147–9
Bey: *Rumeli Beyleri*, 147–8. See under titulature.
Bihişti, 147–8
Al-Biqa'i: victory proclamation of Constantinople, 111–3
Burji (Circassian) period, 5, 48, 64, 72
Bursa: in trade, 16. See under Capital.

Çaldıran, battle of (1514), 177
Caliph, Abbasid, 9–10, 29, 41, 76, 79, 102, 140, 141, 185
Caliph, Fatimid, 43
Caliphate, Abbasid, 9–10, 181, 184
Cape of Good Hope, circumnavigation of, 14, 17, 166
Capital, Transfer of Ottoman, 65; from Bursa to Edirne, 11, 282n62; from Edirne to Constantinople, 50, 52
Captivity: Hersekzade Ahmed Paşa, 141–43; Mihaloğlu İskender Bey, 152–3
Celaleddin al-Kabuni (Ottoman ambassador to the Mamluk court in 1453 and 1456), 110–4, 114–5
Cem (Prince, Bayezid II's brother), 39, 136–8, 145, 168, 169; his son, 145, 265; his daughter, 165, 263, 331n38

Cemaleddin, Hoca (Ottoman ambassador to the Mamluk court in 1429), 98
Ceremonies (practices, traditions, etc.), 183–4; Abbasid, 59; Ayyubid, 24, 59, 184; Bursa, 50–2; Byzantine, 24–5; Cairo, 47–50; Constantinople, 52–7; Edirne, 52–4; Fatimid, 32, 48; Mongols, 24, 59; Seljuks (Great), 24
Champion of faith or Champion of Ghaza, See *Ghazi*.
Chamber of Petitions (*Arz Odası*), 56, 57
Chancery: Mamluk, 33–4, 35; Ottoman, 35–6, 73, 122
Chancery manual, 30–32
Chingiz Khan (d.1224), 6, 8; armies of, 82; heritage in Timurids, 31; parallel with the Safavids, 166; successors, 29, 140; tradition of, 115
Cilicia, 7, 8, 116, 134, 141, 147, 148
Circumcision, 58, 60, 73, 115, 145, 306n27
Citadel (Cairo), as a ceremonial space, 24, 45, 48–49, 49, 55–56, 59; Ottoman missions in, 98, 111, 150–1, 158
Cloth/textile/garment, 16; in diplomacy as gift, 38, 39, 40, 81, 93, 103, 104, 111, 113,115, 116, 120, 140, 148, 159, 201, 203, 207, 212, 221, 257
Çöke, 1–2, 134–6, 139–141
Collection of letters, 31–32
Conquest of Constantinople, 109–10; Mamluk reaction to, 111
Conquest of Syria and Egypt, 178; historiography of, 21–22, 179–80
Correspondence (Letters): Baghdadi sheet in, 29; ending protocol

in, 29–30; epistolary sections in, 29–30; introductory protocol in, 29–30; preparation of, 28–36; presentation of, 49–50 (in Cairo), 56–57 (in Ottoman court); *salutatio*, 67, 87; size of paper, 29
Council Hall: See *Divanhane*.
Crusade, First, 5
Crusaders (Crusader kingdoms, army, etc.), 64, 81, 82, 85, 95, 96, 107
Cyprus, 8, 59, 86, 97; Mamluk attack, 95–6

Dagger (confiscated in Jidda), 138
Damascus, 35, 85, 87, 150, 151, 158, 162
Dar al-'adl. See *Mazalim*.
Dar al-Islam vs. Dar al-Harb, 183
Darende, 7; Bayezid I's attack on, 82–3
Davud Paşa, Tuğrakeş or Nişancı (Ottoman ambassador to the Mamluk court in 1493–4), 157–8
Davud Paşa, 143; attempts to negotiate peace with Qaytbay, 144; 154
devşirme (child levy), 27, 142, 157, 160
Divanhane (Council Hall), 52–3, 55, 56
Divan yolu (Council road), 46, 52, 55
Dawadar, 120; ambassador to the Ottoman court, 158 (*dawadar al-thani*), 168, 170; role in Mamluk ceremonies, 49–50
Dawlatbay, 166, 261, 262, 264, 266, 267
Diwan (Divan): Mamluk, 48–9, 83; Ottoman, 52, 55, 56, 57, 83, 147–48, 184
Dragoman, 47, 49, 50, 57
Dulkadirids, 7–8, 12, 59, 80, 82–3, 93, 95, 124–6, 128–9, 138–9, 143, 145, 146, 167, 173, 177, 179

Elbistan, 7–8; Bayezid I's attack on, 82–3
Elçi Hanı, 46
Etiquette, violation of diplomatic, 126–7, 138, 180–1
Evranos Bey, 70

Faraj (Mamluk sultan, r.1399–1405 and 1405–12), 74, 80, 83–5, 88–90, 96
Fathname (victory proclamation), 30, 35–6, 93, 94–7; Constantinople, 111–3
Fatimids, 5, 14, 32, 43, 48
Fatwa, 106–7 (also see 222), 194, 251
Feridun Bey (d.1555), 32–3, 76, 89–90, 111–3, 162–3, 166
Fur: in diplomacy, 38, 40, 88, 98, 104, 109, 111, 115, 120, 140; in trade, 16

Genoa (Genoese, etc.), 17, 66, 76–7
Generosity, 40, 44, 47, 95, 105–6, 161, 173–4, 187
Gerger, 7, 122–3
Germiyanids, 11, 64, 84, 140; Ibn Nazir al-Jaysh's comments, 68; Al-Qalqashandi's comments, 76; Al-'Umari's comments, 66–68; Wedding, 69–71
Ghaza, 3–4, 12, 40, 51, 65, 76, 86, 91, 94, 106, 114, 115, 116, 147 (while arguing for peace in 1491), 152, 183, 186
Ghazi, (often translated as Champion of Faith), 5, 6, 65, 71–73, 90, 95, 99, 100, 152–3 (while releasing İskender Bey), 156–7, 160–1, 168
Gift, 36–45; animals (other than horses), 38, 40, 113, 140, 159, 257; book of *hadith* collection, 148; genre (*Kitab al-hadaya*), 36–7; head (Abu Sa'id), 41, 130; head ('Ala' al-dawla), 41, 177; head

Index

(Uzbeg Khan), 41; head (Zaynal Mirza), 131; horse, 38, 39, 83, 93, 201, 246; Prophet, 36; Qur'an, 74–5, 103, 148; redistribution of, 44, 70, 95, 120; slave (not *mamluk*), 38, 39–40, 81–2, 83, 88, 94, 95, 98, 109, 111 (including some clergymen from Constantinople), 115, 120, 158 (to the Mamluk ambassador), 160 (to the Mamluk ambassador), 165 (to the Ottoman ambassador), 186; presentation of, 57, 111, 115; prisoners of war (see also slave under gift), 38, 39–40, 81–2, 95, 107, 186; vocabulary for, 37–8; whale's teeth, 140; wheat and oat, 131. See also Balsam, Cloth, Gold artifacts, Silver artifacts, Robe of Honor, Saddles, Spice, Sword.
Gold artifacts: gifts, 38, 74, 113, 229; in Ottoman palace, 51, 53
Golden Horde, 140
Goodwill mission, 91–2, 113–4, 118, 119, 128, 181
Granada, 14–5; Nasrid rulers, 148; reference in correspondence, 93–4
Grand Portico: See *al-Iwan al-Kabir*.
Gülek, 7, 116; key to the castles, 150; returned to the Mamluks, 152
Güvercinlik (Golubevich), 94, 98

Hadım Ali Paşa, 144, 154, 173
Hadith: collection of, 148; concerning the conquest of Constantinople, 11–12; in correspondence, 31, 102–3
Hafsids of Tunis, 15, 95, 139; involvement in Ottoman-Mamluk peace treaty, 148; 154, 173
Hajj: See pilgrimage and pilgrim.
Hajj caravan: See mahmal.

Hamidoğulları, 70
Hawsh, 111, 113
Haydar Ağa, Silahtarbaşı (Ottoman ambassador to the Mamluk court in 1501), 164–5
Head (severed), 40–1, 59, 93, 130, 131, 159, 167, 177
Heerkönig (warrior-king), 8
Hindubay al-Khassaki (Mamluk ambassador to the Ottoman court in 1502), 165
Holy Cities. See Two Holy Cities.
Horse, 38, 39, 83, 93, 201, 246
Hungary: embassy of, 140, 324n23; Hungarians, 97, 98; king of, 94, 99, 139, 214; lands of, 212, 213; 216, 217; Ottoman Treaty with, 99–100, 216; slave of (to the Mamluk court as gifts), 200, 295n137

Ibn Aja (Mamluk ambassador to the Ottoman court in 1472–3), 128, 130
Ibn 'Arabshah (d.1450), 35
Ibn Bahadur, 23, 65, 285n1
Ibn Hajar (d.1449), 106
Ibn al-Himsi, 150, 151
Ibn Iyas, 129, 132, 138, 141, 144, 158, 168, 169, 172, 174–5, 177–8; complimenting the language in Ottoman correspondence, 36, 171
Ibn Kemal, 61, 133, 140, 153, 160
Ibn Khaldun (d.1406), 23
Ibn Nazir al-Jaysh (d.1384), 68, 69, 77, 88, 89, 163
Ibn al-Sughayr, 23, 51, 79
Ibn Taghribirdi (d.1470), 24, 34, 105, 108 (the obituary for Murad II), 114–5, 120–22
Ibrahim Bey (Karamanid ruler, d.1464), 106–7, 122, 124; attack on Mamluk territory, 116;

complaining to the Mamluk sultans (Inal and Khushqadam) about Mehmed II, 114, 126
Ilkhanids, 1, 11, 29, 38, 66; titulature of, 29
Inal (Mamluk sultan, r.1453–61), 20, 110–7; the Karamanids, 116–7
Inal al-Hakim, Amir and the Mamluk governor of Syria, 132
Insha' (İnşa), 33–5, 157; *diwan al-insha'*, 33. See also chancery, *katib al-insha'*.
Investiture, 66; diploma of, 79
Isfendiyarids, 117–8
İskender bey, Mihaloğlu, 145, 150, 152–3
Al-Iwan al-Kabir (Grand Portico): 49, 56

Jalayirids, 80; titulature of, 29
Janbulat (Mamluk ambassador to the Ottoman court in 1491), 150–1; sultan, 162
Janibak, Amir (Mamluk ambassador to the Ottoman court in 1485), 1–2, 134–6, 138, 139–141, 147, 153
Janibak al-Sufi, 101
Jaqmaq (Mamluk sultan, r.1438–53), 20, 86, 102, 106, 109, 185; accession of, 102–4; addressing the Ottoman ruler, 90, 95; attacks on Cyprus and Rhodes, 96; marriage to the Dulkadirid princess, 83; marriage to the Ottoman princess, 100
Al-Jazari, Shams al-din (d.1429), 35, 80; his son Muhammad ibn al-Jazari (also known as Muhammad al-Asghar), 35
Jerusalem, 5, 17, 18; king of, 95; maintenance and security of the roads to, 126; protectorate of, 135, 174

Jewish (and Muslim) expulsion from Iberian peninsula: 14, 15
Jidda, 15, 17; Bahmani envoys in, 138
Jihad: See under Tropes.
Jihan Shah (Qaraqoyunlu ruler, r.1439–67), 63, 116, 225

Kahta, 7
Karaman, 138, 146
Karamanids, 7–8, 11, 12, 50, 64, 70–71, 73, 78, 79, 80, 92–93, 101 (in block quotation), 114, 117, 122, 124–5, 126–127, 129, 130, 132, 179; attack on Mamluk territory, 116; Ibn Nazir al-Jaysh's comments on, 68; Mamluk campaign in, 93, 116–17; Murad II asking *fatwa* from Mamluk scholars concerning, 106–107; succession struggle in, 122–3; titulature of, 29, 68, 182, 184; al-'Umari's comments on, 66–7
Kasabay, Amir (Mamluk ambassador to the Ottoman court in 1510), 170, 271
Kasım i. Ahmed i. Bayezid II, 178
Kasım Bey (the Karamanid), 132
Katib al-insha', 33
Katib al-sirr (the head of Mamluk chancery or confidential secretary), 33–4, 66, 89, 120, 230, 232; in ceremonies, 49–50
Kayseri, 7–8, 131
Kemal Reis (Ottoman ambassador to the Mamluk court in 1498–99 and 1507), 160, 164, 167–8, 171–2
Khadim al-Haramayn al-Sharifayn (The servitor of Two Holy Sanctuaries of Islam; sometimes also *Sultan al-Haramayn*, the Protector of pilgrims and pilgrimage, Protector of the Two Holy Cities, *Hami Sukkan al-Haramayn*

Sharifayn), 8–9, 58, 85, 90, 112, 115, 119, 135, 136, 153, 174, 178
Khassaki, 96, 146, 157, 165
Khassakiyya, 149, 150, 157, 158. See also *devşirme*.
Khayr Bey (Mamluk ambassador to the Ottoman court in 1497), 61, 160–162, 165, 173
Khushdashiyya (camaraderie), 5
Khushqadam (Mamluk sultan, r.1461–7), 20, 116 (when an amir), 117–27, 182
Kissing the ground, 49, 56, 95, 142, 300n228; Ottoman ambassador's refusal to kiss the ground, 119–22
Kissing the hand, 53, 56, 140; Korkud's kissing the hand of Qansuh al-Ghawri, 169; for the brief presence of this practice in the Mamluk court, 302n259
Kissing the letter, 171
Kiswa, 9, 150; tension over (between Barsbay and Shahrukh), 99, 101, 106
Konya, 6, 73, 136
Korkud (Prince), 168–71
Kosova, first battle (1389), 74–5
Kosova, second battle (1448), 107
Al-Kujkuni, Amir Husam al-din Hasan (Mamluk ambassador to the Ottoman court in 1392), 1, 50–1, 78–9, 82
Kul, 142 (translated as slave), 153–4
Kütahya, 11

Madrasa, 10, 74, 183
Mahmal (*mahmil*), 9; cloth or cover for, 98, 99, 106; departure of, 9, 58, 105, 115, 150–1
Mahmud Paşa (Grand Vizier), 131
Malatya, 7, 8, 139, 167; Bayezid I's attack on, 82–4

Malik Arslan (Dulkadirid ruler, r.1454–65), 124
Mamay al-Khassaki (Mamluk ambassador to the Ottoman court in 1490–1 and 1494): his first mission and captivity in Ottoman lands, 146; 148, 149; his second mission, 158; death, 159
Mamluk, 1, 5–6, 16, 28, 31, 112, 135, 142, 153, 154, 156, 157, 182
Maqam Ibrahim (post of Abraham), 150
Al-Maqrizi, 50–1, 92, 209–10, 215–6, 285n1, 301n240, 301n241, 310n76, 337n5
Marj dabik, battle of (1516) 178
Marriage: Aybak al-Turkmani to the Ayyubid child sultan's widowed mother, 5; Bayezid I (Prince) to the Germiyanid princess, 69–71; Bayezid II's daughter to Hersekzade Ahmed Paşa, 142; Bayezid II's daughter to al-Nasir Muhammad (planned), 161–2, 258; Jaqmaq to Dulkadirid princess, 83; Ottoman princess/refugee to Barsbay and then Jaqmaq, 100
Mazalim (*dar al-'adl*): Mamluk, 10, 49, 79, 123, 184; Ottoman, 79, 184
Mecca, 8, 15, 58, 94, 99, 105–6, 113, 126, 135, 167, 174. See also Two Holy Cities.
Medina, 8, 58, 94, 99, 105–6, 135, 167, 174. See also Two Holy Cities.
Mehmed I (Ottoman ruler, r.1413–21), 20, 35, 83, 86–105
Mehmed II (Ottoman ruler, r.1444–48 and 1451–81), 20–1, 109–33, 179–80, 182, 184; Bahmani mission, 137–8; Dulkadirids, 124–6, 128–9, 130, 132; False rumour about his death, 115; first accession, 107–8; gifts to the Venetian dodge, 44; Inal and,

110–7; Karamanids, 114, 116, 117, 122, 123, 124, 125, 126–7, 129, 130, 132; Khushqadam, 117–27; last destination, 132–3; legislation and, 122–23; Molla Gürani, 35–6, 111; Qaytbay, 127–33; role in ceremonials practices, 53–6, 60–1; sending Zaynal Mirza's head to cairo, 131; Title on coinage, 118–9; titulature, 110, 120, 124, 127; Two Holy Sanctuaries and, 126–7, 135; Uzun Hasan,130–1

Menagerie, 40, 55, 159

Merchants: Catalan, 16; European, 17; Genoese, 284n90; Jewish, 284n90; Mamluk, 77, 144, 151; Muslim, 77, 96; Muslim and non-Muslim, 16; Non-local, 18; Ottoman, 16, 77

Mihmandar, 115, 120; ceremonies, 45, 300n230

Molla Arab (d.1496), involvement with the peace treaty, 147–9; 154

Molla Fenari (d.1431), 207, 208

Molla Gürani (d.1488), 356, 111, 134–5, 140, 147

Molla Hüsrev (as the person who prepared two Ottoman letters for the Mamluk court), 223, 227

Mongols, 6–7, 9, 96; influence on Mamluk ceremonies, 24, 59

Al-Mu'ayyad Shaykh (Mamluk sultan, r.1412–21), 20, 35, 44, 86, 90, 90–94, 96, 179

Muhammad Bey (the commander of the Mamluk fleet), 170–1

Muhtasib (market inspector), 115, 130

Muhyiddin Çelebi (Ottoman ambassador to the Bahmani court in 1480–1), 137

Murad I (Ottoman ruler, r.1362–89), 69–73, 73–5

Murad II (Ottoman ruler, r.1421–44 and 1446–51), 20, 35, 38, 40, 42, 43, 62–3, 86, 91–92, 94–108, 118, 179, 185; fatwa against the Karamanid ruler, 106–7; obituary in Ibn Taghribirdi, 108; refugees, 100–1; role in Ottoman ceremonies, 52–3; titulature/title, 88–90, 94–5, 103, 104, 105–6

Mustafa (Prince, son of Mehmed II), 115, 131–2

Mustafa Âli, 148–9

Al-Mutawakkil II, Caliph, 141

Mystic or mysticism (Sufis and Sufism), 10, 27, 43, 159, 186

Nasir al-din Mehmed Bey (Dulkadirid ruler, r.1399–1442), 83, 93, 101 (in block quotation)

al-Nasir Muhammad b. Qaytbay (Mamluk sultan, r. 1496–8), 159, 160, 161, 185

Nasrids, 14–5, 148

Neşri, 72

Nicopolis, battle of (1396), 81–2;

Nişancı, 35,157; in ceremonies, 55–6

Nur al-din 'Ali al-Qurdi (Mamluk ambassador to the ottoman court in 1464–5), 122–4

Nur al-din al-Zangi (Zangid ruler, d.1174), 10

Orhan (Ottoman ruler, r.1324–1362), 66, 67

Orhan (i. Süleyman i. Bayezid I), 100; for his servant who escaped his children to Cairo, 100

Otlukbeli, battle of (1473), 131

Parades: See processions.

Patronage (architectural, artistic, cultural, intellectual): comparative or rivalry, 186–7; Mamluk, 10, 74, 165, 174; Ottoman, 63, 80, 84; 108, 111, 133, 174; peace treaty, 149–55

Pilgrim, 126; Christian, 18–9; Jewish, 18–9
Pilgrimage, 112, 137, 151; 'antiquarian',18; caravan, 9, 58, 105, 115, 150, 160; Christian, 18; routes, 8, 126–7, 135, 174
Portuguese, kingdom of, 15; attack (and/or penetration), 17–18, 21, 36, 156, 164, 167, 169, 173, 174, 176, 178; maritime discoveries of, 17–18, 166–7
Prisoner of war (not as a gift), 141, 145, 150, 170
Procession, 10, 41, 48, 58, 173, 185; ambassador in Cairo, 47–50, 104, 137; ambassador in Bursa, 50–2; ambassador in Constantinople, 46, 54–58, 60–1; ambassador in Edirne, 52–54; other (military, secular, or religious celebrations, etc.) in Cairo, 58–60, 94, 95, 98, 142, 145, 151, 165, 167–8, 169, 170; other in Edirne and Constantinople, 60–1, 160–1
Prophet Abraham (Ibrahim), 134–5
Prophet Muhammad, 11–2, 31, 36, 43, 99, 102–3, 108, 134–5, 164, 169; family or descendants, 105, 108, 184

Qadi Burhan al-din (the ruler of Sivas), 78, 79
Qalawun (the Mamluk sultan, r.1279–90), 15–16; lineage of, 48, 49, 64, 72
Al-Qalqashandi (d.1418), 26, 32, 41, 45–6, 67, 181; comments on the Ottomans, 75–6; titulature (Ottoman), 87, 88, 162–3
Qanibay, Amir (Mamluk ambassador to the Ottoman court in 1456), 115–6
Qanim al-Tajir (Mamluk ambassador to the Ottoman court in 1449), 107

Qansuh al-Ghawri (Mamluk sultan, r.1501–16), 17, 21, 36, 41, 43, 135, 153, 162–3, 156–75, 176–9
Qansuh al-Khazinadari (Mamluk ambassador to the Ottoman court in 1500), 162
Qaraqoyunlus, 13, 62–3, 80, 89, 116
Qawaya (Geyve), 66, 67
Qaytbay (Mamluk sultan, r.1468–96), 20, 21, 41, 127–59; Bayezid II, 134–55; Cem, 136–7; death, 159; Mehmed II, 127–33

Ramazanids, 7, 8, 12, 173, 259–60
Reconquista, 13–4, 148
Refugees: See Ahmad the Jalayirid; Ahmed i. Bayezid (Prince); 'Ala' al-dawla; Cem; Dawlatbay; Inal al-Hakim; Janibak al-Sufi; Kasim Bey (Karamanid); Korkud; Sara i. Orhan; Süleyman i. Orhan; Yusuf (Qara)
Relic, 39, 43, 137
Rhodes, 8, 86, 96, 137, 160
Ridaniye, battle of (1517), 178
Robe of honor, 1, 38, 41–44, 78, 98, 101–2, 104, 105, 113, 114, 121, 129, 141, 150, 158, 165, 168, 170; for ambassadors, 41–2; ambassador in the Ottoman palace, 56; hierarchical order of, 41; Korkud, 169; Mehmed II to 'Ala' al-dawla, 129; Prophet's robe, 43; for rulers, 42; ruler's wardrobe, 43–4; seniority in, 42–43; *Tashrif,* 9–10, 41, 280n51

Saddle (in diplomacy, as gifts), 38, 39; and other riding equipment, 93, 116
Safavids, 4, 12, 13–4, 22, 156, 163–68, 172, 174, 176, 177, 187;

mission in Cairo, 41; mission in Constantinople, 55, 174
Al-Sahmawi (d.1464), 89, 162, 163, 181, 313n10
Salah al-din al-Ayyubi (Ayyubid ruler), 5, 10
Al-Salih Ayyub (Ayyubid ruler, r.1240–9), 5, 6
Sara (?) i. Orhan i. Süleyman i. Bayezid I, 100
Seclusion of Ottoman sultan: 54–5, 56, 184; vis-à-vis Mamluk sultans, 59–60
Selim I (Ottoman ruler, r.1512–20), 12, 173, 176–80; correspondence with Khayr Bey, 161; sending the Dulkadirid ruler's head to Cairo, 41, 177–8
Seljuks, Anatolian, 1, 6, 11, 118
Seljuks, Great, 5, 6, 24, 26
Selman Reis, 171
Smederova (Semendire), 94, 103, 221
Serbia (Serbians, etc.), 36, 39, 51, 71, 94, 98, 114, 115
Shahbudaq (Dulkadirid ruler, r.1465–6 and 1472–80), 124–6, 128–9, 145
Shah Isma'il (Safavid ruler, r.1501–24), 4, 13–14, 41, 164–70, 172, 176–8
Shahrukh (Timurid ruler, d.1447), 42, 95, 101–102, 104–105, 106, 110
Shahsuwar, (Dulkadirid ruler, r.1466–72), 59, 124–6, 128–9
Sharif of Mecca, 113, 230
Shirwanids, 139
Şeyhülislam, 147
Silver artifacts (in Ottoman palace), 51, 53; (in diplomacy, as gifts), 38, 39, 74, 83, 88
Slave, see under gifts and *mamluk*
Spice: in diplomacy, 40; in trade, 16, 18
Succession: Bayezid II's reaction to Mamluk, 161–2, 258, 260;

Dulkadirid, 124, 129, 139; dynastic, 5, 12, 48, 118, 134–5, 184–5; fratricide, 31, 91, 92, 184–5; Karamanid, 122, 123; Mamluk reaction to Ottoman, 92, 134–5, 184–5; Mamluk, 5–6, 48, 102–103, 126, 134–5, 159, 161–62, 184–5; Ottoman reaction to Mamluk, 134–5, 161–2; 184–5; Ottoman, 12, 31, 91–92, 134–5, 136, 184–5; trope of (in diplomatic encounters and correspondence), 2, 31, 102–103; 112–14; 134–5, 161–62; 184–5
Süleyman Bey (Dulkadirid ruler, r.1442–54), 124
Süleyman i. Bayezid I, 84–5, 88, 100, 103, 204, 206
Süleyman i. Orhan i.Süleyman i. Bayezid, 100
Şükrullah, 62
Sword (in diplomacy, as gift), 38, 103, 116, 226–7

Taghribirdi, Amir (Mamluk ambassador to the Ottoman court in 1428), 43, 96, 98
Tamraz al-Shamsi, Amir, 128
Taqlid, 141
Tarsus, 116; keys to the castle, 150; returned to the Mamluks, 152
Tashrif, 9–10, 41, 280n51
Textile/cloth/garment, 16; in diplomacy as gift, 38, 39, 40, 81, 93, 103, 104, 111, 113,115, 116, 120, 140, 148, 159, 201, 203, 207, 212, 221, 257; silk, 39, 104, 115; woolen, 39, 115
Thessalonica (Selanik), 94, 216, 220
Timber: gift, 170–1; trade, 16
Timur, 23, 31, 35, 42, 73, 75, 79–80, 83–85, 184
Timurids, 8, 9, 13, 20, 31, 42, 50, 80, 87, 89, 96, 101–2, 110; Ankara

Index

and its aftermath, 83–5; embassy (to Cairo), 95, 104–105; impact of ceremonies and conventions on Ottoman, 25, 35, 115; titulature of, 29, 76, 104. See also Abu Sa'id and Shahrukh.

Titulature (honorifics, title, appellation), 28–30, 32, 34, 77, 104,162–3; Al-Abwab al-harifa, 77; Ahmedi, 84–5; Amir, 67–8, 89, 90; Bayezid I and Barquq,77, 79; Bayezid II, 162–3, 168; Bey, 84, 114; Caesar (Kaiser, Kayzer), 110; change in, 181, 182; Faraj and Suleyman, 88; Father (*waliduhu*) vs. Brother (*akhuhu*), 119, 163; Feridun Bey, 32, 89–90, 112; Al-Hadra, 162–3; Ibn Nazir al-Jaysh's work, 68, 88, 163; Inal,111–13; Al-Janab (in various combinations), 77, 88–90, 95, 182; Al-Janib (in various combinations), 76, 181; *Khadim al-Harafayn al-Sharifayn*, 8, 178; Khushqadam, 119, 120–1, 123–4 (demotion of); Al-Majlis (in various combinations), 67–8, 77, 87, 88, 162–3, 182; Malik, 68, 90; Al-Maqam (in various combinations), 76, 89, 104, 112, 124, 127, 163, 182, 309fn60; Al-Maqarr (in various combinations), 67–8, 87, 89–90, 95, 103, 104, 112, 114, 115, 120, 124, 127, 163, 182; Mehmed I, 88–9; Mehmed II, 113–14, 115–116, 120–4, 127, 182; Misuse, 110; Murad I, 71–73; Murad II, 88–9, 94–5, 103, 104, 105–6; *Al-Nasiri* (for Mehmed II), 114; *Nusrat al-Ghuzat wa al-Mujahidin*, 100; promotion of Ottoman, 86–90, passim, 182;

Qahraman al-Ma wa al-Tin, 157, 164, 168; al-Qalqashandi's work, 76, 87, 88, 163; Qansuh al-Ghawri, 162–3, 167; *Sahib al-Ujat*, 100, 183; al-Sahmawi's work, 89; Sultan, 84, 114, 119; *Sultan al-Ghuzat wa al-Mujahidin*, 71–73; *Sultan al-Haramayn*, 115; *Sultan al-Islam wa al-Muslimin*, 85, 90, 99, 136, 167; *Sultan al-Mujahidin*, 157, 183; *Sultan al-rum*, 66, 79; *Sultan al-Ujat*, 100, 157, 183; al-'Umari's work, 66–8, 163, 88; Usage, wrong, 120–1

Topkapı Palace: 25; ceremonies before 1478, 52–53; ceremonies after, 54–55; Mamluk missions in, 61, 159

Trade, 15–18, 96, 178; in correspondence, 76–7, 151–2; Ottoman-Mamluk, 15–6, 151–2

Trebizond, 117–8

Tropes (in correspondence, diplomatic encounters, and historical narratives), 20–1, 134–6, 152–55, 156–7, 181–5; age hierarchy (or seniority), 31, 42–3, 72, 112–3, 119, 182; fraternity (brotherhood), 97–100, 182, 183; generosity, 105–6; *Jihad* (holy war), 3–4, 12, 23, 40, 76, 86, 91, 94, 97, 106, 112, 114, 115, 127, 168, 183, 186; leadership in the Islamic world, 164–5, 167; lineage (slave-origin vs. dynastic or noble origin), 1–2, 31, 112–3, 114, 118–9, 127, 134–5, 142, 153–4, 156, 184; longevity, 72; meritocracy, 135, 185; piety (or religiosity), 152, 186; precedence in conversion, 31, 134–5, 156–7, 184–5; Prophet, 31, 99–100,

102–3, 164; Qur'an (or Qur'anic figures), 31, 34, 134–35, 166, 171 (Joseph and Jacob); religion, Ottoman ignorance in, 153, 174, 185; success, maritime, 156–7, 159–60, 164–5; success, military, 183; succession (in diplomatic encounters and correspondence), 2, 31, 102–103; 112–14; 134–5, 161–62; 184–5; Two Holy Cities (and Jerusalem), Protector/Servitor of (or Protectorate of), 135, 174, 183; unity in religion ('two arms from a body'), 31, 77, 182–3 Also see Succession (for additional references), Two Holy Cities (for additional references), *Ghazi* and *Ghaza*.

Tulu, Amir (Mamluk ambassador to the Ottoman court in 1396), 79–80, 81

Turgutoğulları, 173, 259–60

Tursun Bey, 133, 154

Two Holy Cities (or Two Holy Sanctuaries of Islam), 8, 58, 94, 105, 108, 135, 167; endowments to, 44, 105–6, 108, 152, 160, 186. See also Mecca and Medina (separately).

Al-'Umari (d.1348), 66–8, 69, 76, 77, 84, 87, 88, 89, 163

Uthman, Caliph: Qur'an, 103–104

Uzun Hasan (Aqqoyunlu ruler, r.1457–78), 13–4, 41, 54, 110, 122–3, 128, 130–1

Varna, battle of (1444), 38, 94, 107

Venice, 13, 17, 43–44, 141, 160, 172

War, Ottoman–Mamluk (1485–91), 141–9

Water wells (along the pilgrimage routes), 126–7

Weaponry (in diplomacy, as gifts), 38, 39, 113

Window, grilled (*shubbak*), in Cairo, 48, 55; in Constantinople, 55; to pass the gifts in front of, in Constantinople, 57

Yaqub, Sultan (Aqqoyunlu ruler, son of Uzun Hasan, r.1478–90), 13, 139

Yarshbay al-Inali al-Ashrafi (Mamluk ambassador to the Ottoman court in 1453–4), 114–5

Yashbak al-Jamali (ambassador to the Ottoman court in 1473–4), 131

Yashbak min Mahdi (commander), 128, 129, 130

Yazıcıoğlu Mehmed, 74

Yazıcı Salih (Ottoman ambassador to the Mamluk court in 1396 or 1398), 73–4

Yunus al-'Adili, Amir (Mamluk ambassador to the Ottoman court in 1510), 170, 172, 270, 272

Yusuf, Qara (Qaraqoyunlu ruler, d.1420), 80

Zangids, 5, 10

Zeyrekzade Rükneddin Molla, 177

71 51 92 99   10
74 52 97   60
79 58 95   500 ×   90
                   64
                   61
                   67
                   ―――
                   n×l500